MARXISMS
IN THE 21ST
CENTURY

CRISIS, CRITIQUE & STRUGGLE

Editors: Michelle Williams and Vishwas Satgar

WITS UNIVERSITY PRESS

Wits University Press
1 Jan Smuts Avenue
Johannesburg
South Africa

www.witspress.co.za

Published edition © Wits University Press 2013
Compilation © Edition editors 2013
Chapter © Individual contributors 2013
First published 2013

ISBN 978-1-86814-753-3 (print)
ISBN 978-1-86814-754-0 (digital)

Edited by Inga Norenius
Proofread by Alison Lockhart
Index by Clifford Perusset
Cover design by Farm Design – www.farmdesign.co.za
Book design and layout by Hothouse South Africa

DEMOCRATIC MARXISM SERIES

Series Editor: Vishwas Satgar

The crisis of Marxism in the late twentieth century was the crisis of orthodox and vanguardist Marxism associated mainly with hierarchical communist parties, and which was imposed – even as state ideology – as the 'correct' Marxism. The Stalinisation of the Soviet Union and its eventual collapse exposed the inherent weaknesses and authoritarian mould of vanguardist Marxism. More fundamentally, vanguardist Marxism was rendered obsolete but for its residual existence in a few parts of the world, including authoritarian national liberation movements in Africa and in China.

With the deepening crises of capitalism, a new democratic Marxism (or democratic historical materialism) is coming to the fore. Such a democratic Marxism is characterised in the following ways:
- Its sources span non-vanguardist grassroots movements, unions, political fronts, mass parties, radical intellectuals, transnational activist networks and the progressive academy;
- It seeks to ensure that the inherent categories of Marxism are theorised within constantly changing historical conditions to find meaning;
- Marxism is understood as a body of social thought that is unfinished and hence challenged by the need to explain the dynamics of a globalising capitalism and the futures of social change;
- It is open to other forms of anti-capitalist thought and practice, including currents within radical ecology, feminism, emancipatory utopianism and indigenous thought;
- It does not seek to be a monolithic and singular school of thought but engenders contending perspectives;
- Democracy, as part of the heritage of people's struggles, is understood as the basis for articulating alternatives to capitalism and as the primary means for constituting a transformative subject of historical change.

This series seeks to elaborate the social theorising and politics of democratic Marxism.

ACKNOWLEDGEMENTS

This volume was long in the making and because of this we would like to give special thanks to all of the contributors for their patience and perseverance. Thanks also for the two extremely constructive and encouraging blind reviews received from Wits University Press. We are also grateful to the Wolpe Trust, and in particular the former director, Lionel Louw, for funding the original workshop out of which the idea for the volume sprang. We owe special thanks to our students in the National Union of Metalworkers of South Africa's (Numsa) Social Theory and Research course, where we explored and engaged many of the ideas in this volume. We are grateful to our postgraduate students Katherine Joynt, Tatenda Mukwedeya and Andrew Bennie for editing and bibliographic assistance at various stages of the manuscript development. Katherine deserves special mention as she worked through the night (actually a couple of nights) in order for us to meet our deadline. Thanks to our excellent copy editor Inga Norenius. We also thank Roshan Cader and Veronica Klipp at Wits University Press for their enthusiastic support of the project.

CONTENTS

ACRONYMS AND ABBREVIATIONS

Amcu	Association of Mining and Construction Union
ANC	African National Congress
BEE	Black Economic Empowerment
Cosatu	Congress of South African Trade Unions
CPI(M)	Communist Party of India (Marxist)
CPSU	Communist Party of the Soviet Union
CST	colonialism of a special type
DLF	Democratic Left Front
EPLF	Eritrean People's Liberation Front
EPRDF	Ethiopian People's Revolutionary Democratic Front
Frelimo	Front for the Liberation of Mozambique
Gear	Growth, Employment and Redistribution
IMF	International Monetary Fund
MPLA	Popular Movement for the Liberation of Angola
NDR	national democratic revolution
NRM	National Resistance Movement
NUM	National Union of Mineworkers
Numsa	National Union of Metalworkers of South Africa
PAIGC	African Party for the Independence of Guinea and Cape Verde
PCI	Italian Communist Party
PT	Brazilian Workers' Party
RDP	Reconstruction and Development Programme
SACP	South African Communist Party
SPLM	Sudan People's Liberation Movement
Swapo	South West African People's Organisation
Tanu	Tanganyika African National Union
TPLF	Tigray People's Liberation Front
Unita	National Union for the Total Independence of Angola
Zanu	Zimbabwe African National Union

INTRODUCTION

Michelle Williams

Karl Marx's writings on and ideas about social transformation have figured prominently in the Global Left imagination for more than 150 years. Regardless of political hue, scholars, activists and politicos, on the Left and the Right, have engaged with Marx's and Marxists' ideas in some form or another. Marxism's extraordinary influence has been twofold: as a set of analytical ideas and as an ideology influencing the practices of political movements. History is littered with examples of Marx's impact on the world: Marxist-inspired working-class organisations in Europe and the US in the late nineteenth and early twentieth centuries, European socialist and communist parties' lineages of Marxism, Marxist–Leninist political organisations of the twentieth century, Latin American dependency theory's influence on development, Marxism–Leninism in the Soviet Union and Marxist-influenced anti-colonial struggles (for example, in Vietnam, Angola and Mozambique). Whereas Marxist ideas have clearly had enormous impact on the world, many of these experiments have inglorious histories, culminating in the demise of the Soviet Union. At the end of the twentieth century a number of factors seemed to converge to mark the end of Marxism's influence on the world: the collapse of the Soviet Union, the Chinese and Vietnamese move to market capitalism, the shift away from class-based issues to the dominance of identity politics in social movements, and the rise of postmodernism in academia with its anti-Marxist conceptions of power, alienation and marginalisation. As a result, by the late twentieth century the relevance of Marxism was under question.

Neoclassical economists and liberal political theorists were triumphant in the post-cold-war 1990s, not only declaring Marxian ideas dead but that there was no alternative to neoliberalism. Unlike what Marx (and the classical Marxists of the Second International) had predicted, the stages of history did not lead to an emancipated communism, but rather perambulated from capitalism to an even fiercer form of capitalism (for some this journey went via 'state socialism'). Thus, by the turn of the century, it seemed clear that Marxism was, if not already dead, clearly dying an ignominious death. Neoliberal capitalism and the concomitant penetration of the market into all spheres of social life seemed well entrenched for the foreseeable future.

The triumphalism of neoclassical economists was, however, relatively short-lived as their prescriptive ideas wreaked havoc on the global economy as well as on the livelihoods of the vast majority of peoples around the world, helping to reinvigorate Marxist scholarship in the twenty-first century. Not without irony, in the aftermath of the 2008 economic crisis, even mainstream economists – who normally disdain Marxian ideas – publicly acknowledged that Marx's analysis of the dynamics of capitalism has much to teach us (for a fuller discussion see Hobsbawm 2011). There is now widespread agreement that Marx offers a sophisticated and trenchant analysis of capitalism. For example, the tendency toward the concentration of capital has been vividly demonstrated over the twentieth century:

> In 1905, the fifty largest US corporations, by nominal capitalisation, had assets equal to 16 per cent of GNP. By 1999, the assets of the fifty largest US industrial companies amounted to 37 per cent of GNP. [For] the UK's ten largest industrial companies, the rise was from 5 per cent of GNP in 1905 to 41 per cent in 1999 (Therborn 2008: 13).

Just as Marx had anticipated, this concentration of capital came with a massive increase in global industrial unemployment, leaving the vast majority of the world's peoples on the margins of economic activity and creating a 'reserve army' of labour (18–19).

It is not just the analysis of capitalism that has captured the left imagination. Marx's ideas about a future post-capitalist order have inspired political movements for much of the past century and a half. Despite the chequered history of experiments in the name of Marxism, the revival of Marxism is finding new sources of inspiration that revolve around four primary factors:

(i) the importance of democracy for an emancipatory project; (ii) the ecological limits of capitalism; (iii) the crisis of global capitalism and (iv) the lessons to be learned from the failures of Marxist-inspired experiments. The recent revival of Marxism, then, is not simply a return to nineteenth- and twentieth-century understandings of Marxism. Rather, the twenty-first century has seen enormous creativity from movements that seek to overcome the weaknesses of the past by forging fundamentally new approaches to politics that draw inspiration from Marxism along with many other anti-capitalist traditions such as feminism, ecology, anarchism and indigenous traditions (Renton 2004). Thus we have movements led by indigenous peoples in Bolivia, Hugo Chávez's 'twenty-first century socialism' that involves the rural and urban poor in Venezuela, radical democratic decentralisation in Kerala, participatory budgeting in Brazil, the World Social Forum, the Occupy Movement, anti-austerity movements in Spain and Greece and the Arab Spring. These movements do not seek a coherent ideological blueprint, but rather share in their belief that 'another world is possible' through democratic, egalitarian, ecological alternatives to capitalism, built by ordinary people. The Marxism of many of these movements is not dogmatic or prescriptive; rather, it is open, searching, dialectical, humanist, utopian and inspirational. Central to these movements is the importance of radical, direct and participatory democracy in forging an alternative to and an appreciation for the limits of fossil-fuel capitalism.

Whereas there has been a flowering of creativity around the world, in South Africa the main party of Marxism, the South African Communist Party (SACP), has gone the other way by retreating into a scientific, dogmatic Marxism-cum-Soviet communism of the twentieth century.[1] In the new millennium, the SACP has turned away from its open Marxism of the 1990s – which was characterised by deep searching for new Marxist approaches to social transformation rooted in radical democracy, egalitarianism and pluralism – to more orthodox understandings of historical materialism and scientific Marxism. Political education in the SACP focuses on the writings of Joseph Stalin and Vladimir Lenin and the empirical reference points include the former Soviet Union and increasingly the Chinese Communist Party (SACP 2012: 15). For the SACP, democracy can be reduced to vanguard democracy in which the Party plays the pivotal role. Radical democracy and egalitarianism have become rhetorical devices, giving way to populism and authoritarian organisational practices and leaders' elite consumption habits. Unlike many of the movements around the world that look to Marxist theory for assistance in analysing the world and re-finding utopian possibilities, the Marxism of the SACP has retreated to Marxism as a rigid ideology prescribing the laws of history.

Outside of the SACP, there is also a strong Marxist tradition that has been heavily influenced by Leon Trotsky's writings. Trotsky's continued influence on Marxism is unquestionable. His concepts of combined and uneven development, permanent revolution, and his understanding of Bonapartism, for example, are important sources of inspiration for Marxist analysis. Alex Callinicos's (1999) work perhaps best characterises the important and lasting influence of Trotsky's ideas on Marxism. In addition, many movements draw inspiration from his writings. However, in South Africa, like the SACP, many Trotskyist Marxists have been marred by dogmatic certainty. Neither tradition of Marxism – communist or Trotskyist – has grappled sufficiently with the deficiencies of Marxism as a theory, especially with reference to democracy and the changes in world capitalism, as both remain committed to the paramount role of vanguard parties (tied to traditional and limited notions of the 'working class') as the crucial historical agent. The two traditions have also not adequately reflected on the failures of historical experiences, not even the Marxist experiments in Africa, and have not had a thorough-going engagement with democracy, tending to dismiss it as liberal ('bourgeois') democracy and to argue, rather, in favour of 'revolution' and vanguard democracy in which the 'dictatorship of the proletariat', together with the Party, play the leading role in society.

Despite these traditions within the South African context, there has also been a renewed interest in Marxism that seeks to explore new politics grounded in democratic, egalitarian and ecologically sensitive alternatives to capitalism. This renewed interest in Marxism and its intersection with other anti-capitalist traditions has inspired us to produce an edited volume that introduces some of these contemporary approaches to Marxism and explores some of the ways in which Marxism has been engaged in Africa. I now turn to a discussion of the remaining chapters in the volume, which challenge us to see Marxism in often unfamiliar ways by exploring themes such as democracy, globalisation, feminism, critique, ecology, historical lessons and agency, each chapter offering novel and creative approaches to the Marxist tradition. While the range of perspectives in the following chapters might lead some to wonder what is left of 'Marx' in these positions, I would argue it is precisely the plurality of approaches that is the strength of current Marxist theorising and practice.

REFLECTIONS ON MARXISM IN THE TWENTY-FIRST CENTURY

In this volume we explore Marxism as a set of analytical ideas and as an ideology inspiring political movements. Thus, we take stock of various Marxisms today and ask questions about their potential for helping us navigate alternatives. The chapters span a wide range of issues and perspectives, all having to do in some way with Marxism. Part One democratises and globalises Marxism by situating Marxism in debates about democracy (Michelle Williams), reperiodising Marxism along three waves of commodification (Burawoy) and globalising Gramscian Marxism (Satgar). Part Two looks at Marxism's engagement with left politics such as Marxism as critique (Ahmed Veriava), Marxism and feminism (Jacklyn Cock and Meg Luxton) and eco-Marxism (Devan Pillay). Part Three investigates Marxism and socialism in Africa (Daryl Glaser, John S. Saul) and South Africa (Patrick Bond, Ashwin Desai and Trevor Ngwane and Mazibuko K. Jara).

Part One situates Marxism in global capitalism today. In chapter one Williams explores the way in which twentieth-century debates have bifurcated democracy into either liberal or vanguard democracy. Williams shows how mid-twentieth-century scholarship – both liberal and Marxist – promoted either representative democracy or vanguard democracy as the only organising mechanism in society, largely ignoring the importance of direct and participatory democracy. In recent movements, however, Williams finds new sources of inspiration that are explicitly looking to the importance of direct democracy for twenty-first-century alternatives.

Turning from an explicit attention to democracy, the next two chapters focus on globalising Marxism. For most of the twentieth century, Marxism largely confined itself to national developments. However, with the changing and global nature of capitalism today, we have to rethink our Marxism to speak to this global capitalism. In his chapter, Burawoy eloquently challenges us with the simple yet provocative claim: as the world changes so must Marxism. For some this might seem an obvious claim, but for many Marxists it is a fundamental challenge. He suggests that the anti-Marxist euphoria that followed the Soviet Union's demise and China's transition to capitalism (or what the Chinese Communist Party calls market socialism) must be met by a sociological Marxism that seeks neither to immortalise Marx and Friedrich Engels as all-knowing gods whose ideas are laid out in their scriptures, nor to bury Marxism as anachronistic theories for a bygone era. Burawoy is not interested in reconstructing Marx and Engels (and others such as Lenin, Trotsky, Nikolai Bukharin, Rosa Luxemburg, Antonio Gramsci, Franz Fanon and Mao Zedong) as theorists of 'eternal truths', nor does he wish to discard their ideas as irrelevant to understanding our times. Rather, he argues for 'Marxism as a living tradition that enjoys renewal and reconstruction as the world it describes and seeks to transform, undergoes change'. Thus, as globalisation increasingly defines our reality, Marxism too must take on a global character, which requires 'rethinking the material basis of Marxism through the lens of the market, but not in terms of its geographical scope (since markets have always been global as well as local), nor even in terms of neoliberal ascendancy (since markets have always moved through periods of expansion and contraction) but in terms of the novel modes of commodification'.

Suggesting a totally new periodisation of Marxism, Burawoy maps the history of new configurations of Marxism onto three waves of marketisation in which labour, money and nature were commodified. Each wave of commodification engenders a countermovement which corresponds to a new configuration of Marxism – 'classical Marxism based on the projection of an economic utopia; Soviet, Western, and Third World Marxism based on state regulation; and finally, sociological Marxism based on an expanding and self-regulating civil society'. Burawoy is essentially analysing the historical development of Marxism, based on waves of commodification. Thus, as labour was commodified, Marxism responded with visions of breaking free from the chains of exploitation; as money was commodified, Marxism envisioned state regulation of the economy; and, as nature was increasingly commodified, Marxism responded with notions of a fully realised and global civil society shaping governance, production and consumption. Indeed, Burawoy tells us that as 'the state seems to be ever more in thrall to the market, the defence of an independent "civil society" seems to become all the more necessary … third-wave Marxism constructs socialism piecemeal as an archipelago of real utopias that stretch across the world'. In short, Burawoy argues that the third wave of Marxism, the current period, is characterised by transformative projects anchored in concrete experiments in a myriad of local spaces that rely on fundamentally participatory democratic processes. Burawoy is thus providing a radically novel periodisation of Marxism that shows how its evolution has been integrally linked to the essential commodification of labour, money and nature.

Moving from the commodification of labour, money and nature and the concomitant shifts in Marxist theory and practice, Satgar looks to Gramsci to take forward our renewal of Marxism. Satgar powerfully demonstrates how Gramsci's Marxism is renewed by bringing it into discussion with international relations and the global political economy. In his contribution he shows how Gramscian interpretations have reduced Gramsci's theoretical legacy either to a narrow Western Marxist tradition or to that of an Italian thinker. In this framing, Gramsci's Marxism was married to a political economy bounded in the national space. Satgar shows, however, that over the past three decades Gramsci's Marxism has been globalised, which has disrupted the dominance of classical Marxist understandings of imperialism and neo-Marxist approaches to hegemony within the world system. Thus Satgar challenges the version of Gramscian thought that locates Gramsci within Western Marxism or even more narrowly, as an Italian thinker, and he places neo-Gramscian scholarship within Burawoy's third wave of Marxism. Through the efforts of a Gramscian-inspired, transnational historical materialism a new approach to global political economy has emerged. This scholarship has added to critical theory, introducing a new way of understanding power and how social relations constitute global capitalism. In particular, Satgar highlights that a historicised understanding of global capitalist restructuring, the emergence of transnational classes, the disciplining role of transnational neoliberalism, the forms of neoliberal rule evoked by transnational classes (neoliberal constitutionalism and passive revolution) and the importance of counter-hegemonic resistance are some of the crucial themes emerging within a transnationalised neo-Gramscian Marxism to understand, explain and transform the current dynamics of global capitalism. Central in Satgar's embrace of a neo-Gramscian global political economy is the challenge of characterising and understanding post-apartheid South Africa's neoliberalisation as the making of a 'passive revolution'. Satgar concludes by challenging some of the limits within a transnationalising Gramscian Marxism, in particular the need to posit a new analysis of the crisis of global capitalism, the need for a stronger ecological perspective and for greater engagement with anti-capitalist politics and alternatives. Satgar thus provides us with an innovative and creative approach to understanding the global character of capitalism and the importance of resistance.

Having provided new and exciting ideas about the periodisation of Marxism, democracy and global relevance in Part One, in Part Two of the volume we look at the engagement of Marxism with left politics. Here the emphasis is on 'redeeming' Marx through critique, social reproduction and ecological awareness. In the first chapter of this section, Veriava recovers the dying tradition of critique and powerfully argues that at the heart of Marx's ideas about social transformation is the importance of critique. Veriava argues for critique that is 'self-consciously, and militantly, directed at a positive, or better, constitutive task' and asks how critique might play this 'constitutive task' that is required for politics today. He explores this question through the work of Michel Foucault and Marx and ultimately shows how central a component of modern political theory and political practice critique has been historically, and still is, to our understanding of transformative politics today. By reminding us of the importance of critique, Veriava has reinserted a fundamental aspect of political theorising and practice that is often neglected.

Moving from the importance of critique for left politics, Cock and Luxton trace the history of feminist engagement with Marxism, showing how the 'women's question' was seen as a problem of capitalism by classical Marxists, including Engels and Lenin. Cock and Luxton show how later attempts by feminists to integrate feminism with socialism tended toward dualistic and essentialist analyses of the modes of production and patriarchy. They argue that the success of the current Marxist revitalisation hinges on a more equal relationship and that 'this integration is best described as a socialist feminism based on the understanding that "the liberation of women depends on the liberation of all people"'. They trace the debate on domestic labour to the broader concept of social reproduction, which sees society as a totality in which social reproduction is central. Cock and Luxton suggest that gender is no longer collapsed into capitalism nor are there attempts to 'appropriate Marxist concepts of value or productive and unproductive work and apply them uncritically in an attempt to establish the value of domestic work'. They conclude that Marxists must confront the specificity of different women's oppression in specific historical contexts. Cock and Luxton provide an innovative approach, resting on the idea of social reproduction, to bring Marxism into dialogue with feminism.

While Cock and Luxton argue for creative synergies between Marxism and feminism, we also find similar innovative thinking in the dialogue between Marxism and ecology. Pillay introduces the idea that Marx had a deep appreciation for ecology and was not the anti-environmental theorist that many have suggested. Pillay situates the discussion in an analysis of the recent crisis of capitalism that is both a crisis of accumulation and a crisis of nature. Indeed, the economic and ecological moments are interlocked with the one profoundly affecting the other. Like Burawoy, Pillay suggests that humanity's future hinges on our ability to halt capitalism's destruction of nature by acknowledging the limits of a fossil-fuel capitalism that is threatening the planet's capacity to reproduce itself. Pillay shows how most Marxists' readings of Marx highlight the social critique of capitalism and see nature's role as simply instrumental to human exchange. Drawing on recent work by John Bellamy Foster and Paul Burkett, Pillay rediscovers a deeply ecological side to Marx's writings. Pillay provides two sets of analyses: first, he shows how the recent crisis of capitalism is not a financial crisis, as many analysts claim, but has its roots in stagnation in the real economy, and second, he shows an ecological Marx who never saw nature as something simply to be conquered but as something that human existence depends on. With regard to this second point, in particular, Pillay argues that nature was central to Marx's thinking. He maintains that rescuing an ecological Marx is necessary both for our analysis of the link between the social and ecological crises, and for our political mobilisation of alliances between ecologists (green) and socialists/Marxists (red). Pillay thus provides a powerful argument for a greening of Marxism and looks to Marx to pave the way in this effort.

In Part Three, we look specifically at Marxism and socialism in Africa, with an emphasis on South Africa. This section is particularly important as Marxism in Africa is a neglected area within Marxist scholarship. For example, Eric Hobsbawm's monumental *How to Change the World* (2011) gives scant attention to Marxism's influence in Africa as well as Africa's influence on Marxism. Yet Africa's engagement with Marxism is significant and provides important lessons for the twenty-first century (Glaser and Walker 2010).

Glaser takes up this challenge and explores Marxism in Africa, a theme that Burawoy situates in the second wave of Marxism, by developing 'seven theses' on African Marxism. While Marxist–Leninist governance was a failure on the African continent, Glaser shows that important lessons can be drawn for contemporary politics seeking more egalitarian and democratic outcomes. He thus offers seven theses about Africa's Marxist–Leninist governments and movements: (i) there was no clear difference between the 'radicalism' of Marxist–Leninist regimes and the 'African socialist' ones; (ii) there was no clear difference of Marxist commitment between regimes that came to power via military coups and those that came to power through guerilla war; (iii) while Marxism–Leninism was culturally alien to Africa it was brought to Africa via cultural outsiders located in the colonies and ex-colonies themselves; (iv) there emerged a distinctive African Marxist–Leninist tradition; (v) the failure of Marxist–Leninist regimes was above all 'a product of flawed domestic choices';

(vi) the Marxist–Leninist slide into authoritarianism was the product of a flawed theory of democracy; and (vii) Marxism's future in progressive politics depends on its place as one ideological current among others.

Thus there was a distinctive contribution to Marxism, largely authoritarian in its practices, that was coming out of Africa. Whereas socialist movements acknowledged the importance of popular participation and participatory democracy, the vanguard style of party organisation stymied local energies in their efforts to play an active role in society. Indeed, there was very little effort to entrench post-independence democratic practices and challenges to the ruling party were rarely, if ever, tolerated. Not without irony, the turn to representative democracy in the 1990s corresponded with a shift to pro-capitalist projects, neoliberal economic policies and a complete abandonment of socialist projects. Glaser essentially provides a new and powerful reading of engagement with Marxism in Africa and draws important lessons from this history.

Also drawing lessons from Marxism in Africa, Saul takes the discussion to two particular cases – Tanzania and Mozambique – and asks whether these experiences have anything to teach us today, especially in South Africa. Saul homes in on the choices made by the African National Congress (ANC) in its post-apartheid nation-building project and argues that it decidedly chose a capitalist route to development over a socialist one. Drawing on the experience in Tanzania, he problematises the way in which leadership was invoked, noting that South Africa's Black Economic Empowerment entrepreneurial leadership is also deeply problematic. He argues that the problem of leadership is 'one of the most difficult challenges facing those who would create a politics that is at once progressive in import and democratic in substance'. Although enlightened leadership is always needed, he points out that 'no "leadership" can long go unchecked from "below" – not if it is to avoid a fall into high-handedness and self-indulgent elitism'. He then draws lessons about the importance of imaginative planning from Mozambique's experiments with building 'socialism in Africa'. Saul explains that one of the crucial lessons to learn is not 'what not to do', but rather that we cannot afford 'not to dare to be self-reliant and economically imaginative and not to dare to be genuinely democratic and actively committed to the social and political empowerment of the people themselves. For not to so dare is, in our contemporary world, merely to wallow in a stagnant pond of self-serving vanguardism and in a post-Fanonist pattern of elite aggrandisement – even if such attitudes are, in South Africa, sustained within what is now a formally democratic process'. Saul thus makes a bold argument for confident, creative, accountable and imaginative leadership that prioritises people's needs and domestic development on the continent.

The next two chapters look specifically at South Africa and explore the possibilities for developing Marxist-inspired politics today. Bond, Desai and Ngwane explore the issue of 'uneven and combined Marxism', playing on Trotsky's famous 'uneven and combined development'. Bond, Desai and Ngwane take stock of South African politics both within the ANC-led Alliance and within the independent social movements. They argue that we must begin our discussion on the South African Left by recognising the contradictory reality of South African social relations. They argue that '"uneven and combined Marxism" implies a way of considering the difficulties of constructing independent left politics in the conjuncture of a long-term capitalist stagnation in a twenty-first-century South Africa, in which some sectors of the economy – construction, finance and commerce – have been booming while many other former labour-intensive sectors of manufacturing were de-industrialised ... and in which large sections of society are still peripheral to the interests of capital, domestic and global'. Through an analysis of social movement and left politics in South Africa, including the 2012 mineworkers' struggles in Marikana, they convincingly argue that we need to consider 'strategic questions for an agency-centred South African Left', an area that is often neglected. They are, thus, challenging us to think beyond our old certainties and creatively embark on agentic practices.

In the final chapter, Jara explores the way in which the ANC's post-apartheid politics has eschewed a Marxist orientation in favour of controlling and containing social forces, despite its rhetorical uses of 'colonialism of a special type' (CST) and 'national democratic revolution'. Jara shows how the 'ANC's continued use of Marxism has been transformed into attempts to hegemonise and marry the working class to a project to transnationalise and deracialise South African capitalism'. At the same time, the ANC has retribalised and re-ethnicised South African political and social spaces. Using the cases of housing in the Western Cape and legislation targeting rural areas and traditional leadership, Jara powerfully shows how 'the ANC's nation-building project has failed to grapple with racialised post-apartheid social struggles over housing in the Western Cape' and has attempted to retribalise the former bantustans through legislation that reinforces chieftancy and traditional patriarchal forms of leadership. Jara demonstrates that the ways in which the ANC has 'acted on race and nation in the post-apartheid period has opened the door to the reproduction of apartheid racial categories and regressive forms of nationalism including the return of ethnic identity, white supremacist arrogance, regressive racial polarisation, narrow black elite solidarity and Africanist chauvinism particularly in relation to the so-called Indian and coloured racial "minorities"'. He shows how the national democratic revolution (the core of the ANC's Marxism) is 'an exhausted Marxism that is denuded of both its radical impulses and emancipatory logics, particularly when it comes to resolving the national question'. Jara thus embarks on a journey of renewal that has the courage to think with and against Marxism as the basis for a new democratic left politics.

CONCLUSION

In the late 1990s and early twenty-first century there has been a renewed interest in Marxism. Together, the chapters in this volume provide a refreshingly rich and creative engagement with Marxism, and challenge us to think beyond the comfort zone of our certainties and to open our minds to varied approaches to Marxism. While the volume offers a range of perspectives on Marxism, there are also important common strands that hold the diverse viewpoints and themes together. All the chapters take as their starting point a sympathy toward a critical Marxism, a rejection of vanguardism, a desire for and appreciation of involvement in political practice, and a belief that there is enough in Marxism broadly defined to make it relevant and necessary in the contemporary phase of capitalism.

This renewal of Marxism demonstrates a commitment to retrieving the critical impulse in Marxist thought and to drawing on new sources of Marxism to make sense of the contemporary contradictions of global capitalism. What is particularly interesting about the Marxism(s) emerging is the willingness to question the foundations of 'Marxism' and to look reflexively to new ways of integrating Marxism(s) today. The Marxism of today is anchored in new forms of rebellious activity that mark it apart from the deferential, vanguard politics of the twentieth century and has shifted from the academy to struggles led by the exploited themselves through participatory democratic processes. The chapters that make up this volume force us to rethink our dyed-in-the-wool understandings of Marx and Marxism. Issues of democracy, ecology, feminism, critique, globalisation, historical lessons and questions of agency, as well as lineages of thought from a range of anti-capitalist traditions, must feature in our engagements with Marxism for the complex age in which we live.

NOTE

1   Like all political parties, the SACP has varying factions vying for power. The shifts in ideological focus partly reflect which faction has come to the fore at any given time.

REFERENCES

Callinicos, A. 1999. *Social Theory: A Historical Introduction*. New York: New York University Press.

Glaser, D. and Walker, D. 2010. *Twentieth Century Marxism: A Global Introduction*. London and New York: Routledge.

Hobsbawm, E. 2011. *How to Change the World: Tales in Marx and Marxism*. London: Little, Brown and Company.

Renton, D. 2004. *Dissident Marxism: Past Voices for Present Times*. London and New York: Zed Books.

SACP (South African Communist Party). 2012. 'Political Report to the 13th Congress'. Report presented to the 13th Congress of the South African Communist Party, 11–15 July.

Therborn, G. 2008. *From Marxism to Post-Marxism*. London: Verso.

DEMOCRATISING AND GLOBALISING MARXISM

1

MARXISM AND DEMOCRACY: LIBERAL, VANGUARD OR DIRECT?

Michelle Williams

One of the most contentious and neglected issues in Marxism is the content, role and place of democracy in transformative visions and practices. For some, Marxism is antithetical to democracy; for others, vanguard democracy represents the pinnacle of Marxism, and still others pay little attention to democracy at all. Marxism has gone through different phases, each phase with its unique social base and foundational ideas. At the time of the Second and Third Internationals, Marxism's social base was largely in working-class movements and parties, but shifted from the 1950s onwards to intellectuals overwhelmingly located in universities. This growth of and engagement with Marxism among intellectuals was in part due to the phenomenal growth and influence of university education (Hobsbawm 2011: 360). After reaching the peak of its influence in the academy during the 1970s, Marxism weakened through the course of the 1990s. In the late 1990s, however, a renewed interest in Marxism emerged among multi-class movements, middle- and working-class activists and intellectuals. These diverse social strata do not necessarily converge in their understandings of history, or their views of the causes and consequences of the dynamics of capitalism, but rather, share in their belief that 'another world is possible'.

This is the context within which I focus this chapter on literature – both liberal and Marxist – that has explicitly engaged the issue of democracy.[1] Because

Marxist influence over the last half-century has largely emanated from intellectuals located within universities, I focus on the various ways in which liberal and Marxist scholars have placed democracy against and within Marxism. While democracy is a contested concept that often incorporates very different notions of social change and control, with various actors and processes, twentieth-century liberals and Marxists tended to focus on representative and vanguard democracy respectively, largely ignoring the importance of direct and participatory democracy.[2] Bertrand Russell (1946: 14) pithily captured the central distinction: the Western understanding of democracy 'is that it consists in the *rule* of the majority; the Russian view is that it consists in the *interests* of the majority'. Neither tradition emphasised government *by* the people. The bifurcation of democracy into representative democracy versus vanguard democracy severely limited the debate on democracy in the twentieth century. In the twenty-first century, political movements are attempting to transcend this dichotomous view of democracy and have placed direct and participatory democracy at the centre of alternative, emancipatory visions of the future through meaningful deliberation and participation in political and economic life by ordinary citizens.[3]

LIBERAL CRITIQUES OF MARXIST-INSPIRED SOVIET COMMUNISM

In this section, the focus is on scholarship that has equated Marxism with twentieth-century 'communism' as this literature problematises the role of democracy in the communist movement and juxtaposes authoritarianism with representative democracy. Historically, Marxists did not focus their gaze on the importance of direct democracy,[4] content with either vanguard notions of democracy led by the Party together with the advanced working class or with the representative democracy of the Eurocommunists and social democrats. This neglect of the importance of direct democracy and its relation to representative democracy was exacerbated by the liberal tradition's collapsing of Marxism with authoritarianism and juxtaposing this with representative democracy as the only viable alternative.

There is a vast literature on Marxism that has been dominated by studies delving into the totalitarian and undemocratic nature of communism (for example, the work of Gabriel A. Almond, Hannah Arendt, Fernando Claudin, Joseph Schumpeter, Philip Selznick and Jacob Talmon). This image of Marxism as totalitarian, influenced by the larger political milieu of cold-war politics, was uniform in liberal literature on communism, which was concerned with demonstrating the Party's absolute control over the 'masses' (see, for example, the work of Almond, Selznick and Talmon) and continues to influence scholarship, as is evident in Francis Fukuyama's *The End of History and the Last Man* (1992) which posits market capitalism and representative democracy as the pinnacle of human history. Similarly, Stéphane Courtois et al.'s *Black Book of Communism* (1999) concludes that communism is morally similar to Nazism, implicitly positing representative democracy as the only morally acceptable alternative. This anti-Marxist position also influenced the apartheid state, which framed the liberation struggle as part of the 'rooi gevaar' (red danger) coming out of the Soviet Union and influencing the South African liberation movement. The roots of this cold-war tradition hark back to the 1950s.

Many scholars in the mid-twentieth century were heavily informed by the liberal political tradition, taking representative democracy to be the one and only alternative to totalitarian communism (for example, Almond, Schumpeter, Selznick and Talmon). This tradition referred to vanguard democracy as totalitarian because of the way in which the Party (ostensibly made up of the advanced working class and revolutionary activists) enjoyed absolute power in the name of working class majoritarianism (see for example, Selznick 1952). This link between vanguard democracy and authoritarianism had merit, as Joseph Femia's *Marxism and Democracy* (1993) shows how vanguard notions of democracy ultimately lead to absolute elite control in which individual voices are silenced.

Underpinning this allegiance to the liberal tradition was a critique of the dangers inherent in popular participation in politics. With the rise of fascism and the post-World War I establishment of totalitarian regimes (ostensibly based on mass participation), there was a tendency to link 'participation' with the concept of totalitarianism (Pateman [1970] 1999: 2). Thus the liberal tradition conflated totalitarianism with communism, participatory democracy and authoritarianism. In response, by the middle of the century, scholars in the liberal political tradition had cast grave doubts on popular participation in politics. In South Africa this resonated with apartheid policies that sought to exclude the majority from politics and embrace a narrow representative democracy for the white minority. In effect, what the ascendance of the liberal political tradition represented was a shift from a democratic theory centred on participation of 'the people' to a democratic theory based on the participation of an elite minority (104).

For many liberal scholars the intellectual roots of this shift could be traced back to Schumpeter's *Capitalism, Socialism, and Democracy* ([1942] 1975) in which he argues that democracy is not a theory of particular ideals or ends, but rather, is a political method with certain institutional arrangements for arriving at political decisions. Like the scholars he later influenced, Schumpeter (269) looked suspiciously on a participatory and decision-making role for the people and preferred to support the idea that a democratic method was defined by competition for votes among leaders.[5] Schumpeter's characterisation of the democratic method and the dangers of popular participation were widely accepted by the 1950s tradition, which built an entire canon of scholarship on these basic principles (Pateman [1970] 1999: 5). The disregard for popular participation ultimately bifurcated democratic politics into representative and vanguard democracies, both of which rely on elites – elected officials or advanced working class – as the guiding force in society. In many ways, the apartheid state adopted the liberal cold-war view of Marxism, though it was not itself liberal.

One of the most influential statements of the inherent dangers of mass participation and its links with communist totalitarianism was Talmon's *The Origins of Totalitarian Democracy* (1952), in which he traces the history of what he calls 'totalitarian democracy' and is interested in showing how representative democracy and totalitarian democracy, while originating from similar traditions of eighteenth-century political theory, ultimately diverged in opposite directions (3). Demonstrating his distrust of popular participation, Talmon (250) argues that direct democracy, unlimited sovereignty and egalitarian social ideals hold within them the tendency toward totalitarian control of society. He further argues that the modern abstraction of human beings from their social relations (that is classes), which he sees at the core of the Marxian tradition, is a powerful vehicle for totalitarianism. For Talmon, communism is inherently totalitarian and popular participation in politics lends itself toward this end.

Shifting from the political implications of popular participation, the liberal tradition drew a link between individual psychology and vulnerability to communist manipulation (see for example, Almond 1954). Again strongly influenced by the liberal political tradition, scholars were increasingly concerned about the lack of capacity of the general population for democratic politics. Political sociology provided prolific empirical studies into political attitudes that summarised the primary characteristics of citizens from the lower socio-economic categories as not only displaying a lack of interest in politics, but, more importantly, harbouring 'widespread non-democratic or authoritarian attitudes' (Pateman [1970] 1999: 3). This led many in the liberal tradition to conclude that the 'classical' view of a democratic person (capable of participating in decision-making processes) was unrealistic and increased participation would lead to instability of the current system (see for example, the work of Almond, Seymour Martin Lipset and Schumpeter). The liberal tradition, therefore, drew a link between the 'authoritarian' personality traits in the 'masses' and the attraction to communism. For example, Lipset's *Political Man* (1963) adumbrates the link between education, socio-economic status and national development and a tendency toward authoritarianism and an attraction to communist ideology. The average person on the street was, the argument suggests, simply not equipped for participation in the political system.

In general, with their focus on the totalitarian character of Marxist-inspired communist experiments and their juxtaposition of totalitarian communism with representative democracy, these scholars challenged Marxism's relevance in democratic conceptions of social transformation. One of the enduring legacies of the liberal tradition's treatment of Marxism is that it narrowed the discussion of democracy to mean representative, electoral democracy, conflating participatory democracy with vanguard democracy and thus dismissing it as a form of authoritarianism. While the liberal tradition's positioning of communism against representative democracy was largely an ideological tool to delegitimate Marxism, it also served to highlight the contradictory notion of democracy within the Marxist tradition. It also had the further effect of appropriating representative democracy as a liberal invention, distancing representative democracy from radical, egalitarian politics. The liberal characterisation, however, provoked responses from a range of scholars within the Marxist tradition that provided critique of Marxism (and communism) and reintroduced the importance of democracy for Marxism.

MARXIST CRITIQUES OF TWENTIETH-CENTURY SOVIET COMMUNISM

Liberal scholars were not the only critics of Marxist-inspired Soviet communist experiments. Indeed, a whole generation of Marxist intellectuals devoted a significant amount of intellectual energy to distancing Marxism from twentieth-century communism (for example, Theodor Adorno, Claudin, Max Horkheimer, Lukács, Herbert Marcuse and Palmiro Togliatti). 'Western

Marxists', from Antonio Gramsci and Lukács to the Frankfurt School's critical theory to Jürgen Habermas's communicative action, pried open the ideological straightjacket of vanguard party politics to allow theoretical engagement with Marxism to include culture, epistemology, aesthetics and reconciliation (rather than domination) with nature (Anderson 1976; Jay 1984; Therborn 2008: 87–91).

While not explicitly a Marxist, but still critical of the Soviet Union's 'communism', Arendt saw the demise of class society, which she linked to a sense of hopelessness among the populace, providing the basis for totalitarianism. In *The Origins of Totalitarianism* (1951) Arendt (313–314) argues that totalitarianism occurs when class society (and the concomitant institutions in civil society such as parties and labour organisations) breaks down and mass society develops in its stead. Because membership in a class is the primary integrative mechanism linking the individual to civil society, its demise causes people to lose their last remaining link to society, which ultimately makes them particularly susceptible to feelings of anomie (317). She thus shares in the liberal assumption about the psychological basis for attraction to totalitarian communism. For Arendt (351–352), the appeal of totalitarianism is its offer of consistency, predictability, organisation and a vision of the future, which is infinitely more attractive than the uncertainty of reality. Thus, the separation of individuals from meaningful social relations creates the conditions for the emergence of totalitarianism (315–317). Further challenging the liberal tradition, in *The Human Condition* (1958) Arendt develops her conception of the political in which she draws heavily on the participatory democratic tradition. Her critique of communism as totalitarian is fundamentally different from others in the 1950s in that she is interested in counterposing totalitarianism (which she sees as possible in both communism and liberal democracy) against a more direct and participatory democratic conception of politics. While the liberals see representative democracy as integrating people, Arendt (1951: 312) thinks it facilitates societal breakdown by excluding the majority of the population from politics and by weakening civil society as it separates people from each other. Arendt's critique echoes Karl Marx's (1967: 226–227) own critique as he argues that 'liberal' democracy results in alienation and the 'separation of man from his community, from himself, and from other men'. Humans become separated from their communities to such a degree that society comes to exist outside of human beings rather than being integrally connected to the very essence of what it means to be human (Femia 1993: 25).

Similarly, Claudin's monumental two volumes provide an incisive challenge to the liberal rendition of communism by offering his own critique from within the movement. While certainly critical of the totalitarian character of the International Communist Movement, Claudin differs from the liberal tradition in that he does not equate totalitarianism with Marxism or communism. In *The Communist Movement* ([1970] 1975) Claudin follows the history of the Communist Party of the Soviet Union's (CPSU's) slide into totalitarianism, and as he does so he juxtaposes totalitarian communism with democratic and participatory visions of communism that are rooted in a Marxist tradition. Implicitly, Claudin is critiquing vanguard democracy and arguing for direct and participatory democracy within the communist movement. Claudin describes the Comintern as the totalitarian institution par excellence and emphasises the extent to which Soviet foreign policy played a pernicious role in the evolution of communist parties around the world. The CPSU encouraged 'sectarianism and authoritarianism, favoring the dogmatization of Marxism in its Bolshevik version and leading to underestimation of the national originality of other countries' (Claudin [1970] 1975: 93). Importantly, however, Claudin (640) also emphasises the possibility as well as the importance of 'the winning of autonomy' by national communist parties, which he takes to be a necessary condition for the working out of party positions responsive to local conditions and concerns. Unlike the liberal tradition which sees communism as inevitably tending toward totalitarianism, Claudin suggests that autonomy from the CPSU was a precondition for communist parties to develop democratic practices. While his critique of the CPSU often suggests a more participatory understanding of democracy, Claudin ultimately continues to work within the parameters of vanguard democracy in which the national communist party at the helm of the state would be the leading force in national developments. Claudin thus challenges the confines of liberal scholarship on Marxist-inspired alternatives, but does not develop a more participatory and direct understanding of democracy.

Another generation of scholars responding in the 1970s and 1980s were those studying Eurocommunism,[6] a movement that challenged authoritarian communism in general and the authority of the CPSU in particular. Analysts in this tradition tend to draw a distinct line between the pre-1960s, characterised by CPSU hegemony, and the post-1960s characterised by national communist parties' relative autonomy vis-à-vis the CPSU (for example, Boggs and Plotke 1980). Scholars of the Eurocommunist movement were largely interested in showing that certain European communist parties developed deep commitments to representative democratic institutions in the post-1960s era. According to Carl Boggs and David Plotke (1980) the Eurocommunist parties challenged the CPSU's hegemony and reintroduced the importance of democratic practices in the transformation of society. After the Sino-Soviet split and the concomitant demise in CPSU hegemony, communist parties in Europe began rethinking ideological and strategic themes that distinguished them from both social democracy and Marxism–Leninism (7). They argue that in this transition Eurocommunism expanded Marxism by theorising the importance of embracing diverse social groups (for example, the middle class, religious groups, women's groups) in a mass party that engaged in political struggles within the existing representative institutions and was guided by a principled support for social and political pluralism (7). They recognised that representative democracy allowed for diverse social interests to be aggregated by political parties. In short, Eurocommunism reclaimed and expanded on Marxism by merging the commitment to socialism with democracy, seeking the gradual internal democratisation of existing state apparatuses, and hence, advocating a peaceful transition to socialism (Ross 1980: 40). Following Karl Kautsky, the Eurocommunists understood that universal suffrage could make the state an 'expression of popular will' if diligently pursued by the working class (Femia 1993: 59, 100). They rescued the idea that representative democracy can be an instrument of emancipation rather than domination, but this depended on the working class's capacity to shape the state. Eurocommunism's critique of the Soviet Union's vanguard democracy did not translate into an appreciation for direct democracy in conjunction with representative democracy. Nevertheless, this scholarship is useful in highlighting the importance of representative democratic practices in the transition to socialism and helped rescue democracy in Marxism from the liberal scholars' rendition.

Another critical Marxist tradition has challenged the omnipotence of the Soviet Union's influence within national contexts. In this vein, there has been research into the Marxist tradition in the US labour movement in the 1930s and 1940s that contests the totalitarian conception of communist parties. For example, scholarship on the Communist Party's influential role in American unionism in the 1930s challenges the view of pre-1960s Soviet hegemony and argues that of the dynamic unions that emerged from the Depression-era labour upsurge in the United States, communist unions were the most democratic and responsive to their working-class base (see for example, Stepan-Norris and

Zeitlin 2002). Through analysis of historical documents Judith Stepan-Norris and Maurice Zeitlin challenge the scholarship on the totalitarian and undemocratic character of the Communist Party and its pernicious role in American unionism and argue that in the 1930s the Communist Party was not only highly responsive to its working-class base, but was also the main expression of indigenous, working-class radicalism. While this scholarship is important in demonstrating the Communist Party's responsiveness to the working class, it still works within the vanguard understanding of democracy in which the Party plays the pivotal role.

In addition to these responses, a prolific neo-Marxist literature contesting the Western canon focuses on the Bolshevik Revolution of 1917 (for example, Rabinowitch 1968 and [1978] 2008; Smith 1983). This body of scholarship demonstrates the democratic potential in the months before and during, as well as in the first years after the 1917 Revolution and the many forces working against its success. We can also point to the 1956 Hungarian protests, the 1968 Czechoslovakia movement and the 1980s Solidarity movement in Poland for examples of attempts to create democratic practices within communism. In the former East Germany, Rudolf Bahro's *The Alternative in Eastern Europe* (1978) offers a powerful critique of authoritarianism from within and provides a vision of a democratic alternative. Hal Draper (2004) worked with the idea that 'socialism was a process of complete democratic change' that could only happen through 'socialism from below' and thus argued for a third-way socialism that was neither Stalinism (that is vanguard democracy) nor social democracy (that is representative democracy) (Renton 2004: 7, 19). Yugoslavian thinkers such as Mihailo Marković and Rudi Supek argued for shop-floor democracy that is not simply a function of central planning but that decides 'all questions of production and distribution' (Femia 1993: 31). Despite these attempts, direct democracy was not a focus for many twentieth-century Marxists as it throws up serious challenges to top-down central planning and the paramount role of the Party; the more direct participation on the shop floor and the less predictable economic planning from above. Nevertheless, this scholarship challenges the idea that communism is inherently anti-democratic and demonstrates that there was also a deep appreciation for radical forms of democracy within the Marxist tradition. Also in the second half of the twentieth century a thriving scholarship emerged from Marxist historians and philosophers such as Christopher Hill, Hobsbawm, Edward Thompson, C.L.R. James, Marcuse, Horkheimer, Adorno and Jean-Paul Sartre, all of whom pioneered humanist, open Marxism(s) that recognised the importance of spiritual and cultural values. Along these lines, Marxists critiqued 'liberal democracy' for turning people into isolated beings alienated from their social nature (Femia 1993: 20) and argued for the participation of ordinary people (Barber 1984; Bobbio 1976). Other Marxists such as Louis Althusser (1970 and 1972), Ralph Miliband ([1969] 2009) and Nicos Poulantzas (1973) explored questions of the state and its relation to the economy.

In the latter part of the twentieth century, a new generation of Marxists emerged that looked to the world-system and periphery for their inspiration. For example, Immanuel Wallerstein (1974) offers a critique of the Soviet Union when he argues that capitalism operates on a world scale with the politically and economically powerful core profoundly shaping the prospects of the politically and economically weak periphery. In his analysis, cold-war rivalry is no longer understood as a battle between capitalism and an alternative, but rather as Soviet modernisation within the logic of capitalist accumulation. Samir Amin ([1985] 1990) shares Wallerstein's broad perspective, but has also counterpoised the strategy of delinking as an alternative to building socialism in one country in the context of anti-systemic struggles within the global periphery. Amin argues that countries in the periphery must delink from the capitalist system to a degree, in order to achieve development in their national interests. Inspired by 1968 (Wallerstein) and Bandung Third World revolutionary nationalism (Amin), both conclude that, in the light of Soviet authoritarianism, a socialist alternative has to be profoundly democratic.

There has also been scholarship, explicitly on the global South, looking at the way in which Marxism has influenced movements and parties (see Glaser's and Saul's chapters this volume; Ismael and 'at El-Sa'id 1990; Mortimer 1974). Much of this scholarship shows the authoritarian practices of movements in the global South, but also highlights the importance of developing democratic alternatives. For example, Cathy Schneider's (1995) investigation into the Communist Party of Chile's attempt to organise shantytowns in Chile's sprawling townships is an eloquent statement of popular mobilisation from below. There have also been important contributions looking at African socialism and Afro-Marxism that explore the various attempts in post-colonial Africa to chart out socialist paths in varying conditions (Arrighi and Saul 1973; Cabral 1973 and 1979; Fanon 1962; Saul 1990; see also Glaser this volume) as well as important contributions to Marxist theory on the global South from the dependency school that argued that underdevelopment emerged as a result of global capitalism (Baran 1957; Frank 1967). Many of these scholars were taking on issues of extending democracy beyond the political sphere and beyond the Party by recognising power relations in society.

This more recent scholarship helps us re-imagine the importance of direct democracy in transformative politics as we move beyond the twentieth century's bifurcated understanding of vanguard versus representative democracy.

BEYOND BIFURCATION: DIRECT DEMOCRACY IN THE TWENTY-FIRST CENTURY

For twenty-first-century movements such as the World Social Forum, Occupy Movement, Brazilian participatory budgeting and Kerala's democratic decentralisation, direct democracy is a vital part of constituting visions and practices. Movements around the world increasingly demonstrate their distrust of political and economic leaders as the institutions of representative democracy, and vanguard party politics is losing legitimacy, with headline stories splashed across the world of the 1 per cent's (as opposed to the 99 per cent) complicity in the corruption of political processes. These movements demonstrate that ordinary people are tired of paying the price of an under-regulated global economy that provides enormous benefits to the 1 per cent, while the 99 per cent live increasingly precarious lives. Movements are increasingly calling on government to be accountable and responsive to people, rather than to corporations. In this context we have seen an explosion of movements across the globe which, while they vary significantly, share in their belief that 'another world is possible' through the active participation of ordinary people.

What is meant by direct democracy? Direct democracy (often referred to as participatory or radical democracy) is where ordinary citizens are directly involved in the activities of political (and economic) governance. Unlike representative democracy where elected officials act on behalf of citizens, or vanguard democracy where the party acts on behalf of the people, people participate directly in deliberation and decision making in direct democracy. It is about popular empowerment of ordinary citizens to make decisions and carry through with implementation. Key for direct democracy is the actual participation of ordinary citizens (in other words, direct democracy requires participatory practices). Obviously, participation is crucial for this type of democracy. But what is participation? For some it simply means showing up to a meeting where citizens are informed about decisions made. For others it means consulting ordinary people about plans, although the power to make decisions lies with the leaders or officials. Neither of these forms are real participation. Meaningful participation requires that ordinary people engage in deliberation, make decisions and very importantly, have the power to ensure the implementation of the decisions (Pateman [1970] 1999). It is government *by* the people. For direct democracy to have meaning, then, ordinary people must directly participate in and control decision-making processes in the political, economic and social domains and have the power to ensure implementation, which requires access to resources and information. Open and transparent processes are a necessary condition for effective participation. There are examples of weak versions of direct democracy where citizens simply vote yes/no on various initiatives and referendums. There are also strong versions in which citizens directly make decisions about local governance and the distribution of resources.

One of the legacies of the liberal tradition's (mis)appropriation of representative democracy is that direct democracy is often placed in opposition to it. Yet direct democracy is not a replacement for or competitor of representative democracy, but rather, the two forms of democracy are vital institutional spaces for deepening and extending democracy in society. Direct democracy is appropriate and desirable for local-level decision making, while representative democracy is necessary for complex and large societies in which direct decision making by every member of the polity is impossible for every decision. The two types of democracy should not be seen to be in conflict with each other; rather, direct democracy and representative democracy complement and deepen democratic impulses in each other. Indeed, the aspiration of government *by* the people is further realised through combining direct and representative democracy.

This recent emphasis on direct democracy was anticipated by South African scholar Rick Turner, who argued for radical forms of democracy within the liberation movement in South Africa. The search for humanist and participatory dimensions of Marxism was articulated by Turner in his *The Eye of the Needle* (1972). After his assassination in 1978, he became an iconic hero of the liberation movement, but it was only toward the end of the millennium that the ideas embodied in *The Eye of the Needle* started resonating once again with movements. Turner looked to the importance of imagination, human agency, values and consciousness, which, for him, lie at the centre of social *and* human transformation. In other words, social transformation and human freedom only made sense in dialogue with each other as the one could not be attained without the other. He placed worker control and democratic planning at the centre of his understanding of participatory democracy and at the centre of human freedom (1972: 34–47). For Turner, vanguard democracy led by the Party impoverishes human freedom and social transformation.

One of the most famous recent examples of a direct democratic experiment is the Brazilian Workers' Party's (PT as it is popularly called) participatory budgeting in Porto Alegre (Baiocchi 2003; Baiocchi, Heller and Silva 2011; Bruce 2004). In 1986 the PT won the mayoral position in the city, but was not a majority in the city council. This led it to innovate. It decided to open up part of the city's budget for popular participation. It held popular assemblies in neighbourhoods across the city where ordinary people got to decide what the city's development priorities were. By democratising the allocation of part of the city's budget, civil society was transformed into a robust arena of citizen participation. Neighbourhood associations increased from 240 in 1986 to 600 in 2000 and district-level popular councils increased from 2 to 12. Housing cooperatives jumped from 11 to 71 between 1994 and 2000 (Baiocchi 2005: 42). The participatory budgeting process not only gave civil society a voice to determine the investment of some of the city's funds, but also created vibrant institutions in civil society (Goldfrank 2003). This is clearly a model of democracy that is different from vanguard democracy in which the Party dominates, or representative democracy in which elected officials make all the decisions.

Another radical experience in direct democracy is the Communist Party of India (Marxist)'s (CPI[M]) democratic decentralisation campaign in Kerala, India (Williams 2008). While the CPI(M) is a vanguard party in name, in practice it has had to be extremely responsive and accountable to its support base, forcing it to create spaces of mass participation in state governance.[7] Kerala became famous in the developing world in the 1980s for its achievements in human development, but had not achieved economic growth, which was necessary to maintain its redistributive programmes. In the 1990s the CPI(M)-led state government decided to try an exciting and novel experiment in participatory democracy (Williams 2008). The state devolved forty per cent of its finances to local government institutions that had to engage in local development planning with communities. Communities were involved in the deliberations, the decisions made and the implementation of development plans. A few elements of the decentralisation project are worth highlighting. First, a significant part of the funds were earmarked for local economic development projects, mostly through cooperatives. In this way, the state was marrying direct democracy in the political sphere to the economic sphere. Second, the devolution of power and resources was not about bypassing the state, but rather was about using participatory democracy to strengthen (through becoming more accountable and effective) the representative institutions. Third, this shift to decentralisation was not simply a decision of the state, but was integrally linked to the organisational support of the CPI(M). For example, the CPI(M) helped train thousands of community activists, through thousands of hours of training and four thousand pages of training material. The point is that it requires immense organisational support to coordinate grassroots activists. Finally, the project has been successful in galvanising people to become more involved in the development of their communities.

It must be noted, however, that these recent experiments in direct democracy work within representative democracy. It was the PT mayoral election victory that provided the opportunity for participatory budgeting, and the CPI(M)'s involvement in representative democracy that created the space for the radical experiment in direct democracy.

CONCLUSION

What the PT in Brazil and the CPI(M) in Kerala teach us is that radical experiments in direct democracy are part of the twenty-first-century Marxist imagination. What is also particularly noteworthy of these two experiments in direct democracy is that they were spearheaded by political parties. The experiences of Brazil and Kerala suggest that Marxist political parties can transform themselves from vanguard parties to parties that champion direct democracy and representative democracy. While I have focused largely on political democracy, any attempt at achieving democratic, egalitarian, ecologically sustainable, anti-capitalist transformation requires economic democracy in conjunction with political democracy. Thus, the same systems of direct and representative democracy from the political sphere must simultaneously extend into the economic sphere where workers own and control the relations of production and make decisions about how production is organised and about the distribution of surplus. Recent events in Egypt, Syria, Tunisia, Argentina, Bolivia and at the grassroots in South Africa could be described as further examples of such movements in the struggle for political and economic democracy.

NOTES

1   This is not an exhaustive discussion of democracy in either tradition, but rather provides a rough sketch of the way in which liberals and Marxists have viewed democracy within the Marxist tradition.

2   While representative, parliamentary and liberal democracy are often used inter-changeably to refer to elected governments or parliamentary institutions, I prefer to use representative democracy to explicitly refer to systems of government in which representatives are elected by the citizenry (universal suffrage) and consti-tutionalism, division of powers, basic universal and civil rights such as freedom of speech (both written and spoken), the right of assembly and artistic freedom are upheld. Representatives can be there in the role of fiduciary (that is, representing general interests and able to make independent decisions in their best judgements) or delegate (that is, representing particular interests and beholden to decisions made by their constituents) (Bobbio 1987: 47–48).

3   This is not to deny earlier attempts to envision a participatory democratic society. In the 1970s the New Left also pushed the idea of direct democracy, but it did not take root in many of the movements seeking social transformation.

4   There are, of course, important exceptions to this generalisation. The point I am making is that the *dominant* tradition within Marxism was vanguard democracy and not direct democracy.

5   He argued against the political participation of the 'electoral mass', because the 'masses' were only capable of 'a stampede' (Schumpeter [1942] 1975: 283).

6   The Italian, French and Spanish Communist Parties were the main parties that made up the Eurocommunist movement.

7   Like the SACP, the CPI(M) has factions vying for power. Since the 1990s the grass-roots faction has been able to win enough space to shift the party into radically democratic spaces.

REFERENCES

Adorno, T. and Horkheimer, M. (1956) 2011. *Towards a New Manifesto*. London: Verso.

Almond, G. 1954. *The Appeals of Communism*. New Jersey: Princeton University Press.

Althusser, L. 1970. *For Marx*. New York: Vintage.

Althusser, L. 1972. *Politics and History*. London: New Left Books.

Amin, S. (1985) 1990. *Delinking: Towards a Polycentric World*. London: Zed Books.

Anderson, P. 1976. *Considerations on Western Marxism*. London: New Left Books.

Arendt, H. 1951. *The Origins of Totalitarianism*. New York: Hartcourt Brace and Company.

Arendt, H. 1958. *The Human Condition*. Chicago: University of Chicago Press.

Arrighi, G. and Saul, J.S. 1973. *Essays on the Political Economy of Africa*. New York: Monthly Review Press.

Bahro, R. 1978. *The Alternative in Eastern Europe*. Translated by D. Fernbach. London: Verso.

Baiocchi, G. 2003. 'Participation, activism, and politics: The Porto Alegre experiment'. In *Deepening Democracy: Institutional Innovations in Empowered Participatory Governance*, edited by A. Fung and E.O. Wright. London and New York: Verso.

Baiocchi, G. 2005. *Militants and Citizens: The Politics of Participatory Democracy in Porto Alegre*. Palo Alto, CA: Stanford University Press.

Baiocchi, G., Heller, P. and Silva, M.K. 2011. *Bootstrapping Democracy: Transforming Local Governance and Civil Society in Brazil*. Palo Alto, CA: Stanford University Press.

Baran, P. 1957. *The Political Economy of Growth*. New York: Monthly Review Press.

Barber, B. 1984. *Strong Democracy: Participatory Politics for a New Age*. Berkeley: University of California Press.

Bobbio, N. 1976. *Which Socialism? Marxism, Socialism, and Democracy*. Minneapolis: University of Minnesota Press.

Bobbio, N. 1987. *The Future of Democracy*. Minneapolis: University of Minnesota Press.

Boggs, C. and Plotke, D. (eds). 1980. *The Politics of Eurocommunism: Socialism in Transition*. Boston: South End Press.

Bruce, I. 2004. *The Porto Alegre Alternative: Direct Democracy in Action*. London: Pluto Press.

Cabral, A. 1973. *Return to the Source: Selected Speeches by Amilcar Cabral*. New York: Monthly Review Press.

Cabral, A. 1979. *Unity and Struggle: Speeches and Writings*. New York: Monthly Review Press.

Claudin, Fernando. (1970) 1975. *The Communist Movement: From Comintern to Cominform*. Vol. 1 translated by B. Pearce and Vol. II translated by F. MacDonagh. New York: Monthly Review Press.

Courtois, S., Werth, N., Panne, J-L., Paczkowski, A., Bartosek, K. and Margolin, J-L. 1999. *Black Book of Communism: Crimes, Terror, Repression*. Cambridge, MA: Harvard University Press.

Draper, H. 2004. *Socialism from Below*. Alameda, CA: Center for Socialist History.

Fanon, F. 1962. *The Wretched of the Earth*. Harmondsworth: Penguin.

Femia, J. 1993. *Marxism and Democracy*. Oxford: Oxford University Press.

Frank, A.G. 1967. *Capitalism and Underdevelopment in Latin America*. New York: Monthly Review Press.

Fukuyama, F. 1992. *The End of History and the Last Man*. New York: Free Press.

Goldfrank, B. 2003. 'Making participation work in Porto Alegre'. In *Radicals in Power: The Workers' Party (PT) and Experiments in Urban Democracy in Brazil*, edited by G. Baiocchi. New York: Zed Books.

Gramsci, A. (1971) 1992. *Selections from the Prison Notebooks*, edited by Quintin Hoare and Geoffrey Nowell Smith. New York: International Publishers.

Habermas, J. 1996. *Between Facts and Norms: Contributions to a Discourse Theory of Law and Democracy*. Cambridge, MA: MIT Press.

Hill, C. 1984. *The World Turned Upside Down: Radical Ideas During the English Revolution*. London: Penguin.

Hobsbawm, E. 2011. *How to Change the World: Tales in Marx and Marxism*. London: Little, Brown and Company.

Ismael, T.Y. and 'at El-Sa'id, R. 1990. *The Communist Movement in Egypt, 1920–1988*. New York: Syracuse University Press.

James, C.L.R. 1980. *The Black Jacobins: Toussaint l'Ouverture and the San Domingo Revolution*. London: Allison and Busby.

Jay, M. 1984. *Marxism and Totality*. Berkeley: University of California Press.

Kautsky, K. 1988. *The Materialist Conception of History*. Translated by R. Meyer and J.H. Kautsky. New Haven: Yale University Press.

Lipset, S. 1963. *Political Man: The Social Bases of Politics.* New York: Anchor Books.

Lukács, G. 1968. *History and Class Consciousness: Studies in Marxist Dialectics.* Cambridge, MA: MIT Press.

Marcuse, H. 1958. *Soviet Marxism: A Critical Analysis.* New York: Columbia University Press.

Marković, M. 1965. 'Socialism and self-management', *Praxis,* 2 (3).

Marković, M. 1974. *The Contemporary Marx: Essays on Humanist Communism.* Nottingham: Spokesman Books.

Marx, K. 1967. 'On the Jewish Question'. In *Writings of the Young Marx,* edited by L.D. Easton and K.H. Guddat. New York: Doubleday.

Miliband, R. (1969) 2009. *The State in Capitalist Society.* London: Merlin Press.

Mortimer, R. 1974. *Indonesian Communism under Sukarno: Ideology and Politics.* Ithaca, NY: Cornell University Press.

Pateman, C. (1970) 1999. *Participation and Democratic Theory.* Cambridge: Cambridge University Press.

Poulantzas, N. 1973. *Political Power and Social Classes.* London: New Left Books.

Rabinowitch, A. 1968. *Prelude to Revolution: The Petrograd Bolsheviks and the July 1917 Uprising.* Bloomington: Indiana University Press.

Rabinowitch, A. (1978) 2008. *The Bolsheviks in Power: The First Year of Soviet Rule in Petrograd.* Bloomington: Indiana University Press.

Renton, D. 2004. *Dissident Marxism: Past Voices for Present Times.* London and New York: Zed Books.

Ross, G. 1980. 'The PCF and the end of Bolshevik dream'. In *The Politics of Eurocommunism: Socialism in Transition,* edited by K. Boggs and D. Plotke. Boston: South End Press.

Russell, B. 1946. *What is Democracy?* London: Allen and Unwin.

Sartre, J-P. 1976. *Critique of Dialectical Reason.* London: NLB Humanities Press.

Saul, J. 1990. *Socialist Ideology and the Struggle for Southern Africa.* Trenton, NJ: Africa World Press.

Schneider, C. 1995. *Shantytown Protests in Pinochet's Chile.* Philadelphia: Temple University Press.

Schumpeter, J. A. (1942) 1975. *Capitalism, Socialism, and Democracy.* New York: Harper Colophon Books.

Selznick, P. 1952. *Organizational Weapon.* Santa Monica: Rand Corporation.

Smith, S.A. 1983. *Red Petrograd: Revolution in the Factories, 1917–1918.* Cambridge: Cambridge University Press.

Stepan-Norris, J. and Zeitlin, M. 2002. *Left Out: Reds and America's Industrial Unions.* Cambridge: Cambridge University Press.

Supek, R. 1975. 'The sociology of workers' self-management'. In *Self-governing Socialism,* edited by B. Horvat, M. Marković, and R. Supek. White Plains: International Arts and Sciences Press.

Talmon, J.L. 1952. *The Origins of Totalitarian Democracy.* London: Secker and Warburg.

Therborn, G. 2008. *From Marxism to Post-Marxism.* London: Verso.

Thompson, E. 1966. *The Making of the English Working Class.* New York: Vintage.

Togliatti, P. 1979. *On Gramsci and Other Writings.* London: Lawrence and Wishart.

Turner, R. 1972. *The Eye of the Needle: Towards Participatory Democracy in South Africa.* Johannesburg: Ravan Press.

Wallerstein, I. 1974. *The Modern World System I: Capitalist Agriculture and the Origins of the European World-Economy in the Sixteenth Century.* London: Academic Press.

Williams, M. 2008. *The Roots of Participatory Democracy: Democratic Communists in South Africa and Kerala, India.* London and New York: Palgrave-Macmillan.

2

MARXISM AFTER POLANYI

Michael Burawoy

What should we do with Marxism? For most the answer is simple. Bury it! Mainstream social science has long since bid farewell to Marxism. Talcott Parsons (1967: 135) dismissed Marxism as a theory whose significance was entirely confined to the nineteenth century – a version of nineteenth-century utilitarianism of no relevance to the twentieth century. Ironically enough, he penned these reflections in 1968 in the midst of a major revival of Marxist thought across the globe – a revival that rejected Soviet Marxism as a ruling ideology, a revival that reclaimed Marxism's democratic and prefigurative legacy. The revival did not last long but suffered setbacks as revolutionary hopes were vanquished by repression and dictatorship and then by market fundament- alism. With the final collapse of the Soviet order in 1991, and the simultaneous market transition in China, the gravediggers pronounced Marxism finally dead and bells tolled across the world.

Facing such anti-Marxist euphoria, the last hold-outs often appear dogmatic and anachronistic. Marxists have, indeed, sometimes obliged their enemies by demonstrating their religious fervour in tracts that bear little relation to reality, defending Marxism in its pristine form, revealed in the scriptures of Karl Marx and Friedrich Engels. The disciples that followed Marx and Engels – Lenin, Plekhanov, Trotsky, Bukharin, Luxemburg, Kautsky, Lukács, Gramsci, Fanon,

Amin, Mao – were but a gloss on biblical readings of origins. Today's epigones do not place Marx and Engels in their context, as fallible beings whose thought reflected the period in which they lived, but as Christ-like figures and thus the source of eternal truth. In their view the founders can speak no falsehood.

Adopting neither burial nor revelation, a third approach to Marxism has been more measured. Many in the social sciences and beyond have appropriated what they consider salvageable, which might include Marxism's analysis of the creative power of capitalism, the notions of exploitation and class struggle, the idea of primitive accumulation, or even Marxist views of ideology and the state. These neo-Marxists and post-Marxists often combine the ideas of Marx and Marxism with those of other social theorists – Max Weber, Émile Durkheim, Michel Foucault, Pierre Bourdieu, Jürgen Habermas, Simone de Beauvoir, Catharine MacKinnon and so on. Indeed, these latter theorists had themselves absorbed many Marxist notions, often without acknowledging their debt, even as they expressed their hostility to Marxism. The neo-Marxists treat Marxism as a supermarket. They take what pleases them and leave behind what does not, sometimes paying their respects at the checkout, sometimes not. They have no qualms about discarding what does not suit the times.

The fourth approach, the one adopted here, is that Marxism is a living tradition that enjoys renewal and reconstruction as the world it describes and seeks to transform undergoes change. After all, at the heart of Marxism is the idea that beliefs – science or ideology – necessarily change with society. Thus, as the world diverges so must Marxism, reflecting diverse social and economic structures and historical legacies. However, Marxism cannot simply mirror the world. It seeks to change the world, but changing such a variegated world requires a variegated theory, a theory that keeps up with the times and accommodates places.

MARXISM AS AN EVOLVING TRADITION

If Marxism is an evolving tradition, what do all its varieties share that make them part of that tradition? What makes Marxism Marxism? What is its abiding core irrespective of the period, irrespective of the national terrain? What do all branches of Marxism have in common? If we think of the Marxist tradition as an ever-growing tree, we can ask: What are its roots? What defines its trunk? What are its branches?[1]

The roots themselves grow in a shifting entanglement of four foundational claims: historical materialism as laid out in the preface to the *Critique of Political Economy*, the premises of history as found in *The German Ideology*, notions of human nature as found in the *Economic and Philosophical Manuscripts*, and the relation of theory and practice as found in the *Theses on Feuerbach*. The trunk of the Marxist tree is the theory of capitalism, presented in the three volumes of *Capital*, and revised by inheritors over the last century and a half.

Then there are the successive branches of Marxism – German Marxism, Russian-Soviet Marxism, Western Marxism, Third World Marxism – some branches dead, others dying and yet others flourishing. Each branch springs from its own reconstruction of Marxism, responding to specific historical circumstances. German Marxism responded to the reformist tendencies within the German socialist movement of 1890–1920 as well as capitalism's capacity to absorb the crises it generates; Russian Marxism sprang from the dilemmas of the combined and uneven development of capitalism on a world scale, and of the battle over socialism in one country; Western Marxism was a response to Soviet Marxism, fascism and the failure of revolution in the West; and Third World Marxism grapples with the dilemmas of underdevelopment as well as colonial and post-colonial struggles.

When we examine this tree we see that Marxism may have begun as a small-scale project that did indeed link people across national boundaries – think of the First International. As classical Marxism garnered popular support it became tied to national politics (Russian, German, French and so on) from which it expanded into regional blocs – Soviet, Western and Third World Marxism. What is the scale of Marxism today? Even though its popular base has shrunk, I will argue that Marxism can no longer respond only to local, national or regional issues; it has to embrace global issues, issues that affect the entire planet. To reconstruct Marxism on a global scale requires, I argue, rethinking the material basis of Marxism through the lens of the market, but not in terms of its geographical scope (since markets have always been global as well as local), nor even in terms of neoliberal ascendancy (since markets have always moved through periods of expansion and contraction) but in terms of the novel modes of commodification.

In brief, there have been three waves of marketisation that have swept the world: the first spanning the nineteenth century, the second beginning after World War I and the third beginning in the mid-1970s. Associated with each wave is the commodification of a leading force of production, successively labour, money and nature. These are Karl Polanyi's (1944) three fictitious commodities whose commodification, he claimed, destroys their use value. Thus, when labour is subject to unregulated exchange it loses its use value – it cannot be productive; if money is subject to unregulated exchange the value of money becomes so volatile that businesses go out of business; and if nature is turned into a commodity it destroys our means of existence – the air we breathe, the water we drink, the land upon which we grow food, the bodies we inhabit. Each wave of commodification spawns a countermovement that is built on a distinctive set of expanding rights (labour, social and human) organised on an ever-widening scale: local, national and, presumptively, global. Finally, to each countermovement there corresponds a distinctive configuration of Marxism – classical Marxism based on the projection of an economic utopia; Soviet, Western and Third World Marxism based on state regulation; and finally, socio-logical Marxism based on an expanding and self-regulating civil society.

The periodisation of Marxism may be tied to the periodisation of capitalism but the periods themselves are continually reconstructed as a history of the evolving present, a history that makes sense of the present as both distinct from and continuous with the past. Marx (1967) saw only one period of capitalism, Lenin (1963) saw two and Ernest Mandel (1975) saw three. We, too, see three, not based on production but rather on the market as the most salient experi-ence of today. Here I do, indeed, break with the conventional Marxist claim that production provides the foundation of opposition to capitalism. This is no longer tenable: in part because production is the locus of the organisation of consent to capitalism, and in part because in the face of the global production of surplus labour populations, exploitation is rapidly becoming a sought-after privilege of the few. Exploitation continues to figure centrally in the dynamics of accumulation, but not in the experience of subjugated populations. In the Marxian analysis the experience of the market appears as the 'fetishism of commodities', a camouflage for the hidden abode of production, but it is much more than that, shaping multiple dimensions of human existence.

RECONSTRUCTING POLANYI

In making the market a fundamental prop of human existence I draw on Polanyi's theory and history of capitalism. Written in 1944, Polanyi's *The Great Transformation* examines the political and social consequences of the rise of the market from the end of the eighteenth century to the Great Depression. The market, Polanyi argues, had such devastating consequences that it generated a countermovement to protect society. The countermovement, however, could be as destructive as the market it sought to contain. Thus it included fascism and Stalinism as well as the New Deal and social democracy. Indeed, Polanyi concluded that such were its consequences that never again would humanity experiment with market fundamentalism. He was wrong – market fundamentalism struck our planet once again in the 1970s, threatening human existence and annihilating communities.

The reason for Polanyi's false optimism lies in his failure to take the logic of capitalism seriously. While he embraces Marx's early writings on alienation, he rejects Marx's theory of history, whether understood as a succession of modes of production, the self-destroying dynamics of capitalist competition, or the intensification of class struggle. But in rejecting the idea of laws of history, Polanyi also jettisons the logic of capital, in particular its recurrent deployment of market fundamentalism as a strategy for overcoming its internal contradictions. This, of course, is where David Harvey (2003 and 2005) steps in regarding 'neoliberalism' as an ideological offensive of capital against the gains made by labour in the period after World War II.[2]

Recognising the contemporary wave of market fundamentalism leads to questioning Polanyi's homogenising history of capitalism as a singular wave of marketisation giving way to a singular countermovement – what he calls the 'great transformation'. Referring specifically to the history of England, Polanyi recounts in detail the way the Speenhamland system protected labour from commodification until the passage of the 1834 New Poor Law that banished outdoor relief. The year 1834 marked, then, the establishment of a pure market in labour that, through the nineteenth century, generated movements against commodification – from the Chartist movement of 1848 that sought to give workers the vote, to the factory movement that sought to limit the length of the working day, to the abolition of the Combination Acts that sought to advance trade unions, to demands for unemployment insurance and minimum wages. These struggles were not about exploitation, argues Polanyi, but about the protection of labour from its commodification. Society was fighting back against the market.

In Polanyi's history, the commodification of labour was but part of a long ascendancy that continues from the end of the eighteenth century through World War I to the Great Depression. Facilitated by the commodification of money, itself ensured through the regulation of exchange rates by pegging them to the gold standard, the market expanded into the realm of international trade. Opening up an unregulated global market in trade with the fluctuating value of national currencies so destabilised individual national economies that states successively went off the gold standard and undertook protectionist policies. Protectionist regimes took the form of fascism in countries such as Italy, Germany and Austria, took the form of the New Deal in the US, took the form of Stalinism with its collectivisation and central planning in the Soviet Union and took the form of social democracy in Scandinavian countries. In Polanyi's eye the upward swing in commodification ultimately gives way to a counter-movement that could lead to socialism based on the collective self-regulation of society but was just as likely to give way to fascism and the restriction of freedom.

Knowing that Polanyi was wrong about the future, calls into question his account of the past. Thus re-examining Polanyi's argument reveals that there was not a singular upward trajectory in marketisation but at least three waves of marketisation (see Figure 2.1). The first takes us from Speenhamland to World War I and is primarily driven by the commodification of labour, followed by its protection, whereas the second wave takes us from World War I to the middle 1970s. The second wave originates with the commodification of money (and a renewed commodification of labour), leading to a countermovement involving the regulation of national economies. The third wave, known to many as neoliberalism, begins in 1973 with the oil crisis and initiates a third wave of marketisation featuring the recommodification of labour and money, but also the commodification of nature. We are still in the midst of the ascendancy of this third wave of marketisation. Along the way we have passed through struc-tural adjustment administered to the failing economies of the South and shock therapy adopted by the post-Soviet regime and its satellites in East and central Europe. Successive economic failures of state-regulated economies served to energise the ascendant belief in the market. The succession of financial crises in Asia and Latin America during the 1990s, culminating in the financial crisis of 2008, served to consolidate the power of finance capital.[3]

What is unique about the third period, however, is the way the expansion of capitalism has given rise to environmental degradation, moving toward ecological catastrophe. Whether we are referring to climate change or the dumping of toxic waste, the privatisation of water, air and land, or the trade in human organs, the commodification of nature is at the heart of capitalism's impending crisis. The countermovement in the third period will have to limit capitalism's tendency to destroy the foundations of human existence, calling for the restriction and regulation of markets and a socialisation of the means of production which would be as compatible with the expansion of freedoms as with their contraction.

Figure 2.1: Three waves of marketisation

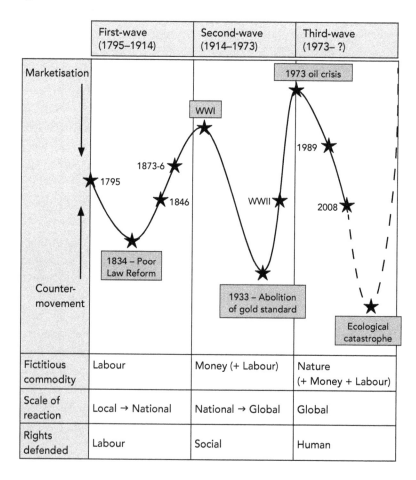

Polanyi's single great transformation, from ascendant marketisation to countermovement, gives way to three waves of marketisation, each with its own real or imagined countermovement. Each wave of marketisation is marked by a leading fictitious commodity. As well as incorporating a new fictitious commodity, each wave of marketisation recommodifies that which had been commodified before, but in new ways. Labour, for example, is commodified, decommodified and then recommodified in successive waves. We should not think of the three waves as compartmentalised and separated from each other, but rather as a form of dialectical progression or, perhaps better, regression.

The rhythm and experience of these waves is different in different parts of the world. Polanyi himself recognises how the first wave of marketisation in the nineteenth century had especially destructive consequences in the colonies where there was, he argues, no capacity to resist the annihilation of indigenous societies. Much as he exaggerated the destruction of the working class in nineteenth-century England, he also exaggerates the destruction of indigenous communities in South Africa.[4] We now know that colonialism actually *limited* land dispossession, so as to create the basis of indirect rule as well as labour reservoirs for industry. Still, in his exploration of colonialism, Polanyi does raise the question of the differential consequences of marketisation according to position in the world capitalist order.

No less important is the historical context. Thus Russia and China today, emerging from a period of state socialism – itself a reaction to second-wave marketisation – face the simultaneity of all three waves of marketisation, that is, simultaneity in the commodification of land, labour and money. In the Russian case, marketisation, at least for the first seven years of the post-Soviet era, was accompanied by an unprecedented economic decline just as in China it was accompanied by unprecedented economic growth. In Russia, wanton destruction of the party state was inspired by market fundamentalism and the belief in a market road to market capitalism, whereas in China the market was incubated under the direction of the party state. The staggering pace of Chinese economic development is a resounding confirmation of Polanyi's own argument that markets require political organisation.

In short, each wave of marketisation is marked by successive articulations of the commodification of labour, money and nature with corresponding countermovements of different scales and defending particular rights. Each wave differentially affects countries according to their history and placement in the world economy. Moreover, as I will now show, each wave also reflects particular contradictions of capitalism, and a particular vision of socialism as well as the defence of a particular set of rights. This movement of history gives rise to a succession of Marxisms: classical Marxism, followed by Soviet, Western and Third World Marxism, which in turn give way to what I call sociological Marxism. Let us take each in turn.

FIRST WAVE: CLASSICAL MARXISM

In the first wave of marketisation, during the nineteenth century, the focus is on the commodification of labour – first the separation of labour from means of subsistence so that it can be bought and sold in a labour market, and then strategies by capital to reduce the cost of labour power through deskilling, employing multiple members of the family and creating a reserve army of labour. This led to struggles that emanated from production, from factories – struggles for labour rights such as limitation of the length of the working day, protection against unemployment, the right to organise into trade unions, the extension of the vote, the development of cooperatives and the development of political parties. The countermovement is of a local character, building toward national working-class organisation to secure state enforcement of labour rights.

To this corresponds the classical Marxism of Marx and Engels and of the golden years of German social democracy, the Marxism of Kautsky, Luxemburg and Eduard Bernstein. It is based on the idea that capitalism is a system of exploitation that is inevitably doomed because the relations of production will finally and definitively fetter the forces of production. Competition among capitalists leads to the accumulation of wealth at one pole of society and its immiseration at the other pole, which in turn gives rise to, on the one side, the deepening crises of overproduction and the recurrent destruction of the means of production and on the other side, the simultaneous intensification of class struggle. What classical Marxism shares is the view that capitalism is doomed by its own laws to destroy itself, thereby giving way to socialism.

The debate between Luxemburg (1970) and Kautsky (1971) (see also Goode 1983) is about precisely when the final crisis will occur, when the forces of production will finally be fettered or whether, as in the view of Bernstein (1961), there is no final crisis because capitalism will *evolve* into socialism. Despite differing views, they all shared the belief that the rise of socialism was guaranteed because capitalism was doomed. As a result socialism remained largely unexamined. It was presumed to develop on the basis of the self-destruction of the capitalist mode of production through the concentration of capital and the collectivisation of labour. In this view socialism is an economic utopia and the negation of capitalism. Classical Marxism depended on laws of history – the succession of modes of production, the dynamics of capitalism that sows the seeds of its own destruction and history as the history of class struggle – that will inevitably lead capitalism toward socialism.

Classical Marxism suffered from three fatal flaws. First, its theory of class struggle was wrong – class struggle does not necessarily lead to its intensification but rather, through the concessions it wins, the working class becomes organised *within* the framework of capitalism. Second, its theory of the state was undeveloped – the state is organised to defend capitalism against capitalists as well as workers. The state recognises and enforces the material interests of workers, in a limited but crucial way, through trade unions and parties, but it also regulates relations among capitalists so that competition does not destroy capitalism. Third, and finally, its theory of socialist transition hardly existed – except in the case of Bernstein who saw it as an evolutionary process based on the inevitable expansion of electoral democracy – thereby confusing the end of competitive capitalism with the end of all capitalism, missing the way the state could contain the ravages of the market and the deepening of class struggle by creating an organised capitalism. Classical Marxists saw the signs of organised capitalism but they mistook it for socialism. In fact, organised capitalism laid the foundations for the second wave of Marxism.

SECOND WAVE: SOVIET, WESTERN AND THIRD WORLD MARXISM

In the Polanyian account, marketisation develops a new burst of energy after World War I, partly in reaction to socialist movements. But now the extent of marketisation involves not just labour but international trade and its regulation by currencies tied to the gold standard. The ever-fluctuating exchange rates that were associated with rampant inflation in Germany and the great crash in the United States led countries to protect their national currencies, and go off the gold standard. Thus, the countermovement now took the form of national regulation of economies. In Germany and Italy it took the form of fascism, in Scandinavia social democracy and in the US the New Deal. After the civil war and with the declaration of the New Economic Policy, the Soviet Union was also taken up with marketisation, but would abandon such policies in 1928 with the inauguration of forced collectivisation in agriculture and central planning. Markets entered a period of retreat across the world and under the influence of Keynesian economics the state assumed regulatory functions. This continued until the mid-1970s when a new round of marketisation began to assert itself.

If the countermovement to the market in the nineteenth century emerged on the ground of local struggles, reflecting the coincidence of exploitation and commodification of labour and the need to advance labour rights, the countermovement to the commodification of money – the source of second-wave marketisation – came from policies of national protection. The commodification of money, concretised in the uncertainty of currency exchange rates, created such economic chaos that national economies withdrew from the international economy. They developed coordinated policies to regulate banking but also to advance the social rights of labour through welfare states that supported those who could not gain access to the labour market, by providing benefits for children, sickness, old age, job loss and so forth. Whether it be fascism, Stalinism or social democracy, social rights for labour underpinned support for the new regime. Thus, second-wave marketisation gave rise to national protection of both capital and labour, and the regulation of the commodification of money.

If the first wave of Marxism is characterised by the contradiction between capital and labour, the second is typified by the clash of the realm of production and the realm of exchange – overproduction under capitalism which called for state administration, and shortage under state socialism which called for the creation of markets (see, for example, Baran 1957; Sweezy 1946).[5] Far from being a utopian construct as in the first period, the notion of socialism in the second period was all too real – based on national economic planning and the protection of social rights.

Marxism, rather than projecting an imaginary socialism that would follow a hypothetical collapse of capitalism, now had to rationalise and legitimate an actually existing socialism. Marxism becomes an ideology that justifies a new form of class domination, the class domination of a party elite, sometimes referred to as the *nomenklatura*. The impending communist transformation and the critique of capitalism became the rallying cry of communist parties all over the world. This Soviet Marxism lost all semblance of a dynamic science, and instead became a dogma, a degenerate branch of Marxism.

It gave rise to a reaction within the Marxist camp – what is known as Western Marxism – that simultaneously contested the Soviet Union's claim to socialism and grappled with the failure of revolution in the West, that is, why the working class was absorbed into capitalism rather than overthrowing capitalism. Here we find, on the one hand, the writings of Lukács and the Frankfurt School which underline capitalism's powers of mystification, and, on the other hand, Antonio Gramsci who explores the way advanced capitalism, and the civil society that accompanies it, organised the consent of the working class through the expansion of social rights, including certain labour rights (see for example, Gramsci 1971; Horkheimer and Adorno 1972; Lukács 1971; Marcuse 1955, 1958 and 1964). Western Marxism, together with the social movements of the 1960s and 1970s, inspired a regeneration of Marxism that examined the question of capitalism's durability and flexibility in the face of the crises and struggles it produced.[6]

Third World Marxism is the third tributary of second-wave Marxism – pointing to the way imperialism creates underdevelopment, calling for insulation from world capitalism and again proposing autarchic forms of state socialism. Leaving China aside, Cuba expresses this form of Third World Marxism, while dependency school theoreticians, such as Andre Gunder Frank (1966) and Amin (1974), wrote from this standpoint. In the African context, Fanon (1967) is a towering figure. Taking dependency as his point of departure, Fanon analyses the balance of class forces within the anti-colonial struggle. Fearing the ascendancy of a 'native bourgeoisie', parasitic on international capitalism, pursuing its own power, compensating for its insecurity with conspicuous consumption, Fanon considers the possibility of a national liberation struggle forged out of the melding of dissident intellectuals and a revolutionary peasantry. Such a struggle for a participatory democratic socialism, averred Fanon, was the only hope for Africa.

Apartheid South Africa generated its own rich and distinctive second-wave Marxism that sat at the crossroads of Soviet Marxism, Western Marxism and Third World Marxism. On the one hand, the South African Communist Party was in thrall to the Communist Party of the Soviet Union (CPSU) and followed its twists and turns, even while responding to local conditions, developing the notion of internal colonialism and 'colonialism of a special type'. Thus, Jack and Ray Simons (1969) wrote the first great Marxist history of South Africa, showing how class and race intertwined in the formation of the South African working class. Harold Wolpe (1972) inaugurated a very different tradition of Marxist analysis, drawing on French structuralism of the 1970s to problematise the very concept of race by rooting it in the articulation of pre-capitalist and capitalist modes of production. This led to a new Marxist historiography, associated with such figures as Colin Bundy, Martin Legassick, Duncan Innes, David Kaplan,

Rob Davies, Dan O'Meara and Mike Morris, that focused on the distinctiveness of the apartheid state and its relation to the capitalist class. At the same time others, such as Charles van Onselen in the tradition of E.P. Thompson, and Edward Webster in the tradition of Harry Braverman, produced highly original work on the formation of the working class by entering into its communities and its work processes. This second-wave Marxism tradition lapsed in the new South Africa, giving way to a third-wave Marxism, aimed at a critique of the post-apartheid order, and embracing the social movements that have given it expression. The essays in this book exemplify this latest wave of Marxism.

THIRD WAVE: SOCIOLOGICAL MARXISM

Second-wave Marxism was concerned with building socialism on earth via a state-regulated economy that ranged from social democracy to the Soviet model of planning, forms of African socialism and the Yugoslav self-managed economy. When markets were not rejected they were seen as an adjunct to the socialist project. Thus, Johanna Bockman (2011) has argued that the early thrust of neoclassical economics was to enjoin markets to a socialist project, whether this was the use of markets to help solve pricing problems of state planning or the organisation of self-management economies. The harnessing of neoclassical economics to capitalism is a more recent phenomenon distinctive to third-wave marketisation, posing once again the question of the meaning of socialism.

If classical Marxism postulated the self-destruction of the capitalist mode of production, projecting an unexamined utopian communism to follow, and if Soviet Marxism acted as a state ideology to represent an actually existing state socialism, the third wave of Marxism focuses not on the economy or the state but on civil society. Here we build on the second-wave Marxism of Gramsci who was the first to centre the importance of civil society as an institutional space distinct from, though connected to, state and economy. Just as Lenin's writings straddled first- and second-wave Marxism, so we can say the same is true of Gramsci and hence his enduring importance. Many of Gramsci's formulations, being in opposition to Soviet Marxism, prefigure the society-centred third-wave Marxism. Gramsci's concern with the relation of state and civil society is, however, too limiting; we need to add Polanyi's concern with the relation of market and society.[7]

In contrast to Gramsci, Polanyi and Fanon, third-wave Marxism thinks of civil society in global as well as national terms – a civil society that defends humanity against mounting ecological disasters that in the final analysis assume a global scale. The commodification of nature, whether this takes the form of privatisation of water, of land or of air, generates crises that affect the entire planet. To be sure, in the short run some will be better equipped to survive disasters of earthquakes, hurricanes and floods than others but in the end we will all suffer – the prototype is disasters such as Chernobyl or the impending catastrophe of climate change. These will call for global solutions based on human rights that protect the foundations of human existence, which in turn require shutting down the capitalist mode of production that systematically destroys the environment in pursuit of profit.

In the third wave of marketisation the commodification of nature may represent the new threat to humanity, but it coexists with a recommodification of labour, as we see everywhere in the development of informalisation, flexploitation and precarity, and with new forms of commodifying money, as we saw in the financial crisis of the 1990s culminating in the financial crisis of 2008. Bailing out finance capital has not altered the tendency to commodification of money but further consolidated it.

The collapse of state socialism in East and central Europe in 1989 and of the Soviet Union in 1991 was, in part, the result of third-wave marketisation, but it also strengthened third-wave marketisation, giving it new energy and discrediting any alternative to market supremacy. As seen from within the Soviet orbit, the illusory potentialities of a market economy were inflated by the fragility and contradictions of state socialism. Always seeking to catch up with capitalism, its incapacity to sustain a dynamic economy led to its downfall. However, during its existence the Soviet order did generate alternative visions of a democratic socialism constituted from below – the cooperatives of Hungary, the Solidarity movement in Poland and burgeoning civil society in Soviet perestroika. This socialism from below rested on the idea of the collective self-organisation of society.

Socialism of third-wave marketisation will not emerge through some catastrophic break with the past as was the case with classical Marxism nor through state-sponsored socialism from above, but through the molecular transformation of civil society, the building of what Erik Wright (2010) calls real utopias – small-scale visions of alternatives such as cooperatives, participatory budgeting and universal income grants that challenge on the one hand, market tyranny and on the other, state regulation. The role of such a sociological Marxism is to elaborate the concrete utopias found in embryonic forms throughout the world. The analysis focuses on their conditions of existence, their internal contradictions and thus their potential dissemination. Sociological Marxism, therefore, keeps alive the idea of an alternative to capitalism, an alternative that does not abolish markets or states but subjugates them to the collective self-organisation of society.

Table 2.1: Three waves of Marxism

	First wave (1795–1914)	Second wave (1914–1973)	Third wave (1973– ?)
Contradiction	Capital–labour	Production–exchange	Production–environment
Socialism	Utopian	State	Societal
Marxism	Classical	Soviet–Western–Third World	Sociological–Global
Debates	Dynamics of capitalism	State regulation	Real utopias
Methodology	Theory guides practice	Practice guides theory→Autonomy of theory	Dialogue of theory and practice
Universalism	Linear	Imposed	Built from below

The methodology employed by each wave of Marxism involves different relations between theory and practice. For classical Marxism theory dictated to practice: theory determined the inevitable collapse of capitalism and rise of socialism, so practice was only affected by knowing where one was in the historical trajectory. For Soviet Marxism practice – national survival at all costs – dictated to theory. Marxism was a thinly disguised ideology of the ruling party state. Sociological Marxism abandons theoretical certainties and practical imperatives and seeks instead to achieve a balance or dialogue of theory and practice. The point is not only to change the world now that we have understood it, but also to change it in order to understand it better. We search out real utopias that can galvanise the collective imagination but also interrogate them for their potential generalisability (see Burawoy and Wright 2002).

If classical Marxism offered a universality based on flawed laws of history, and Soviet Marxism offered a universality based on a singular dictatorial regime, sociological Marxism offers us no guarantees, only an eternal search and reconstruction, a universality that is always contingent, created from the concrete with the help of the abstract (see Hall 1986).

Toward a global Marxism

To some, sociological Marxism is an oxymoron – after all, classical Marxism dismissed sociology as bourgeois ideology, and if Western Marxism borrowed from sociology, especially from Weber and Sigmund Freud, it was not to elevate the idea of civil society. Gramsci himself was dismissive of sociology as concerned only with the spontaneous and thus the trivial.[8]

Why now sociological Marxism? Simply put, sociology's credentials as critic of marketisation and statisation are unquestioned. Whether we turn to the writings of Weber or Durkheim, Georg Simmel or Roberto Michels, Norbert Elias or Parsons, Habermas or Bourdieu, the critique of economic reductionism and instrumental rationality is central. Perhaps the state might have been seen as a potential or partial neutraliser but today that possibility seems to have evaporated. As the state seems to be ever more in thrall to the market, the defence of an independent 'civil society' seems to become all the more necessary. The problem, however, with sociology – and we might say the same of Gramsci and Polanyi – is that the notion of 'civil society' was contained within national boundaries. Today, we have to give the idea a transnational scope.

Marketisation – the commodification of labour, money and nature – is affecting all parts of the planet. No one escapes the tsunami, although some are able to mount more effective dykes. On the face of it, there needs to be a global solution but here we should proceed carefully as solutions can turn out to be as bad as the problem they seek to fix. What could be worse than a planetary totalitarianism, constituted in the name of preventing destruction of the environment? We might be better off knitting together national solutions that centre on society. However, here again we see problems as the state of societies is very different: in South Africa it is fissiparous; in China it is precarious; in Russia it is gelatinous. In every country we need to reconnoitre the trenches of civil society, map out the relations between society and state, society and market. Only in that way can we better understand the possibilities for global connections. Only in that way can we better understand the possibilities for real utopias.

As we think about a global civil society, we must also think of a global Marxism, that is, a Marxism that transcends but also recognises national and regional configurations. If first-wave Marxism was national in scope, and second-wave Marxism was regional (Soviet, Western and Third World), today we have the possibility of a Marxism that still recognises nation and region but also encompasses pressing experiences shared across the world, albeit unevenly. And if first-wave Marxism projected socialism as a utopia guaranteed by laws of history, and if second-wave Marxism became a ruling ideology, justifying socialism as Stalinism – utopia-become-dystopia – then third-wave Marxism constructs socialism piecemeal as an archipelago of real utopias that stretch across the world, attracting to themselves populations made ever more precarious by third-wave marketisation. The Marxist becomes an archaeologist digging up alternatives spawned and wrecked by the storms of capitalism and state socialism.

Finally, and most ominously, we face the creation of another fictitious commodity, one that Polanyi never anticipated – knowledge. We live in a world where knowledge is ever more important as a factor of production, whose production and dissemination is ever-more commodified. The university, once a taken-for-granted public good has become a private good subject to the dictates of the market. Students become fee-paying consumers in search of vocational credentials that guarantee them little but lifetime debt, faculties are diced and spliced into the casualised labour of teachers and researchers, non-academic staff are outsourced while administrators become highly paid managers and corporate executives. The university that cultivated citizens for a democratic polity and produced knowledge to solve societal problems, is being transformed into an instrument of the short-term demands of capital at the very time its contributions to the survival of the planet are most needed. The struggle for the university becomes a struggle not just for its own survival; it has a central role to play in any countermovement to third-wave marketisation, a possible Modern Prince for the defence of modern society.

ACKNOWLEDGEMENT

I would like to acknowledge the comments I have received in the many places I have given variants of this paper before its evolution into the chapter in this book. I'm especially grateful to Stephen Gelb for his thorough-going critique as a reviewer for *Transformation* and to Michelle Williams for encouraging me to continue despite those criticisms.

NOTES

1   There have, of course, been other periodisations of Marxism, but most offer a story of collapse. Thus, George Lichteim (1961) traces the birth and rise of Marxism and then the fall after the Russian Revolution. Writing in the aftermath of the European upsurge, Perry Anderson (1976) focuses on the rise of a classical Marxism, followed by the retreat of Western Marxism into philosophy as it lost touch with its revolutionary mainspring. Leszek Kolakowski (1978) describes Marxism's fall from grace with the rise of the Soviet Union and Western Marxism, followed by its final degeneration with the student movements of the 1960s. Note that all these classic accounts were written before the collapse of communism, whose existence was taken for granted.

2   Harvey identifies the wave of marketisation with accumulation through dispossession, a necessary accompaniment to commodification which Marx had only seen as part of the pre-history of capitalism, what he called primitive accumulation.

3   Naomi Klein (2007) offers a magnificent panorama of capitalism's capacity to exploit the crises it generates through processes of primitive accumulation.

4   Polanyi argues that it is the extreme form of dispossession (disembedding) that leads to working-class revolt whereas later historians, most notably E.P. Thompson (1963) argue that it was the strength of tradition founded in the skilled crafts, in other words a pre-formed working class, rather than its destruction, that accounted for mounting mobilisation.

5   As regards the contradictions of the state socialist economy, see two non-Marxists: János Kornai (1992) and Alec Nove (1983).

6   I refer here to a broad genre of works that would include Louis Althusser (1969 and 1971), Ralph Miliband (1969), Nicos Poulantzas (1973) and William Appleman Williams (1961).

7   I have developed this complementary relation in Burawoy (2003).

8   In this regard Gramsci's critique of sociology applies especially well to Polanyi's invocation of 'society' as a *deus ex machina*. For Gramsci, society or 'civil society' is something that organises but is also organised by specific social and political forces.

REFERENCES

Althusser, L. 1969. *For Marx.* London: Allen and Unwin.

Althusser, L. 1971. *Lenin and Philosophy and Other Essays.* London: New Left Books.

Amin, S. 1974. *Accumulation on a World Scale.* New York: Monthly Review Press.

Anderson, P. 1976. *Considerations on Western Marxism.* London: New Left Books.

Baran, P. 1957. *The Political Economy of Growth.* New York: Monthly Review Press.

Bernstein, E. 1961. *Evolutionary Socialism.* New York: Schocken Books.

Bockman, J. 2011. *Markets in the Name of Socialism.* Stanford: Stanford University Press.

Burawoy, M. 2003. 'For a sociological Marxism: The complementary convergence of Antonio Gramsci and Karl Polanyi', *Politics and Society,* 31 (2): 193–261.

Burawoy, M. and Wright, E.O. 2002. 'Sociological Marxism'. In *Handbook of Sociological Theory,* edited by J. Turner. New York: Plenum Publishers.

Fanon, F. 1967. *The Wretched of the Earth.* Harmondsworth: Penguin.

Frank, A.G. 1966. *Development of Underdevelopment.* New York: Monthly Review Press.

Goode, P. (ed.). 1983. *Karl Kautsky: Selected Political Writings.* London: Macmillan.

Gramsci, A. 1971. *Selections from Prison Notebooks*. New York: International Publishers.
Hall, S. 1986. 'The problem of ideology – Marxism without guarantees', *Journal of Communication Inquiry*, 10 (2): 28–44.
Harvey, D. 2003. *The New Imperialism*. New York: Oxford University Press.
Harvey, D. 2005. *A Short History of Neoliberalism*. New York: Oxford University Press.
Horkheimer, M. and Adorno, T. 1972. *Dialectic of Enlightenment*. New York: Seabury Press.
Kautsky, K. 1971. *The Class Struggle*. New York: Norton.
Klein, N. 2007. *The Shock Doctrine*. New York: Henry Holt & Co.
Kolakowski, L. 1978. *Main Currents of Marxism* (three volumes). Oxford: Oxford University Press.
Kornai, J. 1992. *The Socialist System*. Princeton: Princeton University Press.
Lenin, V. 1963. 'Imperialism: The highest stage of capitalism'. In *Volume 1: Selected Works*. New York: Progress Publishers.
Lichtheim, G. 1961. *Marxism*. London: Routledge and Kegan Paul.
Lukács, G. 1971. *History and Class Consciousness*. Cambridge, MA: MIT Press.
Luxemburg, R. 1970. 'The mass strike, the political party and the trade unions'; 'Reform or revolution'. In *Rosa Luxemburg Speaks*. New York: Pathfinder Press.
Mandel, E. 1975. *Late Capitalism*. London: New Left Books.
Marcuse, H. 1955. *Eros and Civilization*. Boston: Beacon Press.
Marcuse, H. 1958. *Soviet Marxism*. New York: Columbia University Press.
Marcuse, H. 1964. *One Dimensional Man*. Boston: Beacon Press.
Marx, K. 1967. *Capital* (three volumes). New York: International Publishers.
Miliband, R. 1969. *The State in Capitalist Society*. New York: Basic Books.
Nove, A. 1983. *The Economics of Feasible Socialism*. London: Allen and Unwin.
Parsons, T. 1967. 'Some comments on the sociology of Karl Marx'. In T. Parsons, *Sociological Theory and Modern Society*. New York: Free Press.
Polanyi, K. 1944. *The Great Transformation: The Political and Economic Origins of Our Time*. Boston: Beacon Press.
Poulantzas, N. 1973. *Political Power and Social Classes*. London: New Left Books.
Simons, R. and Simons, J. 1969. *Class and Colour in South Africa, 1850–1950*. Harmondsworth: Penguin.
Sweezy, P. 1946. *The Theory of Capitalist Development*. New York: D. Donson.
Thompson, E.P. 1963. *The Making of the English Working Class*. London: Victor Gollancz.
Williams, W.A. 1961. *The Contours of American History*. Cleveland: World Publishing Co.
Wolpe, H. 1972. 'Capitalism and cheap labour power in South Africa: From segregation to apartheid', *Economy and Society*, 1: 425–456.
Wright, E.O. 2010. *Envisioning Real Utopias*. London: Verso.

3

TRANSNATIONALISING GRAMSCIAN MARXISM

Vishwas Satgar

Antonio Gramsci (1891–1937), one of the most original Marxist thinkers of the twentieth century, was imprisoned by Benito Mussolini's regime in 1926 for his radical ideas and his leadership of the Italian Communist Party. He began writing his highly influential *Prison Notebooks* in 1929, the year the New York Stock Exchange crashed and capitalism entered the 'Great Depression'. A central aspect of the problematic informing the *Prison Notebooks* is the ability of capitalism to reproduce itself through ruling-class strategies. At the same time, Gramsci's *Prison Notebooks* pondered how to elaborate a politics capable of transforming capitalism without degenerating into revolutionary voluntarism on the one hand, and economic determinism on the other. Today the world is living through the 'Great Depression' of the twenty-first century. In this context, drawing on Gramsci's theoretical corpus critically is extremely important to provide insight into the nature of the hegemonic crisis of capital; how ruling classes are responding to this crisis and how struggles for alternatives can be waged.

I begin this chapter by clarifying which Gramscian Marxism has to be transnationalised. This is important, given that Gramsci's own Marxism has been overlayed and in some senses obscured by varied interpretations, readings and sometimes abuses. Within twentieth-century Marxism, Gramsci has been reduced to a Western Marxist, an Italian Marxist–Leninist and even a Euro-communist social democrat. First, I reconnect with the universal and critical core of Gramsci's own historical materialism. It is this historical materialism that is central to the project of transnationalising Gramscian Marxism in the twenty-first century. Second, I locate and trace how Gramsci's historical materialism has been brought into international relations and the global political economy. For the greater part of the twentieth century, Gramsci's Marxism has been considered irrelevant to understanding the expansionary tendencies and dynamics of capitalism. However, this has changed as the twentieth-century journey of Gramsci's Marxism inspired the emergence of a neo-Gramscian outgrowth. This transnationalising current of Gramsci's Marxism has challenged the mainstream orthodoxies of twentieth-century Marxism in terms of understanding the international dimension of capitalism.

To a large extent the rise of neo-Gramscian perspectives has engendered a crucial development ensuring Gramsci's Marxism a place in critical analyses of global capitalism and contributing to transformative politics. While this is both a novel and a creative theoretical outpouring, the neo-Gramscian moment is far from complete in terms of transnationalising Gramscian Marxism. This project has come into its own only over the past two decades and mainly in the global North. Although important ground has been covered within a neo-Gramscian framework, there are various unexplored and inadequately developed themes which limit the extent to which Gramscian Marxism is transnationalised in the twenty-first century. In this chapter I specify such themes as a means of deepening the efforts to transnationalise Gramscian Marxism through a South-to-North axis and through a broader research agenda.

RETURNING TO GRAMSCI'S HISTORICAL MATERIALISM

Marxism and its ideological framing is itself a battleground. Engagements with Gramsci's thought have also not escaped this experience. The reception of Gramsci's theoretical framework, mainly his *Prison Notebooks,* has produced important interpretations, elaborations and appropriations throughout the twentieth century. In some ways the fragmentary and unfinished nature of the *Notebooks* lent themselves to various readings. Many of these readings have produced intersubjective understandings of how to understand and 'apply Gramsci', giving us certain dominant modes of approaching Gramsci's thought. Moreover, these understandings have diffused as common sense in the social sciences, in political movements and amongst activists. In this regard, most of Gramscian-inspired theorising from the twentieth century represents Gramsci's Marxism as Western Marxism or a contribution to Italian political thought, particularly Italian Marxism.

The concept of Western Marxism appears in Perry Anderson's (1976) work, mainly to refer to both a generational and geographic shift in Marxist theoretical work. His perspective on the historical development of Western Marxism suggests that it is both generationally distinct from the classical Marxism of the nineteenth century, and was geographically based outside of the Soviet Union after World War I, especially in the West. Besides this formal setting of Western Marxism he goes on to argue that its defining feature, particularly after World War II, was the break between theory and a mass-based class practice. This shift represented a defeated Marxism, but Anderson recognises that this shift was not a spontaneous or teleological inevitability. Interestingly, Anderson highlights that the only exception within the Western Marxist tradition was Gramsci who, shaped by his experience of organising and theorising the Turin factory council movement (1919–1920) and leading the Italian Communist Party (1924–1926), maintained an organic link between theory and practice but also grappled with central questions of historical materialism as it related to socialist advance (Anderson 1976: 45).

The elaboration of Gramsci's place in Western Marxism does not end with Anderson. In other characterisations of Western Marxism, Gramsci's Marxism is reduced to a philosophical tradition, with Georg Lukács's emphasis on a Hegelianised Marxism and its emphasis on 'totality' defining the tradition. Gramsci is placed within this Western philosophical tradition in a rather superficial way. While Gramsci shared with Lukács and Karl Korsch a critique of determinism in sovietised Marxism, and a concern for the need to create a role for collective social agency in history and the importance of superstructures, this did not mean that Gramsci was preoccupied with giving his Marxism a Hegelian philosophic cast (Merquior 1986: 97). On the contrary, one of Gramsci's main preoccupations in the *Prison Notebooks* is a critique of Italy's foremost neo-Hegelian philospher, Benedetto Croce, that focuses on the liberal infusions of his thought and its hold over Italian society. This does not mean that Gramsci dismissed philosophy, however. Central in his approach to Marxism as a 'philosophy of praxis', is placing the unity of theory and practice onto another terrain. Gramsci's intention was not to substitute politics

Marxisms in the twenty-first century

for philosophy, but rather, to recognise that Marxism, with its intellectual resources, could constitute a new civilisation. This opens up an original and new track for philosophy which finds its expression through being grounded in struggle. In short, and for Fabio Frosini (2009: 678), the *Prison Notebooks* is not a book on philosophy and neither should it be read as such, but it does challenge us to think in a new way about philosophy and to think of philosophy as a 'philosophy-politics'.

In addition to placing Gramsci within Western Marxism, there have also been attempts to place him within an Italian tradition. To be sure, Gramsci's Marxism has a distinct Italian flavour about it, given that it grows out of an Italian context. For example, its Italianness is expressed through Gramsci's attempts to build on the work of Antonio Labriola (one of Italy's foremost Marxist thinkers), his engagements with other influential Italian thinkers (for example Niccolò Machiavelli and Croce) and the Italian historical examples he works with (the Risorgimento or North–South question). The Italian Communist Party (PCI) reinforced this in two ways. First, it constructed an iconic place for Gramsci both amongst the Italian left and in Italian society. He was haloed and treated as a patron saint of an Italianised Marxism–Leninism. For Palmiro Togliatti, the leader of the PCI after World War II, any attempts to view Gramsci as an original thinker were dismissed (Femia 1981: 10–11). Togliatti's publication of the *Prison Notebooks* as six thematic volumes, between 1948 and 1951, also presented Gramsci's thought as finished and systematic. For Frosini (2009: 671–672) this meant the *Prison Notebooks* could not be read diachronically as a provisional work that was in progress, open-ended and inviting further research. Essentially, Gramsci was preserved and portrayed as an unreconstructed Marxist–Leninist who was merely translating the Leninist model into Italian circumstances. Many interpretations of Gramsci emanating from the PCI maintained this line even after Togliatti's passing. Moreover, for the PCI, Gramsci was hailed as the theorist of 'revolution in the West' from the 1960s onwards, which laid the basis for appropriating Gramsci as the ideologue of Eurocommunism. Gramsci was evoked to legitimate this ideological current and reduced to being the theorist of class compromise and a social democratic project (Simon 2007: 90).

Readings of Gramsci as theorist of a defeated Western Marxism, a Western philosophical Marxism, a staunch Italian Marxist–Leninist or a reformist social democrat lock us into particular understandings of Gramsci. These instrumentalised understandings came to the fore post-Gramsci. While there may be merits to each of these approaches, they have also become orthodoxies and have circumscribed Gramsci in a manner that takes us away from appreciating the universality and critical edge of his historical materialism. In the twenty-first century our task is to reclaim and return to the universal core in Gramsci's historical materialism. This has to be done in two steps. First, by reading Gramsci through Gramsci. This method of approaching Gramsci's thought has its most sophisticated expression in the work of Adam Morton (2007). For Morton, such an approach to Gramsci's thought is a crucial corrective to the 'austere historicism' which reduces Gramsci to an Italian thinker (or for that matter a Western Marxist). While Gramsci used historical examples, mainly Italian, to illustrate the meanings of his concepts, this does not mean that Gramsci was seized with an Italian problematic. Morton overcomes this demand to place Gramsci narrowly in an Italian context (or a Western context) and instead keeps his historical materialism open to generate new meanings in the present by understanding Gramsci through Gramsci.

To summarise Morton's (2007: 15–36) conception of understanding Gramsci through Gramsci, he gleans from Gramsci's pre-prison and prison writings the following guidelines about appreciating the relevance of historical thought in the present. First, it is important to 'search for the leitmotiv, the rhythm of thought, more important than single, isolated quotations' of a thinker (20). The methodological procedure provided by Gramsci in this regard is a detailed biography of the thinker and an exposition in chronological order of all the works of such a thinker. Second, Gramsci, in his readings of Georges Sorel and Dante, refused to argue that the interpretation of a text was limitless, 'that any reading is valid as any other'. On the contrary Gramsci's methodological advice is to return to the text to establish what was the 'real meat'. Third, the history of ideas has to be understood in terms of the connection between past and present. For Gramsci the past was always part of the present. While ideas are the product of social relations, this does not mean that ideas cannot outlive a historical context. Fourth, according to Gramsci's 'philosophy of praxis', the criteria for the relevance of ideas in the present relate to how an idea assists with clarifying an existing, practical, political problem and the extent to which these ideas become part of mass consciousness. In short, Morton shows that it is possible, through Gramsci's own guidelines, to approach ideas through an absolute historicism which places Gramsci's ideas 'in context but also beyond'. This does not mean that Gramsci's ideas and theoretical concepts are trans-historical but rather, that thinking with Gramsci in new circumstances entails further research and a recognition of his limitations. In others words, reading and understanding Gramsci's concepts through his own absolute historicism also entails going beyond Gramsci.

A further crucial move to take us back to the core of Gramsci's thought is to think in a Gramscian way about historical materialism and social reality. While Gramsci accepted Karl Marx's critique of capitalism and his dialectical understanding of historical change, Gramsci also emphasised the need for historical materialism to be unencumbered by dogmatic, voluntarist and mechanical understandings of history. In this regard, other dimensions of Gramsci's historicism are crucial. First, such a historicism rejects economism, that is, an understanding that history is made only by the 'economic last instance' or fluxes in economic structures. This understanding liberates Marx's 'base-superstructure' metaphor from a deterministic straightjacket and brings to the fore a role for politics, culture and ideology in shaping history.[1] Second, and as corollary to the previous point, Gramsci rejected the positivist and law-like approach to understanding capitalism. This has been explicated with reference to Gramsci's critique of Nikolai Bhukarin's attempt to reduce historical materialism to a structurally determined schema which negates a role for consciousness and social agency.[2]

At the same time, Gramsci's historicism in his *Prison Notebooks* affirmed three important aspects: (i) transience; (ii) historical necessity; and (iii) a dialectical variant of philosophical realism.[3] First, transience refers to the social construction of society and its ever-changing character. Nothing is natural or eternal and there is a 'historicity' about all social phenomena: from states, to class structures, to philosophy, even to capitalism itself. Such a historicised understanding assists in understanding what is old and what is new. Second, historical necessity refers to collective agency as happening 'within the limits of the possible'. These limits (for example, ideas, consciousness, institutions, power relations) are 'not fixed or immutable' but exist within social structures that are subject to the dialectic of historical change: contradiction. Ultimately while social action is shaped and conditioned by social structures, these structures are also transformed by such action. The third element of 'philosophical realism' in Gramsci's historicism refers to how ideas are implicated in and dialectically part of the historical process. This refers to a process of knowledge production which is also open-ended and continuous but integral to the historical process. Philosophy in this context emerges from class struggle and is part of a transformative understanding of social change.

TRANSNATIONALISING GRAMSCIAN MARXISM

In *Capital* Marx expressed his belief that the self-expanding value of capital meant that it would extend beyond national spaces to secure profits. This insight about capitalist accumulation is developed into theories of imperialism by second-generation Marxists such as Karl Kautsky, Rudolf Hilferding, Bukharin, Rosa Luxemburg and Vladimir Lenin. Amongst these Marxist conceptions of imperialism, three contentious issues come to the fore. First, whether the expansion of capitalism was driven by underconsumption or overproduction or both. Second, whether monopoly capitalism was the root cause of inter-imperialist rivalry or rather the end of such rivalry amongst the advanced capitalist countries. Third, whether monopoly capitalism meant inter-capitalist war and revolution or rather, domination of poor countries.

In the twentieth century Lenin's understanding of imperialism and neo-Marxist world-systems theory came to dominate understandings of how the expansionary tendencies of capitalism needed to be understood. For Lenin (1977) imperialism was neither fleeting nor was it a policy that could be changed; rather, it was an expression of an inevitable consequence of monopoly capitalism. With monopoly capitalism, inter-capitalist rivalry ensued and ultimately inter-capitalist war. This understanding of inter-imperialist rivalry and war amongst capitalist countries provided the basis for a political conclusion to overthrow the capitalist system through revolution. It is this understanding of revolution that guided Lenin and his Bolshevik party in 1917 Russia while World War I was being fought. As a result, Lenin's conception of imperialism has been instrumentalised and reified as the basis of revolutionary Marxism. It has become an orthodoxy but as a lens through which to understand contemporary capitalism and its dynamics, it is extremely inadequate. With his emphasis on monopoly capitalism being the 'highest stage of development', Lenin's conception of imperialism is a teleological reading of capitalist development in that it fails to appreciate the dynamics of transnational class formation, the emergence of global capitalist rule through transnational historcial bloc formation and new mechanisms of imperial control and discipline.

From another theoretical tradition within Marxism, world-systems theory expressed the fundamental contradiction of contemporary capitalism as being between the rich North and the poor South (also known as centres and peripheries).[4] This world system has its origins within mercantile capitalism, *circa* the sixteenth century, which evolved different regimes of labour control and a hierarchy of states corresponding to these regimes of labour control (Wallerstein 1974). The core, semi-peripheries and peripheries engender states that enable global accumulation and unequal exhange. Through unequal exchange a polar-ising logic dominates centre–periphery relations, which explains underde-velopment. Hegemonic states with material capacities (political, military and economic) dominate such a world system. Today world-systems theory is at the cutting edge of debates about the decline of the US hegemon and the rise of China. However, while world-systems theory has a lot to offer in terms of contemporary analysis of global capitalism, it is also plagued by its own limita-tions. Beyond its fixation with hegemonic cycles and a 'neo-Smithian definition of capitalism' grounded in a world market, it is not able to appreciate the role of struggles and class conflicts as the basis for social change.

For the greater part of the twentieth century classic theories of imperi-alism (such as Lenin's) and world-systems theory provided common-sense understandings of the international relations of global capitalism, both in the academy and beyond. However, with the reception of Gramsci's work in the English-speaking West in the early 1970s and the evoking of transnational relations to explain how US capitalism has penetrated and dominated post-war western European capitalism, the ground was set for bringing Gramsci's Marxism into international relations (Overbeek 2000). This has given rise to a neo-Gramscian transnational historical materialism, which draws on Gramsci's conceptual framework but attempts to understand the dynamics and structures of global, rather than simply national capitalism. This is a new development in terms of transnationalising Gramsci's Marxism. At the same time, such an approach is further characterised by its openness and willingness to go beyond Gramsci's thought in trying to understand contemporary global capitalism. In many ways, this non-dogmatic approach draws on other critical readings of Gramsci and critical theoretical approaches to explain global capi-talism (discussed in the next section in this chapter).

THE RISE OF NEO-GRAMSCIAN TRANSNATIONAL HISTORICAL PERSPECTIVES

While neo-Gramscians have been designated as belonging to a school of thought by some, this is not the self-understanding that prevails amongst these scholars. Neo-Gramscian scholars draw on Gramsci's Marxism in different ways. They either draw on Gramsci selectively or as part of elaborating a new framework to understand the global political economy of contemporary capitalism. One of the most influential neo-Gramscians, Robert Cox, falls into the latter camp. He has laid the foundations for a neo-Gramscian transnational historical materialism that applies Gramsci to the international while going beyond Gramsci and drawing on other critical theoretical sources.[5] Cox's work is a crucial bridge between the 'nationally bounded' Gramsci and a transnationalised Gramsci. Cox opens the way to bring Gramsci into international relations and global political economy by first challenging mainstream international relations theory as being problem-solving theory rather than critical theory. According to Cox (1995) neo-Gramscian theory is critical theory, which attempts to understand the origins of historical structures and highlights the potential for structural change. It attempts to understand the intersubjective meanings and institutions that have emerged from collective human experience as a response to particular realities. Hence political economy, in his view, is a version of critical theory that contrasts with problem-solving theory, which focuses on 'order' and 'management' within existing structures; the latter takes the status quo for granted. In short, Cox argues that theory is *for* someone and *for* some purpose. Moreover, harnessing Cox's method of historicism calls into question the taken-for-granted aspects of neo-realist international relations: the state as the primary actor of international relations and the aggregation of a 'national interest' through the state. Through a Coxian approach the state is understood as the outward expression of a historically constituted bloc of forces and is contested by domestic and external social forces. Cox (1994) even suggests that the state is a 'transmission belt' for a policy consensus of transnational hegemonic social forces and institutions.

A second crucial step by Cox has been to systematise and elaborate a framework to take Gramsci into international relations.[6] In this regard he draws on and goes beyond Gramsci's historical materialism, mapping a more complex frame to understand power dynamics in relation to hegemony and world order, social relations of force and a historical understanding of structure-agency dynamics within global uneven development. Cox's ontology of the international dimension of capitalism begins with distinguishing modes of social relations of production and the kinds of social forces engendered by such patterns plus state forms (state-society complexes) and world order. These three bases of historical structure have a reciprocal interaction. The configuration of forces shaping such structures are constituted by capabilities (various material resources such as technology and military capabilities), ideational structures (collective images and intersubjective understandings of the world) and institutions (state and non-state, made up of capabilities and ideas). To Cox this ensemble of historical structures and forces is the basis for understanding hegemony and its transformation in the world order.

Cox's work has been critiqued as either a kind of 'Weberian pluralism' or on the basis that his understanding of the state in the neoliberal world order underestimates the state's role in shaping this order (Dufour 2009: 460). Despite these critiques, Cox's foundational work has been built on and taken further by other neo-Gramscians,[7] which has provided a diversity of perspectives and different emphases that bring out the link between transnational historical materialism and the struggle for hegemony within the world order. In this elaboration, the critiques of Cox have also been addressed.

KEY THEMES OF NEO-GRAMSCIAN PERSPECTIVES

There are three critical organising themes in neo-Gramscian theorising: global restructuring of capitalism, transnational class forces and transnational neoliberalism and its fit with the rule of transnational capital. I will address each theme below.

Global restructuring of capitalism

For neo-Gramscians the expansionary tendencies of capitalism are not governed by theological-like laws. Instead, these tendencies have to be explained. Rather than accepting the globalisation narrative and its economic determinism there has been a rigorous attempt to understand change within global capitalism and world order. This has entailed understanding historical change in terms of the event, the conjuncture and the *longue durée* (Gill 2003: 41–44). Change has been understood at different levels and through how it has impacted on historical structures. According to Stephen Gill (1994b: 170) this is a process shaped by a dialectic of disintegration/reintegration in what he describes as 'patterned disorder'. This means social, economic and political structures of the world order are being transformed or are breaking down but the new structures are only beginning to become identifiable.

Moreover, instead of embracing globalisation discourse, neo-Gramscians have historicised and placed it in the context of the accumulation crisis of the 1970s. Globalisation in this context has been understood as a response to this crisis. It is about restructuring capitalism through a new hegemonic 'concept of control' (Overbeek 1993). Such a concept of control has provided an ideational convergence that has led to globalising post-Fordist relations of production, financial markets and liberalised trade. In this global process of restructuring capitalist historical blocs, state forms, state–civil society relations and international relations have been remade. In other words, a conjunctural project has emerged which expresses a class strategy to facilitate the rule of capital and discipline labour. This capitalist strategy has ensured that the interests of the dominant class fraction become the general interests at a societal level; it has propagated an ideological outlook through intersubjective understandings and world-order institutions.

For Gill (2003: 116–138), beyond a new class consensus for a hegemonic project shaping the restructuring of global capitalism over the past three decades, there has also been a deeper historical shift taking place. This shift goes to the systemic level, or the *longue durée*, in that capitalism has been remaking itself in civilisational terms. Essentially, the global restructuring of capitalism has led to the emergence of a 'global market civilisation' which is premised on possessive individualism and competition. In other words, the world view of transnational capital has articulated with and become part of the common sense of everyday life such that commodification of social relations, the socialisation of private risk and the 'civilising role of financial markets' have become naturalised.

Transnational class forces

The centrality of class analysis within social science has generally been contested by postmodernism's search for non-universalising categories and new subject identities as the basis of understanding social change. This has coincided with and feeds into the neoliberal ideological onslaught which is best expressed in Margaret Thatcher's well-known declaration in the 1980s that 'society is dead'; the subject of neoliberal society is merely the greedy and possessive individual with a fetish for commodites. However, for neo-Gramscian perspectives the global restructuring of capitalism cannot be understood without the centrality of class analysis, particularly *transnational class analysis*. According to Bastiaan van Apeldoorn (2002: 21–22) late twentieth-century Marxist class analysis tended to polarise between two extremes. At the one extreme, stood a Poulantzian-inspired structural approach to class in which class was not prior to structure but was merely an expression of structure. Put differently, there was a structural over-determinism that accounted for class agency; class agency was 'mechanically determined' by structure. At the other extreme, E.P. Thompson rejected structure and focused on class as a historically constituted category. It was necessary to historicise class formation in order to appreciate the social agency of class.

Drawing on Gramsci, neo-Gramscian theorists have brought to the fore a structure-agency understanding of transnational class analysis. Such a position appreciates the structural location of transnational capital within globalised production, financial and trade structures. However, this in itself does not constitute a transnational capitalist class; ultimately, such a class has to be constituted politically and ideologically. For Gramsci, capitalist class forces are incomplete in their formation unless they transcend corporate and sectoral consciousness and ultimately achieve a political consciousness about how their interests articulate with the overall direction of society. Such an approach recognises the limits of class location as not necessarily translating into class position. An understanding of the structural and agential nature of a transnational capitalist class has engendered three crucial dimensions to neo-Gramscian transnational class analysis.

The first dimension relates to appreciating the fractionation of the transnational capitalist class. Due to competition, capital is not necessarily disposed to find common perspectives.

However, to understand the agency of transnational capital in this context, neo-Gramscian perspectives engage fractionation of capital, at an abstract and at a concrete level. For Henk Overbeek (2000) and Kees van der Pijl (1984 and 1998), transnational class formation has to be located within Marx's scheme in which the functional forms of capital are determined within the overall reproductive circuit of capital. Moving from the abstract forms of money capital and productive capital to more concrete forms such as merchant houses, financial firms and industry, this approach emphasises how capital fractions exist at an abstract level and how these fractions constitute transnational capital more concretely; the shift from the abstract to the concrete does not mean class formation is automatic. Instead, the constitution of capital fractions at a concrete level also brings in a role for historicising class formation as it relates to politics and ideology. Van der Pijl (1984) demonstrates this empirically in his study on the formation of an Atlantic ruling class, demonstrating how capital fractions formed and linked in particular circuits of accumulation. At the same time, these fractions constitute and contest the direction of historical blocs as part of the making of an Atlantic ruling class. In this sense, hegemonic concepts of control are negotiated, bargained and articulated under the leadership of a particular class fraction. The outcome determines the direction of the historical bloc in terms of accumulation models, state forms, state–civil society relations and international relations.

A second dimension regarding transnational class analysis is the nature of transnational class power. For Gill and David Law (1988: 84–95) a transnational capitalist class and its managerial cadre emerges through the restructuring of global capitalism. As production relations transnationalise, the structural and direct power of capital is reconstituted. Structural power refers to the mobility of capital, for example, and how this contrains the nation state. Footloose and mobile capital is able to play off states, push regulatory standards downwards and ensure the risk to capital prevails even over democratic imperatives. The latter expresses itelf through 'international and domestic business climates' which are a mechanism to articulate limits and functions for states. Direct power refers to networks of influence and lobbying to advance the interests of transnational capital.

A third dimension of transnational class analysis refers to the national versus transnational level and the ideological disposition of transnationalising capitalist classes. Van Apeldoorn (2002: 29–30) highlights how productive fractions of capital, while generally oriented to national protection, tend to transcend this in the concrete process of being transnationalised. Increasingly the degree and depth of the transnationalisation of an economy shifts the outlook of productive capital towards economic liberalism. This increasing disembeddedness and ideological shift prompts a national oriented productive/industrial capital to embrace policies that challenge national protection.

Transnational neoliberalism and the rule of transnational capital

For neo-Gramscians global restructuring of capitalism led by transnational capital has been linked to neoliberalism and how transnational capital rules the current world order. This prompts an attempt to understand how historical blocs are constituted in national spaces and how this links to other state–civil society complexes to reproduce a form of class rule. Following Gramsci, hegemony is understood as a form of class rule in which leadership is based on consent rather than naked coercion. For neo-Gramscians hegemony has to be rooted in a national context as the basis for projecting it outward into the realm of international relations. Mark Rupert (1995) in his study of US hegemony shows how it has its roots in relations of production, state–society complexes and in ideational structures. In the context of the Pax Americana after World War II, a national hegemony grounded in Fordist relations of production, a welfarist state and 'embedded liberalism' provided the basis for projecting US hegemony externally. In other words, national hegemony became the necessary condition for projecting a US global hegemony.

However, with the global restructring of capitalism over the past three decades a new concept of control has come to the fore: transnational neoliberalism.[8] Such a concept of control is the world view of transnational capital, and is founded on a 'market civilisation' – a market-based accumulation model – and it determines new requirements for the functions of state power. This concept of control has provided the basis for a new class consensus and transnational capitalist class project in which the transnational fraction of finance capital has prevailed. This has provided a new basis for renewing US hegemony, grounded in production relations, state forms and a new balance between coercion and consent. Besides explaining neoliberalism as part of reproducing global hegemony, neo-Gramscian perspectives have traced the origins of transnational neoliberalism and how it works.

In the context of the heartlands of capitalism and particularly European monetary integration, neoliberalism has been characterised as a new disciplinary constitutionalism. For Gill (2001) this is about insulating parts of the state from mass scrutiny and democratic accountability. It is about hollowing out democracy, while at the same time, ensuring state functions are changed to meet the requirements of transnational capital. In the peripheries of capitalism and given uneven development, neoliberalism has been embedded in a manner that reproduces the rule of transnational capital through 'passive revolutions' (Morton 2007). Such forms of non-hegemonic rule from above have also demonstrated how the internalising of neoliberalism in specific contexts takes on a national character and articulation. In other words, neo-Gramscian perspectives have gone beyond generic or abstract understandings of neoliberalisation and have attempted to analyse concrete ways in which transnational class rule is reproduced through neoliberalisation. This is developed further below.

UNDERSTANDING POST-APARTHEID SOUTH AFRICA AS A 'PASSIVE REVOLUTION'

For Gramsci, in the *Prison Notebooks*, the concept of passive revolution refers to a form of politics in which there is a 'revolution without revolution'; it is a non-hegemonic form of bourgeois class rule. There are three crucial dimensions defining the politics of passive revolution. First, it is primarily a politics of social change led from above with a conscious effort to limit mass initiative and subaltern hegemony. Passive revolution exists in a context in which there is a stalemate in the relations of force; a thorough social revolution has not occurred in which bourgeois hegemony can be established and economic structures developed on these lines. The form and role of the state constituted in this process is determining in this regard. For Gramsci (1998: 246–274), the form and roles of the state are not just determined by internal forces but also by international influences. Ultimately the state form and the social relations that constitute it advance a restoration of power relations determined by dominant class and social forces; power relations are not reconstituted substantively but rather, dominant power relations are reproduced. Second, passive revolution is about gradual or 'molecular transformation' which does not seek to transform the social order. Various ideological concepts of control are articulated to suggest that a universal project of social transformation is underway, involving a broad base of class interests, but yet the content of reforms merely meets the needs and requirements of dominant class and social forces; some concessions are made to the subaltern. Third, through passive revolution the modification of economic structures engenders capitalist social relations that produce either a 'bastardised capitalism' (marriage of pre-capitalist and capitalist structures) or variants of state capitalism. These historical choices, which are malformed copies of capitalist development but reflecting advances of capitalist modernity, eclipse more radical possibilities for social transformation and are underpinned by more degenerate authoritarian political forms like 'Caesarism' (rule by a strong political personality or even a corrupt parliament) and *trasformismo*. *Trasformismo* refers to the co-option of leaders and elements of subordinate groups in order to pacify, neutralise and tame such forces. It is about ensuring that a working-class-based opposition does not emerge. In these senses, passive revolution is a form of politics that exists between consent and coercion; it is 'corruption-fraud'; it is a politics aimed at containing the working class and subaltern social forces. It is not a politics for the working class.

Gramsci's concept of 'passive revolution' derives from two important principles (1998: 106–107):

1. That no social formation disappears as long as the productive forces which have developed within it still find room for further forward movement.

2. That a society does not set itself tasks for whose solution the necessary conditions have not already been incubated.

As a 'criteria of interpretation' (or analytical concept), passive revolution is a complex concept which should not be understood fatalistically or teleologically, but rather, should find its meaning in historical contexts of class and social struggle. In the *Prison Notebooks*, Gramsci utilises various historical analogies to explicate the concept and develop a theory of passive revolution in which state formation, advances of capitalist modernity in the context of uneven capitalist development and international forces are linked. There are three crucial historical analogies utilised. First, for Gramsci the 1789 moment of the French Revolution expressed the narrow and self-interested set of demands of the bourgeoisie. Hence, the Jacobins (1792–1794) represented the apogee of the bourgeois revolution in France. Their revolutionary dictatorship succeeded in achieving a 'national popular' character through developing an alliance in which the bourgeoisie had to make sacrifices, landed estates had to be broken up so that land could be given to the peasantry and a bourgeois state had to be constituted as an expression of the French nation. While for Gramsci the Jacobins represented the most radical expression of bourgeois hegemony, this was a limited class hegemony that remained on 'bourgeois ground'. This was expressed through crackdowns on workers' rights of assembly and limits on workers' wages in order to control inflation. The importance of Jacobin hegemony is used by Gramsci to highlight the limits of the broader historical pattern of bourgeois rule that unfolded in Europe up to 1870. In terms of 'temperament' and 'content' all subsequent forms of bourgeois rule were 'passive revolutions', but they did not achieve the radical social transformation of Jacobin bourgeois hegemony and were moments of reform-based 'restoration-revolution'; aristocratic and feudal elites continued to thrive as Western societies transitioned to capitalism.

Second, and as a corollary to the previous point, in the nineteenth century the emergence of the unified Italian state under the leadership of the bourgeoisie did not go as far as the French Revolution (despite feeling the threat of its long historical march since 1789 and the defeat of the working class in 1848). The *Risorgimento*, as it was called, led to a form of state in which an alliance of the industrial bourgeoisie in the north and the landlords in the south prevailed. While there were some benefits provided to the petite bourgeoisie in the state bureacracy and a centralised government established with limited suffrage, the lack of widespread popular participation defined the 'passive' character of this 'passive revolution'.

Third, with the emergence of fascism in Europe, Italy did not escape its influence. Gramsci characterised fascism as a 'passive revolution'. Fascism in

Italy attempted to introduce the advanced industrial practices of American capitalism through corporatist arrangements, underpinned by a broad alliance of industrial capitalists, workers and with a primary role for the petite bourgeoisie. This class alliance co-opted and neutralised the working class through 'corporativism' which gave it a 'passive' character. Its 'revolution' character derived from two dimensions: the shattering of a weak liberal order and its transformation of the economic structure, through moderate steps, from a competitive economy to a semi-planned economy.

For neo-Gramscians it is crucial to go beyond the literal historical analogies used by Gramsci to explicate his concept of passive revolution so as to grasp the rhythm of his thought and historical method (discussed above). With this in hand, the concept of passive revolution can be deployed in contemporary historical contexts to understand the global restructuring of capitalism, neoliberalisation and state formation. This is about locating passive revolution in the context of transnational relations and uneven capitalist development. It is about understanding how neoliberal globalisation, as a form of transnational class rule, prevails over national states, state–civil society complexes and accumulation models. In the following section I utilise a neo-Gramscian approach to initiate another way of thinking about post-apartheid South Africa's embrace of global neoliberal restructuring. I suggest that this is about reproducing a form of transnational capitalist class rule at the expense of advancing a working-class-led popular democratic and hegemonic transformation project. I argue that neoliberal post-apartheid South Africa engendered a passive revolution, a form of non-hegemonic transnational capitalist class rule.

This is not a fully fledged analysis, but rather a thought experiment of how a neo-Gramscian approach can be utilised to understand and contest existing explanations of South Africa's much-vaunted transition to democracy and global capitalism. The starting point for this exercise is an engagement with a rival interpretation of post-apartheid South Africa which ostensibly explains contemporary South Africa as an expression of hegemonic politics. Thereafter there is an attempt to identify the key aspects characterising South Africa's embrace of global capitalist restructuring as the making of a 'passive revolution'.

Rival interpretations of post-apartheid South Africa's transition

Hein Marais's *South Africa Pushed to the Limit – The Political Economy of Change* (2011) provides an analysis of South Africa's transition from above. It is a rigorous take on historical shifts, policy agendas and strategic choices that have come to the fore to define post-apartheid development. Thus it provides a comprehensive overview of the macro political-economy picture and a useful policy scan of crucial challenges for and limits of the African National Congress (ANC) rule. However, a key claim and assertion of this book is that post-apartheid South Africa's political economy is explained as the ANC's 'hegemonic work in progress'. This intervention in the debate about post-apartheid South Africa, while wanting to come across as a sophisticated reading in its rich historicised and empirical descriptions, tends to be a rather muddled and confused explication of post-apartheid South Africa.

Marais's assertion and use of 'ANC's hegemonic work in progress' evokes a crucial Gramscian analytical category but in ways that do not work. It reads as a desperate attempt to fit reality into theory. There are three serious limitations to Marais's theoretical characterisation of post-apartheid South Africa's transition as the 'ANC's hegemonic work in progress'. First, this formulation suggests, despite Marais's historicising of South Africa's embrace of neoliberalism, that the ANC's rather contingent and tenuous hegemony is about advancing a neoliberal post-apartheid South Africa; the ANC and all South Africans must embrace the realities of a capital-led process of neoliberal economic transformation, he argues, with a few ideological embellishments thrown in to provide ideological tension (Marais 2011: 395). Moreover, it is claimed the working class has gained and still can gain from this project. He seems to suggest that consent for the neoliberalisation of South Africa, with a national liberation gloss, is what the ANC has secured in civil and political society. Second, for Marais (390) hegemonic consent is really about clinching and winning the balance of forces in South African society and this is what the ANC has achieved, but for a few setbacks and weaknesses (such as mass unemployment and deepening inequality). For Marais the prospects of renewal and fixing the ANC's unravelling hegemony come to the fore at the ANC's national conference in Polokwane, which saw the rise of Jacob Zuma. This simply means the ANC must get on with addressing some of its weaknesses and recommit to marshalling 'broad based consent' (394). Such an understanding of hegemonic consent, which gives a determining role to the balance of forces, seems to imbue the ANC with the ability to switch hegemony on and off like a light switch. However, by itself the balance of forces is not a sufficient condition to ensure a hegemonic politics. In fact, such a conception of hegemony could be more about a degenerate dominance than a class-based intellectual and moral authority to lead society. Furthermore, hegemony is never fixed and has to be constantly worked for on the terrain of civil and political society, to provide moral and intellectual solutions, to find the right balance between the dialectic of consent and coercion once being organised within the state, to constitute a national popular imagination around a progressive South African nation-state, to maintain the ideological cohesion of a leading historical bloc of forces and to be organised through democratic political instruments. These are necessary conditions for hegemony to come into being and persist, but are non-existent vis-à-vis the ANC's vaunted 'hegemonic work in progress'.

Finally, in relation to the conceptual thrust of 'hegemony', Marais does not explicitly ground this concept in a class-based analysis and understanding of South African society. Instead he inserts the centrality of capital in different parts of his analysis, highlighting that some of its fractions have been the main winners of South Africa's transition (Marais 2011: 390). Yet, at the same time, hegemony is explicitly presented as a *declassed* category beyond the overdeter-minations of the class struggle (391–392). Hegemony is reduced to the hege-mony of a political party: the ANC. Reducing hegemony to a political party lends itself to substitutionism, vanguardism and authoritarianism. Gramsci's major contribution to Marxist theory, through the *Prison Notebooks* and in particular his concept of hegemony, 'is a moment of rupture with the concep-tuality of the bourgeois epoch analysed in the *Prison Notebooks*' (Thomas 2009: 134). In other words, hegemony has to have a class character and it would seem Marais uses the formulation of 'ANC hegemonic work in progress' as a proxy for capitalist hegemony rather than working-class hegemony; Gramsci would have analysed such a power configuration but would not have advocated it for the subaltern and society.

Moreover, there are three coherent, but not entirely compelling arguments made by Marais (2011: 397–401) against a characterisation of post-apartheid South Africa as the making of a 'passive revolution'. First, he argues against a passive revolution analysis by imputing a normative basis to the argu-ment. Thus he suggests that the alternative to a globalised and capitalist post-apartheid South Africa was a socialist South Africa almost akin to a soviet-ised 'socialism in one country'. This counterfactual argument is disingenuous and a misleading caricature. To utilise a passive revolution analysis does not mechanically suggest all-out revolution as the alternative, but it does point to more radical and transformative possibilities than what has been realised in South Africa, within the limits of the conjuncturally determined balance of forces and necessary conditions to develop a rival class hegemony in South Africa. Such transformative possibilities are profoundly about democratic Left alternatives including, but not limited to, food sovereignty, climate jobs, a solidarity economy, de-growth, a socially owned renewable energy sector, a basic income grant, participatory budgeting, integrated mass public transport, decent housing and public health care and ultimately, more democracy not less. In short, the use of a passive revolution analysis allows us to disentangle progressive transformation in the interests of the majority from bourgeois transformation in the interests of an elite, which is necessary for advancing twenty-first-century Left alternatives, including a reimagined democratic eco-socialist South Africa as the basis of a working-class-led politics.

Second, Marais suggests that the ideological disciplining of the working class is what hegemony is all about. Hence a passive revolution analysis that suggests the linchpin concept of national liberation ideology, namely the 'National Democratic Revolution', is a 'disciplinary abstraction' bereft of a grounding in the contemporary political economy of South Africa, is misplaced. Put differently, Marais argues that it is in the interests of the working class in South Africa to be misled, duped and enticed by the ANC's 'hegemonic work in progress'. There are two fundamental problems with Marais's understanding. First, as pointed out above, it lacks a class analysis, and is about control in the interests of the elite rather than the working-class hegemony. Second, his understanding of ANC capitalist hegemony is about assimilating, disciplining and limiting the opposition capacities of the working class, which then means he is actually talking about a passive revolution. This, of course, is notwithstanding the ANC's historical commitment to 'working-class leadership of the National Democratic Revolution'.[9]

Finally, Marais reveals a selective and superficial reading of Gramsci on the passive revolution. He suggests the passive revolution merely manifests in the context of failed hegemonic politics. He goes on to argue that the premise for a passive revolution did not exist in South Africa because apartheid was not about hegemony, in particular a politics of universal consent, and therefore a passive revolution analysis is irrelevant in the post-apartheid context. Gramsci utilised various historical analogies to explicate his concept of passive revolution, which highlight two important issues. First, passive revolution refers to various historical moments including transitions from feudalism to capitalism (like the *Risorgimento* in Italy), liberal advance (through crisis and defeat of working-class forces in the nineteenth century, such as in 1848 and 1871) and the emergence of fascism after a great upheaval, namely World War I. These moments should not be read mechanically to verify (or reject) the application of a passive revolution theoretical analysis in the present, as Marais does. Instead, if the concept of passive revolution is to help us understand our contemporary times, it needs to find its own meaning and relevance in different historical contexts, whether preceded by hegemony or not; it is not a frozen analytical concept tied into a rigid historical sequence. Second, the passive revolution is about the inability of the bourgeoisie to be a progressive force in history and to lead social transformation. Gramsci thus points to the limits of capitalist modernity with the use of the concept of passive revolution. This, of course, is too ghastly and challenging for Marais to contemplate.

Approaching post-apartheid South Africa as a passive revolution

The theory of passive revolution, when applied to South Africa, has to speak to South Africa's transition to democracy and deep integration into global capitalism as part of highlighting the limits to capitalist-class rule. It shows how the formation of the post-apartheid state gave rise to the dominance of transnational capitalist-class rule and the deepening of apartheid patterns of political economy (the passive side of the couplet) and how it ended formal, political apartheid (the revolution side of the couplet). Such an analysis teases out the specific and concrete dimensions of this form of class politics. What follows is an attempt to propose key dimensions of such an analysis to be developed; this is not a fully fledged analysis of South Africa's passive revolution but a proposed approach to such an analysis.[10]

The first crucial element is historicising and periodising South Africa's transition. This task is necessary to highlight the origins and line of development of the passive revolution. There is a need to bring out the historical contingencies, the twists and turns, and the complexities as part of this narrative. In this regard, there are two overlapping historical conjunctures which are crucial. A conjuncture, which can last decades, refers to a political project or its counter of class strategies that attempt to determine the form and role of the state. South Africa's transition can be historicised and delineated into two overlapping conjunctures. The first is the conjuncture of the democratic corporatist state (1990–1996) and the second is the conjuncture of constituting the Afro-neoliberal state (1996 to the present). The former conjuncture can be delineated into two phases: (i) the phase of negotiations (1990–1993) and (ii) the phase of democratic advance (1994–1996). The conjuncture of constituting the

Afro-neoliberal state is delineated by a long phase of low-intensity co-option, division and defeat of the working class (1996 to the present). Each of these conjunctures and phases can be unpacked with regard to historical evidence demonstrating the strategic class and state practices that come to the fore.

For the sake of illustration, our starting point has to be a recognition that resistance to the apartheid state did not produce an outright victory for either the contending class or the popular forces. Neither did the phase of negoti-ations (1990–1993) yield such an outcome. At the same time, a working-class-led alternative project was not automatically co-opted or defeated. Rather the defeat of a working-class alternative project has been politically constituted through neutralising a working-class-led hegemonic project and through the making of an Afro-neoliberal state. The conjuncture of constituting a demo-cratic corporatist state highlights the way in which the hegemonic working-class-led project was neutralised (and defeated) by cementing working-class commitment to ANC-led state rule.

By 1994 the Congress of South African Trade Unions (Cosatu), the most organised section of South Africa's working class, had put in place the following strategic elements to define a hegemonic working-class-led, post-apartheid project: (i) to form an alliance with the ANC and the South African Communist Party (SACP), rather than Cosatu forming a workers' party to contest elec-tions; (ii) a crucial commitment from South Africa's emergent democratic state and transnationalising monopoly capital to engage in a democratic corporatist framework to determine macro-economic policy; (iii) the Reconstruction and Development Programme (RDP) as a basis for electoral support for the ANC. The RDP was meant to provide a basis for redistribution, the realisation of basic needs, domestic-centred and externally oriented industrial development and deepening democratisation. Workers in Cosatu mobilised in their commu-nities and workplaces for the ANC's electoral victory in 1994, believing that the RDP would determine the content of state policy. All three elements in Cosatu's strategic initiative provided for the making of a democratic corporatist state. To cement this in place the ANC brought on to its electoral list several leading trade unionists in Cosatu, including key leaders of Cosatu such as Jay Naidoo (he was appointed RDP minister) and Alec Erwin (who eventually became minister of trade and industry) who were given places in Nelson Mandela's cabinet. By 1995 Cosatu's commitment to institutionalised and democratic corporatist bargaining was crystallised into the National Economic Development and Labour Council (Nedlac). Despite Cosatu's political commitment to the ANC state and seeming assertion of a hegemonic strategic initiative, it was ultimately neutralised and then defeated in the conjuncture of the Afro-neoliberal state. However, the phase of democratic advance ensured that working-class self-organisation, initiative and commitment to an ANC-led democratic corporatist state yielded a fleeting moment of ANC hegemony and held out the potential for the ANC to embody a working-class-led hegemonic project.

By 1996 Cosatu was on its way to being effectively defeated and losing the strategic initiative to transnationalising capital. This focuses us on the second element in our analysis regarding the making of post-apartheid South Africa as a passive revolution. How did South Africa's neoliberal shift come about? The emergence of an indigenised neoliberal accumulation model and state form is crucial, as it gave African characteristics to neoliberalism. The historicising of South Africa's Afro-neoliberal shift is located in the context of the conjuncture of constituting an Afro-neoliberal state and the eclipsing of a democratic corporatist state form. Such a shift relates to the following:

- The contestation of the petit bourgeois leadership of the ANC by monopoly capital. This begins in the 1980s with various dialogues between the ANC and white monopoly business and the undertakings given by the ANC to secure the interests of capital. Moreover, post-1990 witnessed various initiatives by capital to contest the perspectives of the ANC through scenario planning exercises. Ultimately a deal is struck between the dominant faction of the ANC, which embraces the deracialisation of monopoly capital through Black Economic Empowerment (BEE), and transnationalising white monopoly capital wanting to globalise through neoliberal reforms.
- After being elected, the ANC's economic policy choices were neoliberal policies, starting with South Africa's first democracy budget in 1994 which echoes key strictures of International Monetary Fund (IMF) neoliberal thought, the liberalisation of trade and exchange controls and the adoption of a neoliberal macro-economic policy: the infamous 1996 Growth, Employment and Redistribution (Gear) macro framework, which is followed in 2006 by micro-economic policies to reduce costs to business, referred to as Accelerated Shared Growth Initiative for South Africa. All of these policy choices created the conditions to globalise South Africa from within and externally, while at the same time, remaking the state. In this regard, the role of the minister of finance, Trevor Manuel, and his department, are crucial as a state within the state.

- There was an emphasis on transnational class formation through domestic restructuring and the constitution of a historical bloc of forces committed to a globalised South Africa. Three structural determinants of transnational class formation are crucial: first, the role of neoliberal reforms in externalising South Africa's import-substitution industrialisation model; second, the movement of monopoly capital into Africa and beyond; and third, the attraction and inflows of foreign direct investment. All of this expressed itself through the existence of transnational capital and various social forces (sections of the media, economists working for capital, state managers, parastatals, a dominant faction in the ANC, transnational corporations and international forces such as the World Bank, the IMF, the World Trade Organisation and the World Economic Forum) championing deep globalisation of the South African economy, through a non-hegemonic historical bloc.

Finally, understanding post-apartheid South Africa as the making of a passive revolution requires us to bring into view ANC state–civil society relations in the conjuncture of the Afro-neoliberal state. Cosatu's political defeat regarding a democratic corporatist state was further reinforced with the structural squeeze on the working class once neoliberalisation kicked in. Retrenchments, rising costs of living and high unemployment all serve to undermine the structural and direct power of labour. In this context the ANC (also working through the state) effectively won over key leadership strata of Cosatu to business unionism, careerist paths in ANC politics and BEE deals. Moreover, state practices around BEE mired the state in corruption and patronage relations. Finally, ANC state–civil society relations evolved from the demobilisation, to the instrumentalisation, then to the bureaucratisation and finally to the outright criminalisation of civil society. The most telling in this regard is the recent violent attacks by the ANC state against the Marikana mineworkers. The state's response ranged from a police massacre of 34 workers, to collective purpose murder charges being laid against the mineworkers, to a police and military crackdown on the community. This tragedy ended with a death toll of 46 (44 workers and 2 police officers), all because mineworkers wanted to challenge apartheid working conditions – working conditions the ANC state has refused to challenge as it manages a globalised economy.

In short, post-apartheid South Africa can be explained as a passive revolution in which the rule of transnational capital eclipsed a working-class-led hegemonic project for a democratic corporatist state. Since 1996, with the onset of self-induced neoliberalisation, the ANC state has been remade to manage a globalised accumulation model, mitigating risk to capital, facilitating transnational class formation and limiting the realisation of democratic citizenship rights for workers and South Africans in general. Essentially civil society has been ensnared in the politics of 'corruption-fraud' and increasingly state-orchestrated violence. This is an unviable project and is most certainly not about hegemony, a politics in which the general interests of society is expressed through the particular interests of a class or dominant fraction.

NEW THEMES FOR A TRANSNATIONALISING NEO-GRAMSCIAN MARXISM

Neo-Gramscian Marxism (transnational historical materialism) has successfully transnationalised Gramsci's Marxism beyond a 'nationally bounded' Marxism and beyond our received understandings of Gramsci's thought from the twentieth century. It has done this both in academic spaces (particularly with regard to international relations and the global political economy) but also within transnational activist currents. However, it is an unfinished project. This is so because of its own open-endedness but also because of the ever-changing vicissitudes of global capitalism. As a result we need to identify new themes and research agendas to continue the transnationalising of Gramsci's Marxism as part of neo-Gramscian transnational historical materialism. In this regard there are three crucial research themes that need to be developed.

First, the current crisis of global capitalism, since 2007, has brought to the fore various 'organic' crisis tendencies that register and impact on both the systemic and the conjunctural level. This has also disrupted the hegemony of a US-led historical bloc of forces. This prompts us to research and grapple with the following questions: How have relations of production been transformed in the context of the global capitalist crisis? How is the US state–society complex dealing with the crisis of hegemony? How are state–society complexes adjusting in the heartlands and peripheries of capitalism? What is happening to existing historical blocs? What are the new concepts of control coming to the fore from various transnational class and social forces to 'solve' the global capitalist crisis? What are the limits of these new class strategies? Has neoliberal hegemony ended in the world order? Is this a crisis *of* neoliberalism or a crisis *in* neoliberalism? Is this the end or the beginning of the end of neoliberalism? Is the world order in transition to global passive revolution or to global supremacy? In short, there is a need for a systemic and conjunctural understanding of the current global capitalist crisis from a neo-Gramscian perspective.

A second crucial theme that needs to be developed to enhance the trans-nationalising of Gramsci's Marxism is the ecological dimension of Gramsci's thought. In this regard, new readings and interpretations are required of Gramsci's Marxism, both to identify how Gramsci grappled with nature within his historical materalism and to begin a conscious 'greening' of Gramscian categories that will make sense of the ecological crisis of global capitalism. This needs to be related to the greening of neo-Gramscian thought as a whole. In other words, the ecological limits of Coxian-inspired neo-Gramscian theory have to be revisited. The relationship between power, production and ecology must be rethought. This provides another crucial research plank for transna-tionalising neo-Gramscian Marxism.

Finally, while a transnationalising neo-Gramscian research agenda has and will continue to provide politically committed analysis of the capitalist world order, which has important implications for strengthening anti-capitalist politics, this has to be taken further. In other words, a more explicit research and theoretical commitment has to come to the fore in order to support how alternatives to contemporary anti-capitalist politics are articulated. More work has to be done on understanding ideologies of anti-capitalist movements, the alternatives being articulated, how these relate to transforming historical blocs both nationally and beyond, the nature of the power being expressed by such anti-capitalist forces in state–society complexes, new forms of counter-hegemonic practice and new ways of contesting common-sense understand-ings of the world.

CONCLUSION

Transnationalising Gramscian Marxism in the twenty-first century entails disrupting existing orthodoxies about Gramsci's Marxism by retrieving its core. This entails reading Gramsci through Gramsci and thinking in a Gramscian way about historical materialism and social reality. This is not about finding a true Gramsci or a Gramsci with all the answers. Instead it is about thinking with Gramsci, as expressed through his own work, while also going beyond

Gramsci. At the same time, transnationalising Gramsci's Marxism has meant taking Gramsci beyond the national scale of politics and into international relations by applying Gramsci's concept of hegemony to world order and global political economy.

Neo-Gramscian approaches and elaborations of Gramsci's Marxism are a crucial bridge. Neo-Gramscian analysis has historicised the social structures of global capitalism, including globalisation, has elaborated a transnational class theoretical approach to global capitalism and has explained how transnational capitalist rule works in the context of neoliberalisation. This is an unfinished transnational historical materialism. In the twenty-first century a neo-Gramscian transnational historical materialism has to be taken further with a historicised analysis of the crisis of capitalism, the greening of Gramsci's Marxism and with a new appeciation for anti-capitalist struggles. Such an elaboration is happening through a South–North diffusion of ideas, grounded in an appreciation that all history according to Gramsci is 'world history'.

NOTES

1   See Gramsci's (1988: 189–221) notes on hegemony, relations of force and historical blocs which provides a non-reductionist understanding of ideology.

2   See Gramsci's (1998: 419–72) 'Critical notes on an attempt at popular sociology' in which he critiques Nikolai Bukharin's *Theory of Historical Materialism: A Popular Manual of Marxist Sociology.*

3   Gill (2003: 17–20) elaborates on these three elements and suggests these elements form a crucial basis for neo-Gramscian perspectives. In Gramsci's (1998: 321–418) notebooks these themes are brought out in his notes on the study of philosophy, namely, 'Some preliminary points of reference and problems of philosophy and history'. For his discussion about the problems of Marxism, see his notes 'Some problems in the study of the philosophy of praxis and critical notes on an attempt at popular sociology'.

4   World-systems theory is part of an ongoing research agenda within which there are different emphases and perspectives. For example, Giovanni Arrighi, Immanuel Wallerstein and Samir Amin have had divergent views on various aspects and dynamics within the world system.

5   Leysens (2008) provides an important interpretation of Cox's thought. He highlights the various influences on Cox's historical dialectical approach which include Gramsci, Giambattista Vico, Marx, Braudel and Collingwood, amongst others.

6   See Cox's (1987) classical work *Production, Power, and World Order: Social Forces in the Making of History.*

7   Amongst others, see Gill (1994a).

8   See Overbeek (1993) and Gill (2003).
9   All the ANC strategy and tactics documents have evoked the primacy of the work-
    ing class as the leading social force for change in South Africa.
10 See Satgar (2008 and 2012) and a forthcoming book entitled: *Africa's Passive
    Revolution – From Self-reliance to Afro-neoliberalism.*

REFERENCES

Anderson, P. 1976. *Considerations on Western Marxisim.* London: New Left Books.
Cox, R.W. 1987. *Production, Power, and World Order: Social Forces in the Making of
    History.* New York: Columbia University Press.
Cox, R.W. 1994. 'Gramsci, hegemony, and international relations: An essay in method'.
    In *Gramsci, Historical Materialism and International Relations,* edited by S. Gill.
    New York and Cambridge: Cambridge University Press.
Cox, R.W. 1995. 'Critical political economy'. In *International Political Economy:
    Understanding Global Disorder,* edited by B. Hettne. New Jersey: Zed Books.
Dufour, F.G. 2009. 'Historical materialism and international relations'. In *Critical
    Companion to Contemporary Marxism,* edited by J. Bidet and S. Kouvelakis.
    Chicago, IL: Haymarket Books.
Femia, J.V. 1981. *Gramsci's Political Thought: Hegemony, Consciousness, and Revolutionary
    Process.* Oxford: Clarendon Press.
Frosini, F. 2009. 'Beyond the crisis of Marxism: Gramsci's contested legacy'. In *Critical
    Companion to Contemporary Marxism,* edited by J.Bidet and S. Kouvelakis. Chicago,
    IL: Haymarket Books.
Gill, S. 1994a. *Gramsci, Historical Materialism and International Relations.* New York:
    Cambridge University Press.
Gill, S. 1994b. 'Structural change and global political economy: Globalizing elites and
    the emerging world order'. In *Global Transformation: Challenges to the State System,*
    edited by Y. Sakamoto. Tokyo, New York, Paris: United Nations University Press.
Gill, S. 2001. 'Constitutionalising capital: EMU and disciplinary neo-liberalism'. In
    *Social Forces in the Making of the New Europe – The Restructuring of European Social
    Relations in the Global Political Economy,* edited by A. Bieler and A.D. Morton. New
    York: Palgrave.
Gill, S. 2003. *Power and Resistance in the New World Order.* New York: Palgrave-Macmillan.
Gill, S. and Law, D. 1988. *The Global Political Economy: Perspectives, Problems, and
    Policies.* Baltimore: Johns Hopkins University Press.
Gramsci, A. 1988. *An Antonio Gramsci Reader,* edited by D. Forgacs. New York: Schocken
    Books.
Gramsci, A. 1998. *Selections from the Prison Notebooks,* edited by Q. Hoare and G. Nowell
    Smith. India: Orient Longman.
Lenin, V. 1977. *Selected Works – Imperialism, the Highest Stage of Capitalism.* Moscow:
    Progress Publishers.
Leysens, A. 2008. *The Critical Theory of Robert W. Cox.* New York: Palgrave-Macmillan.
Marias, H. 2011. *South Africa Pushed to the Limit – The Political Economy of Change.*
    Cape Town and London: UCT Press and Zed Books.
Merquior, J. G. 1986. *Western Marxism.* London: Paladin Books.

Morton, A.D. 2007. *Unravelling Gramsci: Hegemony and Passive Revolution in the Global Economy*. London and Ann Arbor, MI: Pluto Press.

Overbeek, H. (ed.). 1993. *Restructuring Hegemony in the Global Political Economy – The Rise of Transnational Neoliberalism in the 1980s*. London and New York: Routledge.

Overbeek, H. 2000. 'Transnational historical materialism: Theories of transnational class formation and world order'. In *Global Political Economy: Contemporary Theories*, edited by R. Palan. London and New York: Routledge.

Rupert, M. 1995. *Producing Hegemony – The Politics of Mass Production and American Global Power*. Cambridge: Cambridge University Press.

Satgar, V. 2008. 'Neoliberalised South Africa: Labour and the roots of passive revolution', *Labour, Capital and Society*, 41 (2): 38–69.

Satgar, V. 2012. 'The post-apartheid state: Developmental or Afro-neoliberal?', *Africa Spectrum*, 47 (2/3): 33–62.

Simon, R. 2007. 'Eurocommunism'. In *Twentieth Century Marxism*, edited by D. Glaser and D.M. Walker. Oxon: Routledge.

Thomas, P. 2009. *The Gramscian Moment – Philosophy, Hegemony and Marxism*. Chicago, IL: Haymarket Books.

Van Apeldoorn, B. 2002. *Transnational Capitalism and the Struggle over European Integration*. London and New York: Routledge.

Van der Pijl, K. 1984. *The Making of an Atlantic Ruling Class*. London: Verso.

Van der Pijl, K. 1998. *Transnational Classes and International Relations*. London and New York: Routledge.

Wallerstein, I. 1974. *The Modern World – System I – Capitalist Agriculture and the Origins of the European World Economy in the Sixteenth Century*. San Diego, CA and London: Academic Press Inc.

MARXISM AND LEFT POLITICS

4

NOTES ON CRITIQUE

Ahmed Veriava

Critique, we have recently been told, has 'run out of steam', making it a poor weapon for engaging in contemporary theoretical battles. Worse still, not only does critique appear blunted, even anachronistic, but the enemy is wise to the critical trick and has turned its back on 'our' forces. Field marshals of the academy are even calling for a regrouping, a new assessment of the strategic disposition that has come down to us via the critical tradition (see Latour 2004).

Today, even in politics, there is less patience for interventions that take a critical form (and which cannot always be dismissed as a capitulation to power). For instance, in my own experience, criticism of dominant political narratives and practices are often met with the objection: 'Your criticisms are all very well and good, but what does it say about the alternative?'

If we (sometimes) concede the sincerity of such statements, and admit the need to direct ourselves towards finding an alternative, why should we bother with critique? 'Write all the critical words you want,' they might even say, 'but it's the new world that we're really interested in.'

By presenting the problem in these terms, I do not mean to suggest that we all, and always, mean the same thing when we talk about critique or criticism. Summarising the wide spectrum of practices that go under the name 'critique', a recent contribution by Michael Hardt (2011: 19) speaks of 'relatively generic means of fault-finding; methods to question the truth of authority; techniques to reveal the figures of power that operate in dominant discourses or ideologies; and even specific Kantian procedures of investigating the human understanding, reason, or judgment'.[1] Nevertheless, for Hardt (2011: 19), in spite of the differences between ways of doing critique – conceived in his paper as the primary mode of practising theory as political intervention – they all remain open to the charge of being 'insufficient as political methods in so far as they lack the capacity both to transform the existing structures of power and create alternative social arrangements'.

I have respect for 'this critique of critique', which motivates for politically engaged modes of doing theory, self-consciously and militantly, directed at a positive, or better, constitutive task. Indeed, in this chapter, I trace a similar path to that of Hardt in his insistence on a 'militancy of theory', but here, in the name of critique. It seems to me that we lose much more than we gain by writing off critique and it might well be that without it, our new worlds will remain only as words. Still, the challenge raised by Hardt is a crucial one: what (if anything at all) does critique have to do with 'the constitutive political tasks' which fall on us today?

As a way of addressing this important question, I begin by tracing a line between and within what have been, for me, important landmarks for 'doing critique'. In the latter sections of this chapter I focus on the work of Michel Foucault, which is not only a formative point of reference for a number of contemporary critical perspectives, but also the primary point of inspiration for the mode of 'philosophical and political militancy, beyond critique' advocated by Hardt (2011: 20). In the next section, however, I begin marking Foucault's relation to something more familiar, perhaps in the same way that one searches for a nearby landmark in order to establish a preliminary bearing.

A line, then, that runs from Karl Marx to Foucault.

LANDMARKS

Maurizio Lazzarato (2002: 102) has noted that Foucault's writings on political economy and government are at once very close to and very far from Marx. Even more generally, however, Foucault's relationship to Marx is a double relation: a certain tension combined with a shared set of concerns and often real methodological and political intersections between the two projects. On the one hand, Marxism (if not Marx himself) has often appeared in Foucault's writings, lectures and interviews as the subject of polemical statements or inferred critique. On the other hand, his later work, in particular his lectures on the genealogy of modern government, will, as Bob Jessop (2007: 34) has noted, move towards an 'appropriation and development of insights from Marx himself'.

Already in 1975, however, Foucault had indicated that his relationship to Marx was more complex than what might appear to be the case skimming through reference sections of any one of his works. It would seem, rather than ignoring Marx, his 'negligence' in offering up the appropriate citation might have been linked to his aversion to a certain cultish character he associated with Marxism:

> I often quote concepts, texts and phrases from Marx, but without feeling obliged to add the authenticating label of a footnote with a laudatory phrase to accompany the quotation. As long as one does that, one is regarded as someone who knows and reveres Marx, and will be suitably honoured in the so-called Marxist journals. But I quote Marx without saying so, without quotation marks, and because people are incapable of recognising Marx's texts I am thought to be someone who doesn't quote Marx. When a physicist writes a work of physics, does he feel it necessary to quote Newton and Einstein? He uses them, but he doesn't need the quotation marks, the footnote and the eulogistic comment to prove how completely he is being faithful to the master's thought (Foucault 1980: 52–53).

There can be little doubt, however, that the relationship between these two projects, their various intersections and fissures, runs deeper than the anxieties of offering (or not) the 'appropriate citation'. As Thomas Lemke (2000: 1), following Etienne Balibar, has noted, Foucault's thought is characterised by a 'genuine struggle' with Marx, a struggle that will prove one of the 'principle sources of its productivity'. If Foucault's (1980: 57) criticisms of Marxism – whether with respect to its inattention to the question of 'the body' or Foucault's (1990a: 92–102) refusal of an analytic practice that would reduce relations of power to relations of production or a bipolar field of social antagonism, or even, for that matter, the sense in which Foucault's (2004: 30–33) methodological elaboration seems to self-consciously run in the opposite direction from Marxism's 'descending' method – are suggestive of a theoretical antagonism, it is no less true that his later work will increasingly throw light on what has been called a broader 'tactical alliance' (Balibar 1995 in Lemke 2000: 1) between the two projects. As Lazzarato (2002: 102) notes, in both Foucault and Marx, what will be crucial will be the forms through which relations between men, or 'between man and "things"', become the object of strategies to 'coordinate and command' human action with an eye to the extraction of a surplus (of power in Foucault and value in Marx). And in both Marx and Foucault, these strategies will unfold in ways that produce effects that are neither simply economic, nor even political, but also ontological.

It seems to me, however, that a more subtle affinity between Marx and Foucault – and which, in an odd way, underlies and reinforces the sense of a 'tactical alliance' between their respective projects – goes beyond the thematic or analytic intersections between their respective works, to clarify their respective approaches to critique.

Such a connection is, however, by no means self-evident and the suggestion of an affinity between Marx and Foucault with respect to critique is not made without an element of (hermeneutic) risk. After all, on all the occasions where Foucault (in Kelly 1994: 148) draws the line of influence that gives the tradition within which he locates his own work, there is the un-ignorable and consistent exclusion of a proper name 'from Hegel, through Nietzsche and Max Weber, to the Frankfurt school' – the scandal of a critical tradition without the name Marx!

Although these risks are lessened by Foucault's confession – 'a citation without citation' – a gesture perhaps motivated by his desire for the 'unburdening and liberation of Marx in relation to party dogma' (Foucault in Kelly 1994: 135) and thus the possibility of reading Marx's place in the silences and in-between spaces of a list of proper names, risk is re-inscribed in the strategy of this essay, which makes its case in relation to 'The Young Marx', or at least, a younger one.

BEGINNINGS

In 1843, as the 25-year-old Marx was preparing to leave behind the 'oppressive air' of Germany after being forced to resign as editor of *Rheinische Zeitung* (which was shut down less than one month later), he was already working on his next project, the 'critical journal' *Deutsch–Französische Jahrbücher* (German–French Annals). Although only one issue of the journal was published, with the majority of the print run eventually finding its way into the hands of the police, the contribution the journal makes to 'critique' is, if not an important one, then at least not an altogether uninteresting one; no less for giving us a glimpse into the attitude that shaped the philosophical practice of a young Marx (whatever its limitations) – one of the many 'beginnings', however contingent,[2] on the way to his *Critique of Political Economy* (1867).

Notably, in addition to Marx's *On the Jewish Question* (1844), the journal also published two texts explicitly written in the tradition of critique: Friedrich Engels's *Outline of a Critique of Political Economy* (1844), and Marx's own *Introduction for a Contribution to a Critique of Hegel's Philosophy of Right* (1844). Leaving aside questions of what Louis Althusser called the 'enormous layer of ideology' (2005: 74) that the young Marx was said to be still struggling to escape from, we can note that, along with these texts, the journal also published a series of correspondences, concluding with Marx's stirring letter to Arnold Ruge (the co-editor of the journal), encouraging 'relentless criticism'. Beyond the militant lyricism of a young Marx, what makes these letters particularly intriguing is the light they throw on a 'critical attitude', an attitude that I suspect is, in part, what establishes Marx in a critical relationship to his own beginnings; what Althusser (2005: 84) called his 'ferocious insistence on freeing himself from the myths which presented themselves to him as truth' and his insistence on the grounding of intellectual practice in the 'experience of real history' that will elbow 'these myths aside'. But, if there is a binding thread in these letters and the approach that they take to critique, it is their immediately political character and their commitment to the task of making revolution. And it is this question, that is, of 'revolution', or rather the potential for one, which is a deeper thread that runs through the exchange.

A RELENTLESS CRITICISM

Marx's analysis of political conditions in Germany (whose very air he complained 'makes one a serf') are interesting for a number of reasons, not least of which are its subtle reflections on the political and the question of autonomy (see Veriava 2013). What I want to underline here, however, is that this is a thought already inserted in what, elsewhere, I call the militant's questioning: 'at the level of every move' making an assessment of 'our ability to resist control, or of our submission to it'.[3] And here, the work of criticism stands as a way to 'expose' the old in order to 'shape the new along positive lines' (Marx 1967: 211).

In Marx's final letter, where he outlines the perspective of the proposed journal, the task appears intimately tied to the 'self-understanding (critical philosophy) of the age concerning its struggles and wishes' (Marx 1967: 215). This self-understanding that the 'present time' must arrive at, or at any rate move toward, is, however, at once the task of the critic and that of the world (or in anticipation of Foucault, we could say, the work of the critic as witness and participant in the unfolding processes of the world). Marx (214) is emphatic: this does not mean raising up one or other 'dogma' through which the world can know itself – '[h]ere is the truth, kneel here!'. Instead, criticism will only develop new principles out of criticism of 'the world's own principles' (214).

I do not want to exaggerate the importance of the letter. Although not obscure, it is more of a beginning (one of many) than anything else. What I want to do is to simply mark several points that I think are helpful for thinking about the movement of Marx's thought.

Firstly, much of the letter is devoted to defining the role of the journal, a role that is explicitly related to a practice of criticism and the role of the critic. In Marx's terms, this implies a concern with both the 'theoretical' existence and the 'practical' existence of 'man'. In this Marx, there is still little that motivates one over the other and the socio-political contexts in which people find themselves, their forms of life and 'economic processes', for instance, stand alongside religion as an object of criticism. Secondly, Marx, with a marked Hegelian accent, sets up a striking opposition between a 'reason' that has always existed and the 'reasonable form' that has eluded it, noting that not only does the 'modern state' take on the demands of reason, but because of this, it everywhere becomes caught in a contradiction between its 'function and its real prerequisites'.[4] The third aspect of Marx's critical practice I want to highlight is, in a sense, its deeply political character. In fact, Marx (1967: 214, Marx's emphasis) writes: 'nothing prevents us … from starting our criticism with criticism of politics, with taking sides in politics, and hence *actual* real struggles, and identifying ourselves with them'.

It is necessary to also say that Marx's thought, and the questions that move his critical practice are here still bound to a 'problematic' that, just a few years later, he turns his critical sights on, and in so doing, remakes the terms and question of this political-intellectual project. The motto given to criticism in the letters, for instance, still bears the mark of a set of questions 'all up in the head', posed as 'the reform of consciousness' through 'analysing the mystical consciousness' that has become incomprehensible to itself. And it does so in order to bring to light what is already latent to it, with Marx (1967: 214) offering that 'it will be evident, then, that the world has long dreamed of something of which it only has to become conscious in order to possess it in actuality'. More crucially, however, Marx's critic will only carry out this work within historic-ally given limits – both in relation to a historical process, as well as to the ways in which individuals have come to see themselves in relation to this process (that is in relation to subjectivity) – precisely by confronting these limits. In an impassioned, and also daring passage, Marx outlines an intellectual practice that marks out a relationship to the existing state of things, his present, as one of 'relentless criticism':

> Even greater than the external obstacles seem to be the inner ones. Even though there is no doubt about the 'whence', there does prevail all the more confusion about the 'whither'. It is not only the fact that a general anarchy has broken out among the reformers; each one will have to admit to himself that he has no exact idea of what is to happen. But this is exactly the advantage of the new direction, namely, that we do not anti-cipate the world dogmatically, but rather wish to find the new world through criticism of the old. Until now the philosophers had the solutions to all riddles in their desks, and the stupid outside world simply had to open its mouth so that the roasted pigeons of absolute science might fly into it. Philosophy has become secularized, and the most striking proof for this is the fact that the philosophical consciousness itself is drawn into the torment of struggle, not only outwardly but inwardly as well. Even though the construction of the future and its completion for all times is not our task, what we have to accomplish at this time is all the more clear: *relentless criticism of all existing conditions*, relentless in the sense that the criticism is not afraid of its findings and just as little afraid of the conflict with the powers that be (Marx 1967: 212, Marx's emphasis).

Marx's story does not end here. In the letters, 'the philosophical consciousness' is already bending with the 'torment of struggle', but it will only 'shift base' by regrounding itself in the perspective of the 'real movement' that Marx, in 'taking sides in politics', in 'actual real struggles', allows to reshape the terms of his critical intellectual project. In fact, the Marx we find in the letters fits well with Althusser's complaint that the critical practice of the young Marx remained prisoner to 'a rationalist conception of critique', whose essential problem remained distinguishing the true from the false, conceived as a form of questioning to guard against 'errors, prejudices and illusions' (Althusser 2006: 17).

Doubtless, Marx's treatment of the question of the state in these letters is one of the sources of this impression. More importantly, however, when Marx (1967: 212) later turns his critical thought to the ideological world of his own beginnings, we see emerging 'an altogether different meaning and function' for critique (see Marx and Engels [1847] 1998). While the full significance of these shifts is in many ways still beyond my own powers of philosophical-textual appreciation, it is less difficult to get a sense of the (political) temporality that marks the development of Marx's thought in this period: its constant and unflinching confrontation of its own limits and the deepening urgency it gives to re-evaluating the 'tasks of the present' from within a *new perspective*. Althusser, in fact, insists on a certain 'pace' in the development of Marx's thought, itself marked by the contingency of beginnings and which progressively calls into question the very problematic that gives the initial questions and terms of his critical philosophy.

Although I suspect that a work might produce results that go beyond the problematic that inspired it, Althusser's reading of Marx and the specific development of his conception of critique, has turned out to be an important signpost in mapping the intellectual terrains I grapple with.

BECOMING MARXIST

Engels famously reported that Marx, the founder of Marxist philosophy, had once remarked that he (Marx) was not a Marxist.[5] To be sure, Marx was not here repudiating his own thought, nor rejecting the possibility that this thought should take on a political life apart from him. It is more likely that Marx was responding to what in Marxism is (already within his own lifetime) beginning to take on the character of dogma ('[h]ere is the truth, kneel here!') and what years later Foucault found cause to insist Marx needed to be liberated from, as I have already mentioned. Althusser points out that the intellectual kinship that Marx's works solicits is with a thought that is already thinking for itself, a thought grounded in real history and the struggles that belong to it. And it was in fact precisely on these materialist terms that Marx presented his critique of political economy for critique.[6]

This fact, however, takes nothing away from the confidence of Marx's texts, nor from Marx's confidence in his texts. Marx was very much a Marxist in this sense: as Althusser (2006: 15) says, 'he believed in his work'. Marx was not, however, a Marxist where this indexed subjection to a 'total or totalizing unity, constituting a body of thought that could be labelled Marxism'. In fact, rather than a tenet of thought, in the late Althusser, Marx's identity as a Marxist turns on the form of critique his intellectual practice comes to be regrounded in.

As is well known, the tremendous contribution, significance and controversy of Althusser's writing is in no small part connected to his thesis that the development of Marx's thought is marked by an 'epistemological break' – characterised by a certain mode of 'shifting ground', by 'the changing out of the elements' of this thought – as Marx moves from the problematic that marked his early writings,[7] to the properly materialist perspective that is beginning to emerge with his *Theses on Feuerbach* (1888) and *The German Ideology* (1932). What I want to emphasise, however, is the manner in which Althusser links this break in Marx's thought to a shift in the 'meaning and function' this thought gives to critique. For where Althusser sees the young Marx's critical practice stranded to a rationalist conception of critique that was bound to the idealist problematic of the state of reason, this practice shifts ground precisely by *regrounding* itself in the perspective of the 'worker's movement' that the Marx of 1843 was soon to discover.[8]

While I have some reservations about the reduction of the critical practice of the young Marx to the 'rationalist conception of critique' that is clearly determining many of its questions and terms, it is the latter point that I find the most convincing and Althusser's fixing of the shifts in Marx's critical practice to the tempo of political struggle:

> [C]ritique is not, for Marx, the judgment which the (true) Idea pronounces on the defective or contradictory real; critique is critique of existing reality by existing reality (either by another reality, or a contradiction internal to reality). *For Marx, critique is the real criticizing itself,* casting off its own detritus itself, in order to liberate and laboriously realize its dominant tendency, which is active within it. It is this materialist sense that Marx's critique could, as early as 1845, treat communism as the very opposite of the 'ideal', the deepest tendency of the 'real movement'. But Marx did not content himself with this still abstract notion of critique. For which 'reality' is in question here? ... Marx tied critique to that which in the real movement, grounded critique: for him, in the last

instance, the class struggle of the exploited ... (Althusser 2006: 17, Althusser's emphasis)

I want to pause on this passage whose intelligence for me is the connection it makes between a conception of critique and 'the real movement' and thus the very definition Marx gives for communism in *The German Ideology*. In fact, between the letters of 1843, and Marx and Engels's definition of communism in 1845, one might note an interesting shift, a kind of 'changing out of elements', in which the critic of 'the relentless criticism' of the present state of things, changes out with 'the real movement' whose '*practical* critique' is now the author of the destruction of the existing state of things: 'Communism is for us not a state of affairs which is to be established, an ideal to which reality (will) have to adjust itself. We call communism the real movement which abolishes the present state of things' (Marx and Engels [1847] 1998: 57).[9]

This real movement – whose condition is that of the class struggle itself – is in fact the real that Marx poses against reality, the real that, in Althusser's words, is 'the true author (the agent) of the real's critique of itself' (Althusser 2006: 18). Marx becomes Marxist by grounding critique in the real movement, in presenting the real, as the reality of the class struggle, from the perspective of the workers' movement.

We can now turn to Foucault.

IN FITS AND STARTS

Between the publication of the first volume of Foucault's *The History of Sexuality* (Foucault 1990a [1976]) and the two volumes that follow it (1990b [1984] and 1990c [1984]), there is a space of eight years. This 'gap' is, however, often thought of as more than a temporal one, dividing the two lines of Foucault's later research; on the one hand a series of studies concerned with the problem of power and on the other, a set of investigations that take up the question of the subject. In spite of Foucault's clarification in his 1982 essay, 'The subject and power', that it was the 'subject' and 'not power', that was the 'general theme' of his research (2002: 327) and his explicit confrontation of this 'gap' in the introduction to the second volume of *The History of Sexuality* (titled *The Use of Pleasure*), this shift has, if not confounded Foucauldian scholars, then at least presented itself as a problem needing resolution.

The great enthusiasm that accompanied the publication of Foucault's lectures at the College de France is thus accounted for not only by the very real break-through it makes for a theoretical approach to the 'government of state', but also, it would seem, for the ways in which it helps fill in this apparent gap, drawing together these two apparently 'disparate projects'. The blurb of the first English edition of *Security Territory Population* in fact carries, in these very terms, the endorsement of the *Continental Philosophy Review*, characterising the lectures' publication as a 'major event' that 'might properly be called the "missing link"' revealing 'the underlying unity of Foucault's later thought' (Foucault 2007).[10]

There is certainly a real sense in which this is correct and the posthumously published lectures on government help us to understand and draw together the different lines emerging from Foucault's later work. Nevertheless, we should still ask whether this is the way one ought to read Foucault. As Gilles Deleuze (1992: 159) says in his essay on Foucault's concept of the 'dispositif', '[g]reat thinkers are somewhat seismic; they do not evolve but proceed by means of crisis, in fits and starts'. And, indeed, it is often the 'holes' in a philosopher's work that contain the signs of these crises, the place of new beginnings.[11]

Would it therefore not be better to do something else? To assume discon-tinuity, breaks and even crises, along with the continuities, leaps and break-throughs, but within a field that is opened up by our own questions, our own grappling with the present? In any case, a reading that is less about offering an account of the unity of the work, but instead (borrowing an analogy) which traces a 'line of force', linking and aligning elements that would give us the basis of a use, here-now. This is what Harry Cleaver (2000) calls a political reading, given of course that we ask the right questions.[12]

Along these lines, I want to say that here, in relation to this 'hole' in a work, a political *problem* clarifies. As I argue elsewhere, while 'the question of resist-ance is far from being already closed from the start in Foucault',[13] there is still an open question about what forms of political action might be most effective within a dynamic in which power is implicated in the very constitution of the subject who resists (Veriava 2013; see also Hardt 2010).

BEGINNING AGAIN

There is something uneasy, difficult even, about Foucault's writings on critique, a superficial accessibility that covers over the affective work of the text, forcing us to return to it every time we try to say something about it, searching for something already there, and yet, not-yet.

Their subtlety arises in part from the question form these works take ('What is critique?', 'What is enlightenment?'), which presents a conception of critique through 'enacting a certain mode of questioning which will prove central to this activity' (Butler 2001: 2–3). Here the question – what is critique? – becomes the place of a displacement, the redrawing of a fold, *daring* us to think otherwise … 'to stray afield' of ourselves.[14]

Doubtless, the most well-known of Foucault's texts on critique is his essay 'What is enlightenment?' (1997) which takes up a novel reading of Immanuel Kant's essay by the same name. One can, however, find scattered throughout Foucault's later work a number of references (some direct, others less so) to these threads, which collectively represent something of a sustained engagement with the theme of critique and with Kant's essay.

In relation to these texts it is sometimes noted that Foucault allows us to 'rethink critique as a practice' and to rethink it in a way that is at a remove from what it wants to critique (see Butler 2001). This is true. However, it is important not to lose sight of the ways in which, in these threads, Foucault also comes to talk about the focus of his own intellectual work and the philosophical objects upon which this work centres.

In this section, I want to suggest that in these texts, next to his reading of Kant's essay on the Enlightenment and in fact, in relation to it, Foucault also wants to underline a historically determined 'relation', or even 'correlation' between, as he once put it, 'the government of self and the government of others'. Moreover, the practice of critique finds 'no external support', not only emerging with the 'dispositifs' or apparatuses that characterise modern power, but also (as Deleuze might say) belonging to it. It is at this impasse that Foucault offers us a reflection on the significance of his own work, in a way that not only details the methodological relations it establishes as a consequence, but also, I think, in a way that wants to underline the political and indeed also, ontological stakes this mode of critique is playing for.

AN-OTHER POWER

One of the things that is exciting about working between the lines of the texts on critique, or marking the development of concepts between these successive statements, is the very real sense one gets of the movement of a thought coming to a 'better perspective' on itself. That is to say, of thought problematising its own practice, in ways that both clarify it and point a path beyond it: a thought crossing over behaviours and representations to find thought itself and with this movement, coming to the thought of the subject – what this thought was already becoming. And yet, or perhaps, for this reason, they are not straightforward, shifting terms and strategies, developing new ones even as they re-turn, every time, to the same place. Indeed it is Kant's essay that exerts a particular gravity for this analysis.

However, I want to set aside Foucault's commentary on Kant's essay for the time being. As we will see, what he ascribes to this short piece by Kant is a new way of posing the question of the present. But he also locates the emergence of the 'critical attitude' that he links to Kant's essay within a wider historical process.

In his lecture at the Sorbonne in 1978, Foucault suggests that between the lofty 'Kantian enterprise and the small polemical-professional activities that bear the name "critique"' one can find 'a certain manner of thinking, of speaking, likewise of acting, and a certain relation to what exists, to what one knows, to what one does, as well as a relation to society, to culture, to others, and all this one might name the critical attitude' (Foucault 1996: 382).

This work, which marks the first explicit formulation of Foucault's conception of critique, and which was delivered shortly after his course *Security Territory Population* (focused on the problem of government), is interesting for the ways in which the emergence of this 'critical attitude' is linked to what he calls the 'simultaneous movement of governmentalisation' (384). This 'movement', which Foucault's course at the College de France took as its subject, refers to the process, beginning from around the fifteenth and sixteenth centuries, whereby a particular mode of directing the conduct of men – which had grown out of the institutional form of the Christian church – will increasingly shift, or rather be 'displaced' and expand into 'civil society',[15] while at the same time becoming more focused (Foucault speaks about the 'proliferation' of treatise on conduct; on 'conducting the conduct' of children, the poor, cities, states, one's body, one's mind and so on) (383–384). And Foucault comes to speak about these treatises in terms of an 'art of government'.

There is, however, a subtle point that is often overlooked in commentary on Foucault's work on government, but which emerges far more starkly in this 1978 lecture on critique: *the process of governmentalisation is in a sense always double*. It is the virtue of Hardt and Antonio Negri (2009: 56), in their recent book *Commonwealth*, to point to this 'doubleness' in Foucault's theorisation of power, which they see at work in his monumental studies *Discipline and Punish* (1995) and the first volume of *The History of Sexuality* (1990a). For Hardt and Negri, there is in Foucault's theory of power always an 'other' of power 'or even an other power', in relation to what Foucault calls resistance. And if this is true of books like *Discipline and Punish* and the *History of Sexuality* (Volume 1) as Hardt and Negri suggest, it is also true of Foucault's courses on government as well as these statements on critique.

Echoing the formulation in his course *Security Territory Population*, in 'What is critique?' Foucault (1996: 384) tells us that a 'fundamental question' for the fifteenth and sixteenth centuries was 'How to govern?', a question to which 'all the institutions of government' – pedagogical, economic, political – would come to respond. It is worth pointing out that in *Security Territory Population* the immediate backdrop of this new art of government was what he called the 'insurrections of conduct', linked to a whole series of revolts. In the Sorbonne lecture, he thus notes that this question ('how to govern'), which for him was in a very real sense characteristic of the period, 'cannot be dissociated' from a second question, 'how not to be governed'. It is important to point out, however, (in spite of his 'slip' at the end), that this question does not so much mark a rejection of government for Foucault, as it comes to function as a form of 'constant contestation' of the particular mode in which government might be realised:

> In the great anxiety surrounding that way to govern and in the inquiries into modes of governing, one detects a perpetual question, which would be: 'How not to be governed like that, by that, in the name of these prin-ciples, in view of such objectives and by means of such methods, not like that, not for that, not by them?' (Foucault 1996: 384)

And it is exactly in relation to this 'double movement' – between the question 'How to govern?' and 'How not to be governed?' – that the drama of govern-mentalisation unfolds. However, what is crucial for the discussion on critique is that it is in relation to this 'simultaneous movement of governmentalisation, of society and individuals' (Foucault 1996: 384),[16] and specifically in relation to this question of 'How not to be governed?', that Foucault uncovers 'something close to what might be called the critical attitude':

> Against this, and like counterpoint, or rather at once partner and adversary of the arts of governing, as a way of suspecting them, of challenging them, of limiting them, of finding their right measure, of transforming them, of seeking to escape these arts of governing, or in any case to displace them, as an essential reluctance, but also in that way as a line of development of the arts of government, there would have been something born in Europe at this time, a kind of general cultural form, at once a moral and political attitude, a way of thinking ... (384)

The 'preliminary definition' that the 1978 lecture gives to critique is thus the 'art of not being governed so much' (Foucault 1996: 384). Critique, as that which is linked to the other side of the process of governmentalisation, will thus find its specific points of development, or rather, what Foucault calls the 'anchoring points' of the critical attitude, in those domains that the 'art of government' takes as its source and support.[17] In fact, Foucault sees emerging from this 'game of governmentalisation and critique' many of the forms of discursive reflection that characterise modern thought.

In this text we already get a strong sense of how, in relation to the genealogy of critique (which figures almost as the other side of the genealogy of government), Foucault wants to think of the relations between the three broad lines running through his work, which is in fact precisely what he reads as the focus of critique; that is, the relations that bind together knowledge, power and the subject. In 'What is critique?' Foucault shows us the ways in which critique emerges with a form of power and subjection whose mechanism forms a tight set of relations with knowledge. Moreover, in so far as the process of governmentalisation must be thought of as well as in relation to processes of subjection/subjectification, critique belongs to an alternate 'movement', a force of 'desubjectification':

> If governmentalisation is really this movement concerned with subjugating individuals in the very reality of a social practice by mechanisms of power that appeal to a truth, I will say that critique is the movement through which the subject gives itself the right to question truth concerning its power effects and to question power about its discourses of truth. Critique will be the art of voluntary inservitude, of reflective indocility. The essential function of critique would be that of desubjectification in

the game of what one could call, in a word, the politics of truth (Foucault 1996: 386).

And it is in this context that the 1978 lecture turns to the question of Enlightenment (*Aufklarung*) and the ways in which Kant's essay foregrounds the question of knowledge within an analysis coordinated along the axes of the question of autonomy and obedience to authority.

I would, however, like to linger a bit on Foucault's characterisation here of the strategic field in which critique finds itself intervening. He describes it as a game and calls this game 'a politics of truth'. To be sure, we are talking about a politics in which the contestation of power will, in a certain sense, also invest relations of knowledge, a contestation of a form of power marked by specific relations between power and knowledge (that is, specific relations between mechanisms to affect conduct and the systems of knowledge that determine their 'application and validity'). However the subject of this politics, her conducts, and even her critical conduct, are already inserted into this terrain and in a strong sense take their form within it.

In this tight passage, this game, as a politics of truth, is in fact defined in relation to two forces, or rather two types of force; in the lecture Foucault calls them 'movements'. The first is the movement of governmentalisation, by which Foucault indexes the process through which a particular form of power takes hold of life, subjugating it to specific forms of conduct and, as Foucault would have said, 'through mechanisms that appeal to truth'. The second, alternative movement is characterised by a force of 'inservitude' and 'indocility', 'a force of desubjectification'. In relation to this other side of the process of governmentalisation, in *Security Territory Population* Foucault speaks about revolts of conduct and suggests the term 'counter-conducts' in relation to the 'struggle against the processes implemented for conducting others' (2007: 201). In the Sorbonne lecture, where Foucault seems far more focused on the specific ways in which struggles at the level of knowledge rebound on 'this game', the alternative or countermovement is described in terms of critique. What I want to highlight, which speaks to the truly profound stakes of this '*double movement*' which characterises the politics of truth, is that it is in relation to it that the subject of this politics is decided. What makes Foucault indispensable to my own project is that he allows us to refocus our critical energy, beyond this or that particular intervention in the game, to the constitution of the game itself.

PROBLEMATISING GOVERNMENT

There are a number of questions about Foucault's relationship to Kant's essay. Unquestionably, there is something in it that Foucault finds inspiring. Yet this is not the whole story, since what he finds inspiring is perhaps not unrelated to the paradoxical relations this text potentially forms with its canonical terms. In fact, what seems to me crucial in grasping Foucault's relationship to Kant's essay is grappling with the way it is linked to a particular problematisation that is fundamental to modernity: the problematisation of government. Doubtless the specific difficulties that instigate thought to reflect on the special form of conduct we call government (which is after all the conduct of conduct itself) – to problematise it, so to speak, in terms of the question of 'how to govern?' (which cannot be disassociated from the question of 'how not to be governed?') is what Foucault first reflects on under the heading of 'the insurrections of conduct', linked to the pastoral revolts of the fifteenth and sixteenth centuries. If, under the heading of 'Governmentality', Foucault sought to grapple with solutions that the age of reason presented to this problem and the practices that grew with them, the theme of critique was for Foucault 'a still open dossier' running alongside this crucial thread in his work (and he says as much).

The 1978 lecture highlights the ways in which Kant's way of defining enlightenment links up with Foucault's own way of defining the 'critical attitude', in terms of intervention in a game that binds power, knowledge and the subject. Although, in this lecture, Foucault moves somewhat quickly through them, I want to pause on those aspects that he underlines in relation to Kant's 'definition' of the Enlightenment since they collect – in raw form – many of the consistent themes of his engagement with this text.

Firstly, he tells us that Kant defined enlightenment in relation to 'a certain state of immaturity in which humanity would be maintained and maintained authoritatively' (Foucault 2007: 386). This immaturity, or minority (following Thomas Abbott's translation of Kant's essay) is, in a sense, 'self-incurred', at least in so far as it is here related to a 'lack of determination and courage' (Kant 2001: 135). But determination and courage for what? Kant tells us, 'minority is the incapacity to use one's intelligence without the guidance of another', or as Foucault (1997: 305) explains in 'What is enlightenment?', it is 'a certain state of our will which makes us accept someone else's authority to lead us in areas where the use of reason is called for'. The *problem* here centres on the question of subjectivity, since, as Foucault makes clear in his 1983 lecture (in his series *The Government of Self and Others*), it is not by an act of violence that we are prevented from thinking for ourselves, but instead, because of ourselves, or more precisely, *because 'of a certain relationship' we have 'to ourselves'* (2010: 33, my emphasis).

What I think is important here, and I will return to it, is that this state of minority is marked by a certain relation – Foucault also calls it a 'correlation' – between authority and a certain disposition with respect to the subject; as Foucault puts it in his reading of Kant, 'a certain correlation between an authority that is exercised and that maintains humanity in this state of immaturity... [and] a lack of decision and courage' (1996: 386).

Secondly, Foucault highlights that Kant defines enlightenment as 'exit' from minority, through an 'appeal to courage' that is itself connected to the public labour of philosopher. In the 1978 lecture this element of Foucault's reading of Kant's text is not well developed, but, I suspect that it was what formed the deeper basis of Foucault's fascination with this text, and as Hardt (2011) has noted, is in no small part related to what he takes inspiration from. As Foucault emphasises in 'What is enlightenment?' and the 1983 lecture, Kant calls enlightenment an 'exit' (see Kant 2001: 135), a 'way out' (Foucault 1997: 305) from this state where our judgement is ceded to the authority of another. Where in 1978 Foucault underlined a certain correlation, in 'What is enlightenment?' this is formulated in slightly more rigorous terms, such that the 'exit' of enlightenment is here 'defined by a modification of *the preexisting relation linking will, authority, and the use of reason*' (1997: 305, my emphasis).

Part of the ambiguity of Kant's text, which Foucault powerfully draws out, is that here enlightenment is at once a moment and a particular phenomenon, a process in which men are at the same time a part or element of, and as Foucault emphasises, also a 'task and an obligation' that will have to be undertaken (1997: 305). It is a collective process, but one which implies as well an individual disposition. In this sense then, there is enlightenment because people are actors within this process, and this process occurs only to the extent that they 'decide to be its voluntary actors' (1997: 306). And Kant's motto for the Enlightenment, which is at the same time its very condition, is 'Sapere aude! [Dare to know!] Have the courage to use your own intelligence' (Kant 2001: 135).

What seems to move Foucault deeply here is the ways in which the essay connects Kant's own intellectual enterprise to the moment in which he is writing, a moment that, in part, comes to assume its specific difference 'because he is writing' (1997: 309). Enlightenment then, is in this sense a way of relating to the 'present' and the collective subject, the we, that constitutes this present. This questioning of the present, of the 'we' that belongs to it, and which is also an insertion in the present, a way of belonging to it and an intervention in the making of it, marks the specific difference, the new way of raising the question of modernity, introduced by Kant. This is undoubtedly the most important part of what Foucault takes from Kant's essay, formulated as the question 'Who are we today?'.

A NEW DISTRIBUTION

One aspect of what Foucault wants us to see is the ways in which Kant's essay becomes part of enacting, by articulating, a certain strategy for exiting a correlation that links the exercise of authority to forms of subjectivity. It seems to me, however, that Foucault's interest in the text is just as much about the new correlation it is suggesting and indeed, in a certain sense helping establish. In fact, I wonder if staging this paradox for the present is not part of the pleasure Foucault takes from his public readings of this essay.

In the 1978 lecture, when he reminds us of the motto of the Enlightenment, he therefore also immediately sets it next to a second, that of the sovereign, Frederick II, who says: '[l]et them reason as much as they want as long as they obey' (1996: 387). There is a particularly interesting ambiguity here, for this movement of a subject exiting minority – who, as we saw, is at once agent and element of the necessarily collective undertaking called enlightenment – is 'correlated' with that of another at a second pole, that of the sovereign. In 'What is enlightenment?' Foucault writes:

> Enlightenment, as we see, must not be conceived simply as a general process affecting all humanity, it must not be conceived only as an obligation prescribed to individuals: it now appears as a political problem. The question, in any event, is that of knowing how the use of reason can take the public form that it requires, how the audacity to know can be exercised in broad daylight, while individuals are obeying as scrupulously as possible. And Kant, in conclusion proposes to Frederick II, in scarcely veiled terms, a sort of contract – what might be called the

contract of rational despotism with free reason: the public and free use of autonomous reason will be the best guarantee of obedience, on condition, however, that the political principle which must be obeyed itself be in conformity with universal reason (1997: 308).

Foucault offers a rich discussion of the particular opposition between public and private that Kant's thought is grounded in. All I want to do, however, is to underline the crucial significance Foucault seems to want to give this relation. In fact, in the 1983 lecture, Foucault suggests that, for Kant, it is Frederick (with some difficulty) who is given the role of the agent of the Enlightenment, for the way his mode of governing removes the 'obstacles' standing in the way of people using their own understanding:

> [W]e have ... through Frederick's ... way of governing, that adjustment between, on the one hand, a government of self which will develop in the form of the universal (as public discussion, public reasoning, and public use of understanding) and, on the other, the obedience to which all those who are part of a given society, state, or administration will be constrained. Frederick of Prussia is the very figure of Aufklarung, the essential agent who makes the right redistribution in the interplay between obedience and private use, universality and public use (Foucault 2010: 38).

An interesting aspect of the 1983 lecture is the way in which it clarifies the ground of development for this 'correlation' by setting it at the base of political modernity. Foucault suggests that Kant's 1784 text was not the only time he presents a reflection on his present and points to his comments on the French Revolution in *The Conflict of the Faculties*. There the phenomenon of enthusiasm for the revolution now replaces the sovereign as the agent of the Enlightenment:

> The difficulty Kant clearly experienced in giving the King of Prussia this role as agent of Aufklarung no doubt partly explains the fact that, in the 1798 text ... the agent of Aufklarung, the very process of Aufklarung, will be transferred to the Revolution. Or, more exactly, it will not be transferred to the Revolution, but to that general phenomenon of

revolutionary enthusiasm produced around the Revolution. In the 1798 text, revolutionary enthusiasm replaces or succeeds the King of Prussia in the role he was given in the 1784 text as agent of Aufklarung (Foucault 2010: 39).

Although Foucault himself does not put it in these terms, it is not unjustified to think about this statement in relation to the crucial transition through which the question of political modernity is often thought: that is the transition from royal sovereignty to popular sovereignty.

More importantly in his 1983 lecture on Kant's essay, when Foucault motivates beginning with this text, he suggests that, 'to formulate it in rigorous terms' it is exactly in line with the 'relationship between the government of self and the government of others' (Foucault 2010: 7). It should be equally unsurprising then, that in the lecture that follows, he should come to refer to Kant's Enlightenment as a 'new dividing up', a 'new distribution of the government of the self and the government of others'.

METHOD

When, at the start of the 1983 course, *The Government of Self and Others* (after clarifying the terms of his project as 'a history of thought'), Foucault turns to Kant's essay on enlightenment, he describes this discussion as 'not exactly an excursus [... but] a little epigraph' (Foucault 2010: 7). Just a few sentences later he also admits that Kant's text is something of a 'blazon' and a 'fetish' for him. Now an epigraph, at least in the literary sense, is a short piece of text (often a quotation) which precedes a work, and which, in some way, suggests or connects with its theme. By contrast, in heraldic vexillology, a blazon is a type of discursive description of an emblematic sign (such as a coat of arms or a flag), marked by specific grammar for progressively specifying the elements of an emblem.

These characterisations of Kant's essay raise two questions. Firstly, in what sense is this detailed discussion of Kant's essay – what at any rate appears as a digression or excursus – an epigraph for the course that follows, centred on the theme of 'parrhesia' in ancient Hellenic writing. This question – of the relationship between the course's discussion of Kant's essay and its treatment of the theme of parrhesia – is in fact what is taken up in Hardt's (2011) recent essay on the course. The second question is more along the lines of what I have been trying to get at in this last section, that is, to answer the question relating to the relationship between Foucault's project and these discussions of Kant's essay: how does Foucault's discussion of 'What is enlightenment?' and his way of speaking about this text, come to specify the elements of something that would be an emblem for him, for his project as 'a history of thought'? And what seems crucial here is the relationship that these public readings of Kant's text form with something that Foucault sets next to it – what, for lack of a better way of putting it, is a discussion on method.

In relation to Kant's question – that is, this question of 'who we are today?'– Foucault (1997: 315) wants to say something about what he is doing, about what is specific to his way of doing critique: that is a 'philosophical ethos consisting in a critique of what we are saying, thinking, and doing, through a historical ontology of ourselves'. Kant's question, in fact, becomes definitively Foucault's for the way in which it comes to feature as the central element, or in keeping with the heraldic analogy, the principle 'charge', of what the discussions on method call the 'historico-philosophical approach' (in 'What is critique?'), or 'historico-critical analysis' (in 'What is enlightenment?').

Reading across these texts it seems clear to me that Foucault (1996: 393) wants to set himself apart from various contemporary strands of a rationalist conception of critique. Then critique, for Foucault, cannot be a matter of fault-finding or searching for that 'false idea knowledge makes of itself'. Rather, critique is directed at the relations that bind rationalisation to modes of domination, in order to identify what it is already possible for us to go beyond. If Foucault refuses to temper a critical disposition with respect to the forms of rationality that belong to modernity, he equally wants to underline the impossibility of making an intellectual practice outside of it. In fact, part of what is interesting about his displacement of the question of enlightenment in these essays, is his insistence on separating enlightenment from humanism and the way in which he poses against the latter's static conception of the subject 'the principle of critique and a permanent creation of ourselves in our autonomy' (Foucault 1997: 314).

Against a mode of critique that would fall for 'the blackmail of the Enlightenment', or make an intellectual practice on the grounds of humanism, then, Foucault affirms an ethos no longer simply defined by its mode of opposition, but which, in 'What is enlightenment?', he now characterises 'as a limit attitude'; an ethos going 'beyond the outside-inside alternative' to work at 'the frontiers' of who we are now (1997: 315). We are in fact now properly on the positive side of the new ethos of criticism:

> Criticism … consists of analyzing and reflecting upon limits. But if the Kantian question was that of knowing what limits knowledge must renounce exceeding, it seems to me that the critical question today must be turned into a positive one: In what is given to us as universal, necessary, obligatory, what place is occupied by the singular, contingent, and the product of arbitrary constraints? The point, in brief, is *to transform the critique conducted in the form of necessary limitation into a practical critique that takes the form of possible crossing-over.* … This entails an obvious consequence: that criticism is no longer going to be practised in search of the formal structures with universal value but, rather, as a historical investigation into the events that have led us to constitute ourselves and to recognize ourselves as subjects of what we are doing, thinking, saying (Foucault 1997: 315, my emphasis).

FRANK TALK

What is going on here, in these 'still open dossiers' on critique? Is it that Foucault is searching, as Hardt (2010) suggests, for a way of going beyond a particular conceptual and also political dead end?

The problem arises with the implications of 'the doubleness of power' that Foucault's work allows us to grasp. While the immense value and political potentiality of Foucault's work on power is to open our thought to a 'strictly relational' dynamic in which 'resistance comes first' (see Deleuze 1999), it nevertheless struggled to show the possibility of a mode of resistance that is also an autonomous constitution of an alternative form of life.

The importance of Foucault's thought on critique is its suggestion of a mode of 'practical critique' that would take the form of a 'crossing over' of the correlations and forms of subjection that characterise modern configurations of power (see also Hardt 2011).[18] This, I would argue, is precisely the importance of Foucault's reflections on Charles Baudelaire (in 'What is enlightenment?') and parrhesia (in the course that follows his lecture on Kant's essay, *The Government of Self and Others*).

It is from this vantage point that I would like to return to Hardt's (2011) essay. For it seems to me that the importance of this reading of Foucault is to emphasise the place of his (Foucault's) reflections on parrhesia, where the political vocation of the latter is to mark out a model that pushes beyond the interplay of resistance and power, toward the constitution of a new collective subject, that is at the same time a making of the present and the forms of life that belong to it. The tremendous value of this reading to my own work is the perspective on later Foucault it opens up and its radicalisation of a con-ception of an 'ontology of the present and ourselves', which now takes on an explicitly political sense that is bound to 'the making' of a collective political subject:

> By ontology here Foucault is clearly not referring to immutable, eternal being, as do conventional conceptions. The ontology of the present and ourselves, of ourselves in the present, can only be a process of becoming. This seemingly paradoxical notion of ontology as process in the present, a being of becoming, is key to Foucault's conception of the potential role of theory and the theorist. The philosophical relation to the present is an active and collective relation that is not merely a matter of register-ing or even evaluating the present but acting on and transforming it. The task of theory is to make the present and thus to delimit or invent the subject of that making, a 'we' characterised not only by our belong-ing to the present but by our making it. It is not clear yet, though, how Foucault imagines we can accomplish the transformative and constitu-tive task (Hardt 2011: 21).

In Hardt's account of the significance of Foucault's lectures on parrhesia, and especially the forms it comes to take in the militant practice of the Cynics, is then the suggestion that it offers a model for this 'ontology of ourselves'. As I have already noted, Foucault's discussion of Kant's essay and critique is followed by his development of this thematic of parrhesia, which is taken over to the following year's course as well. Defined by Foucault as 'true discourse in the political realm' (2010: 6), or free, frank speech ('*franc-parler*'), the courses illustrate three distinct appropriations of parrhesia at different moments in the ancient world. While the specific work of this chapter is to underline the points of inspiration for my own way of doing critique, thus setting a detailed commentary on this thematic beyond my immediate tasks here, it seems to me important to point out the extremely interesting relation between Foucault's discussion on parrhesia and his discussion of critique.

In the second lecture of the course, *The Government of Self and Others*, in which Foucault introduces his audience to this theme of parrhesia, he says:

> [W]e have, if you like, a whole structure, a whole bundle of important notions and themes: care of self, knowledge of self, art and exercises of oneself, relationship to the other, the truth on the part of the other. You can see that with parrhesia we have a notion which is situated at the meeting point of the obligation to speak the truth, procedures and techniques of governmentality, and the constitution of the relationship to self. Truth-telling by the other, as an essential component of how he governs us, is one of the essential conditions for us to able to form the right kind of relationship to ourselves that will give us virtue and happiness (2010: 45).

As Hardt (2010: 151) notes, this excursion into the ancient world and its concept of parrhesia is by no means 'innocent' and has contemporary political issues at its root. And I would argue that if, as we have suggested, at the centre of Foucault's discussion of critique is the problem of the 'correlation of the government of self and others', then the profound importance of the theme of parrhesia is the manner in which it seems to turn the (modern) forms of such correlations on their head. Indeed, what we find in parrhesia, in particular in the form it takes with the Cynics, is correlation between a subject's (autonomous) constitution and self-government and this subject's subversion and antagonistic relation to 'the government of others'; apolitical practice that militantly attempts to make the world anew:

> [T]he Cynic life defined itself as a royal life, and even as the royal life par excellence, fully sovereign over itself. I think that this sovereignty, by which the Cynic life characterized itself, expressed a double derision towards political sovereignty, the sovereignty of kings of the world. First, because Cynic sovereignty asserted itself aggressively, in a critical, polemical mode, as the only real monarchy. What basically was at issue in the meeting between Diogenes and Alexander was which of them was the true king. And Diogenes, of course, asserted himself and revealed

himself as the true king, facing Alexander, who held his monarchy, in the true sense of the term, only inasmuch as he too shared in the sovereignty of that wisdom ... On the other hand – this was the other side of the Cynic derision of monarchies – the Cynics' real monarchy inverted all the signs and distinguishing features of political monarchies (Foucault 2011: 307–308).

One in fact finds in Foucault's discussion many passages highlighting the ways in which Cynic parrhesia inverts forms of correlating the government of self and others. However, by way of summary, I want to quote (at length) Hardt's reading of this complex and rich thread in Foucault's work:

> The Cynics practised Parrhesia, Foucault explains, through a kind of public, critical preaching, often aimed against social institutions. They also sought to enact the truth through scandalous behavior that exposed to public view aspects of life that are generally hidden ... Two fundamental principles of the true life for the Cynics were exposure and poverty: not only destroying any division between private and public, but also releasing the Cynic from the limits of individuality, so as to be able to construct a life addressed to humanity as a whole ... The *askesis* of the ancient Cynics, Foucault claims, is a 'militancy that aims to change the world, much more than a militancy that would seek to furnish its adepts with the means to arrive at a happy life'. The life the Cynics proposed is a militant left that struggles to change both ourselves and the world ... [In the cynics' struggle for social change t]he care of the self is enlarged to the care not only of a few others but humanity as a whole ... In terms of philosophical doctrine, Foucault argues, the ancient Cynics contributed little, merely adopting and transforming various traditional formulations. Their singular contribution instead is to make life the centre of a philosophical and political project ... Foucault defines Cynics' primary goal as 'militant life, the life of combat and struggle against the self and for the self, against other and for others'. The only true life for the Cynics is a life transformed, and the only way to achieve such a life is to create another world out of this one ... The key to the shift accomplished by the Cynics is the development of the terrain of life – a militant life, a revolutionary life – as the locus of politics (Hardt 2010: 158–159).

However, apart from the suggestion that the modern heirs of Cynic parrhesia are 'revolutionaries whose lives enact a – sometimes violent – rupture with the conventions and values of the dominant society' (Hardt 2010: 158–159), neither Foucault nor Hardt gives us a sense of what parrhesia in the modern context might look like, let alone something as an example. This, of course, is not their job. Elsewhere, I suggest that 'we', here at the southern tip of Africa, already have a rich instance of parrhesia to draw upon and one whose affective power already marks our world and works. For it seems to me that the clearest and most immediate referent (for us) of a parrhesia in the modern – that is, of a 'frank talk' that articulates a mode of correlating a strategy for making ourselves in our autonomy, with a strategy for remaking the world in which we live – is Steve Biko. What we find in Biko is an antagonistic style of life that breaks the interplay between resistance and power (see Biko 2004). This seems to me the form of practical critique that the best Foucault might be said to point towards.

It could well be objected that in Hardt's reading such is not even critique, but what he poses as an alternative to this mode of political-intellectual engagement. For me, however, this is merely a semantic issue. By my reading, Hardt's objections to critique arise from his dissatisfaction with a politics that becomes trapped in modes of opposition and negativity, a dissatisfaction with ways of doing critique that cannot articulate positive, or rather, constitutive practice. In fact, I suspect that the primary target of Hardt's statement is not the mode of doing critique that I have attempted to outline in my discussion of Marx and Foucault,[19] but rather, what takes the name of critique in today's academic publics, and which has little to do with the real movement through which militant subjects and radical collective forms of life are constituted politically. By contrast, the militant critique I take from Marx and (a radicalised) Foucault already belongs to such a movement, is already grounded in the production of the common.

CONCLUSION

Marx to Foucault. This is the provisional line I want to draw, and which sets our critical aspirations apart from, and even against, 'a rationalist conception of critique'.

There are of course many – and deep – differences between Marx and Foucault. Mine is not an attempt at synthesis, or at least not the type of synthesis that would want to erase these differences.

Where Marxism has often appeared in Foucault's work as the object of 'critique', this is in part for the ways in which Marx appears to the Foucault of 1978 as an imposed limit, or the object of a particular 'struggle', as Lemke and Balibar might say. Conversely, what consolidates their 'tactical alliance' is a critical attitude towards the inherited epistemological field; Foucault's critique as a 'limit-attitude' that calls into question our most intimate 'ways of knowing' and what Balibar (1995: 2) calls Marx's 'anti-philosophy', neither 'the doctrine' nor 'the system of an author called Marx', but a constant 'displacement of the sites, questions, and objectives of philosophy' (5) that calls this very practice into question. Could the matter have been any other way? After all, is it not that, as Hardt once suggested, materialism cannot be a body of thought, but is instead 'a constant questioning of the priority thought gives to itself' (see Read 1999: 2)?

From Marx then, I take the potential for grounding a critical work in the perspective of the real movement for the destruction of the present order. It is for me a matter of presenting *a* perspective on the struggles of a post-apartheid South Africa from '*our side*', that is, from the side of the antagonistic movements that have grown out of these struggles and posing this perspective in the reality of the political order against every perspective in support of the order. From Foucault, I take the potential to think about the constitution of the very game that will determine the character of the strategic terrain these movements and their struggles emerge upon and which, in different ways, affects any perspective such a movement might come to form of itself and its struggles.

We should not, however, lose sight of our own differences. After all, the subject Marx was concerned with was the European working class; for Foucault, it was 'western man as the subject of desire' and it is only by the violence of a dislocation that we should find something about our story in these respective his-stories. But clarity can be found in the very silences and absences of these texts, the place of our own 'productive struggles' with Marx and Foucault.

We read Marx and Foucault for the weapons they might contain, or the tools for making new ones. It is on these terms that we negotiate our tactical alliance with both Marx and Foucault.

NOTES

1   In fact, depending on how we define critique, it might well be necessary to move away from a straightforward association of this term with what we ordinarily mean when we speak of 'criticism'.

2   As Etienne Balibar (1995: 6) notes, 'Marx is the philosopher of eternal new beginning', constantly leaving behind projects and drafts, changing direction and shifting onto new paths. See also Louis Althusser's 'On the young Marx' (Althusser 2005) for a discussion of the 'contingent' beginnings of the young Marx.

3   These quotations are lifted out of an interview with Deleuze conducted by Negri (Gilles Deleuze and Antonio Negri 1990). Elsewhere I use it to help explain the disposition of the militant (Veriava 2013).

4   What is emphasised by the young Marx, however, is that historically determined state forms in which conflicts appear as a consequence, stand as a 'table of contents' for the practical struggles of a particular society (a role that religion is said to have played in relation to mankind's 'theoretical struggles').

5   Engels wrote: '[W]hat is known as "Marxism" in France is, indeed, an altogether peculiar product – so much so that Marx once said to Lafargue: 'Ce qu'il y a de certain c'est que moi, je ne suis pas Marxiste' (If anything is certain, it is that I myself am not a Marxist) (Engels 1882). See also Althusser (2006) from whom this line of argument is borrowed.

6   Althusser points to Marx's 'invitation' in the preface to *Capital* to his reader to 'think for himself', welcoming 'every opinion based on scientific criticism' (2006: 14).

7   In Althusser's reading, this period comes to be weighted down by the untenable marriage between a 'Hegelianized-Feurbachian philosophy of alienation' and 'the mythical ideology of a political economy adopted without a critique' (2006: 28).

8   Drawing on Auguste Cornu's writing on the life of the early Marx, Althusser suggests that an important turning point was Marx's time in France where he became a communist, around 1843–1844.

9   On the website www.marxists.org practical critique is explained as follows: 'Marxism is a tendency *within the workers movement* and it is concerned with both *theoretical* and *practical* critique. By "*practical critique*" is meant *political action* which undermines and "exposes" the object and mobilises opposition to it.' (Blunden 2012)

10   This is in fact precisely how it appeared in Thomas Lemke's formulation: 'The "missing link" between these two research interests is the problem of government. It is a link because Foucault uses it exactly to analyse the connection between what he called technologies of the self and technologies of domination and the formation of the state' (Lemke 2000: 2).

11   Remarking on an eight-year period of silence in his work Deleuze wrote: 'It's like a hole in my life, an eight year hole. That is what I find interesting in lives, the holes that they have, the lacunas, sometimes dramatic, sometimes no … Perhaps it is in the holes that movement takes place' (Deleuze in Hardt 1993: xix).

12   For Harry Cleaver, what distinguishes a political reading is that it 'self-consciously and unilaterally structures its approach to determine the meaning and relevance of every concept to the development of working-class struggle. It is a reading which

eschews all detached interpretation and abstract theorising in favour of grasping concepts only within that concrete totality of struggle whose determinations they designate' (Cleaver 2000: 30).

13　That is, it is by no means certain that power necessarily always trumps resistance (which is internal to power relations).

14　The phrase is borrowed from the introduction of the *Use of Pleasure*: '[W]hat would be the value of the passion for knowledge if it resulted only in a certain knowledgeableness and not, in one way or another and to the extent possible, in the knower's straying afield of himself?' (Foucault 1990b: 8).

15　Foucault speaks here about civil society. However, I suspect what is more decisive is a certain shifting or crossing-over from the sacred to the profane world.

16　In the context of what I said about resistance above, it is possible to misread this quote and what Foucault means here. To be clear, in this context, Foucault means by the 'simultaneous movement of governmentalisation', the simultaneity of the movements through which, on the one hand, society is governmentalised, and on the other, individuals.

17　Not surprisingly then, critique is for Foucault in the first place 'historically biblical' (1996: 385) and looks for a source of support in scripture. Secondly, critique takes on a juridical character, taking the form of a 'problematisation' of law. Finally, the question of 'how not to be governed' underlines the problem of truth and a questioning of what authority presents as true. In this regard Foucault says that critique will imply accepting authority 'only if one thinks oneself that the reasons for accepting it are good' (385). Critique's third anchoring point is therefore the problematisation of 'certainty in the face of authority' (385).

18　Elsewhere I trace in more detail the development of Foucault's thought on critique (Veriava 2013).

19　In fact, for me, the original source of a formulation that makes critique both a 'destruction of the existing state of things' and the articulation of a constitutive project is Michael Hardt and Antonia Negri's 'critique of the state form' (see Hardt and Negri 1994: 6).

REFERENCES

Althusser, L. 2005. *For Marx*. London and New York: Verso.

Althusser, L. 2006. *Philosophy of the Encounter: Later Writings, 1978–1987*. London and New York: Verso.

Balibar, E. 1995. *The Philosophy of Marx*. London and New York: Verso.

Biko, S. 2004. *I Write What I Like*. Johannesburg: Picador Africa.

Blunden, A. 2012. 'Marxism'. Accessed 15 April 2012, http://www.marxists.org/reference/subject/philosophy/help/marxism.htm.

Butler, J. 2001. 'What is critique? An essay on Foucault's virtue'. Accessed 4 March 2013, http://eipcp.net/transversal/0806/butler/en.

Cleaver, H. 2000. *Reading Capital Politically*. Leeds: AK Press.

Deleuze, G. 1992. 'What is a dispositif?' In *Michel Foucault: Philosopher*, edited by T.J. Armstrong and R. Machado. Hemel Hempstead: Harvester Wheatsheaf.

Deleuze, G. 1999. *Foucault*. London: Continuum.

Deleuze, G. and Negri, A. 1990. 'Control and becoming'. Accessed 11 April 2012, http://www.generation-online.org/p/fpdeleuze3.htm.

Engels, F. 1882. 'Letters: Frederick Engels to Eduard Bernstein'. Accessed 15 April 2012, http://www.marxists.org/archive/marx/works/1882/letters/82_11_02.htm.

Foucault, M. 1980. *Power/Knowledge: Selected Interviews and Other Writings, 1972–1977.* New York: Pantheon Books.

Foucault, M. 1990a. *The History of Sexuality Vol. 1: An Introduction.* New York: Vintage.

Foucault, M. 1990b. *The History of Sexuality Vol. 2: The Use of Pleasure.* New York: Vintage.

Foucault, M. 1990c. *The History of Sexuality Vol. 3: The Care of Self.* New York: Vintage.

Foucault, M. 1995. *Discipline and Punish: The Birth of the Prison.* Translated by A. Sheridan. New York: Vintage.

Foucault, M. 1996. 'What is critique?' In *What Is Enlightenment?: Eighteenth-century Answers and Twentieth-century Questions*, edited by J. Schmidt. London: University of California Press.

Foucault, M. 1997. *Ethics: Subjectivity and Truth.* New York: New Press.

Foucault, M. 2002. *Power: Essential Works of Foucault, 1954–1984 (Vol. 3).* London: Penguin.

Foucault, M. 2004. *Society Must be Defended.* London: Penguin.

Foucault, M. 2007. *Security Territory Population: Lectures at the Collège de France, 1977–1978.* New York: Palgrave-Macmillan.

Foucault, M. 2010. *The Government of Self and Others: Lectures at the Collège de France, 1982–1983.* New York: Palgrave-Macmillan.

Foucualt, M. 2011. *The Courage of Truth (The Government of Self and Others II): Lectures at the College de France, 1983–1984.* New York: Palgrave-Macmillan.

Hardt, M. 1993. *Gilles Deleuze: An Apprenticeship in Philosophy.* Minneapolis, MN: University of Minnesota Press.

Hardt, M. 2010. 'Militant life', *New Left Review*, 64: 151–160.

Hardt, M. 2011. 'The militancy of theory', *South Atlantic Quarterly*, 110 (1): 19–35.

Hardt, M. and Negri, A. 1994. *Labour of Dionysus.* Minneapolis, MN: University of Minnesota Press.

Hardt, M. and Negri, A. 2009. *Commonwealth.* Cambridge, MA: Harvard University Press.

Jessop, B. 2007. 'From micro-powers to governmentality: Foucault's work on statehood, state formation, statecraft and state power', *Political Geography*, 26 (1): 34–40.

Kant, I. 2001. *Basic Writings of Kant*, edited by A.W. Wood. New York: Modern Library.

Kelly, M. 1994. *Critique and Power: Recasting the Foucault/Habermas Debate.* Cambridge, MA: MIT Press.

Latour, B. 2004. 'Why has critique run out of steam? From matters of fact to matters of concern', *Critical Inquiry*, 30 (2): 225–248.

Lazzarato, M. 2002. 'From biopower to biopolitics', *PLI: Warwick Journal of Philosophy*, 13 (2): 100–111.

Lemke, T. 2000. 'Foucault, governmentality, and critique'. Accessed 4 March 2013, http://www.andosciasociology.net/resources/Foucault$2C+Governmentality$2C+and+Critique+IV-2.pdf.

Marx, K. 1967. *Writings of the Young Marx on Philosophy and Society*, edited by L.D. Easton and K.H. Guddat. New York: Anchor Books.

Marx, K. and Engels, F. (1847) 1998. *The German Ideology*. New York: Prometheus Books.

Read, J. 1999. 'The antagonistic ground of constitutive power: An essay on the thought of Antonio Negri', *Rethinking Marxism*, 11 (2): 1–17.

Veriava, A. 'The South African diagram: The governmental machine and the struggles of the poor'. PhD thesis, Department of Political Studies, University of the Witwatersrand, Johannesburg.

5

MARXISM AND FEMINISM: 'UNHAPPY MARRIAGE' OR CREATIVE PARTNERSHIP?

Jacklyn Cock and Meg Luxton

In this moment of economic and ecological crisis a feminist anti-capitalist politics could generate a transnational solidarity that is larger and more powerful than anything we have yet seen.[1] Such a politics requires both Marxism for its trenchant critique of capitalism and the class inequalities essential to it and feminism for its commitment to gender equality. Both require a commitment to anti-racism.[2] In this chapter we trace the uneasy relations between Marxism and feminism showing the contributions each has made to the other and argue that the success of the current Marxist revitalisation hinges on a more equal relationship. This integration is best described as a socialist feminism based on the understanding that 'the liberation of women depends on the liberation of all people' (Rowbotham 1972: 11).

Feminism is both an intellectual project and a political movement, so its theoretical debates are also political and strategic. Feminists tend to be drawn together by their commitment to oppose women's oppression, but they are also engaged with different theoretical and political paradigms, differences that are sometimes obscured by the apparent unity of 'feminist theory'. There are multiple 'feminisms'. Typically, mid- to late twentieth-century feminism included several distinct political currents: liberal feminism aspiring to formal legal equality and access to equal opportunities with men; radical feminism, which assumed that unequal gender relations are the primary contradiction of social organisation and that women's oppression underlies all other inequalities; Marxist feminism, which assumed that women's liberation depended on over-throwing or dismantling capitalism; and socialist feminism which combined the historical materialism of Marxism with an analysis of gender-based inequalities.

In an influential intervention published over thirty years ago, Heidi Hart-mann complained that the relationship between Marxism and feminism was marked by extreme inequality. She compared it to the marriage between husband and wife depicted in English common law at the time: 'Marxism and feminism are one, and that one is Marxism'. She concluded that 'either we need a healthier marriage or we need a divorce' (Hartmann 1981: 2). Her hope for a healthier marriage was based on a conviction that each had strengths the other needed:

> [W]hile Marxist analysis offers essential insight into the laws of histor-ical development, and those of capital in particular, the categories of Marxism are sex-blind. Only a specifically feminist analysis reveals the systemic character of relations between men and women. Yet feminist analysis by itself is inadequate because it has been blind to history and insufficiently materialist.

While Hartman was writing from a US perspective, Belinda Bozzoli (1983: 142), writing from a South African perspective, noted that 'the dominant tendency in analyses of women in South Africa' collapses 'female oppression into the capit-alist mode of production'. Bozzoli's and Hartmann's interventions were part of a heated and extensive debate that raged throughout the 1980s. A central ques-tion was whether Marxism could be reworked to integrate gender and whether class-based political movements would integrate feminist demands into their practices. Many left-wing feminists shared the concern that feminism was at risk in engagements with Marxism, especially in political organising (Shelton and Agger 1993). Roberta Hamilton's mischievous position (1978: 104) that socialist feminists should avoid marriage with Marxism, opting instead for shacking up together, captures what has typically happened. Socialist feminism remains an autonomous political current engaged with both Marxism and other currents of feminism, theoretically and politically (Sangster and Luxton 2013).

At stake in these debates was the issue of how to understand the relationship between class and gender hierarchies and, based on that understanding, how to most effectively mobilise politically to fight for a world in which class exploitation and gender oppression are eliminated for all peoples. Sexism, heterosexism, racism and different class interests, as well as a diversity of other systemic inequalities, easily undermined the ability of activists to work together in solidarity. The capacity of scholars to develop an integrated analysis of gender, race and class, or what Kimberlé Crenshaw (1991) called 'intersectional analysis', remains challenging, partly because of radically different objects of analysis and partly because of the uneven strength of various political movements. Both Marxism and feminism have long histories of struggling with issues of race, racism, colonialism and the subjugation of indigenous peoples. Both traditions, theoretically and politically, have been 'race-blind', forcing anti-racist and post-colonial scholars and activists to simultaneously develop their own work while challenging Marxism and feminism to integrate their perspectives (Joseph 1981; Sunseri 2011).

Through the 1990s and early 2000s, the collapse of most communist governments, especially the USSR, and China's turn to the market undermined Marxist politics. At the same time, English-language scholarship turned to postmodernism and post-structuralism in ways that denied the value of historical materialism and undermined its presence in academic thought. The current period disrupts those tendencies, inviting a re-engagement with Marxism and re-animating a socialist feminist politics. We argue that socialist feminism offers a vital corrective to twentieth-century Marxist politics and has the potential to inform new forms of struggle and compelling alternative visions.

Central to the contribution of socialist feminism is its commitment to integrating analyses of gender, race and class. This is not an easy task. Despite a voluminous literature and decades of political struggle, many Marxists have resisted feminist interventions. Similarly, many feminists have dismissed Marxism as economistic and reductionist.

FROM MARXISTS AND FEMINISTS TO MARXIST FEMINISM

No Women's Liberation without Socialism!
No Socialism without Women's Liberation!

This slogan of the 1970s' women's liberation movement expressed the political convictions of movement activists and reveals important political tensions that have confronted such activists. Identified variously as women's liberation movement activists, left-wing feminists, radical feminists or socialist feminists, they live the tensions and contradictions of adhering to both Marxism and feminism. They are drawn to Marxism for its critique of capitalism, its commitment to class struggle and its vision of a future world free of class exploitation. Marxism also provides a theoretical perspective that rejects arguments that women are a uniform social category inevitably subordinated to men, instead linking women's oppression to specific historical circumstances and providing some political strategies for overcoming that oppression.

However, throughout the twentieth century Marxist political movements failed to seriously address sexism, heterosexism, racism or the systemic subordination of women. One of the goals of socialist feminists is to put women's oppression and liberation and anti-racism at the heart of Marxism and to integrate gender, race and class in Marxist analyses and politics.

At the same time, socialist feminists are drawn to other feminists by their shared commitment to develop both critiques of 'malestream thought' (including Marxism) and a shared feminist politics around basic demands intended to challenge sexism, heterosexism and racism. Such demands are intended to ensure for women at least the same legal rights and cultural norms as men, to reduce women's economic vulnerabilities, give them greater control over biological reproduction and foster at least some degree of social support or collective responsibility, both from men and the society as a whole, for care of people. Practically, feminist politics includes demands such as improved maternal and child health, access to free, safe birth control and abortion, paid parental leave, childcare, micro credit, access to clean water, housing, sanitation, an end to men's violence against women, an end to police and legal harassment of indigenous people and people of colour, access to education and good secure jobs, and greater involvement by men in care work. In different times and places, some of these demands have been partially met, especially in welfare states where women have been able to organise strongly, and where employers need women's participation in the labour force.

But these are resolutely social democratic demands that do not challenge the essential dynamics of capitalist economics. As the recent global economic crisis illustrates, these gains are among the first to be attacked when profits are threatened, and even the most advanced social democratic policies do not eliminate the subsidy that women's unpaid care work ensures for the private profit-making essential to capitalism (Braedley and Luxton 2010: 12–16; Connell 2010). Another of the goals of socialist feminists is to integrate an anti-racist class analysis into feminist theory and to win wider support among feminists for the recognition that 'the liberation of women depends on the liberation of all people' (Rowbotham 1972: 11).

No women's liberation without socialism!

The assertion that efforts to end women's subjection to men and the oppression they face because they are women are not possible in a capitalist society has its roots in early nineteenth-century socialism in Britain and France. Rejecting the social organisation of the new capitalist societies that were emerging, activists formed communal or collective communities where they tried to create alternative ways of living, some of which were explicitly anti-capitalist (Hayden 1982; Taylor 1983). Writing about their ideas, William Thompson and Anna Wheeler ([1825] 1983) argued that in any society based on competition and private ownership of wealth, women would be at a disadvantage because of their responsibilities for pregnancy, childrearing, care provision and household management. Instead, they envisioned communities in which all members would cooperate to generate livelihoods and look after each other. Domestic responsibilities, including care, would be shared by all. They argued that such communities would free women from the burdens imposed by private individual families and households. As fully integrated members of the community, women would be able to realise their full potential and subjection and discrimination would no longer be possible.

Karl Marx and Friedrich Engels identified such ideas as 'utopian socialist' because they failed to take account of class differences and they assumed that total social transformation involving the elimination of individualism, competition and private property is possible, failing to recognise that it is impossible to create cooperative societies in a world where elites retain power and wealth. In *The Communist Manifesto*, Marx and Engels wrote:

> The undeveloped state of the class struggle, as well as their own surroundings, causes Socialists of this kind to consider themselves far superior to all class antagonisms. They want to improve the condition of every member of society, even that of the most favored ... Hence, they reject all political, and especially all revolutionary, action; they wish to attain their ends by peaceful means, and endeavor, by small experiments, necessarily doomed to failure, and by the force of example, to pave the way for the new social Gospel ([1848] 1998: 23).

Instead, they insisted on the necessity of class struggle and the revolutionary role of the proletariat in accomplishing the transition.[3]

However, like Thompson and Wheeler, Marx and Engels assumed that women's oppression was linked to the historical development of private property and family forms based on private property. In that context, women were isolated in private family households under the authority of their husbands, subjected to a sexual division of labour that made childrearing and running the household women's responsibilities and excluded them from public life. For Marx and Engels, the solution to women's subordination required their full participation in public life, especially in production. Women's ability to do so required the socialisation of household labour and childrearing, something Marx and Engels advocated but did not elaborate on.

Marx ([1867] 1976: 718) stressed that 'the maintenance and reproduction of the working class remains a necessary condition for the reproduction of capital'. What he neglected was that this 'maintenance' and 'reproduction' involved a great deal of work done by women. Classical Marxism analysed the consumption of labour power, but left the production of people to their own self-interest, assuming that the production of labour power occurs naturally as people live their lives. It never challenged the domestic and family forms that produce labour power for capitalist or communist markets. The result is the social organisation of childbirth, infant care and socialisation, and the care of adults is 'naturalised' (relegated to the realm of the 'natural') by default.

The sexism and essentialism of this analysis reverberated through the communist and socialist politics of the twentieth century. While Marxism recognised women's oppression, its treatment of 'the woman question' focused on the relationship of women to the economic system of production for the market rather than on sex/gender divisions of labour or on gender relations. The early Marxists failed to examine gender differences, particularly on the difference between women's and men's experiences under capitalism. In his *Origins of the Family, Private Property and the State* ([1884] 1972), Engels argued that as women were incorporated into wage labour, they would become economically independent; the authority of the male head of the household would be weakened and patriarchal relations destroyed.

Early twentieth-century thinkers and revolutionary activists influenced by Marxism, such as Alexandra Kollontai, Clara Zetkin, Vladimir Lenin, Leon Trotsky and August Bebel, likewise argued for the integration of housewives into the paid labour force and for the collectivisation of housework (Davis

1981). However, unlike the early nineteenth-century European socialists who called for collectivisation of social life, including the abolition of the nuclear family and who experimented, albeit in very small communities, with ways of living communally, most Marxists did not spell out what collectivisation of 'housework' would mean. They assumed that paid teams of employees with access to advanced technologies could clean houses, produce meals, do laundry and other household tasks more efficiently than unpaid housewives working alone in their individual homes (Davis 1981, chapter 13). No attention was paid to the gender of those 'employees'.

Several of these women understood the family to be the source of women's oppression. Some developed scathing critiques of marriage and family relations, calling instead for free love. Kollontai, for example, is remembered mainly as the proponent of the 'glass of water theory', the theory that sex should be as easy and uncomplicated as drinking a glass of water (Kollontai [1921] 1972).

In the excitement of the first years of the new communist Soviet society, Kollontai ([1920] 1977: 259) articulated her vision of the new order:

> The workers' state needs new relations between the sexes, just as the narrow and exclusive affection of the mother for her own children must expand until it extends to all the children of the great, proletarian family, the indissoluble marriage based on the servitude of women is replaced by a free union of two equal members of the workers' state who are united by love and mutual respect. In place of the individual and egoistic family, a great universal family of workers will develop, in which all the workers, men and women, will above all be comrades. This is what relations between men and women, in the communist society will be like. These new relations will ensure for humanity all the joys of a love unknown in the commercial society, of a love that is free and based on the true social equality of the partners.

Assuming that the new communist society would eliminate exploitation in the workforce, Kollontai understood the family as the source of women's oppression. She wrote of the necessity of introducing public services of every kind that would free women from the 'petty cares' of everyday life. Sensitive to the double load of housework and wage work, she emphasised the solution to women's oppression as the collectivisation of domestic labour under socialism. This provision of such public services was necessary to bring women into politics. She argued that 'society should relieve women of all those petty house-hold cares which are at present unavoidable (given the existence of individual, scattered, domestic economies)' and take over 'responsibility for the younger generation' (Kollontai [1920] 1977: 68).

She envisioned and fought for a workers' state that would create ideal conditions for women and children, by taking collective responsibility for them:

> The workers' state aims to support every mother, married or unmarried, while she is suckling her child, and to establish maternity homes, day nurseries and other such facilities in every city and village, in order to give women the opportunity to combine work in society with maternity (Kollontai [1920] 1977: 259).

For Kollontai and others, the struggle for women's liberation was part of the struggle for socialism. In their view there should be no separate women's movement. Kollontai was dismissive of 'the feminists' because 'they seek equality in the framework of the existing class society; in no way do they attack the basis of this society' ([1920] 1977: 59).

Similarly, Lenin understood women's positions in both the household and the paid workforce as problematic and was dismissive of feminism. For Lenin, a housewife was a domestic 'slave' and women's unpaid labour within the family was a major obstacle to progress. Writing in 1919 Lenin (cited in Vogel 1983: 121) points out that despite 'all the laws emancipating women, she continues to be a domestic slave, because petty housework crushes, strangles, stultifies and degrades her, chains her to the kitchen and the nursery, and she wastes her labor on barbarously unproductive, petty, nerve-racking, stultifying and crushing drudgery'. Hence Lenin argued strongly for the socialisation of domestic labour, to 'transform petty housekeeping into a series of large-scale socialised services: community kitchens, public dining rooms, laundries, repair shops, nurseries, kindergartens and so forth' (in Vogel 1983: 122).

The dreams of these early communists were destroyed by the events of the 1920s and 1930s (Zizek and Douzinas 2010). In practice, the communist states of the twentieth century pushed for women's entry into the labour force but did nothing to challenge the deep sexism and sex/gender divisions of labour that relegated women to low-paying jobs and made them vulnerable to sexual harassment. They provided childcare to facilitate women's labour force participation but did little or nothing to encourage collectivisation or democratisation. Instead of free love and new relations of joy, they imposed heterosexual marriage, made homosexuality illegal and manipulated mothers to have many children or to limit childbirth to one child. Instead of 'true equality', they romanticised and reinforced the private, heterosexual, nuclear family and the prevailing sex/gender divisions of labour, stressing women as workers and mothers but failing to provide support for them.[4]

Communist states became infamous for inadequate housing and poor domestic services such as the provision of water, sewage or electricity. Most women in communist countries worked a double day with few supports for their domestic responsibilities and little acknowledgement of the systemic sexism women faced. Given the explicit state opposition to an autonomous feminist movement, women in communist countries were rarely able to mobilise in order to challenge or change their oppressive conditions (Molyneux 2000; Urdang 1989).

In capitalist countries and the so-called Third World countries of the twentieth century, communist and socialist parties and movements relied for the most part on the political analyses of classical Marxism. The narrow legacy of 'the woman question' produced a tendency for left-wing and revolutionary movements to insist that women's concerns were of secondary importance and divisive of working-class struggles. Women were told that their issues would naturally resolve themselves 'after the revolution'. Left-wing organisations rarely integrated women into their leadership, usually downplayed issues deemed 'women's' and ignored the sexism of their men as well as the sexual harassment their women were subject to. As Hartmann (1981: 2) noted, women's issues were seen: 'at best [as] less important than class conflict and at worst divisive of the working class'. While there have always been Marxists and activists in the communist and socialist movements who took up women's issues, that dismissive context limited women's capacity to analyse their specific oppression, undermined their ability to organise and struggle for their issues and constrained efforts to analyse the interconnections of gender, race and class.

No socialism without women's liberation!

With the re-animation of the women's movement in the 1960s and 1970s, women's liberation activists took up and began to rework the earlier Marxist critiques. In doing so, they simultaneously drew on the insights, debates and struggles of the larger feminist movement while trying to make Marxism more receptive to gender and race politics (Hennessay and Ingraham 1997; Rowbotham 1992). They agreed that participation in the paid labour force was essential for women's economic independence and agreed with the need for a wide range of benefits and social services designed to socialise care and household labours, but they went further.

They developed complex analyses of the social construction of gender, showing how deeply and profoundly gender hierarchies have penetrated all aspects of social life, from psychic patterns of gender identity and embodied being (Benjamin 1988; Bordo 1993) to political and economic structures (Armstrong and Armstrong 1987). Sex, for example, they argued, was infinitely more complicated than drinking a glass of water (Segal 1994). They showed that changing people's ways of being was much more challenging than the early Marxists had anticipated and argued that socialism had to take into account all aspects of personal life as well as people's experiences in the workplace (Rowbotham, Segal and Wainright 1979).

At the same time, they struggled with issues of race and racism. Anti-racist feminists revealed the ways in which the women's movement of Western Europe and North America failed to take up racism analytically or politically (Amos and Parmar 1984; Bhavnani 2001; Bulbeck 1998; hooks 1995). Socialist feminists recognised that struggles for women's liberation in one part of the world were always linked to other struggles against exploitation and oppression (McClintock 1995). They took for granted that women in 'advanced capitalist' societies had much to learn from the struggles of women in other parts of the world, especially those resisting imperialism and colonialism and those participating in revolutionary movements against capitalist and authoritarian regimes (Ferree and McClurg Mueller 2004; Rowbotham 1972). But despite their interest in and solidarity with anti-imperialist movements, they were slow to attend to the racism permeating their theorising and practice. Much of their work assumed that the family forms, work experiences and political strategies of Western Europe and North America (often referred to as 'Western feminism' or the 'global North') could be generalised. For example, Michèle Barrett and Mary McIntosh's (1982) critique of the nuclear family as an 'anti-social institution' which monopolised the caring and sharing that should be spread more widely in society, did not resonate with the experience of African women in South Africa who saw the family as an arena to defend from the encroachments of capitalism and the state. Subsequently, anti-racist socialist feminists have deepened the analytical capacity of socialist feminism to integrate race with its analysis of gender and class (Mohanty 2003), thus operationalising the early socialist feminist insistence that the liberation of women depends on the liberation of all peoples.

Although Marx and Engels limited their solution to 'the woman question' to integrating women into the labour force by collectivising household labour and providing childcare, and failed to integrate a gender or race analysis into their understanding of class, Engels's work offers two important insights that Marxist feminists have built on.

In his 1844 *The Condition of the Working Class in England*, Engels reports on the devastation caused by the appalling working conditions in the factories of Manchester. He tells the story of an unemployed man who is found by his mate, at home, mending his wife's stockings. His mate is shocked to see a man doing women's work, but poor embarrassed Jack explains that he has been unemployed for a long time and has no prospects of getting employment while his wife works long hours in the factory earning the only income their household has. Jack defends his inappropriate gender practice by explaining that his wife is exhausted by her employment and Jack does what he can to relieve her. Engels concludes this account with a profound insight. There is something terribly wrong, he says with:

> this condition, which unsexes the man and takes from the woman all womanliness without being able to bestow upon the man true womanliness, or the woman true manliness – this condition which degrades, in the most shameful way, both sexes, and, through them, Humanity (Engels [1844] 1987: 147).

He goes on to offer an embryonic analysis of the social construction of gender:

> [W]e must admit that so total a reversal of the position of the sexes can have come to pass only because the sexes have been placed in a false position from the beginning. If the reign of the wife over the husband, as inevitably brought about by the factory system, is inhuman, the pristine rule of the husband over the wife must have been inhuman too.

His critique of the normative sex/gender divisions of labour and family relations prevalent in his time was elaborated 40 years later in *Origins of the Family,*

Private Property and the State ([1884] 1972). He argued that different modes of production, based on different labour relations, coincided with different family forms and therefore with different patterns of relations between women and men. He linked the rise of private property to 'the world historic defeat of women' (120), thereby laying the basis for later analyses that women's liberation depends on their integration into production and the collectivisation of social resources. He also provided a key theoretical insight about how to understand the interconnections of gender and class in his discussion of reproduction.

The idea of social reproduction had its origins in Marx's analysis of capitalist society. In Volume 1 of *Capital,* he pointed out that 'every social process of production is at the same time a process of reproduction' ([1867] 1976: 71). Although his work was concerned specifically with economic processes relating to production of goods and services for exchange in the market, Marx also examined the processes of the reproduction of capitalist social relations. He and Engels applied these ideas to all modes of production, leading to Engels's ([1884] 1972: 71) formulation that

> [a]ccording to the materialist conception of history, the determining factor in history is, in the final instance, the production and reproduction of immediate life. This, again, is of a two-fold character: on the one side, the production of the means of existence, of food, clothing and shelter and the tools necessary for that production; on the other side, the production of human beings themselves, the propagation of the species.

Despite the importance of this insight, neither Engels nor the leaders of the early twentieth-century communist movements inspired by Marx and Engels, realised the full implications of this analysis (Maroney and Luxton 1987: 13). Instead, they equated the production of the means of existence with labour and assumed the production of human beings could simply be left to 'drives for self-preservation and propagation' (Marx [1867] 1976: 718). They left this untheorised and ignored the fact that 'maintenance' and 'reproduction' involved a great deal of work done by women. However incomplete and unsatisfactory, this insight nonetheless proved a fertile starting point for later feminist interventions on gender and class.

MARXIST FEMINISM: THEORISING CLASS AND GENDER

One of the central preoccupations of women's liberation activists was to challenge the primacy Marxists gave to class. Initially women's liberation activists
and theorists struggled to understand how class and gender could be understood in relation to each other. Some, especially US radical feminists such as
Kate Millet (1970) and Shulamith Firestone (1972) were influenced by Marxism
but identified unequal gender relations as the primary contradiction of social
organisation. Both Firestone and Millet give patriarchy an analytical primacy.
Their project is to substitute sex for class as the driver of history. Drawing on
Weber's use of the term 'patriarchy' to describe a particular form of household organisation, in which the father dominated and controlled the economic
production of the household, Millet argues for patriarchy as a system of male
domination that is analytically independent of any economic mode including
feudalism and capitalism. In capitalist society all women are characterised by
an economic dependency which 'renders her affiliation with any class a tangen-
tial, vicarious and temporary matter' (Millett 1970: 32). Drawing on Engels's
concept of the production and reproduction of immediate life, Firestone argued
that 'the economy' and 'the family' are distinct sites generating class and gender
hierarchies. She argued that the subordination of women was a necessary
precondition for the development of class inequalities (Firestone 1972: 175).

Dual systems theories
Some socialist feminists, similarly influenced by Engels's production/reproduc-
tion formulation, worked with the same dichotomy but understood the two sides
of the divide as related and equally important.[5] Some rejected the notion of an
unchanging universal patriarchy, offering instead a separate system of social relations and divisions of labour that organises human sexuality, nurturance, affec-
tion and biological reproduction. They argued that this system, what Gayle Rubin
(1975) calls 'the sex/gender system', or 'sex/affective production' (Ferguson 1989
and 1991) has different historical modes, just as Marx argued that economies do
(Ferguson and Folbre 1981). Others retained patriarchy, positing two separate
structures: the mode of production and patriarchy (Eisenstein 1979; Ferguson
and Folbre 1981). Some of the attempts at developing a more cohesive Marxist-
feminist framework have involved some very convoluted theoretical formulations (Folbre 1987; Walby 1990). For example, in attempting such an integration,
the concept of a 'patriarchal mode of production' has been proposed.

[This] is a theoretical model of class relations between a class of patriarchs who, as heads of households, control the access of other household members to the means of production and a class of patriarchal
dependents, wives and working children, who gain access to the means
of production and consumption by providing surplus labour to the
class of patriarchs (Henn 1988: 28).

In another variant of this dualistic analysis, which reduced patriarchy to an ideological structure, Juliet Mitchell wrote of 'two autonomous areas: the economic
mode of capitalism and the ideological mode of patriarchy' (1974: 412). A more
materialist definition is provided by Hartmann (1981) who defines patriarchy
in terms of men's control of women's labour power in terms of both their sexuality and their access to resources. However, patriarchy remains a universal,
transhistorical category which lacks a material basis and easily falls into the
trap of assuming men are innately oppressive (Beechey 1979; Young 1981). As
Bonnie Fox notes, 'this understanding of patriarchy does not involve a clear
specification of its origins, its structure, and its direction. Because the motive
force is not specified, the shortest step (usually taken) is to invoke male agency,
and by implication, an innate desire for power on the part of men' (1988: 170).

This analysis is not just sexist in assuming men's proclivity for domination,
but as Meg Luxton has argued elsewhere, it is also analytically incoherent:

Like Engels, many feminists tend to equate production, labour and men
with the economy and reproduction and women with the family, even
while they recognize women's involvement in subsistence economies or
in the paid labour force. That formulation fails to understand the family
as both a set of economic relations and a part of the economic workings
of society. It also generates conceptual chaos as 'reproduction' embodies
several overlapping but contradictory meanings, including human biological reproduction, the socialisation of children, the reproduction of
labour power and the reproduction of the mode of production or of the
society as a whole (Luxton 2006: 27).

The expanded mode of production concept
In opposition to the dual system approach, other Marxist feminists took up
Marx's observation that in the capitalist mode of production, 'the most indis-
pensable means of production' is the worker and that the 'maintenance and

reproduction of the working class remains a necessary condition for the reproduction of capital' (Marx [1867] 1976: 718). They also took up Engels's formulation that 'the determining factor in history is, in the final instance, the production and reproduction of immediate life' (Engels [1884] 1972: 71). In contrast
to those arguing that patriarchy as a mode of reproduction and capitalism as
a mode of production were two separate systems of domination operating in
relation to each other, they argued for an alternative approach based on an
'integrated system or expanded mode of production model'. Instead of positing
two distinct systems of economics and family and thus of class and gender, they
argued that no mode of production can exist without its labouring population ('life itself') (Morton 1972). Instead, they conceptualised an alternative
approach based on an expanded concept of mode of production that includes
the propagation of the species, particularly the production and reproduction of
people on a daily and generational basis (Seccombe 1992: 14).

They argued that central to any mode of production is the production of
its people. From this perspective, the social organisation of childbirth, infant
care and socialisation and the care of adults are as much a part of any mode
of production as the labours involved in producing goods and services for
exchange (Seccombe 1983). In short, the way in which the population as a
whole is produced is as critical to the organisation of any mode of production
as the organisation of objects (raw materials) and forces of production (tools).
Both the production of the means of life and the production of life itself are
distinct but interrelated necessary social processes.

Wally Seccombe, a leading proponent of this approach, argues:

> All human societies are necessarily involved in three interrelated pro-
> ductions: the production of the means of production; the production of
> the means of subsistence; and the production of labour-power. The
> reproduction cycle of each is constituted by means of the regular repair
> and periodic replacement of the productive force in question. Standard
> Marxist accounts of the mode-of-production concept are confined to
> the first two 'departments'. The on-going production of labour-power
> – its daily rejuvenation and generational replacement – is missing. Yet
> this is primarily what families do: they people societies, restoring their
> members' energies and replacing worn-out labourers with the 'fresh
> blood' of youth. The exclusion of labour-power's daily and generational
> reproduction from the conception of modes of production has made it

almost impossible to see families, as labour teams, pumping the life-blood through socioeconomic systems. From a feminist perspective, this tunnel vision is deadly, since the social control of women is based upon the control of their reproductive capacity in a broad range of societies (Seccombe 1992: 11).

Three significant challenges to prevailing assumptions about social relations followed. First, the sex/gender divisions of labour that exist in most societies are not natural and are not based on biological differences between women and men, but are historically and socially constructed and subject to change (Rubin 1975). Second, the activities involved in sustaining and reproducing daily life – having babies, raising children, caring for frail seniors, people with disabilities and looking after each other – and the related domestic work of procuring food and other goods and services for immediate household consumption – cooking, cleaning, laundry and so on – are not just expressions of the way people naturally live their lives, but constitute socially determined work (Luxton 1980). Finally, the labours involved in looking after people are not just private activities involved in intimate kinship, family and personal relations, but work that is socially necessary and central to the production of both subsistence and wealth in any society. In the capitalist economies most of us currently live in, that labour is essential to the process of capital accumulation (Bakker and Gill 2003).

Indeed, one of the most important insights of the global feminist movement has been the recognition that capitalist economies depend for their existence on the unpaid care work of women (and a minority of men). Feminist scholars have shown that unpaid care work acts as a significant subsidy for the private profit-making essential to capitalism and that the divisions of labour which make this work central to women's lives are key to women's oppression and subordination. Class and gender operate as one integrated system (Pollert 1996).

The domestic labour debate

Socialist feminists identified the primarily women's unpaid, non-market work that was required to maintain working-class households and ensure the daily and generational reproduction of labour power, as 'domestic labour' (Luxton 1980; Morton 1972; Seccombe 1974). They argued that it is socially necessary work that contributes to the production of the labour power that is essential to the capitalist mode of production. At the end of the working day, a worker returns home depleted, tired and hungry. The time off work is necessary as part of the process of replenishing the worker, so that she or he is ready and able to return to work the next day. Similarly, from a social and structural perspective, in raising their children, parents are ensuring the generational reproduction of the working class. This analysis theorised households, families and kinship systems as crucial relations in any social formation and exposed the material basis of working-class women's subordination and its links to the political economy of capitalist society. It demonstrated housework's contribution to maintaining the capitalist system and showed the important link between working-class housewives and capitalist economics.

Unfortunately, the theoretical gains of this perspective were undermined by at least three related problematic developments. Some contributors to the domestic labour debate tried to bring this work – housework and child-rearing – into the sphere of Marxist analysis by arguing that housewives' unpaid labour reduces the value of labour power and thus cheapens the cost of wage labour to capital (Dalla Costa and James 1970; Seccombe 1974; Zaretsky 1973). Mariarosa Dalla Costa claimed that housewives were not only essential to capital by reproducing the labour force, but also produced surplus value. The implication was that women should demand wages for housework. Orthodox Marxists objected, arguing that non-commodity-producing labour (housework, childcare, subsistence agriculture and so on) is incommensurable with capitalist wage labour (Henn 1988: 29). This provoked an extensive and largely arid debate about whether or not domestic labour contributes to capital accumulation (Molyneux 1979). The focus in this debate was on capital and tended to subsume the feminist struggle into the struggle against capital, ignoring relations between men and women. Hartmann (1981: 9) stresses that for most contributors their Marxism dominated their feminism; they failed to recognise how women's domestic labour benefited men 'who as husbands and fathers receive personalized services at home'. They also failed to account for the negative impacts of men's power on women.

At the same time, feminists studying the oppressive and exploitative conditions of paid household workers such as nannies, cleaners and home care providers, applied the term 'domestic labour' to the paid work of such employees (Giles and Arat-Koc 1994). Others use domestic labour to refer to the activities of women and men of the managerial classes or even the elites (Stone 2007). Such usages remove the focus on social relations, so that domestic labour loses its analytical capacities and becomes just a descriptive term for either the paid work some do for others or the unpaid work all people do in their own homes. Missing from such formulations is the understanding of the importance of the social relations in defining the organisation of labour. If a working-class woman does certain tasks in her own home for her family, she is doing unpaid, non-market, domestic labour that contributes to the production and reproduction of labour power on a daily and generational basis. If she does the same tasks in someone else's home for pay (in other words, if the work is commoditised) she is a paid employee or wage labourer. The distinction lies in the social relations of the work, not in the tasks themselves or the physical and emotional exertions performed by the worker. By ignoring the class relationships involved, the term domestic labour lost its analytical power as a term describing a set of social relations, becoming instead a simple adjective applied to the performance of a range of tasks (Luxton 2006: 34).

Furthermore, the domestic labour debate left unexplained why women retain primary responsibility for domestic labour, even when they are fully integrated into the paid labour force – an oppressive reality in most countries (Bittman 2002; McMahon 1999). Instead, its adherents tended to generate a Marxist functionalism or reductionism which reduces women's oppression to an effect of the operations of capital (Barrett 1980). As Bozzoli (1983: 142) wrote, 'The problem of functionalism rests in the fact that descriptions are presented as explanations. Because female oppression performs certain functions for capitalism, this does not mean that it was a pre-creation of capitalism.'

That existing sex/gender divisions of labour are oppressive to women does not explain why or how sexual differences produce gender hierarchies. Theory must address the apparent empirical reality that in almost every society at least two dominant genders, feminine and masculine, are recognised and anchored by divisions of labour in which specific labours are associated with one to the exclusion of the other. Feminists asked some key questions: (i) under what circumstances does women's childbearing result in childrearing and other related household and caring work being socially allocated as women's responsibility? (ii) why are women's labour and women's spheres of responsibility so frequently of lower social status than men's (especially when cross-cultural and historical studies confirm the elasticity of gendering)? (iii) to what extent is the sex/gender division of labour based on women's childbearing and responsibility for childcare a cause or effect of women's oppression? and (iv) under what conditions do biological females become oppressed women? To date, neither Marxism nor feminism has provided satisfactory or conclusive answers.

Social reproduction

Marxism and feminism have made a major contribution to current theorising about the concept of 'social reproduction' which is derived from Marx's analysis of ongoing, related social processes: 'When viewed ... as a connected whole, and in the constant flux of its incessant renewal, every social process of production is at the same time a process of reproduction' ([1867] 1976: 711). In his analysis of capitalism Marx notes:

> The capitalist process of production, therefore, seen as a total connected process, that is, a process of reproduction, produces not only commodities, not only surplus value but it also produces and reproduces the capital-relation itself: on the one hand the capitalist, on the other the wage-labourer (724).

By integrating the sex/gender systems essential to the reproduction of a capitalist mode of production, Marxist feminists give a centrality to women's oppression and establish the undissolvable links between gender and class.

Feminists have defined social reproduction in contested ways. Underlying theories of social reproduction are the different ways in which social relations and organisation are understood and the various kinds of economic and social structures its theorists aspire to. However, Isabella Bakker and Stephen Gill point out that most identify three dimensions: firstly, 'the biological reproduction of the species'. This involves both the material and cultural aspects of giving birth and raising children in different social contexts. According to Bakker and Gill (2003: 32) it includes 'the social constructions of motherhood in different societies'. The second aspect or component of social reproduction involves the reproduction of the labour force. This involves a range of social institutions including the family and various educational institutions to provide the necessary informal socialisation as well as formal education and training. The third aspect Bakker and Gill point to is 'the reproduction of provisioning and caring needs that may be wholly privatized within families, or socialised or, indeed provided through a combination of the two'. They stress that each of these dimensions relate to a 'gender order' which refers to a set of social relations grounded in a sexual division of labour. These are the analytical tools used to examine the transnational process of neoliberal restructuring which has exacerbated inequalities in many parts of the world.

This approach is taken further by Kate Bezanson and Luxton (2006) who argue that an analytical framework based on social reproduction leads to new ways of understanding women's situation in capitalist society. The:

> concept builds on and deepens debates about domestic labour and women's economic roles in capitalist societies ... it offers a basis for understanding how various institutions (such as the state, the market, the family/household) interact and balance power so that the work involved in the daily and generational production and maintenance of people is completed (Bezanson and Luxton 2006: 3).

As Barbara Laslett and Johanna Brenner (1989: 382) note, social reproduction refers to:

> ... the activities and attitudes, behaviours and emotions, responsibilities and relationships directly involved in the maintenance of life on a daily basis and intergenerationally. Among other things, social reproduction includes how food, clothing and shelter are made available for immediate consumption, the ways in which the care and socialisation of children are provided, the care of the infirm and the elderly, and the social organisation of sexuality. Social reproduction can thus be seen to include various kinds of work ... aimed at providing the historically and socially, as well as biologically defined care necessary to maintain existing life and to reproduce the next generation.

Not all the work involved takes place in the family-household. There is the complementary work provided by state services such as education and health care, by the voluntary sector and the community such as children's sports or food banks, or in the market.

Based on the expanded mode of production approach, the emphasis is on analysing society as a totality, a totality in which social reproduction is central at various levels. As Bezanson (2006: 28) writes, 'Social reproduction is ... a central aspect of the capitalist economic system:

1. at the level of *production*, because labour is considered a produced input to production but one that is produced outside that sphere;
2. at the level of *distribution*, because savings on the costs of social reproduction of the labouring population lead to higher profits;

3. at the level of *circulation*, because the consumption of wage goods is the largest component of aggregate demand;

4. at the *institutional level*, because insecurity of access to the means of repro-duction is the fundamental source of command over work processes;

5. at the *political level*, because the process of social reproduction implies a radical conflict between profit and the living standards of the whole labouring population.'

A class analysis is necessary to understand how production and reproduction are linked in a single process. Luxton (2006: 37) argues:

> By developing a class analysis that shows how the production of goods and services and the production of life are part of one integrated pro-cess, social reproduction does more than identify the activities involved in the daily and generational reproduction of daily life. It allows for an explanation of the structures, relationships and dynamics that produce those activities.

Further drawing from Marx means recognising that these class relations render the capitalist totality fundamentally unstable. This is because there is a central contradiction between capital accumulation and social reproduction, which is anchored in the capital–labour contradiction and:

> is expressed when workers through their unions try to improve working conditions, pay and benefits to ameliorate their livelihood, while employers resist and, under pressure to make profits, try to cut labour costs by reducing pay, benefits and working conditions (Bezanson and Luxton 2006: 8).

Following this approach means that contemporary analyses of institutions, such as commodified household labour, pay close attention to the race, class, ethnic and gendered dimensions involved. Furthermore, the scope of analysis is expanded: for instance, on how household labour is increasingly globalised, as women from the global South and European post-socialist countries have been recruited to service an exploding demand for household workers in the United States, Canada, the European Union, Hong Kong and the Middle East. This is 'the global care chain' of women moving from poor to rich countries (Ehrenreich and Hochschild 2003), involving work for low wages under poor working conditions in what has been termed 'the feminisation of survival' (Sassen 2000). It is part of a rich and growing scholarship on the 'care economy'.

Social reproduction has generated an extensive literature that has stimulated new analyses of capitalist political economy and challenged the political and economic theories of mainstream economics that promote capitalism as the ideal or only viable economic system (Picchio 1992). This wealth of material demonstrates the value of a Marxist–feminist alliance, a historical materialist approach that integrates gender, race and class. However, it remains hampered by two difficulties: its relative isolation as a scholarly field and its own, as yet, unresolved theoretical questions. On the one hand, social reproduction remains primarily of interest to socialist feminists and has hardly been taken up either by Marxists or by broader feminist scholarship. On the other hand, trying to develop a new way of looking at the world is profoundly challenging. At the same time as it must deconstruct prevailing theories by revealing their class and gender biases and their failure to account for race, ethnic and other systemic discriminatory regimes, it must also reconstruct new theories based on the valorization of all aspects of social reproduction. Despite frequent assertions that the intersections of gender, race and class are core topics of study, very few studies actually succeed in dealing adequately with all three.

A final challenge relates to social reproduction as a way of theorising the politics of everyday life. Since the late 1970s, neoliberalism has forced a move away from national or public commitments to universal forms of social reproduction such as citizenship rights, welfare and development services, through which working classes, peasants, some indigenous peoples and other marginalised groups had some claims to public services and assistance. There has been a move to marketised and exclusive forms of social reproduction. Both public and private forms operate within a capitalist framework and neither provides secure conditions of social reproduction for the majority, although the former modified somewhat the vulnerabilities produced by market economies while the latter has undermined the capacities of a growing population to ensure its own social reproduction. We suggest that a major challenge facing those of us who are concerned about these issues is to envision what kinds of political, social, cultural, ecological and economic initiatives would foster revitalised forms of social reproduction. And what would a politics that takes social reproduction seriously look like?

CONCLUSION

Much progress has been made in the relation between Marxism and feminism since Bozzoli's claim that in southern African studies 'no substantial challenges to androcentric tendencies within Marxism have been made' (Bozzoli 1983: 140). The 'collapsing of female oppression into the capitalist mode of production' is no longer the 'dominant tendency in analyses of women in South Africa' (142). Marxism's earlier claim to provide a comprehensive theory of human history and society has been shown to be flawed by its marginalisation of experiences and aspects of life traditionally associated with women.

The solution to a 'healthier marriage' that Hartmann offered in the 1980s lay in giving equal weight to patriarchy and capitalism. Historical materialist feminist scholarship has since shown that such a dualistic analysis dehistoricises women's oppression (Lerner 1987). Patriarchy is not a universal system and cannot be understood as distinct from the relations of production or outside of a specific historical context. Instead, with socialist feminism's concept of social reproduction, domestic, procreative and caring activities and relationships are understood as part of the material basis of society.

No one now attempts to appropriate Marxist concepts of value or productive and unproductive work and apply them uncritically in an attempt to establish the value of domestic work (Cock 1981). The accusations of a white-feminist epistemological imperialism are no longer apt. No one assumes that a socialist order will necessarily guarantee gender equality. No one now presents women, irrespective of class, race, nationality, ethnicity, or sexual preference as comprising a homogeneous group bound together by their shared 'oppression'. The theories developed through the engagement of feminism and Marxism over the past century offer important tools of social, political and economic analysis to their practitioners. The challenge in the current period is to use those tools as weapons in a resurgence of a socialist feminist politics. Both Marxism and feminism contain insights into an alternative social order and point to the means of reaching it. Mapping this alternative vision would challenge 'the deepest shadow that hangs over us (which) is neither terror, environmental collapse, nor global recession. It is the internalised fatalism that holds there is no possible alternative to capital's world order' (Kovel in Kelly and Malone 2006: 116).

NOTES

1   As Marxist feminists who came of age during the previous period of left-wing
     mobilisations and the global revitalisation of feminism in the 1960s and 1970s, and
     who have lived through the defeats of left-wing politics and the rise of neoliberal
     capitalism during the 1980s and 1990s, we have been energised and excited by the
     recent mobilisations. Living in different parts of the world, in countries with very
     different histories (South Africa and Canada), we understand that the mobilisation
     in different parts of the world will reflect and be shaped by the constraints and
     possibilities of local situations. But we are also struck by the ways in which our
     experiences and our related political analyses are similar. One of the challenges fac-
     ing those who are trying to develop new approaches to Marxism is how to attend
     simultaneously to global patterns and local specificities.
2   The struggles of women of colour, indigenous women and others to make white
     feminism aware of its own racism and to integrate race and gender has been long
     and difficult. Socialist feminism has often shared the racism, indifference and
     resistance that the larger women's movement manifests. However, socialist fem-
     inism starts from the premise that the liberation of women depends on the libera-
     tion of everyone. At least in theory, that means that socialist feminism integrates
     both class analysis and an anti-racist politics (Mohanty 2003; Rowbotham 1972).
3   For a brilliant socialist feminist commentary on Marx and Engels's analysis of
     'the woman question' from the perspective of a 'utopian socialist', see Sheila
     Rowbotham's 'Dear Dr. Marx: A letter from a socialist feminist' (1999: 221–237).
4   By the 1980s, woman leaders of the main women's organisations insisted that they
     had too much emancipation; they called for less. What they seemed to mean by
     this is that they equated emancipation with integration into the paid labour force,
     forcing them to manage a double day they found exhausting and overwhelming.
     They wanted an opportunity to 'stay home' as housewives. They had no vision of
     collectivisation of domestic labour (Luxton and Reiter 1991).
5   As far as we know, Simone de Beauvoir (1952) was the first theorist to use the pro-
     duction/reproduction dichotomy in analysing women's oppression.

REFERENCES

Amos, V. and Parmar, P. 1984. 'Challenging imperial feminism', *Feminist Review*, 17: 3–20.
Armstrong, P. and Armstrong, H. 1987. 'Beyond sexless class and classless sex: Toward
     Marxist feminism'. In *The Politics of Diversity*, edited by R. Hamilton and M.
     Barrett. London: Verso.
Bakker, I. and Gill, S. (eds). 2003. *Power, Production and Social Reproduction: Human In/
     security in the Global Political Economy.* New York: Palgrave-Macmillan.
Barrett, M. 1980. *Women's Oppression Today.* London: Verso.
Barrett, M. and McIntosh, M. 1982. *The Anti-social Family.* London: Verso.
Beechey, V. 1979. 'On patriarchy', *Feminist Review*, 3: 66–82.
Benjamin, J. 1988. *The Bonds of Love: Psychoanalysis, Feminism and the Problem of
     Domination.* New York: Pantheon Books.
Bezanson, K. 2006. *Gender, the State and Social Reproduction: Household Insecurity in
     Neo-liberal Times.* Toronto: University of Toronto Press.
Bezanson, K. and Luxton, M. 2006. 'Introduction: Social reproduction and feminist
     political economy'. In *Social Reproduction: Feminist Political Economy Challenges*

Neo-Liberalism, edited by K. Bezanson and M. Luxton. Montreal and Kingston: McGill-Queens University Press.

Bhavnani, K-K. (ed.). 2001. *Feminism & 'Race'*. New York: Oxford University Press.

Bittman, M. 2002. 'The visible and the hidden: States, markets and non-market activity', unpublished PhD thesis, RMIT University, Melbourne.

Bordo, S. 1993. *Unbearable Weight. Feminism, Western Culture, and the Body*. Berkeley, CA: University of California Press.

Bozzoli, B. 1983. 'Marxism, feminism and South African studies', *Journal of Southern African Studies*, 9 (2): 139–171.

Braedley, S. and Luxton, M. 2010. 'Competing philosophies: Neoliberalism and the challenges of everyday life'. In *Neoliberalism and Everyday Life*, edited by S. Braedley and M. Luxton. Montreal and Kingston: McGill-Queens University Press.

Bulbeck, C. 1998. *Re-orienting Western Feminisms: Women's Diversity in a Postcolonial World*. Cambridge: Cambridge University Press.

Cock, J. 1981. '"Disposable nannies": Domestic workers in contemporary South Africa', *Review of African Political Economy*, 43: 40–56.

Connell, R. 2010. 'Understanding neoliberalism'. In *Neoliberalism and Everyday Life*, edited by S. Braedley and M. Luxton. Montreal and Kingston: McGill-Queens University Press.

Crenshaw, K. 1991. 'Mapping the margins: Intersectionality, identity politics, and violence against women of color', *Stanford Law Review*, 43 (6): 1241–1299.

Dalla Costa, M. and James, S. 1970. *The Power of Women and Subversion of the Community*. Bristol: Falling Wall Press.

Davis, A. 1981. *Women, Race and Class*. New York: Random House.

De Beauvoir, S. 1952. *The Second Sex*. Translated by C. Borde and S. Malovany-Chevalier. London: Jonathan Cape.

Ehrenreich, B. and Hochschild, A. (eds). 2003. *Global Woman: Nannies, Maids and Sex Workers in the New Economy*. New York: Metropolitan Books.

Eisenstein, Z. (ed.). 1979. *Capitalist Patriarchy and the Case for Socialist Feminism*. New York: Monthly Review Press.

Engels, F. (1844) 1987. *The Condition of the Working Class in England*. Harmondsworth: Penguin.

Engels, F. (1884) 1972. *Origins of the Family, Private Property and the State*. Harmondsworth: Penguin.

Ferguson, A. 1989. *Blood at the Root: Motherhood, Sexuality and Male Domination*. New York: Pandora/Unwin and Hyman.

Ferguson, A. 1991. *Sexual Democracy: Women, Opression and Revolution*. Boulder, CO: Westview Press.

Ferguson, A. and Folbre, N. 1981. 'The unhappy marriage of patriarchy and capitalism'. In *Women and Revolution: A Discussion of the Unhappy Marriage of Marxism and Socialism*, edited by L. Sargent. Boston: South End Press.

Ferree, M.M. and McClurg Mueller, C.2004. 'Feminism and the women's movement: a global perspective'. In *The Blackwell Companion to Social Movements*, edited by D.A. Snow, S.A. Soule and H. Kriesi. Oxford: Blackwell.

Firestone, S. 1972. *The Dialectic of Sex: The Case for Feminist Revolution*. New York: William Morrow and Co.

Folbre, N. 1987. 'Patriarchy as a mode of production'. In *New Directions in Political Economy*, edited by R. Albeda and C. Gunn. New York: M.E. Sharpe.

Fox, B. 1988. 'Conceptualizing "patriarchy"', *Canadian Review of Sociology and Anthropology*, 25 (2):163–182.

Giles, W. and Arat-Koc, S. (eds). 1994. *Maid in the Market: Women's Paid Domestic Labour.* Halifax: Fernwood.

Hamilton, R. 1978. *The Liberation of Women: A Study of Patriarchy and Capitalism.* London: George Allen and Unwin.

Hartmann, H. 1981. 'The unhappy marriage of Marxism and feminism: Toward a more progressive union'. In *Women and Revolution: A Discussion of the Unhappy Marriage of Marxism and Socialism,* edited by L. Sargent. London: Pluto Press.

Hayden, D. 1982. *The Grand Domestic Revolution: The History of Feminist Designs for American Homes, Neighborhoods and Cities.* Cambridge, MA: MIT Press.

Henn, J. 1988. 'The material basis of sexism: A mode of production analysis'. In *Patriarchy and Class: African Women in the Home and the Workforce,* edited by S. Stichter and J. Parpart. London: Westview Press.

Hennessay, R. and Ingraham, C. (eds). 1997. *Materialist Feminism: A Reader in Class, Difference, and Women's Lives.* New York and London: Routledge.

hooks, b. 1995. *Feminist Theory: From Margin to Center.* Cambridge: South End Press.

Joseph, G. 1981. 'The incompatible menage à trois: Marxism, feminism and racism'. In *Women and Revolution: A Discussion of the Unhappy Marriage of Marxism and Socialism,* edited by L. Sargent. London: Pluto Press.

Kelly, J. and Malone, S. 2006. 'Ecosocialism or barbarism'. In *Socialist Register 2007: Coming to Terms with Nature,* edited by C. Leys and L. Panitch. London: Merlin Press.

Kollontai, A. (1920) 1977. 'Communism and the family'. In *The Worker,* 1920; *Selected Writings of Alexandra Kollontai.* London: Allison & Busby.

Kollontai, A. (1921) 1972. *Sexual Relations and the Class Struggle: Love and the New Morality.* Bristol: Falling Wall Press.

Laslett, B. and Brenner, J. 1989. 'Gender and social reproduction: Historical perspectives', *Annual Review of Sociology,* 15: 381–404.

Lerner, G. 1987. *The Creation of Patriarchy.* New York: Oxford University Press.

Luxton, M. 1980. *More Than a Labour of Love: Three Generations of Women's Work in the Home.* Toronto: Women's Press.

Luxton, M. 2006. 'Feminist political economy in Canada and the politics of social reproduction'. In *Social Reproduction,* edited by K. Bezanson and M. Luxton. Montreal and Kingston: McGill-Queens University Press.

Luxton, M. and Reiter, E. 1991. 'Overemancipation? Liberation? Soviet women in the Gorbachev period', *Studies in Political Economy,* 34: 53–73.

Maroney, H.J. and Luxton, M. (eds). 1987. *Feminism and Political Economy: Women's Work, Women's Struggles.* Toronto: Methuen.

Marx, K. (1867) 1976. *Capital: A Critique of Political Economy (Vol. 1).* London: Penguin.

Marx, K. and Engels, F. (1848) 1998. *The Communist Manifesto.* Translated by Samuel Moore. Halifax: Fernwood.

McClintock, A. 1995. *Imperial Leather: Race, Gender, and Sexuality in the Colonial Context.* New York: Routledge.

McMahon, A. 1999. *Taking Care of Men: Sexual Politics in the Public Mind.* Cambridge: Cambridge University Press.

Millet, K. 1970. *Sexual Politics.* Garden City, NY: Double Day & Company, Inc.

Mitchell, J. 1974. *Women's Estate.* Harmondsworth: Penguin.

Mohanty, C. 2003. *Feminism Without Borders: Decolonizing Theory, Practising Solidarity.* Durham: Duke University.

Molyneux, M. 1979. 'Beyond the domestic labour debate', *New Left Review,* 1 (116): 78–97.

Molyneux, M. 2000. *Women's Movements in International Perspective: Latin America and Beyond.* London: Palgrave.

Morton, P. 1972. 'A woman's work is never done'. In Corrective Collective no. 6, *Women Unite!* Toronto: The Canadian Educational Women's Press.

Picchio, A. 1992. *Social Reproduction: The Political Economy of the Labour Market.* Cambridge, MA: Cambridge University Press.

Pollert, A. 1996. 'Gender and class revisited: Or the poverty of patriarchy', *Sociology,* 30 (4): 639 –659.

Rowbotham, S. 1972. *Women, Resistance and Revolution.* London: Penguin.

Rowbotham, S. 1992. *Women in Movement: Feminism and Social Action.* New York: Routledge.

Rowbotham, S. 1999. 'Dear Dr. Marx: A letter from a socialist feminist'. In *Threads through Time: Writings on History and Autobiography.* London: Penguin.

Rowbotham, S., Segal, L. and Wainwright, H. 1979. *Beyond the Fragments: Feminism and the Making of Socialism.* London: Virago.

Rubin, G. 1975. 'The traffic in women: Notes on the "political economy" of sex'. In *Toward an Anthropology of Women,* edited by R. Reiter. New York: Monthly Review Press.

Sangster, J. and Luxton, M. 2013. 'Feminism, co-optation and the problems of amnesia: A response to Nancy Fraser'. In *The Question of Strategy,* edited by L. Panitch, G. Albo and V. Chibber. New York: Monthly Review Press.

Sassen, S. 2000. 'Global cities and survival circuits'. In *Global Woman: Nannies, Maids and Sex Workers in the New Global Economy,* edited by B. Ehrenreich and A. Hochschild. New York: Metropolitan Books.

Seccombe, W. 1974. 'The housewife and her labour under capitalism', *New Left Review,* 83: 3–24.

Seccombe, W. 1983. 'Marxism and demography', *New Left Review,* 1 (137): 28–40.

Seccombe, W. 1992. *A Millennium of Family Change.* London: Verso.

Segal, L. 1994. *Straight Sex: Rethinking the Politics of Pleasure.* London: Virago.

Shelton, B. and Agger, B. 1993. 'Shotgun wedding, unhappy marriage, no-fault divorce? Rethinking the feminism–Marxism relationship'. In *Theory on Gender/Feminism on Theory,* edited by P. England. New York: Aldine de Gruyter.

Stone, P. 2007. *Opting Out? Why Women Really Quit Careers and Head Home.* Berkeley: University of California Press.

Sunseri, L. 2011. *Being Again of One Mind: Oneida Women and the Struggle for Decolonization.* Vancouver: UBC Press.

Taylor, B. 1983. *Eve and the New Jerusalem: Socialism and Feminism in the Nineteenth Century.* London: Virago.

Thompson, W. and Wheeler A. (1825) 1983. *Appeal of One Half the Human Race, Women, Against the Pretensions of the Other Half, Men, to Retain Them in Political, and Thence in Civil and Domestic Slavery.* London: Virago.

Urdang, S. 1989. *And Still They Dance: Women, War and the Struggle for Change in Mozambique.* New York: Monthly Review Press.

Vogel, L. 1983. *Marxism and the Oppression of Women: Toward a Unitary Theory.* London: Pluto Press.

Walby, S. 1990. *Theorising Patriarchy.* Oxford: Blackwell.

Young, I. 1981. 'The limits of dual systems theory'. In *Women and Revolution: A Discussion of the Unhappy Marriage of Marxism and Socialism,* edited by L. Sargent. London: Pluto Press.

Zaretsky, E. 1973. *Capitalism, the Family and Personal Life.* New York: Harper.

Zizek, S. and Douzinas, C. (eds). 2010. *The Idea of Communism.* London: Verso.

6

MARX AND THE ECO-LOGIC OF FOSSIL CAPITALISM

Devan Pillay

There is now increased recognition of the severity of the ecological crisis facing our planet, to the extent that even the president of a leading industrialised nation recently questioned the growth/consumption paradigm based on the abundant availability of natural resources, in particular fossil fuels such as oil.[1] The sustainability of economic growth is in doubt because of the rapid depletion of non-renewable fossil fuels (particularly peak oil) and because of carbon emissions from the use of these fossil fuels in production and consumption processes. This has caused climate change resulting in, amongst other things, melting polar ice caps, rising sea levels, floods, drought and a host of other human-induced 'natural' disasters which can destroy the earth as we know it (Gore 2009; Magdoff and Foster 2011). In addition, other pollutants from industrial processes, such as acid mine drainage, acid rain and other toxins have polluted the air and rivers, destroying livelihoods and causing a wide range of public health problems, including new diseases that modern medicine is unable to cure (Hallowes 2011). The rapid advancement of industrial and urban growth is also destroying delicate local ecosystems, making a wide range of flora and fauna extinct, thus threatening the planet's precious biodiversity that holds the key to much of the hitherto-unknown inner workings of the entire ecosystem that governs the earth's existence (Cock 2007).

This 'eco-logic' of industrial capitalism (Friedman 2008) is an intricate web of economic and ecological processes that feed off each other, with very specific social consequences. While the social critique of capitalism (pivoted around the capital–labour contradiction) is associated with Marxist and neo-Marxist paradigms that have emerged over the past century and a half, the ecological critique has been mainly the preserve of environmentalists who have drawn inspiration from non-Western thought (including Native American and Eastern philosophical thought). Indeed, Marx and the varieties of Marxism that flowed out of his thinking over the past century have usually been lumped together with other products of the Enlightenment, allegedly sharing a similar anthropocentric belief in the domination of nature (itself a product of Christian thinking), but departing from Christianity in its belief in the wonders of science and technology and the idea of historical *progress* (Barry 2004; Ponting 2007).[2]

In other words, while Marxism is associated with a critique of capitalism, and the idea of social equality, it allegedly shares with neoclassical capitalist thought (free market and Keynesian) the belief that economic growth is based on the infinite supply of fossil fuel and other natural resources (as 'gifts of nature') and that the main task of socialism and communism is the equal distribution of the fruits of labour expended during the production process. In this view, nature in and of itself has no intrinsic value – it has only use-value for human beings (and, under capitalism, exchange-value, as a commodity to be bought and sold).

Drawing on a growing corpus of work rethinking Marx's ecological credentials (see for example, Burkett 2005; Foster 1999 and 2009; Foster, Clark and York 2010; Magdoff and Foster 2011; O'Connor 1998; Pepper 1992 and Williams 2010), this chapter assesses whether Marx's thinking, in light of the ecological crisis, is irredeemably Promethean in its blind faith in the power of technology and industrial development and thus anti-ecological, or is it relevant to an understanding of the eco-logic of capitalism?

FOSSIL CAPITALISM AND THE CRISIS OF PROMETHEAN MARXISM

The historical trajectory of what Elmar Altvater (2006) calls 'fossil capitalism', relies on the burning of fossil fuels as the basis for rapid economic growth. This has its own logic, accumulation for the sake of accumulation, which enriches (in the form of profits, dividends and high salaries) a tiny minority of the earth's population, while leaving the vast majority living in squalor and misery (Amin 2008).

Industrial capitalism, in other words, has an 'eco-logic' in three interrelated senses. Firstly, its reliance on the easy availability of non-renewable fossil fuels (particularly oil) in abundance is reaching a tipping point (peak oil), such that in 50 to 100 years' time the oil will run out. This underlines the natural limits to industrial capitalist development (or economic growth) as we currently conceive of it. Secondly, increasing pollution of various kinds, including carbon emissions produced by the burning of fossil fuels (oil, gas and coal), as well as other pollutants produced by production–consumption–urbanisation processes, threaten the very existence of earth as we know it (through amongst other things, the manifold impacts of climate change). Thirdly, rapid deforestation and declining biodiversity (flora and fauna) as a result of these processes threaten delicate ecosystems, which have wide-ranging and devastating impacts. The earth's carrying capacity to provide resources for exploitation, as well as to act as a sink for waste produced by the production–consumption treadmill, is rapidly reaching its limits (Clapp and Dauvergne 2008).

For a while this terrain of analysis was dominated by environmental economics, which seeks to internalise the costs of environmental damage into the market/growth logic of capitalism and the more radical ecological economics (see Burkett 2005). The latter is critical of economic growth and tends toward at least for the developed economies, considerations of 'steady state' economies – namely a return to the pre-capitalist rates of production and consumption based on 'sufficiency' rather than incessant, unsustainable growth (Kovel 2002).

This latter group, while at least implicitly anti-capitalist, has nevertheless also been critical of Marxism as an allegedly 'anthropocentric' paradigm. Even if Marxism looks forward to the transcendence of capitalism in the form of socialism and communism, where the material abundance produced by industrialisation is continued under different relations of production, such that the fruits of production are more equally distributed to people throughout human society, it nonetheless, like market liberalism and Keynesianism, sees capitalist growth as necessary for human progress (see Barry 2004; Ponting 2007).

This productivist, Promethean logic based on the marvels of technological progress has been the standard signifier of twentieth-century orthodox Marxism (particularly its Leninist and social democratic forms) that came to define the legacy of Karl Marx and Friedrich Engels.

For orthodox Marxism, capitalism's demise will emerge out of the social contradictions embedded in capitalism – namely, the capital/labour contradiction
through which capitalism creates its own gravedigger in the form of the organised
working class (Marx and Engels [1848/1888]1999). The area of debate around
strategy and tactics, which divided the Bolshevik Leninists from the Menshevik
social democrats in Russia before the 1917 revolution, and which forever split
Marxism throughout the world thereafter between revolutionary Leninism
(whether Stalinist or Trotskyist) and social democracy and later 'Eurocommunism'
(or 'evolutionary' Marxism), was over the manner in which socialism would
emerge. For the Bolsheviks (or Marxist–Leninists), the revolution needed to be
induced from the outside (through the voluntarist action of a revolutionary party
of the working class, or in Antonio Gramsci's [1971] terms, a 'war of manoeuvre'
against the capitalist state), while Marxists such as Eduard Bernstein and Karl
Kautsky believed that the endemic crises arising out of capitalism's internal
contradictions would bring about its own downfall (thus allowing social democratic parties to participate in the electoral system of 'bourgeois democracy'
through Gramsci's 'war of position', building counter-hegemony within the interstices of capitalism, such that when the crisis reaches its ultimate tipping point, a
socialist ethos would prevail within the working class and broader society).

Arguably Joseph Stalin's emphasis on the two-stage revolution (first the
national-democratic stage and then later the socialist stage), which imprinted
itself on all Marxist–Leninist–Stalinist communist parties over the past century,
meant that during the 'first stage' communist parties would in substance be
'left' versions of social democratic parties – except that politically they would
be aligned with either the Soviet Union or China during the cold war (whilst
social democratic parties invariably aligned themselves with the US-led
West). Gradually, many social democratic parties dropped their overt links to
Marxism and their vision of a transition to fully fledged socialism (in favour of
the Keynesian compromise between capitalism and socialism).

Today, with the fall of Soviet statism (see Wright 2010) and the crisis of
the Marxist revolutionary project,[3] most established Marxist–Leninist parties,
such as the South African Communist Party (SACP) or the communist parties
in India,[4] are in substance, if not in form, social democratic parties (usually
occupying the left space abandoned by self-declared social democrats since
the 1980s and still looking forward, in the very long term, to a rather abstract
socialism and eventually communism). In other words, a great displacement
has happened – traditional social democrats (such as the British Labour Party,

or the German Social Democratic Party [SPD]) have moved to the right, and become market liberal with a dash of welfarism, while communists have become true social democrats in the spirit of Kautsky (even while denouncing him, as Vladimir Lenin did, as a renegade for opposing the dictatorship of the proletariat after the Russian Revolution of 1917).

The long march from capitalism to socialism and, seemingly, back to capitalism during the 1990s' triumph of the West, was seemingly evidence of the 'end of history' (Fukuyama 1992) – namely, the end of Marx's vision of historical stages from capitalism to socialism to communism. Capitalist democracy, it seems, was the final stage: Allow the market its freedom across the globe and all boats will rise, as economic development will apparently sweep the world out of poverty (but not inequality, which is conveniently regarded by most neoliberals as the necessary catalyst for growth and development).

With Russia and its former East European satellites going for full-blown free market 'disaster capitalism' (Klein 2008), other so-called socialist countries such as China and Vietnam increasingly embraced the market mechanism (if not the political form of multi-party liberal democracy), to become mixed or 'state capitalist' economies

In the 1990s and early 2000s Marxism, it seemed, was, if not dead, then dying a slow death. Indeed, even the new social movements that rose to fight the social ills caused by disaster capitalism – ranging from environmental degradation to free trade, privatisation, land dispossession and various forms of identity politics – seemed keen to embrace postmodern or post-Marxist conceptions of struggle. The industrial working class and traditional trade unionism had lost their social weight as the historical agent of social liberation in most countries (except perhaps South Africa and Brazil), particularly as their numerical weight declined with the rise of informalised labour and unemployment worldwide.

Even in academia, Marxism seemed on the decline, as a de-classed, decentred and apparently non-dogmatic postmodernism swept forward to explain power, alienation and marginalisation under globalised capitalism. Marx remained important as a historical figure – as a founding father of the social sciences – but he was exhausted, no longer really relevant (except in isolated corners of intellectual life, where a more Gramscian Marxism tried, in dialogue with postmodernism, to redeem the dialectical, nuanced Marx from the dregs of his more dogmatic Leninist progeny). The certainties of the twentieth century were replaced by the uncertainties of the globalised twenty-first century, dominated by global capital under the tutelage of US hegemony.

THE CAPITALIST CRISIS AND A REVIVAL OF MARX

Along with the rise of 'twenty-first century socialism' in Latin America, given the dramatic failure of neoliberalism in that region, the recent capitalist crisis has revived popular interest in Marx (for his analytical insight) and an open Marxism (for its revolutionary potential).

However, it is not business as usual. Three factors have now become central to any reconsideration of the Marxist project: first, multi-party democracy based on principles such as freedom of expression and association (given the horrors of Stalinist dictatorships); second, the enduring efficacy of the market mechanism, albeit subordinated to society (à la Karl Polanyi [1944]), in the production and distribution of goods and services (given the failures of statist production/distribution, which often facilitate networks of patronage); and third, the ecological limits to capitalist growth, as a 'second contradiction' or gravedigger of capitalism.

The current capitalist crisis has evoked a variety of responses: from the very narrow, one-dimensional approaches (free market and Keynesian-lite), which see the crisis as a purely financial one, to broader Marxist (and Keynesian–Marxist) approaches which conceptualise the crisis as economic, rooted in the stagnation of the real economy (particularly the falling rate of profit in the manufacturing sector), to the very broad, multidimensional eco-Marxist approaches, which see the crisis as a complex interaction between economic, ecological and social crises that has its roots in industrialisation based on fossil capitalism.

The free market (or orthodox neoclassical or 'neoliberal') approach, whilst currently under severe attack, nevertheless remains embedded amongst economists as a default set of assumptions. As British heterodox economist Ben Fine remarked recently,[5] the economics profession has, since the 1980s, been so drenched in neoclassical economic thinking – which both disembeds the economy from society as well as the economics profession from the other social sciences – that economists in the former British government found it difficult to respond to the Labour Party's drift towards Keynesian thinking at the political level, which they barely understood.

As the crisis temporarily subsides, free market thinkers are becoming bolder again. However, the generally accepted view is that, in the words of *Time* magazine's Peter Gumbel, 'the markets have failed, and in doing so they have destroyed the conventional wisdom about how to run an efficient economy'

(2 February 2009). The finger is pointed firmly at the financialisation of capitalism, due to the deregulation of capital movements, beginning in the 1980s.

But is the finger pointing at greedy bankers a sufficient explanation of the
crisis? And will Keynesian fiscal stimulation (mainly bailing out banks with
billions of dollars) and financial regulation (including the increasingly popular
Tobin tax on global financial transactions) address the roots of the crisis, or
merely patch over the cracks until the dam bursts open again, only more fiercely?

Marx inspired a deeper political economy-historical perspective that traces
the roots of the crisis to deeper, structural faults in the entire system. As many
Marxists argue, the financialisation of capitalism is not the *cause* of the capitalist crisis, but was itself a *response* to the manufacturing crisis of the 1970s
(Arrighi 2007; Brenner 2009; Harvey 2010). Inherently crisis-ridden, this new
financial 'fix' has spawned a number of short-term crises in different parts of
the world over the past two decades. The current financial crisis, which hit the
core, developed countries directly, is the deepest since the Great Depression.

John Bellamy Foster and Fred Magdoff (2009), in an extension of the Paul
Baran and Paul Sweezy (1968) analysis, characterise the new stage of capitalism as monopoly-finance capitalism. It is based on ever-increasing concen-
trations of capital, under the rule of mega-financial institutions that straddle
the globe, where manufacturing firms are intermeshed with financial firms
and investments.

It is a system of accumulation based on mass consumerism (the creation of
everlasting wants). However, particularly in the US centre of global capitalism,
these new wants could not be satisfied because potential consumers, experiencing
stagnant or declining real wages, did not have the means to purchase the commodities produced. The only way out was increased indebtedness – creating fictitious
wealth built on sand, which would eventually collapse, as it did. The 'recovery' is
mired in rising unemployment and growing inequality, as the bankers dole out
billions of dollars in bonuses to themselves. In 2009, in the midst of the crisis,
India's number of billionaires doubled (just as the Maoist rebellion on behalf
of displaced farmers grew [Perry 2010]). Despite the talk, there are no signs that
Western governments are able to stand up to the power of Wall Street. It seems
that Western politicians, like modern-day shareholders of companies, can think
only short term – to the next election, or the next big payout (Harvey 2010).

Marx, according to David Harvey (2010), argued that capitalism is based
on an average of three per cent compound growth per annum (accumulation for the sake of accumulation). It is now reaching its limits in two senses –

where do the super-rich, sitting on trillions of dollars, invest this capital, other than in fictitious commodities? And if they do find some avenues of invest-ment in real commodities, can the earth sustain more mining, deforestation and industrial pollution?

MARX'S ECOLOGY

If Marx is still relevant as a prescient analyst of capitalist economic crisis (what James O'Connor [1998] calls the first contradiction of capitalism), does Marx have anything to offer in terms of the ecological crisis (O'Connor's second contradiction)?

There are at least four possible ways of viewing Marx on the matter:[6] the dominant view, depicted above, is that Marx was anti-ecological and his think-ing was indistinguishable from Soviet practice (see Ponting 2007). Alternatively, many environmental sociologists feel that Marx had moments of ecological insight, but that these were minor compared to his pro-technology, pro-growth (or Promethean) stance (Barry 2004). Others, including many ecological Marxists such as Ted Benton (1996), David Pepper (1992) and James O'Connor (1998), go further and argue that Marx had a theory about ecological degrada-tion in agriculture and in his sober moments valued nature as much as labour, but that this was separate from his core social analysis, as Marx (and Engels) were ambiguous about nature.

Finally, there are the views of Foster and Paul Burkett, who have inspired a new generation of Marxist ecologists who are adamant that, all along, Marx had a *systemic* approach to nature and to environmental degrada-tion (Burkett 2005; Foster 1999) – even if he gave prominence to the social contradiction (between capital and labour), given the pressing issues of his time. Had Marx lived today and witnessed the extent of the ecological crisis, it is most likely that he would have placed it alongside the social crisis, with equal emphasis.

It is debatable as to whether it is analytically feasible to speak of one, inter-connected set of capitalist contradictions, or two – the first, or economic, and the second, or ecological (O'Connor 1998), in the sense that the two have separate rhythms of their own, even if they collide and at times reinforce each other. Nevertheless, even if ecological crises can be found to precede capitalism (such as the Roman's plunder of natural resources [Ponting 2007], ecological degradation has intensified exponentially on the capitalist production tread-mill. Burkett (2005: 7) criticises O'Connor for arguing that Marx does not 'adequately account for the natural and social conditions of production' and then, in a functionalist's manner, grafting such conditions 'onto a Marxian model of accumulation and crisis'. This, according to Burkett, has prevented a full engagement between ecological economists and Marxists and allowed 'the infiltration of neoclassical visions and concepts into ecological economics' (8) – particularly the supply-and-demand framework and in the process weakening the anti-market current within the discipline and reducing its interdisciplinary plurality.

Burkett (11) points to recent research that has established that Marx's and Engels's 'engagement with the natural sciences was more intensive and extensive than anyone could previously have imagined'. The natural sciences, including Charles Darwin's *Origins of the Species* ([1859] 2012) and what is currently known as ecological analysis, were central to their materialist approach. In other words, the allegation that they ignored natural limits, thought that humans should dominate nature, embraced an anti-ecological industrialism, under-appreciated capitalism's reliance on materials and energy and saw wealth only in terms of labour, 'have been thoroughly debunked' (Burkett 2005: 11).

Indeed, Foster (2009: 266) asserts that Marx and Engels, throughout their writings, grappled with the main ecological problems of society:

> … the division between town and country, soil depletion, industrial pollution, urban maldevelopment, the decline in health and crippling of workers, bad nutrition, toxicity, enclosures, rural poverty and isolation, deforestation, human-generated floods, desertification, water shortages, regional climate change, the exhaustion of natural resources (including coal), conservation of energy, entropy, the need to recycle the waste products of industry, the interconnections between species and their environments, historically conditioned problems of overpopulation, the causes of famine, and the issue of the rational employment of science and technology.

Foster's *Marx's Ecology* (1999) is a detailed and highly persuasive examination of Marx's ecological insights, starting with his PhD thesis and maturing with his later work, when he delved deeply into the problems of soil fertility and the nutrient cycle. The following quotes give a sample of Marx's views on nature and the ecological contradiction embedded in capitalism – and casts significant doubt on the Promethean view of Marx expressed by Marxists and non-Marxists over the past century. This quote from the little-read volume three of *Das Kapital* reveals an explicit view of 'sustainable development' a century before the famed Brundtland Commission of 1982, which defined 'sustainability' as development that preserves the natural environment for future generations (Clapp and Dauvergne 2008). According to Marx ([1894] 1981: 911):

> Even an entire society, a nation or all simultaneously existing societies taken together, are not owners of the earth, they are simply its possessors, its beneficiaries, and have to bequeath it in an improved state to succeeding generations, as *boni patres familias* [good heads of households].

Of course Marx goes way beyond Brundtland, which was a compromise between environmentalists who wanted real ecological sustainability and big business that wanted continued economic growth. The end result was 'sustainability' that was subsumed under the growth imperative – allowing corporations to proceed with accelerated accumulation over the past 30 years, resulting in increased carbon emissions and heightened climate change – but under the cover of 'greenwashing' (Bruno and Karliner 2004).

For Marx, the social relations of production – the private ownership of productive resources, or the rule of capital – must change before real sustainable human development can occur. Although many believe that Marx conceptualised the labour theory of value to the neglect of nature as a source of value, he saw both labour and nature as sources of value:

> All progress in capitalist agriculture is a progress in the art, not only of robbing the worker, but of robbing the soil; all progress in increasing the fertility of the soil for a given time is a progress toward ruining the more long-lasting sources of that fertility … Capitalist production, therefore, develops technology, and the combining together of various processes into a social whole, only by sapping *the original sources of all wealth – the soil and the labourer* (Marx [1887]1954: 475, my emphasis).

Marx's theory of the metabolic rift between town and countryside, which he mentions in the *Communist Manifesto*, is also about the rift between humans and nature. Marx, unlike anthropocentric thinkers, saw humans as part of nature and who, as such, had to respect the laws of nature. In *Capital* (volume one) he says:

> Labour is, in the first place, a process in which both man and Nature participate, and in which man of his own accord starts, regulates, and controls the material reactions [metabolism] between himself and Nature. He opposes himself to Nature *as one of her own forces*, setting in motion arms and legs, head and hands, the natural forces of his body, in order to appropriate Nature's productions in a form adapted to his own wants. By thus acting on the external world and changing it, he at the same time *changes his own nature* ... it is the necessary condition for effecting exchange of matter [the metabolic interaction] between man and nature; it is *the everlasting Nature-imposed condition of human existence*. (Marx [1887] 1954: 173–179, my emphasis)

This intimate, interconnected (or dialectical) view of humans and nature, is so holistic that most deep ecologists would find little fault with it. For Marx, capitalism has torn asunder this metabolic interaction, creating a rift between humans and nature that is now threatening the existence of earth. While Marx did not, in his time, foresee the full detail of the consequences of this rift, he saw enough to warn us of its dangers. It may not have captured the headlines of his thinking, but Marx had a systematic view of humans and nature, stemming from his PhD thesis (Foster 1999).

Marx understood, following the work of Justus von Leibig (Foster 2002), that the metabolic rift between town and country – a central feature of capitalism, as urbanisation envelops the earth – leads to two things. Firstly, the soil is deprived of its nutrients, which are taken to the cities (in the form of food and clothing, for example) and then dumped into rivers or landfills in the cities. Human and non-human animal waste, which had previously been used to fertilise the soil in a continuous process of recycling, are, under capitalism, sources of pollution and potential danger to public health. Secondly, this has led to a crisis in agriculture and the frantic search for fertiliser in the form of guana (bird-droppings) amongst other things, leading to the colonisation of islands rich in guana, until this, too, dried up. Eventually artificial fertiliser had to be created, and this still forms the basis of capitalist agriculture, with recycling occurring only at the margins of global agriculture.

This example of the metabolic rift between town and country received focused attention from Marx, particularly in his later years, and is strong evidence of an ecological imagination that was quite advanced for his time. This is how Marx himself put it:

> Large landed property reduces the agricultural population to an ever decreasing minimum and confronts it with an ever growing industrial population crammed together in large towns; in this way it produces conditions that provoke an *irreparable rift in the interdependent process of the social metabolism*, a metabolism prescribed by the *natural laws of life* itself. The result of this is a *squandering of the vitality of the soil*, which is carried by trade far beyond the bounds of a single country ([1894]1981: 949, my emphasis).

In *Capital* (volume one) Marx ([1887]1954: 474) makes the following point: 'Capitalist production ... violates the conditions necessary to lasting fertility of the soil. By this action it destroys at the same time the health of the town labourer and the intellectual life of the rural labourer.'

Marx is referring here to the *isolation* of rural communities from developments in the sciences and the arts in cities. Indeed, this observation of Marx and Engels in the widely read *Communist Manifesto* was mistranslated, as Hal Draper (1978: 344) discovered in the 1970s, as the 'idiocy of rural life',[7] and for the past century this has been quoted extensively to prove that Marx and Engels looked down upon the peasantry – giving force to the Promethean perspective that capitalist industrialisation was a necessary precursor to socialism/communism. As Foster (1999) argues, Marx at the same time as he wrote the *Manifesto* also expressed great admiration for peasant leaders such as Thomas Muntzer.

Unlike Marxists such as Reiner Grundmann (Benton 1996; Foster 2009), who sought to justify the popular view of Marx as an anthropocentric advocate of the *domination* of nature, the above quotes give a different picture of Marx and Engels, as advocating the *mastery* of nature in accordance with nature's laws.[8] In other words, far from being a blind technological determinist, Marx was much more nuanced in his thinking about the limits and possibilities of technology as a solution to the problems of human society. Technology, for it to be socially useful, had to be subjected to social priorities (as opposed to market priorities) in accordance with the laws of nature.

MARX AND MARXISM

If all this was so self-evident, why has a century of Marxism gone by without ecology being at the forefront of Marxist thought? Well, as Marx once said, 'I am not a Marxist' (Wheen 1999).

According to Foster (1999) Marxists did address ecological issues in the early part of last century – including Lenin, Rosa Luxemburg, Nikolai Bukharin and early Soviet scientists. However, after Lenin died, Stalin embarked on a rapid industrialisation path and obliterated the ecological movement within the Soviet Union. The blind pursuit of industrial development at all costs, in the form of state capitalism (Wallerstein 1979; Foster 2009), was little different to the production treadmill of the capitalist West – except that a bureaucratic bourgeoisie was at the helm. This path was celebrated by Soviet-inclined Marxists in the post-war race with the West, as various Soviet leaders promised to outpace the West in industrial development.

While the horrors of Stalinism produced a wide range of responses from more democratically minded Marxists – ranging from followers of Leon Trotsky to various strands of Western Marxism (McLellan 1979), few of these departed from the Promethean emphasis of Stalin. Indeed, as Foster (1999) observes, Western Marxism's aversion to positivism and the natural sciences led to a neglect of Marx's ecology, with a few exceptions amongst British Marxists, in particular Christopher Caudwell. It is only from the 1970s, with the rise of the environmental movement, that Marxists have begun to take ecology seriously again.

Was Marx at least partly to blame for this? As mentioned above, some Marxists (such as Benton 1996) believe that, despite his ecological insights, Marx does reveal a certain ambiguity regarding the ecological question – thus allowing for the Promethean emphasis of most twentieth-century Marxists. Burkett (2005) and Foster (1999) are adamant that this is not the case, that nature is embedded in the core of Marx's analysis. Foster, however, concedes that Marx did expect the imminence of the socialist revolution, based on the *social* contradiction, as the working-class movement grew during his time. He thus focused more on the exploitation of labour as the gravedigger of capitalism, than on the contradictions of nature. He consequently devoted more attention to ecology in post-capitalist society, as a form of sustainable human development. This features prominently in the latter (but little understood) part of the *Communist Manifesto*, where explicit reference to the need for a metabolic restoration between town and country is made.

THE RELEVANCE TODAY

The Indian Marxist Randhir Singh (2010: 167) notes that Engels warned followers 'not to pick quotation from Marx or from him as if from sacred texts, but think as Marx would have thought in their place'. In this light, why is it important whether Marx had an ecological perspective or not?

Three reasons spring forth: firstly, to set the record straight, as Marx remains a foundational thinker within the social sciences; secondly, to provide a deeper analysis of the ecological crisis and point to possible limitations in current ecological thinking around the internalisation of environmental costs, without looking at the social relations of production; and thirdly, to build a broader, red-brown-green alliance against fossil capitalism, where traditional Marxist groups revise their approach towards ecology, and environmental groups likewise see the interconnections between environmental issues and capitalism as an economic system.

As a purely intellectual exercise, the work of Burkett and Foster serves a purpose, since it debunks a century of misunderstanding regarding Marx's and Engel's ecological insights. It goes along with the rediscovery of the ecological insights of other foundational sociological thinkers, such as Max Weber, who 'recognised the finitude of the world's fossil resources and the "heedless consumption of resources for which there are no substitutes"' (Urry 2011: 39–40). This serves to undermine the traditional separation of 'social facts' from 'material facts' and helps us to understand more fully the carbon resource bases of modern societies. Social scientists are slowly beginning to see the necessity of asserting the social back into an analysis of climate change and environmental degradation and of displacing economics as the primary discipline in such analyses (see White 2004). Marx, in particular, encourages a holistic perspective that undermines the boundaries between the natural and the social sciences, along with the subordination of economics to both.

The rediscovery of Marx's ecology also has important political implications. With the failure of the working-class movement to live up to its potential as the gravedigger of capitalism in the twentieth century – either through failed Stalinist/Maoist revolutions, or the absorption of the industrial working class as junior partners or labour aristocrats into social pacts with capital, *nature* has now stepped forward as a candidate to become gravedigger of capitalism. The depletion of fossil fuels to drive further industrialisation, climate change as a result of carbon emissions, various forms of pollution that threaten public health, as well as the destruction of ecosystems, all threaten our planet.

Responses to this impending doom have been varied. At the one extreme is the eco-centric (or bio-environmentalist) view, which tends to privilege 'nature' over humans. A key focus of their critique is not industrial capitalism in the first instance, but overpopulation and urbanisation, which has encroached on the living space of non-human animals and damaged delicate ecosystems (Clapp and Dauvergne 2008). In other words, the battle is between nature and humans and the underlying principle is that nature has *intrinsic* value – that is, value in itself, as opposed to use-value for the benefit of humans, or exchange-value for capitalism. The political implications of such a perspective are varied, ranging from green anarchism and deep ecology to neo-Malthusianism, where population control is a key policy instrument, as well as the return to nature, or living in small, localised communities in complete harmony with nature.

Marx and Engels were not romantic environmentalists, who sought a return to living in small rural communities. As Foster (2002) argues, they were neither anthropocentric nor eco-centric, but saw the two as a false dualism. Human beings do occupy the upper rung of the animal ladder, but they should use that position with care and sensitivity to the rights and laws of nature. Humans do not possess knowledge and understanding of the complex workings of nature. If they arrogantly think they do – witness the fanciful proposals to control the weather – then only disaster can befall humankind. In other words, it is neither humans nor nature but the dialectical interaction between the two, rooted in Darwin's theory of evolution (which Marx greatly admired as scientific proof of his materialist conception of history).

At the other end of the spectrum is the anthropocentric 'ecological modern-isation' perspective, which has two broad variants – the market liberal and the institutionalist (Clapp and Dauvergne 2008). For market liberals, sustainability is subordinated to economic growth, while institutionalists seek to regulate the market at global and national levels, without questioning the logic of accumula-tion. For these perspectives, the internalisation of environmental costs means 'getting the prices right' (Friedman 2008), with market liberals favouring instru-ments such as carbon trading, which implies a more complete commodification of nature. In addition, accumulation can proceed as long as greater efficiencies in resource consumption are made and green technologies are found to replace fossil fuels. More radical Keynesians propose incentives as well as taxation to encourage entrepreneurs to invest in wind, solar and hydro technologies – and believe that Germany has shown that it is feasible to produce all its electricity needs by 2050 with renewable sources (Dullien, Herr and Kellerman 2011).

While for some, unproven 'clean coal' technology is advocated, for most ecological modernisers the key is nuclear power (Friedman 2008). Indeed, as Alexander Cockburn (2011) laments, most environmentalists in the US support nuclear power, as does the radical British environmentalist, George Monbiot, on the grounds that it is now safer in all respects, including waste disposal. This seems to be the compromise between environmentalists panicked by the impending climate disaster and the need to find a quick fix and the corporate-led accumulation/consumption treadmill, which both consumers and producers are reluctant to move off. Is this not a case of having one's cake and eating it? As Cockburn (2011: 79) concludes:

> Look at the false predictions, the blunders. Remember the elemental truth that Nature bats last, and that folly and greed are ineluctable parts of the human condition. Why try to pretend that we live in a world where there are no force 8–9 earthquakes, tsunamis, dud machinery, forgetful workers, corner-cutting plant owners, immensely powerful corporations, permissive regulatory agencies, politicians and presidents trolling for campaign dollars? Is that the shoal on which the progressive movement in America is beached? This shameful pact between the nuclear industry and many big greens has got to end.

SUSTAINABLE (HOLISTIC) HUMAN DEVELOPMENT

A more holistic, Marxist analysis makes the connection between pollution, plunder and poverty. In what Harvey (2005), following Marxist Luxemburg, calls a process of 'accumulation by dispossession', capitalism has resulted in a form of enclave development whereby wealth and power is concentrated in certain regions of the world (the core) and within a super-class (Rothkopf 2009) of a few thousand people (the core within the core). The rest of the (mainly post-colonial) world continues to be characterised by extreme inequality, poverty and dispossession, with a few exceptions. While rapid economic growth in parts of the semi-periphery, particularly the BRICS countries (Brazil, Russia, India, China and South Africa), threatens to spread this wealth and power in the supposedly great levelling process called 'globalisation', this amounts to little more than enlarging the core within the periphery, without significantly altering the global or national core-periphery division of labour, wealth and power (Amin 2008; Wallerstein 1979).

The only exceptions to this scenario have been in parts of South East Asia (most notably Japan and the Asian tigers South Korea, Taiwan, Singapore and Hong Kong), under special geo-political conditions during the cold war. The expectation that this model of state-led development, based on rapid industrialisation, can spread to the rest of the world, is more hope than reality. The reality, in fact, is that this model, based on non-renewable sources of energy, seems as doomed as the free market (or neoliberal) model. Any 'solution' to the capitalist poly-crisis (the intertwined social and natural limits) that is not holistic will be piecemeal and of benefit to the few who have already concentrated wealth into their own hands – green, gated communities behind immigration walls in developed countries, or fenced-off wealthy suburbs in islands of excess amidst seas of poverty. If one leaves aside the immorality of growing social inequality, this is a recipe for instability on a national and global scale.

In other words, the natural limits to growth cannot be addressed without confronting the social contradiction arising out of the accumulation process – namely, the social relations of production. For ecological Marxists, the socio-economic and ecological crises have a common origin – industrial capitalism – and ultimately, a lasting solution to these crises cannot be found within capitalism. The very nature of capitalism needs to be transcended to find solutions for all of humanity, in harmony with the natural environment. The question is, what does this mean in practice?

If Marx is still relevant to the analysis of fossil capitalism, does it then follow that his belief in socialism/communism, as a form of sustainable human development (Foster 2009; Burkett 2005) is also still relevant? In other words, is sustainable human development for all only realisable under communism? If so, and if 'communism' is *not* the state-dominated authoritarian experiment in 'actually existing socialism', where democracy was emptied of most of its content, what is it? Does it include a role for the market and the state, or is it an ideal of workers'/citizens' self-management that will always remain an aspiration rather than a realisable utopia? Foster and Burkett do not directly address these questions – except to point to the potential inherent in the Latin American movements towards 'twenty-first-century socialism', as well as the participatory planning achievements of the Indian state Kerala and the Brazilian city of Porto Alegre (Foster 2009). These 'islands of hope', including Cuba's widely admired organic urban community gardens, remain fragile amidst 'the class and imperial war imposed from above by the larger system' (Foster 2009: 276). The exact shape of a future where the state and market are subordinated to society remains a question of struggle and further theoretical reflection, as an open-ended set of questions in keeping with Marx's approach to continuous critical enquiry (see Wright 2010).

The red-brown-green alliance those in the environmental justice movement are calling for (Cock 2007) is a deep engagement, based on mutual respect, between Marxists (red) and environmentalists that are engaged in both urban ecological struggles dealing with pollution and waste issues (brown) as well as the more traditional conservation issues (green). It is a recognition that while Marx and Engels may have had an ecological imagination that permeated their thinking, they could not have foreseen the depth, extent and complexity of the multifaceted ecological crisis facing the planet. As much as environmentalists need to infuse their understanding of ecological crises with a class perspective (Magdoff and Foster 2011), so do Marxists need to build on the insights of Marx and Engels, with a deeper understanding of ecological crises and the natural limits to growth (Angus 2009; Pepper 1992). For this alliance in struggle to succeed, it must combine with a necessary convergence of research and thinking between natural and social scientists.

CONCLUSION

Terry Eagleton, in his book *Why Marx was Right* (2011), argues that to be a Marxist does not mean agreeing with everything Marx has written. However, he asserts that Marx was right enough of the time about enough important issues, including the natural environment and its relationship to capitalism, the historical object he was the first to identify, 'to show how it arose, by what laws it worked, and how it might be brought to an end' (xi). The foundational insight of his work remains critical for as long as capitalism exists as a crisis-prone system based on incessant accumulation and the exploitation of land (that is the natural environment) and labour, which are for Marx the original sources of all value.

An eco-Marxist or eco-socialist school of thought is emerging to give added depth to the growing belief that capitalism may be reaching its natural limits. The ecological consequences of hyper-accumulation have become so apparent that few dare ignore it.

The work of ecological Marxists, in particular that of Burkett and Foster, has sparked considerable interest around the world – particularly in China which, despite its drift towards state capitalism in recent decades, is still officially a 'socialist' or 'Marxist' state, increasingly grappling with the ecological contradiction. Zhihe Wang (2012) notes that since 2001 there has been an explosion of articles published in this area, from 45 during the period 1991 to 2000, to 598 during the 2001 to 2010 period, as well as 9 books, 75 MA theses and 15 doctoral dissertations. Wang (2012: 2) observes:

> Today ecological Marxism is part of the totality of Marxism in China. Ecological Marxism is regarded by some Chinese Marxists as not only 'one of the most influential movements in contemporary Western Marxism' and 'a new development of Marxism', but also as 'a very important force among various ecological theories'. Some Marxist scholars even argue that ecological Marxism is 'the most creative aspect of American Marxist Philosophy'.

In South Africa, there is a growing awareness within the labour movement about the links between capitalism and the ecological crisis – outstripping that of the SACP, which a few years back began linking the economic and ecological crises (see Bond 2009; Cronin 2009) before becoming immersed in government and endorsing tame green policies such as the New Growth Path, which subordinates sustainability to the logic of accumulation. The National Union of Metalworkers of South Africa (Numsa), one of the largest affiliates of the Congress of South African Trade Unions (Cosatu), is at the forefront of an emerging ecological Marxist perspective. Its president recently declared that 'it must always be clear that capitalism has caused the crisis of climate change that we see today. There is an urgent need to situate the question of climate change in a class struggle perspective' (Gina 2011). This echoes the thinking of an embryonic formation, the Democratic Left Front (2011) which explicitly promotes an eco-socialist form of politics.

Of course, in both China and South Africa the prospects of ecological Marxism becoming dominant forms of thinking are as yet remote. China may be ruled by a communist party, but its adherence to Marxism is questionable, even though Marxism remains the official doctrine and Marxist studies are promoted. Nevertheless, the emergence of an ecological Marxism has begun to challenge the dominant growth-at-all-costs perspective, as China increasingly comes to terms with the ecological costs of rapid growth.

In South Africa, Numsa's strident anti-capitalism is constrained by its alliance, through Cosatu, with the ruling party, the African National Congress and the SACP, which obliges it to, at best, negotiate policies that seek greater state intervention in the economy, as opposed to a more substantive democratic, holistic developmental path. In other words, in both China and South Africa, the best that can be hoped for in the immediate future is some form of social-democratic 'new deal', whereby the excesses of capitalism are regulated at the global and national levels.

Whether one adopts a green 'new deal' perspective, or a more radical eco-socialist perspective, both pose fundamental challenges to capitalism's growth-at-all-costs tendencies. The transcending of capitalism is of course not on the immediate agenda – although in parts of Latin America, countries like Bolivia and Ecuador have given the earth constitutional rights, with strong support from rural indigenous communities (within the highly contested framework of pursuing twenty-first-century socialism in alliance with Venezuela, Nicaragua and Cuba – as well as the political support of Brazil, Argentina and Uruguay). These experiments are hemmed in by global constraints and the temptation of urban elites to pursue extractive development paths, in order to more quickly deliver social benefits to the population.

Whether or not a 'green new deal' is pursued as a stepping stone towards more fundamental options in the longer term, it is worthwhile remembering these words of Bolivian President Evo Morales (2009: 168):

> It is nothing new to live well. It is simply a matter of discovering the ways of our forebears and putting an end to the kind of thinking that encourages individualistic egoism and the thirst for luxury. Living well is not living better at the expense of others. We need to build a communitarian socialism in harmony with the Mother Earth.

NOTES

1   The former right-wing president of France, Nicolas Sarkozy, had a moment of rare insight in 2008, during the height of the financial crisis.
2   In one sense, all humans are 'anthropocentric' in that we conceptualise the world through a human lens, even when we advocate extreme eco-centric views that seemingly pit nature against humans. The only human community that comes close to true 'eco-centrism' are the Jains in India, who refuse to harm any living creature whatsoever. Here we distinguish between a 'hard' anthropocentrism that seeks the domination and exploitation of nature, with little or no regard for its sustainability and softer versions that seek greater harmony between humans and the natural environment. The term 'anthropocentric' is used here in the harder sense.
3   Amongst Marxists there is a long-standing debate about whether these regimes were more state socialist or state capitalist – the term 'statism' leaves this debate open. Neither critical Marxists nor the Soviet regimes themselves ever called their systems 'communist' – this was a stage of statelessness for the long-term future.
4   Since the SACP became enmeshed in the Zuma administration after 2007, it has acted less as a 'social democratic' party in the radical sense of the term and more as left fig-leaf for the continuation of neoliberal policies under the guise of the 'national-democratic revolution', even supporting authoritarian moves to narrow democratic space in the country. On the other hand, the Communist Party of India (Marxist) in Kerala, despite its recent internal problems which saw it removed from power, has promoted participatory democratic forms of governance that took it way beyond traditional social democracy (see Williams 2008).
5   This remark was made at a Global Labour University workshop in Johannesburg, 22 September 2009.
6   This is derived from Foster (2009).
7   As Foster (1999: 136) points out, the word *Idiotes* in ancient Greek meant 'to be cut off from public life'. In addition, in *The German Ideology* (1932) Marx and Engels referred to the division between town and country as a form of division between mental and manual labour, resulting in a restricted town-animal (cut off from nature) and a restricted country-animal (cut off from 'all world intercourse, and consequently from all culture' [quoted in Foster 1999: 137]).
8   Foster (2009) likens domination to the desire to exploit and crush, while mastery is more subtle – such as the mastery of the violin, where the musician lovingly learns how to harmonise his inner being with the laws of the instrument.

REFERENCES

Altvater, A. 2006. 'The social and natural environment of fossil capitalism'. In *Socialist Register 2007: Coming to Terms with Nature*, edited by C. Leys and L. Panitch. New Delhi: LeftWord Books.

Amin, S. 2008. 'Preface'. In *Labour and the Challenges of Globalisation: What Prospects for Transnational Solidarity?*, edited by A. Bieler, I. Lindberg and D. Pillay. London: Pluto Press.

Angus, I. 2009. *The Global Fight for Climate Justice: Anticapitalist Responses to Global Warming and Environmental Destruction*. London: Resistance Books.

Arrighi, G. 2007. *Adam Smith in Beijing*. London: Verso.

Baran, P. and Sweezy, P. 1968. *Monopoly Capitalism*. Harmondsworth: Penguin.

Barry, J. 2004. *Environment and Social Theory*. London: Routledge.

Bell, M. 2012. *An Invitation to Environmental Sociology*. London: Sage.

Benton, T. (ed.). 1996. *The Greening of Marxism*. London & New York: Guilford Press.

Bond, P. 2009. 'Comments on "The current financial crisis and possibilities for the Left" by Jeremy Cronin'. Accessed 15 June 2010, http://www.ukzn.ac.za/ccs/default.asp?2,68,3,1681.

Brenner, R. 2009. 'Overproduction not financial collapse is the heart of the crisis: The US, East Asia, and the world'. Interview with Jeong Seong-jin, *The Asia-Pacific Journal*, 6 (1).

Bruno, K. and Karliner, J. 2004. *Earthsummit.biz: The Corporate Takeover of Sustainable Development*. Oakland: Food First Books.

Burkett, P. 2005. *Marxism and Ecological Economics*. Leiden: Brill.

Clapp, J. and Dauvergne, P. 2008. *Paths to a Green World*. New Delhi: Academic Foundation.

Cock, J. 2007. *The War Against Ourselves: Nature, Power and Justice*. Johannesburg: Wits University Press.

Cockburn, A. 2011. 'In Fukushima's wake: How the Greens learned to love nuclear power', *New Left Review*, 68: 75–79.

Cronin, J. 2009. 'The current financial crisis and possibilities for the Left'. Joe Slovo Memorial Lecture, Chris Hani Institute, 28 January. Accessed 15 June 2010, http://www.ukzn.ac.za/ccs/default.asp?2,68,3,1681.

Darwin, C. (1859) 2012. *Origin of the Species*. London: HarperCollins.

Democratic Left Front. 2011. 'Unite to make another South Africa and world possible!' Pamphlet issued by the National Convening Committee for the first national conference of the Democratic Left, Wits University, Johannesburg, 20–23 January.

Draper, H. 1978. *Karl Marx's Theory of Revolution: The Politics of Social Classes*. New York: Monthly Review Press.

Dullien, S., Herr, H. and Kellerman, C. 2011. *Decent Capitalism: A Blueprint for Reforming our Economies*. London: Pluto Press.

Eagleton, T. 2011. *Why Marx was Right*. New Haven & London: Yale University Press.

Foster, J.B. 1999. *Marx's Ecology*. New York: Monthly Review Press.

Foster, J.B. 2002. *Ecology Against Capitalism*. New York: Monthly Review Press.

Foster, J.B. 2009. *The Environmental Revolution*. New York: Monthly Review Press.

Foster, J.B., Clark, B. and York, R. 2010. *The Ecological Rift: Capitalism's War on the Earth*. New York: Monthly Review Press.

Foster, J.B. and Magdoff, F. 2009. *The Great Financial Crisis*. New York: Monthly Review Press.

Friedman, T. 2008. *Hot, Flat and Crowded*. London: Allan Lane.

Fukuyama, F. 1992. *The End of History and the Last Man*. New York: Avon Books.

Gina, C. 2011. Opening address to the Numsa International Seminar on Climate Change and Class Struggle, Durban, 4 December.

Gore, A. 2009. *Our Choice: A Plan to Solve the Climate Crisis*. London, Berlin & New York: Bloomsbury.

Gramsci, A. 1971. *Selections from Prison Notebooks*. London: Lawrence and Wishart.

Hallowes, D. 2011. *Toxic Futures: South Africa in the Crises of Energy, Environment and Capital*. Pietermaritzburg: UKZN Press.

Harvey, D. 2005. *The New Imperialism*. Oxford: Oxford University Press.

Harvey, D. 2010. *The Enigma of Capital*. London: Profile Books.

Klein, N. 2008. *The Shock Doctrine: The Rise of Disaster Capitalism*. London: Penguin.

Kovel, J. 2002. *The Enemy of Nature: The End of Capitalism or the End of the World?* London: Zed Books.

Magdoff, H. and Foster, J.B. 2011. *What Every Environmentalist Needs to Know about Capitalism*. New York: Monthly Review Press.

Marx, K. (1887) 1954. *Capital: A Critique of Political Economy (Vol. 1)*. London: Lawrence and Wishart.

Marx, K. (1894)1981. *Capital: Volume 3*. London: Penguin.

Marx, K. and Engels, F. (1848/1888) 1999. 'Manifesto of the Communist Party'. In *A World to Win: Essays on the Communist Manifesto*, edited by P. Karat. New Delhi: LeftWord Books.

McLellan, D. 1979. *Marxism after Marx*. London: Macmillan.

Morales, E. 2009. 'How to save the world, life and humanity'. In *People First Economics*, edited by D. Ransom and V. Baird. Oxford: New Internationalist Publications.

O'Connor, J. 1998. *Natural Causes: Essays in Ecological Marxism*. New York: Guilford Press.

Pepper, D. 1992. *Eco-Socialism: From Deep Ecology to Social Justice*. London: Routledge.

Perry, A. 2010. *Falling off the Edge: Globalization, World Peace and Other Lies* (second edition). London: Pan Books.

Polanyi, K. 1944. *The Great Transformation*. Boston: Beacon Press.

Ponting, C. 2007. *A New Green History of the World*. London: Vintage Books.

Rothkopf, D. 2009. *Superclass: How the Rich Ruined Our World*. London: Abacus.

Singh, R. 2010 *Struggle for Socialism: Some Issues*. Delhi: Aakar Books.

Urry, J. 2011. *Climate Change and Society*. Cambridge: Polity Press.

Wallerstein, I. 1979. *The Capitalist World-Economy*. Cambridge: Cambridge University Press.

Wang, Z. 2012. Ecological Marxism in China, *Monthly Review*, 63 (9). Accessed 13 March 2012, http://monthlyreview.org/2012/02/01/ecological-marxism-in-china.

Wheen, F. 1999. *Karl Marx*. London: Fourth Estate.

White, R. 2004. *Controversies in Environmental Sociology*. Cambridge: Cambridge University Press.

Williams, C. 2010. *Ecology and Socialism: Solutions to Capitalist Ecological Crisis*. Chicago: Haymarket Books.

Williams, M. 2008. *The Roots of Participatory Democracy*. London: Palgrave.

Wright, E.O. 2010. *Envisioning Real Utopias*. London: Verso.

CRISES OF MARXISM IN AFRICA AND POSSIBILITIES FOR THE FUTURE

CHAPTER

7

RETROSPECT: SEVEN THESES ABOUT AFRICA'S MARXIST REGIMES

Daryl Glaser

Africa joined three other continents in the twentieth century's experiment in Marxist–Leninist governance. The first African regimes to claim Marxism as one source of inspiration were established in the late 1950s with the commencement of the European decolonisation of Africa, some forty years after Russia's October Revolution. The first orthodox Marxist–Leninist regimes appeared in the early 1960s, with the orthodox tide cresting in the mid- to late 1970s. The Marxist–Leninist regimes dissolved at the beginning of the 1990s, their dissolution by then just one moment in the global 'collapse of communism'. These regimes are of enduring historical interest, but their experience also yields lessons for those seeking a progressive or egalitarian way forward for twenty-first-century Africa.

The experience of Marxist–Leninist governance was disastrous by virtually any defensible metric. The lessons it offers for contemporary social democrats and democratic socialists are thus largely negative. New generations of activists and intellectuals in South Africa and elsewhere often seem too ready to forget or deny these in their rush to embrace slogans, concepts and iconography reminiscent of authoritarian rather than democratic socialism.

Bearing in mind both the historical interest value of Africa's Marxist regimes and the need, more than two decades after their demise, to learn what we can from their failures, I offer below seven theses about Africa's Marxist–Leninist governments and the movements undergirding them.

The theses refer to the doctrines and practices of parties, movements and political currents that claimed to be Marxist and were guided to a significant degree by particular interpretations of Marxist theory. The chapter does not address academic Marxism, and it sidesteps the question of whether these regimes were 'truly' Marxist, whether they correctly interpreted the canon or indeed whether it constitutes a category error to refer to a regime as Marxist (as opposed to, say, popular-democratic or socialist). I do, however, conclude with some critical comments on Marxist theory as such and take the view that Marxist theory is probably implicated, along with other factors, in the failure of the 'Marxist regimes'.

THESIS ONE

There was no clear qualitative difference between the levels of radicalism displayed by the Marxist–Leninist regimes and the preceding African socialist ones.

Defenders of the African Marxist regimes generally viewed them as marking a clear break from the immediately preceding (and partly overlapping) phenomenon of 'African socialism', the movement that dominated the first phase of post-independence African governance. There certainly were differences between the two 'moments'. The 'African Marxist' regimes hewed more closely to Marxist–Leninist orthodoxy, both doctrinally and in their approach to party organisation. In contrast to the African socialist emphasis on mass parties and African communal solidarity, they established vanguard parties of the working class and girded for class struggle. Eschewing African socialism's celebration of a communalistic African personality and its goal of recovering the ethos of pre-colonial agrarian socialism, the African Marxists were for the most part relentlessly modernising and universalistic. They also established a tighter relationship with the Soviet Union and the socialist bloc than did the more non-aligned African socialists. The new cohort of African Marxists positioned themselves relative to the African socialists much as Marx and Engels had done vis-à-vis the utopian socialists, contrasting the scientific character of their approach with the eclecticism, romanticism and naiveté of the African socialists.[1]

One would be hard-pressed, though, to identify clear qualitative differences between the levels of social radicalism exhibited by the two types of regime. The more committed African socialist governments initiated programmes of nationalisation, rural cooperative-building and popular mobilisation that look pretty radical by today's lights. They were moreover not rustics: in key cases, like Kwame Nkrumah's Ghana and Ahmed Ben Bella's Algeria, they vigorously promoted programmes of industrialisation.[2] They did not believe that a dormant African egalitarianism stood ready to reassert itself the moment colonialism was thrown off; like the orthodox Marxists, they envisaged an active cultural effort to create a socialist 'new man'.[3] The assumption that they were consistently voluntaristic (or naively humanistic) is also false: the African socialist regimes were, like their Marxist successors, prone to authoritarianism and resorted to coercion of the peasantry. Confronted by peasants who appeared far less keen on socialism than the theory of African communalism had supposed them to be, Guinea's Sékou Touré and Tanzania's Julius Nyerere coerced them into villages (Ottoway and Ottoway 1986: 45–59). And while the African socialists maintained some distance from the Soviet bloc, the more radical amongst them were keen anti-imperialists and eager to secure their countries' independence from the capitalist world economy.

THESIS TWO

There was little difference between the levels of Marxist commitment, social radicalism or democratic zeal displayed by the coup-engendered military Marxist regimes and those that came to power via protracted guerrilla war.

The prominence of the military in African Marxism elicited controversy amongst both African civilian leftists and academic commentators. Marxist–Leninism came to power by military *coup d'état* in Congo-Brazzaville (1963), Mali (1968), Somalia (1969), Dahomey (1972), which was later renamed Benin, Ethiopia (1974), Madagascar (1975) and Upper Volta (1983), later renamed Burkina Faso. Marxist military takeover was not envisaged in the Marxist classics; nor did it acquire, like guerrilla war, a subsequent iconic status in Marxist revolutionary theory. It involved armed forces delivering revolution from on high rather than the people securing it from below. Leftist critics saw soldiers as more likely to install regimentation than participatory democracy. The military's uneven acquaintance with Marxism, its weak popular roots and preoccupation with power certainly made soldiers improbable bearers of socialist deliverance (Giorgis 1990: 54; Halliday and Molyneux 1981: 35–38). Perhaps not surprisingly, quite a few academic observers concluded that these regimes were not really Marxist. They were thus denied recognition of their leftist authenticity in the same way that earlier African socialists had been.[4]

These critics underestimated the Marxist–Leninist commitments of military leaders, just as many had earlier underestimated the seriousness of the radical African socialists. There are no grounds for thinking that the military regimes were more authoritarian, or less authentically Marxist, than those established by guerrilla war. These regimes *were* authoritarian, acted pragmatically rather than ideologically in certain instances, were vulnerable to coups and warlordism and spent a lot on the military. But the same could be said of, for example, Angola's ruling Popular Movement for the Liberation of Angola (MPLA) in the 1980s. Military-ruled Somalia set aside ideological affinity to invade Marxist Ethiopia – but the non-African cases of China and Vietnam remind us that Marxist–Leninist regimes brought to power by mass-based guerrilla war also invaded Marxist-ruled neighbours (Vietnam and Cambodia respectively).

The fact is that officers, especially in junior ranks, were often highly radicalised. Some, like Captain Thomas Sankara of Burkina Faso, were politicised in advance of the revolutionary process while others, like Benin's Lieutenant-Colonel Mathieu Kérékou, swung left in the course of it.[5] In Congo, Ethiopia and Madagascar, arguably also in Benin, the military came to power as part of popular movements.[6] Once in power they cooperated or competed with civilian leftists on matters ideological, generally with radicalising effect (Ayele 1990: 16–17; Covell 1987: 6; Keller 1988: 192, 196). Military leaders issued symbolically important Marxist–Leninist pronouncements, notably the Derg's Programme for the National Democratic Revolution, Madagascar's Revolutionary Charter, Sankara's 'Political orientation speech' and General Mohamed Siad Barre's 'Blue-and-white-book'.[7] Aware that rule by soldiers violated Marxist canons, military governments also constructed ostensibly civilian Marxist–Leninist parties. While in Congo and Somalia the transition from military to civilian-party rule was a façade, in Benin and Madagascar it marked a genuine if incomplete process of civilianisation.[8] Finally – the proof of the socialist pudding, some might say – military governments instituted central planning, widespread nationalisation and serious efforts to improve health, education and literacy.[9] Where the military-civilian government in Madagascar deviated from the Leninist script it was in order to preside over the most pluralistic Marxist regime in Africa.

The other route to power for African Marxists was guerrilla warfare. Armed struggle broke out in countries where intransigent regimes – colonial and African, white and black – refused to relinquish colonies (Portugal, independent Morocco), abandon white minority rule (Rhodesia, South Africa), grant regional autonomy (Ethiopia, post-independence Sudan) or stem human rights violations and ethnic favouritism (independent Uganda). Anti-colonial guerrilla war brought to power the MPLA in Angola (1975), the African Party for the Independence of Guinea and Cape Verde (PAIGC) (1975), the Front for the Liberation of Mozambique (Frelimo) (1975), the Zimbabwe African National Union (Zanu) (1980) and the South West African People's Organisation (Swapo) in Namibia (1990). Guerrilla war played some part in the victory of the African National Congress (ANC) in South Africa (1994). The Eritrean People's Liberation Front (EPLF) won independence for Eritrea (1991) following a guerrilla war against Marxist–Leninist Ethiopia. Guerrilla war also enabled the Tigray People's Liberation Front (TPLF) to gain power in Ethiopia at the head of a multinational Ethiopian People's Revolutionary Democratic Front (EPRDF) in 1991, the National Resistance Movement (NRM) to win power in Uganda in 1986 and forces originating in the Sudan People's Liberation Movement (SPLM) to achieve independence for South Sudan in 2011. Of these various formations, only MPLA and Frelimo set up Marxist–Leninist regimes or made a serious effort to implement socialism. Several others were Marxist or Marxist-oriented at some point before achieving power (PAIGC, Zanu, Swapo, EPLF, TPLF, NRM, SPLM and the ANC) but never tried or else failed to establish recognisably socialist states or economic systems. Zanu's post-2000 re-radicalisation is, at best, an arguable exception to this rule (I will return to this later). An originally Marxist-orientated guerrilla movement, the Popular Front for the Liberation of the Saguia el Hamra and Rio de Oro (Polisario), is still contending for power (though currently only diplomatically) in Western Sahara. It does not intend to establish a socialist regime.

With arguable exceptions such as the ANC in the early 1960s, Africa's leftist guerrilla movements sought power by waging a variant of the people's war strategy developed by Mao Zedong, General Vo Nguyên Giáp and others in Asia, rather than the more elitist and militaristic *foco* warfare associated with guerrilla movements in Cuba and South America (Munslow 1986: 8–9; Young 1997: 33). People's war entailed extensive political preparation of the peasantry, who supplied the physical force behind armed struggle, the privileging of political leadership over military command and the establishment of 'liberated zones' in which movements could establish rear bases and build embryonic socialist orders. Frelimo and PAIGC were the most successful in securing liberated zones; other groups achieved more brittle or fleeting successes.[10] The PAIGC's Amilcar Cabral, exponent of petit bourgeois 'class suicide' and 'returning to the source' to live amongst the peasantry, became Africa's most famed contributor to the theory of this kind of warfare.[11]

For their admirers in the 1970s and early 1980s, the movements that had engaged in people's war were definitely to be taken more seriously as Marxists than either the reformist first wave of African socialists or the later Marxist military regimes (Ethiopia perhaps excepted).[12] According to some commentators, Frelimo, MPLA and PAIGC in particular, were products of a 'logic of protracted struggle' that inculcated democratic habits and socially transformative zeal. Because these movements depended on peasant support, they understood the value of popular participation and because their leaders had to fight so long and hard, honing their politics along the way in rivalry with reformist or reactionary elements, they were likely to be theoretically more astute and committed. In contrast to the African socialists, they were genuinely radical; in contrast to the military Marxists, they were, at least potentially, authentically democratic. Having already roused the population from passivity, their reconstruction efforts were moreover likely to benefit, post-revolution, from a release of popular energy.[13]

Viewed retrospectively, these positive claims made for 'protracted struggle' and 'people's war' seem unconvincing. It is far from clear, for example, that the guerrilla movements were less militaristic than the Marxist military regimes. It may be no coincidence that Africa's most successful anti-colonial guerrilla army, the PAIGC's Revolutionary Armed Forces of the People (FARP), provided a base for opposition to the first post-colonial government, that of Cabral's brother Luís, which it overthrew in 1980 (Dhada 1993: 138); or that the leader then installed, Joao Vieira, was himself deposed in the course of a bloody civil war in 1999. The MPLA, for its part, assigned substantial areas of Angola to military control in the 1980s, spent an estimated seventy per cent of government revenue on its armed forces and was besieged by recurrent warlordism both in opposition and power (Ciment 1997: 130, 160; Somerville 1986: 65).

It is also striking how little the experience of liberated zones did to entrench post-independence democratic practice or to cement a lastingly sympathetic relationship between Marxist governments and the peasants they had earlier depended upon. Frelimo, for example, discarded the participatory priorities and pro-peasant orientation of its guerrilla-war days to set up, post-1975, a centralised pro-industrial regime willing to employ coercion against its rural subjects. It is anyway doubtful whether the liberated zones were ideal incubators of future democratic practice. The exigencies of warfare were as likely to inculcate habits of military command as they were to cultivate democratic instincts. And finally, there is no evidence that Marxists honed by protracted struggle stuck to socialism any more tenaciously than military-Marxist or even African-socialist regimes when confronted by economic crises in the 1980s and the hard bargaining of international lending agencies.

THESIS THREE

While orthodox Marxism–Leninism was not imposed on Africa by external powers, its local champions were cultural outliers.

How did a European-hewed doctrine like Marxism make its way to Africa? It is certainly true that, as many alleged during the cold war, the international communist bloc provided important impetus. The Union of Soviet Socialist Republics (USSR or Soviet Union), the German Democratic Republic and Cuba were the key international Marxism-exporters. China – and Maoism – were early contenders, but fell by the wayside.[14] The Soviet bloc's capacity to provide military aid gave it significant leverage, especially with those (like the MPLA and Ethiopia's ruling Provisional Military Administrative Council, or Derg) who were fighting desperate wars for survival. There is also no doubt that the Soviets reinforced Leninist orthodoxy – for example, by encouraging the Ethiopian and Somali military governments to set up vanguard parties, offering political and technical education courses in the Soviet Union and supplying teachers versed in dialectical materialism to universities and ideological schools in Africa.[15] When the Soviet Union embarked on a path of pro-market reform and disentanglement from cold war proxy conflicts in the mid-1980s, Africa's Marxist regimes had little choice but to join its ideological retreat.

Yet it would be wrong to suppose that Africa's Marxist movements adopted Marxist policies in order to secure Soviet arms or Cuban troops. Their Marxism usually preceded the relationship with the Soviet bloc or developed independently of it. Tension occasionally broke out between Marxist governments and the Soviets, for example when the MPLA leadership suspected Moscow's hand in a 1977 coup attempt (Ciment 1997: 163–164; Keller 1988: 237, 268–270; Ottoway and Ottoway 1986: 5–10, 34). Marxist governments in Mozambique, Guinea-Bissau and Benin kept lines of communication open with the West in order to offset dependence on the Soviets, while others, like Angola, invited Western capitalists to help them develop extractive industries – much as African-socialist Guinea had done.[16] Nor, contra John Saul and others (Ottoway and Ottoway 1986: 80–81; Saul 1985: 28, 138, 145–146; Saul 1993b: 73), can the authoritarian tendencies of African Marxist regimes be ascribed in any substantial measure to Soviet-bloc influence: they were largely the home-grown product of African Leninism.

Nor did Marxist–Leninist regimes exhaust the list of external communist and leftist 'suppliers' of Marxism. Ironically, colonial networks themselves performed a vital part in Marxism's transmission to Africa. Activists in the colonies acquired a fair proportion of their Marxism through contact with communist and labour movements based in colonial metropoles. The contact occurred when African students studied in European capitals, notably in Lisbon in the case of the PAIGC and the MPLA and it occurred when European socialist and communist parties and trade union federations – especially French federations – established branches in the colonies. Touré, for example, started out as an organiser in the communist-dominated Confédération Générale du Travail. Much earlier, the British labour movement had closely influenced the beginnings of South African Marxism. Portugal implanted settlers whose numbers included a leftist anti-Salazarist fringe.

A second route that Marxism took to Africa passed via class, racial, ethnic and cultural outsiders living in African urban centres such as Brazzaville, Luanda, Bissau and the Rand in South Africa. These included educated sectors, notably students, teachers and sometimes civil servants; relatively privileged African *assimilados* in Lusophone Africa; mixed-race *mestiços* in Angola and Mozambique and Western Cape 'coloured' people in South Africa; and immigrants who were in important senses culturally distant from both black indigenes and established white settler populations, notably Indians in South Africa and the Portuguese colonies (many of the latter Goans) and Jews who emigrated to South Africa from the Russian Empire.[17] Universities also provided bases for an academic Marxism. These included notably the University of Dar es Salaam and various universities in South Africa, though academic Marxism was plugged into a network that extended to North America, Britain, France and the Netherlands (Bozzoli and Delius 1990; Turok 1986: 59–60). These various groups were educated enough to generate avid readers of Marxist texts and enjoyed cultural connections with a wider world. For *assimilados*, Marxism offered a formula for anti-colonial struggle that kept faith with Western modernity. White, Indian and *mestiço* leftists found in Marxism's prioritisation of class over race an analytic approach that did not associate them indelibly with the system of racial oppression (in the case of the white leftists) or exclude them from exercising an active and equal – critics would claim a more than equal – influence in struggles against colonialism and apartheid. Many South African Jewish immigrants, for their part, had previously belonged to the Russian labour movement, whose ideals they brought to the new country.[18]

Outsider groups like these, together with mostly small cores of organised workers (Allen 1989: 62, 68–69; Radu and Somerville 1989: 160), formed Marxist milieus in the capital cities of independent African states. These were to be found not only in African countries that 'went Marxist', but in many that did not (Turok 1986). The component groups of the radical milieus interacted dynamically with Marxists in power, cooperating with them in some cases, in others competing, sometimes violently (Allen 1989: 31–32, 68–69; Keller 1988: 177, 199–200, 218–219). The milieus also threw up a variety of 'left oppositions'.[19]

The anchorage of Marxist regimes in the radical, racially mixed milieus of capital cities goes some way to account for the distrust felt towards them among two groups: rural Africans and inhabitants of regions beyond capital-city hinterlands. Thus in Angola, the National Union for the Total Independence of Angola (Unita) appealed with some success to the resentments of African peasants, especially those located outside the MPLA's Kimbundu heartland. In Mozambique the Marxist southerners who dominated Frelimo contended with the suspicions of both northern Makonde traditionalists and Africanist leaders from the central regions.[20] The submersion of Marxist regimes in metropolitan milieus helps, further, to explain their modernist zeal. Marxist rulers were hostile to traditional authorities, religions and practices while favouring rapid industrialisation, high technology and large-scale mechanised farming.[21]

THESIS FOUR

Despite the orthodox Marxist–Leninists' insistence upon their unoriginality, Africa's Marxism exhibited some distinctive features.

Was there a distinctive African contribution to Marxist theory and practice?[22] Curiously, many of Africa's Marxist leaders answered this question emphatically in the negative. Arriving in the wake of the initial wave of African socialism, the new cohort of Marxist–Leninist leaders coming to power mainly in the 1970s insisted on their orthodoxy. If African socialists had sought a path to socialism that appealed to African particularity, the later cohort insisted that there could be no specifically African socialism or Marxism, that there was just one universal Leninist Marxism, albeit one that needed to be fitted to local conditions in Africa as everywhere else it was employed.

Yet the story of Marxism in Africa was not entirely bereft of original contributions.

First, African socialism's narrative cannot be cleanly separated from Marxism's. At least two of the most prominent African-socialist leaders, Touré and Nkrumah, viewed Marxism as a part of their theoretical lineage and Nkrumah became explicitly Marxist after being thrown out of power.[23] We can therefore choose to view African socialism as itself contributing – and as imparting originality – to African Marxism.

And doctrinally at least, African socialism was interesting and creative in both programme and organisational style. Its ideologues held that that the spirit of an essentially communalistic pre-colonial African society could be invoked by those building post-colonial societies. Africa's early communal experience (the theory went) qualified new African states to advance to socialism without passing through the period of capitalist development and class conflict that, according to Marxist orthodoxy, was supposed to precede it.

In addition, African socialists appealed to an essential African-ness (what Léopold Sédar Senghor called 'Negritude') in their efforts to mobilise popular energy behind economic development.[24] Negritude was one instance of an African-socialist appeal to humanistic themes, one that emphasised voluntarism and solidarity, sought alternatives to Western instrumental rationality and engaged intimately with the aesthetic, psychological and cultural as opposed (or in addition) to the material, economic and scientific tasks of the African liberation struggle.

Because they believed that Africa could attain socialism without class struggle, radical African socialists moreover organised mass parties rather than Leninist revolutionary vanguards. Nkrumah's Convention People's Party at one stage claimed a membership of 2 million in a total population of 4.7 million (Nkrumah 1964a: 105; Ottoway and Ottoway 1986: 15, 20). Guinea's Touré 'experimented with an enormous variety of institutions in his painful search for an overall system which would embody his vision of socialism' (Ottoway and Ottoway 1986: 55). His ruling Parti Démocratique du Guinée started life as a mass organisation, morphed into a vanguard party, re-emerged as a party for all the people and finally reinvented itself as a 'party-state'. In this last permutation it sought literally to dissolve the state by absorbing society into the party (Ottoway and Ottoway 1986: 52–59).

Second, and professions of conformity notwithstanding, some of the orthodox Marxist-Leninists themselves made distinctive practical and theoretical contributions to Marxism.

The very possibility of applying Marxist revolutionary theory to Africa and generally to the European colonial realm depended on innovation within Marxist theory, if not necessarily innovation led by African and other colonial subjects. Marxists, as bearers of a doctrine concerned with revolution under advanced capitalism, had to explain Marxism's relevance to Europe's underdeveloped colonies – and sub-Saharan Africa represented an acute instance of a region that was definitely not economically developed or even, outside South Africa, subject to the sort of 'combined and uneven' development that brought pockets of urban proletarian modernity to imperial Russia.

As is well known, Karl Marx and Friedrich Engels expected the proletarian revolution to break out and socialism to be established, in advanced capitalist societies. They allowed that societies with recently strong communal traditions (notably Russia) might be able to skip capitalism, but they never developed this thought into a theory (Cox 1966: 47–48; Marx 1881). Leon Trotsky and Vladimir Lenin took a different route to justify revolution in largely agrarian Russia: they argued that Russia had too weak a liberal bourgeoisie to establish a successful bourgeois-democratic order, yet just enough of capitalism and a working class to enable workers and peasants to take power. The nature of their revolution remained for long unclear, but Lenin came increasingly round to Trotsky's view that it would be socialist rather than bourgeois-democratic (Liebman 1975: 62–83, 180–189). While they believed Russia was ripe for revolution, both Lenin and Trotsky thought that the post-revolutionary state's survival, and certainly its flourishing, would depend on supportive proletarian revolutions breaking out in more advanced capitalist societies. It was the failure of these to materialise, and the prospect of an isolated socialist Russia, that prompted communists to turn their attention to the colonies (Cox 1966: 47–48; Drew 2000: 95; Padmore 1964: 225). Some began to think that the world capitalist system might be sooner and more successfully attacked at its weak colonial link than in its metropolitan heartland. During the 1920s, the Moscow-led Communist International threw its weight behind the aspiration of colonised people to national independence.

In the decades after World War II the Soviet Union and the international communist movement faced an exciting new circumstance: a decolonising Africa and Asia falling into the hands of post-colonial leaders who were often determined to build socialism. The Soviets remained orthodox enough Marxists to doubt whether the newly independent countries were ready to embark on socialist construction. They nevertheless adapted their theory sufficiently to enable them to take advantage of new opportunities to project Moscow's influence abroad. Soviet theorists began to argue in the 1950s that a 'non-capitalist' path of development had been opened for Third World countries by the presence of an international socialist bloc led by a relatively advanced Soviet Union. Later Soviet theorists posited the possibility of 'societies of socialist orientation'. While this theoretical refinement rationalised close ties with Marxist–Leninist regimes in Africa, its formulators remained somewhat doubtful about the prospects for socialism, as opposed to Moscow-friendly regimes, in Africa.[25] Naturally, the Soviet Union's proud Marxist–Leninist allies in Africa did not share their scepticism (Cox 1966: 49–50; Halliday and Molyneux 1981: 277–283; Keller 1987: 5–6; Somerville 1986: 194–196).

Africa's Marxist–Leninist leaders and attendant thinkers themselves mostly applied a single template to the continent. Though eager socialists, they acknowledged that Africa was not immediately capable of achieving full socialism, let alone communism. The initial phase of revolution was 'national democratic' and would yield what Marxist ideologues termed 'people's democracy' or 'people's democratic dictatorship'. People's democracy would eliminate feudal vestiges and, bypassing the capitalist stage of development, lay the basis for socialism and the dictatorship of the proletariat.[26] Political leadership during this stage would fall to a vanguard party representing an alliance of workers, peasants and the progressive petite bourgeoisie. Workers would be the leading element in the alliance but, in the absence of a substantial proletariat, their leading role would in effect be exercised by proxy through the party. This core class alliance might cooperate with other social elements where tactically necessary, but it would fight any existing or aspirant classes that blocked progress to socialism (Somerville 1986: 99). Such was, roughly speaking, the path that all 'societies of socialist orientation' were expected to ply according to a Marxist script shaped over decades by Lenin's theories of imperialism and national self-determination, the experience of popular-front politics in the 1930s through to the mid-1940s and post-war Soviet foreign policy. In this respect African Marxists had little distinctive to offer: they considered that the above represented a universal formula, albeit one that required local adjustments.

African-based academic Marxism was in some instances more independent-minded and willing to challenge orthodox Marxist templates, helping itself to theoretical advances within non-Soviet Western Marxism and reproducing some of its debates. For example, South African academe in the late 1970s and early 1980s saw debates between E.P. Thompson-style social historians and structuralists influenced by Louis Althusser and Nicos Poulantzas. With some notable exceptions (for example, the influence of Marxist academics on 'workerist' trade unionism in South Africa in the 1970s), academic Marxism was nonetheless marginal to actual political developments. Trotskyist groups too, were small, as were other left oppositions and in any case, most of these groups competed for the mantle of true Marxism–Leninism rather than seeking to challenge it. They sometimes invoked left-libertarian councilist and syndicalist strands within Marxism, but did not for the most part eschew party vanguardism or celebrate political pluralism.

Ironically, Africa's ostensibly orthodox Marxist regimes and movements may have displayed a greater originality. Perhaps the most idiosyncratic was General Siad Barre's attempt to synthesise Marxism and Islam (Samatar 1988: 108–109; Library of Congress c.2005).[27] The philosophico-theological innovations of Siad Barre echo, though within a more explicitly Marxist discourse, the earlier efforts of Algeria's Ben Bella and his successor Houari Boumedienne to develop an 'Arabo-Islamic' socialism (Humbaraci 1966: 90, 109, 237–270). While these amounted to explicit syntheses, most socialist and Marxist movements operating in Muslim-majority societies felt compelled to accommodate Islam to one degree or another. Notwithstanding his confrontation with the Muslim Brotherhood, Egypt's Gamal Abdel Nasser benefited from the theological support of the *ulema*, the country's official religious leaders (Woodward

1992: 35). And Islam remained the official religion, taught in schools, of the People's Democratic Republic of Yemen (Lackner 1985: 109–110).

The EPLF and TPLF made an interesting addition to Marxist thinking on the national question. The EPLF insisted that nations had a right to secession even from socialist states, while the TPLF proposed that African states should recognise national differences and constitute themselves where necessary on a multinational basis. In both cases the movements were invoking Leninist norms, but these were, at best, inconsistently applied in the Soviet Union and were positively frowned upon in post-independence Africa, with its insistence on ethnicity-transcending nation-building and its aversion to the rearrangement of existing state boundaries. The EPLF and TPLF took these ideas very seriously, as the former showed when it brought about Eritrean secession, the latter in its governing practice at the head of Ethiopia's ruling EPRDF (Pool 1979: 56–71; Young 1997: 214).

On an *institutional* level, Africa's most baleful innovation may appear to be military-coup Marxism. Although there have been non-African instances of Marxists coming to power by military coup (for example, Afghanistan and Grenada in the late 1970s), Africa was undoubtedly the chief exemplar of this form. Whether it was also a pioneer depends on how one classifies the economically nationalist, left-leaning regimes installed by militaries in countries such as Syria and Burma in the 1960s. While these regimes were not orthodox and explicitly Marxist they certainly bore kinship with some later African Marxist military regimes. The true prototype for this more hybrid left-nationalist form may however itself be in an African country: the socialist-oriented Nasserite regime in Egypt, established by a coup in 1952.

I have already mentioned another, earlier instance of institutional innovation, Touré's experimentation with the mass-party. This form, like the Marxist–Leninist party, assumed that popular democratic participation would unfold within a unitary polity, either within the ruling party or guided by it. A more pluralistic institutional innovation occurred in Madagascar. There, a military-civilian regime, in a formula possibly unique in the world, permitted a competitive multi-party democracy limited to socialist and Marxist parties. To qualify for admission to electoral politics, parties had to subscribe to a founding revolutionary document, the Charter of Malagasy Revolution. While the regime established its own party, the Avant Guard of the Malagasy Revolution (Arema), it joined its cooperative competitors in a National Front for the Defence of the Revolution (Covell 1987: 1–2, 60–62,

119). This pluralism-within-the-left arrangement instantiated the sort of politics that some more democratic-minded revolutionary leftists advocated from time to time in the last century. Malagasy Marxism was more generally eclectic; in the early 1980s, for example, it sought a philosophical rapprochement with Christianity, which in Madagascar had developed along fairly progressive lines.

Malagasy Marxists never turned their pluralistic formula into a theory: indeed many were Leninists who saw their political system as a temporary and rather unsatisfactory compromise dictated by circumstances. Even so it represented, by comparison with other, more rigid African Marxisms, a not wholly unattractive accident.

Few of these innovations had a lasting influence. Some, like Madagascar's, never spread beyond its country of origin. Others died with African socialism and African Marxism. If there is a Marxist African revolutionary who still holds many in his thrall it is probably Frantz Fanon, the Martinique-born, adoptively Algerian revolutionary thinker. Fanon's unorthodox Marxism, originating in the moment of African socialism and in Marxist existentialism and humanism, speaks directly to the contemporary intellectual climate of the radical left. His defence of violence as therapeutic is generally downplayed by his current supporters for normatively good reasons, but it placed him alongside Georges Sorel as one of the two most explicit and striking celebrants of violence within the history of left-wing revolutionary thought. Fanon's anticipation that the African nationalist elite would sell out the revolution, replacing the colonial oppressor with a new indigenous one, is generally taken as prescient. Perhaps the main reason for Fanon's renewed popularity is that he speaks to 'post-colonialist' theoretical concerns with the West's discursive construction of the Other. Fanon's depiction of colonialism as a psychopathological force that crushes indigenous cultures and induces natives to internalise the objectifying white gaze serves as one important starting point for the identity-based, sometimes nationalist-tinged cultural politics that seems to have expanded into the activist-cum-intellectual space vacated by economistic Marxism. Exactly what socio-historical alternative Fanonism offers, beyond a general exhortation to resist cultural colonialism and post-independence leadership betrayal, remains up for debate.[28]

THESIS FIVE

The failure of the Marxist–Leninist regimes was a product of flawed domestic choices rather than of 'scarcity plus encirclement'.

The life of African Marxism was pretty short. Most of the Marxist regimes were set up in the mid-1970s and most had begun to liberalise economically by the mid-1980s. During 1990 and 1991 almost all of them renounced Marxism and embraced representative democracy (Hall and Young 1997: 202–219; Hodges 2001: 50–59, 70–102; Waterhouse 1996: 11). African socialism's commencement dated back further – to the later 1950s – but its remaining regimes followed a similar trajectory of decline and redefinition in the later 1980s and early 1990s. The overwhelming consensus amongst participants and observers was that the Marxist and African-socialist experiments had both failed. None of the socialist economies had escaped underdevelopment; some ended the 1980s amongst the world's most destitute.

As earlier noted, formerly Marxist or Marxist-influenced movements that came to power in the 1980s and 1990s did not even attempt to institute socialist experiments. Some might see in Zimbabwe's post-2000 land seizures a reprise of the 'Marxist-Leninist-Maoist' radicalism of Robert Mugabe's guerrilla-war days, but the episode is better understood (ideologically speaking) as an instance of crisis-driven racial nationalism.[29] Whatever the precise ideological content of Zanu's radicalism, its economic results have been calamitous and there is little evidence of either a popular or an elite push across Africa to replicate it.

So what happened to the attempt to build socialism in Africa? And does its abandonment offer lessons for attempts in the current (unpropitious) time to advance a left-social democratic project, in Africa or elsewhere?

It is possible to identify a range of factors that contributed to the failure of the African socialist and African Marxist regimes.

Some of these fit the classic 'scarcity plus encirclement' scenario that sympathisers often use to explain the difficulties faced by leftist governments. Socialist governments in Africa inherited undeveloped agrarian economies in which growth had centred on a few enclaves. Colonial education systems gener-ated scandalously few skilled people, the ranks of whom were further depleted when settlers and expatriates in Guinea-Conakry, Mozambique and Angola fled after independence. A long history of land degradation in the Ethiopian highlands was at least contributory to the famine of 1983–1986 in which a million people died (Kebbede 1992; Ottoway 1990: 4). The MPLA and Frelimo faced extremely costly, externally backed armed insurgencies that wrecked promising social programmes. Ethiopia was invaded by US-backed Somalia in 1977 and challenged from within by armed secessionists; the Somali regime and the Derg were both finally toppled by insurgents in 1991. Angola and the Horn of Africa became cold-war battlegrounds while apartheid South Africa spread 'destabilisation' across much of southern Africa. Though commentators from the late 1980s began, properly, to underline the extent to which socialist governments brought their difficulties upon themselves (Kaure 1999: 2–3; Saul 1993a), inherited underdevelopment and (once underway) military pressure were enough on their own to render economic reconstruction formidably difficult under any ideological rubric.

Endogenous failings were nevertheless many. One was a radical impatience that led African socialists and Marxists to require too much, too soon of states that were hampered by insufficient skilled personnel and other resources.[30] Overconfident socialist rulers did not hesitate to vest the central planning of entire economies in the hands of flimsy state systems. They also overestimated the capacity of their societies to industrialise rapidly from a low base in a context of capital and skill shortages and limited economies of scale. The fallout of this over-ambition included bureaucratic paralysis, loss-making enterprises and, in several cases, high levels of debt. Given what we know now about the necessity for some sort of market under feasible socialism, it would have been more prudent for these governments to provide space for private enterprise while developing the state's capacity to collect revenue, supply social benefits, redistribute wealth and engage in overall economic steering. And given the costs and uncertainty attending large-scale, capital-intensive projects, it would have been more sensible not to take on external debt to finance them. Rapid debt accumulation was the undoing of socialism in Benin and Madagascar (Allen 1989; Covell 1987: 63–68).

In keeping with their radical ambition, socialist governments overestimated the ripeness of the countryside for fast-track socialism or indeed rapid modernisation. Socialist incumbents tried, understandably, to rearrange rural life to facilitate welfare provision, higher productivity, egalitarian land distribution and social cooperation – and in Ethiopia, in the mid-1980s, simply to avoid mass starvation (Kebbede 1992: 79–84). The methods they chose to achieve these objectives were generally disliked by rural populations. It is not that the peasants were pro-capitalist: they did not, for the most part, want a free market in land and opposed attempts by the TPLF in Ehtiopia and Frelimo in Mozambique to introduce one in the 1990s; they mostly welcomed redistribution of land from state holdings and big landowners (Ottoway and Ottoway 1986: 139–142; Waterhouse 1996: 23; Young 1997: 198–199). At the same time, peasants did not usually wish to work on cooperatives or collective farms or, in Ethiopia, to be relocated to supposedly more fertile land hundreds of miles away. Faced with peasant reluctance to join such arrangements, Marxist governments, like some of their African-socialist predecessors, resorted to force.[31] Many peasants also resented the way urban-based leaders disparaged entrenched animist beliefs and sidelined traditional leaders, often coercively.

Peasant agriculture suffered from a range of factors that were not fully under state control, from drought and war to shortages of capacity, but the use of coercion against peasants must be counted as a reckless forfeiture of goodwill. If there is a clear message from countries like Mozambique, but also, say, Afghanistan under the Soviets, it is that urban elites need to treat the countryside and its ways with care, employing methods of consultation and persuasion wherever possible rather than force, in realising modern values. Alienation of peasants directly fuelled armed opposition in Mozambique, Angola and Ethiopia and passive non-cooperation in other cases.

It is generally striking how ready Marxist regimes were to alienate, gratuitously, whole swathes of the societies they sought to govern. Until the mid-1980s the governments of Mozambique and (to a lesser degree) Angola harassed already suspicious Christian churches, guaranteeing their outright hostility.[32] While foreign capital was courted, domestic capital often faced an undifferentiating animus. The honing of vanguard parties required systematic purges that isolated party elites from society (Hodges 2001: 48; Radu and Somerville 1989: 172–173; Somerville 1986: 56–57, 90, 92–95). Ethnic identity was demeaned, for example, by denial of indigenous language rights, while ethnic out-groups were under-represented in state bodies.[33] Eritrean demands for independence were ignored by a Derg determined to transform the Ethiopian empire into an effectively unitary state (Iyob 1995: 118–119; Keller 1988: 202–203, 240; Ottoway 1990: 607). Clearly, socialist governments were convinced that, in imposing modernisation, history was on their side. When things went wrong, they needed scapegoats. Nor should we forget how much more left-sympathetic was the temper of the 1960s and 1970s – a temper conducive to what Saul called 'cockiness' (Saul 1993b: 72–73). But whatever the explanation, the politics seem desperately inept.

A comprehensive diagnosis of African socialism and African Marxism's lack of success is made difficult because it lay at the intersection of two larger failures: of Marxist governance globally, and of African governance irrespective of ruling ideology. It is fair to say, though, that the African-socialist and Marxist regimes bore the imprint of both failures: those stemming from post-independence Africa's economic marginality, ethno-regional complexity and state weakness together with those engendered by Marxism–Leninism's totalitarian tendencies, centralising statism and ambitious industrial modernism.

THESIS SIX

The authoritarianism of the Marxist–Leninist regimes was a product less of their weak commitment to democracy than of their flawed theory of democracy.

African Marxism's failure was, to an important extent, a failure in its theory and practice of democracy. Socialist movements and regimes considered popular participation necessary to the realisation of democratic values and to the canalisation of popular energies into development tasks. Their democratic idealism impressed not a few observers, as did the neighbourhood committees, workplace councils, peasant associations and sectoral mass organisations established in liberated zones and within the jurisdiction of the new socialist states.[34] Some observers thought that this participatory democracy more than compensated for the absence of representative-democratic institutions. Yet it is clear, now, that this democracy was a sham. In the playing out of the dialectic between leadership and mass action referred to by Saul and others, a commandist concept of leadership seemed relatively quickly to win out once socialists were in power. The result was a downgrading of participatory democracy (Hall and Young 1997: 74–76; Ottoway and Ottoway 1986: 200–207; Saul 1990: 55). In many cases its demotion was prompted by the fact that factional opponents of the government or military – youth-wing militants in Congo, oppositionists in Benin's Committees for the Defence of the Revolution, leftist conspirators in Luanda's *poder popular*, the Ethiopian People's Revolutionary Party in Ethiopia's neighbourhood *kebeles* – had established bases in the participatory organs. In other cases participatory organs, like the *grupos dinamizadores* in

Mozambique and workers' self-management bodies in Algeria, Angola and Mozambique, were sacrificed to governments' scramble for discipline and centralised coordination.[35]

More important, these organs were part of a misconceived model of democracy in the first place. When African-socialist and African Marxist regimes spoke of participation they meant mobilisation of the population to realise collective ends, defined by a ruling party. To be sure, this might require popular input through discussion and criticism, and such input might influence the choice between regime-vetted candidates, the technical details of policies and even the clauses of constitutions.[36] But participants were not meant to, nor could they, challenge the ruling party or its ideological direction. For the regime, participatory bodies served primarily as venues to explain already-decided policies; alternatively, as mechanisms for co-opting dissent and subjecting the population to surveillance (Ciment 1997: 145). The so-called 'mass organisations' of youth, workers, women and others were designed, for their part, to function as transmission belts between the regime and the population.[37] With a few exceptions, no autonomous associations were allowed to develop outside them.[38] Nor were there other, compensating checks on the concentration of power. Elected national representative assemblies served as rubber stamps.[39] Leninist democratic centralism eviscerated internal party democracy (Giorgis 1990: 62–63; Radu and Somerville 1989: 192–193; Saul 1985: 78–79). Ruling parties were anyway invariably subordinated to powerful presidencies or (in Congo and Somalia) to military cabals.[40]

A deeper democratic philosophy informed the operation of the participatory bodies. The democracy the socialist regimes put in place was teleological rather than representative. Its architects sought a state structured around the singular goal of building socialism rather than one enabling citizens to choose among diverse collective projects. If the system 'represented' anyone it was not an actual, but an ideal, or higher people: that is, the people as they would think and act if they were free of false consciousness and able to apprehend their real interests or the real good of society. In this sense, Africa's socialist regimes made a Rousseauian distinction between the will of all and the general will, with the party embodying the latter thanks to its scientific grasp and far-sightedness.[41]

The theory and practice of democracy in African Marxist states (Madagascar apart) differed in no significant way from that operative in the generality of Marxist–Leninist regimes extant until 1989–1991. It can be described as the Leninist approach to democracy, legitimated by the particular interpretation that the Bolsheviks and subsequently the Communist Party of the Soviet Union gave to the often ambiguous work of Marx and Engels, generalised globally by the Comintern (Glaser 1999). In the end, this conception was not sustainable because it failed to take account of irreducible social diversity, whether of values or interests and because it left regimes open to delegitimation by enemies – Western governments, local insurgents – who plausibly portrayed them as oppressive dictatorships. In the early 1990s several (ex-) socialist governments and movements discarded the teleological democratic model in favour of a more open-ended, representative one. In these cases citizens can now, at least in principle, choose amongst competing collective projects embodied in rival programmes and parties. This is the framework, bereft of guarantees of power, in which socialist or social-democratic parties of the future will have to seek office. It means governing only with the revocable consent of actual, empirical peoples.

THESIS SEVEN

Marxism can have a useful future in progressive politics only as one ideological and discursive source amongst others.

It not only seems futile, but is morally wrong, to seek to resurrect the Marxist–Leninist state in the twenty-first century. In Africa, that form of state denied its people elementary democratic rights, bankrupted economies and, in the worst cases, brought in its tow civil war, interstate war and famine – all for highly questionable gains that could arguably have been secured (and then some) by more humane and democratic methods.

It does not follow that socialism, or indeed Marxism, has no place in a progressive contemporary politics. The fact that Africa's capitalism generates such vast venality and inequality is proof enough of the need for an opposition to the status quo that can offer a vision of a more egalitarian, participatory and caring future. Still, we should not think of that as a specifically Marxist, or even Marxist-inspired, future. Marxism has useful critical points to make about capitalism's crisis-prone nature, the human cost of hyper-commoditisation and profit-driven economics, the threat to democratic equality posed by unequal economic power and the failure of democracy to penetrate the 'hidden abode' of capitalist production. But Marxism also gets crucial things wrong. Reducing the political to class dynamics, it cannot comprehend the value of the so-called 'bourgeois' democratic liberties in limiting despotic power and enabling all citizens, the poor included, to organise in defence of their interests. Guided by a sense of history as impelled by material reality rather than ideas, it offers no comfortable space for moral and ethical reasoning, especially concerning the limits of what can be done to individuals in pursuing grand social goals. Marxism's immanent critique of the environmentally destructive consequences of self-propelled capital accumulation is vitiated by its preoccupation with the ever-expanding human productivity demanded by communism. Marxist theory offers little guidance on the organisation of a feasible socialist economy.

Because of these flaws and limits – the repercussions of most of which were visible in the period of African Marxist governance – Marxism is defensible today only as one ideological and discursive source amongst others within a democracy-respecting oppositional culture. Within such a culture, it can be joined in fruitful dialogue with democratic liberalism about the proper relationship between procedural and substantive democracy, with analytical political philosophy about the meaning of social justice and with social democracy, ecologism and other currents about the shape of a sustainable mixed economy harnessed to social needs. These are just some of the possible dialogic axes.

This last thesis has departed from the African materials, allowing itself a more general and prescriptive bent. But it is, I think, the upshot of any proper consideration of the African Marxist experiment with power, as well as of any more wide-ranging reflection upon the lessons of Marxist government and the limits of Marxist theory. It is thus the right way to conclude.

NOTES

1   See Nkrumah (1973: 77, 79, 82); Adamolekun (1976: 35); Ottoway and Ottoway (1986: 1, 25–30); Keller (1987: 3, 7–8, 11); Clapham (1988: 66); Radu and Somerville (1989: 173, 187); Hall and Young (1997: 61).

2   See Nkrumah (1963: 110, 119); Nkrumah (1964b: 260–262); Senghor (1965: 264); Ottoway and Ottoway (1986: 59–65).

3   See Nyerere (1964: 242); Dia (1964: 249); Nkrumah (1963: 124, 130); Nkrumah (1964b: 263).

4   See Covell (1987: 4–5, 158, 162); Clapham (1988: 81); Keller (1988: 191); Harbeson (1990).

5   See Allen (1989: 31–32, 62); Baxter and Somerville (1989: 248); Radu and Somerville (1989: 173); Ayele (1990: 15).

6   See Halliday and Molyneux (1981: 11–50); Ottoway and Ottoway (1986: 128); Covell (1987: 1–2, 161); Keller (1988: 173); Allen (1989: 31–32); Radu and Somerville (1989: 164–165); Ayele (1990: 15).

7   See Covell (1987: 97–100, 158); Clapham (1988: 66); Keller (1988: 197–198); Allen (1989: 50–51); Baxter and Somerville (1989: 249); Library of Congress (c.2005).

8   See Covell (1987: 115–119); Clapham (1988: 96); Samatar (1988: 110–113, 152–153); Allen (1989: 70–71, 121); Radu and Somerville (1989: 174–178, 200).

9   See Ottoway and Ottoway (1986: 151–152); Covell (1987: 100); Keller (1988: 219–223); Samatar (1988: 87–89, 98, 100–104); Allen (1989: 37); Baxter and Somerville (1989: 250); Radu and Somerville (1989: 189–190, 229).

10 See Chaliand (1980: 51); Houtart (1980: 99–107); Ottoway and Ottoway (1986: 71–72); Dhada (1993: 136–137).

11 See Cabral (1969: 71–72, 83–93); Cabral (1973: 59–64, 67–69); Cabral (1979: 44–46, 57–60, 85, 94–97, 143–153); Davidson (1979: xi); Cohen (1986: 50).

12 On Ethiopian exceptionalism, see Halliday and Molyneux (1981) and Lefort (1983).

13 See Machel (1980: 199); Davidson ([1969] 1981: 97–99); Davidson 1992: 296–308); Saul (1985: 9–10); Munslow (1986: 8–11).

14 See De Andrade (1979: xxix); Munslow (1986: 8–9); Ottoway and Ottoway (1986: 34); Keller (1988: 195); Radu and Somerville (1989: 172); Ciment (1997: 42); Hall and Young (1997: 62–63); Young (1997: 33, 77, 80, 84).

15 See Saul (1985: 28, 138, 145–146); Ottoway and Ottoway (1986: 6–10, 34, 80–81, 154–155); Somerville (1986: 26); Clapham (1988: 67–68, 84); Keller (1988: 266–267); Samatar (1988: 111); Saul (1993a: 73); Ciment (1997: 11, 128, 162); Hall and Young (1997: 62–63).

16 See Adamolekun (1976: 13); Ottoway and Ottoway (1986: 52–59, 118–119); Marcum (1987: 78); Allen (1989: 116, 129); Hanlon ([1984] 1990: 178–179, 234–236); Davidson (1992: 305); Ciment (1997: 168); Kaure (1999: 37–38).

17 See Marcum (1969: 37–41); De Andrade (1979: xxiii); Ottoway and Ottoway (1986: 69); Lewis (1987); Marcum (1987: 69); Clapham (1988: 65); Keller (1988: 176–177); Baxter and Somerville (1989: 247); Radu and Somerville (1989: 160); Allen (1989: 62); Ciment (1997: 11, 123, 128); Hall and Young (1997: 83–84); Kaure (1999: 29).

18 See De Andrade (1979: xxiii–xxiv); Ottoway and Ottoway (1986: 101); Ciment (1997: 38); Hall and Young (1997: 64–66, 73–74); Drew (2000: 24).

19 See Ottoway and Ottoway (1986: 134–137, 201); Somerville (1986: 48–53); Covell (1987: 124–127); Clapham (1988: 66–68); Allen (1989: 33, 47); Radu and Somerville (1989: 172); Ayele (1990: 19–21); Young (1997: 106–112).

20 See Somerville (1986: 102); Marcum (1987: 75); Ciment (1997: 126–127, 140–141, 143); Hall and Young (1997: 83).

21 See Davidson ([1969] 1981: 73–74); Samatar (1988: 107–108); Allen (1989: 65–66); Saul (1993a: 61, 64–65); Waterhouse (1996: 56–57); Hall and Young (1997: 83–87); Ciment (1997: 63, 66, 160–161, 168–169, 172); Kaure (1999: 24–25, 30–31).

22 I am here primarily concerned with Marxist movements and their attendant ideologies, rather than with academic Marxism.

23 See Nkrumah (1963: 129); Nkrumah (1964a: 79, 89–90, 103); Nkrumah (1973: 75-83); Cox (1966: 83); Rivière (1977: 86–87); Munslow (1986: 27); Ottoway and Ottoway (1986: 18–24); Keller (1987: 1).

24 See Friedland and Rosberg (1964: 4–9); Nyerere (1964: 239–243, 246); Nkrumah (1964a: 78–79, 106); Nkrumah (1964b: 263); Senghor (1965: 264–266); Ottoway and Ottoway (1986: 13–17).

25 See Ottoway (1978); Halliday and Molyneux (1981: 273–283); Ottoway and Ottoway (1986: 32–33); Somerville (1986: 194–195); Turok (1986: 65).

26 See Ottoway and Ottoway (1986: 77–78); Somerville (1986: 54, 82–83, 98); Clapham (1988: 66); Keller (1988: 197–198); Radu and Somerville (1989: 190); Iyob (1995: 127–129); Young (1997: 80–84, 99–100).

27 The only other significant movement I know to attempt something similar is the People's Mojahedin (Mojahein-e-Khalq) in Iran.

28 See Fanon (1965); Fanon (1967a); Fanon (1967b); Fanon (1967c). On whether Fanon was a critic of nationalism or sought to radicalise it, see the survey and intervention by Lazarus (1993). On Fanon's democratic thought (which basically amounted to advocating participatory decentralisation within a non-liberal, most likely one-party regime), see Adam (1993). For a critique of Fanon on violence, see Kebbede (2001). On Fanon more generally, see Gibson (2003) and Tronto (2004). The renewed popularity of Steve Biko also owes something to this Fanonian moment.

29 The beneficiaries of the land seizures included landless peasants but also politically connected, aspirant large-scale landowners; its victims were white farmers but also black foreign nationals and black workers evicted from farms. The rhetoric accompanying the seizures was more anti-colonial, anti-white, anti-urban and xenophobic than Marxist or socialist. No effort was made to establish state or collective farms. The seizures are best seen as part of the larger effort by the Mugabe regime to Africanise the country's mixed market economy.

30 See Somerville (1986: 108); Keller (1988: 214–215, 263); Ottoway (1990: 3); Hall and Young (1997: 80–82); Hodges (2001: 46).

31 See Keller (1988: 225–227); Giorgis (1990: 64–66); Kebbede (1992: 6, 79–84, 90); Waterhouse (1996: 30–31); Ciment (1997: 63); Young (1997: 29, 145, 169–170).

32 See Marcum (1987: 74); Ciment (1997: 172, 185); Hall and Young (1997: 85–87).

33 See Somerville (1986: 102); Marcum (1987: 75); Keller (1988: 239); Hall and Young (1997: 212).

34 See Houtart (1980: 106); Saul (1985: 80–81); Ottoway and Ottoway (1986: 56, 71–72, 82, 104); Somerville (1986: 115–122); Covell (1987: 54, 57, 61–62, 94–5, 111–113); Keller (1988: 196, 232–235); Allen (1989: 35–37, 54); Baxter and Somerville (1989: 249, 255); Radu and Somerville (1989: 165); Iyob (1995: 130); Waterhouse (1996: 61); Young (1997: 104).

35 See Ottoway and Ottoway (1986: 60–61, 75, 81–82, 86–92, 108–109, 113–120, 149–151, 227–228); Somerville (1986: 115–122); Keller (1988: 232–234); Allen (1989: 38–39, 53); Radu and Somerville (1989: 165–168); Ciment (1997: 66–67); Hall and Young (1997: 74–76).

36 See Saul (1985: 92–93); Keller (1988: 239); Allen (1989: 42); Hanlon ([1984] 1990: 204); Waterhouse (1996: 23).

37 See Saul (1985: 81–82, 96–97); Somerville (1986: 115–122); Keller (1988: 218–219); Samatar (1988: 112–113); Allen (1989: 54, 68–69); Radu and Somerville (1989: 166).

38 See Marcum (1987: 72–73); Allen (1989: 71–73, 122); Waterhouse (1996: 9, 61); Ciment (1997: 127).

39 See Ottoway and Ottoway (1986: 83); Clapham (1988: 94–95); Allen (1989: 46–47); Dhada (1993: 136–138); Ciment (1997: 177); Hall and Young (1997: 71–72, 77–78).
40 See Somerville (1986: 92); Covell (1987: 101); Clapham (1988: 79–81); Keller (1988: 240); Samatar (1988: 110–113, 152–153); Allen (1989: 51–52); Giorgis (1990: 55–67); Hall and Young (1997: 70–73, 77); Hodges (2001: 48–51).
41 During the transition to socialism and communism, strictly speaking the regime presumed to represent the higher will of only the proletariat and its class allies, though they in turn supposedly served as intimations and forebears of a still-to-come classless people.

REFERENCES

Adam, H.M. 1993. 'Frantz Fanon as a democratic theorist', *African Affairs*, 92 (369): 499–518.
Adamolekun, L. 1976. *Sékou Touré's Guinea: An Experiment in Nation Building*. London: Methuen.
Allen, C. 1989. 'Benin'. In *Benin, The Congo, Burkina Faso: Economics, Politics and Society*, edited by C. Allen, M.S. Radu, K. Somerville and J. Baxter. London: Pinter Publishers.
Ayele, N. 1990. 'The Ethiopian revolution: Political aspects of the transition from PMAC to PDRE'. In *The Political Economy of Ethiopia*, edited by M. Ottoway. New York: Praeger.
Baxter, J. and Somerville, K. 1989. 'Burkina Faso'. In *Benin, The Congo, Burkina Faso: Economics, Politics and Society*, edited by C. Allen, M.S. Radu, K. Somerville and J. Baxter. London: Pinter Publishers.
Bozzoli, B. and Delius, P. 1990. 'Radical history and South African society', *Radical History Review*, 46 (7): 13–45.
Cabral, A. 1969. *Revolution in Guinea: Selected Texts by Amilcar Cabral*. Redhill, Surrey: Love and Malcolmson.
Cabral, A. 1973. *Return to the Source: Selected Speeches by Amilcar Cabral*. New York: Monthly Review Press.
Cabral, A. 1979. *Unity and Struggle: Speeches and Writings*. New York: Monthly Review Press.
Chaliand, G. 1980. 'The guerilla struggle'. In *Behind the War in Eritrea*, edited by B. Davidson, L. Cliffe and B.H. Selassie. Nottingham: Spokesman.
Ciment, J. 1997. *Angola and Mozambique: Postcolonial Wars in Southern Africa*. New York: Facts on File, Inc.
Clapham, C. 1988. *Transformation and Continuity in Revolutionary Ethiopia*. Cambridge: Cambridge University Press.
Cohen, R. 1986. 'Marxism in Africa: The grounding of a tradition'. In *Africa: Problems in the Transition to Socialism*, edited by B. Munslow. London: Zed Books.
Covell, M. 1987. *Madagascar: Politics, Economics and Society*. London: Frances Pinter.
Cox, I. 1966. *Socialist Ideas in Africa*. London: Lawrence and Wishart.
Davidson, B. (1969) 1981. *No Fist is Big Enough to Hide the Sky: The Liberation of Guinea and Cape Verde*. London: Zed Press.
Davidson, B. 1979. 'Introduction'. In *Unity and Struggle: Speeches and Writings* by A. Cabral. New York: Monthly Review Press.

Davidson, B. 1992. *The Black Man's Burden: Africa and the Curse of the Nation-State*. London: James Currey.

De Andrade, M. 1979. 'Biographical notes'. In *Unity and Struggle: Speeches and Writings* by A. Cabral. New York: Monthly Review Press.

Dhada, M. 1993. *Warriors at Work: How Guinea Was Really Set Free*. Niwot, CO: University Press of Colorado.

Dia, M. 1964. 'African socialism'. In *African Socialism*, edited by W.H. Friedland and C.G. Rosberg. Stanford, CA: Stanford University Press.

Drew, A. 2000. *Discordant Comrades: Identities and Loyalties on the South African Left*. Aldershot: Ashgate.

Fanon, F. 1965. *A Dying Colonialism*. Harmondsworth: Penguin.

Fanon, F. 1967a. *Black Skin, White Masks*. New York: Grove Press.

Fanon, F. 1967b. *The Wretched of the Earth*. Harmondsworth: Penguin.

Fanon, F. 1967c. *Towards the African Revolution*. New York: Grove Press.

Friedland, W.H. and Rosberg, C.G. 1964. 'The anatomy of African socialism'. In *African Socialism*, edited by W.H. Friedland and C.G. Rosberg. Stanford, CA: Stanford University Press.

Gibson, N. 2003. *Fanon: The Postcolonial Imagination*. Cambridge: Polity.

Giorgis, D.W. 1990. 'The power of decision-making in post-revolutionary Ethiopia'. In *The Political Economy of Ethiopia*, edited by M. Ottoway. New York: Praeger.

Glaser, D. 1999. 'Marxism and democracy'. In *Marxism and Social* Science, edited by A. Gamble, D. Marsh and T. Tant. Basingstoke: Macmillan.

Hall, M. and Young, T. 1997. *Confronting Leviathan: Mozambique since Independence*. London: Hurst and Company.

Halliday, F. and Molyneux, M. 1981. *The Ethiopian Revolution*. London: New Left Books.

Hanlon, J. (1984) 1990. *Mozambique: The Revolution under Fire*. London: Zed Books.

Harbeson, J.W. 1990. 'State and social transformation in modern Ethiopia'. In *The Political Economy of Ethiopia*, edited by M. Ottoway. New York: Praeger.

Hodges, T. 2001. *Angola: From Afro-Stalinism to Petro-Diamond Capitalism*. Oxford: The Fridtjof Nansen Institute and the International African Institute, with James Currey.

Houtart, F. 1980. 'The social revolution in Eritrea'. In *Behind the War in Eritrea*, edited by B. Davidson, L. Cliffe and B.H. Selassie. Nottingham: Spokesman.

Humbaraci, A. 1966. *Algeria: A Revolution that Failed: A Political History since 1954*. London: Pall Mall Press.

Iyob, R. 1995. *The Eritrean Struggle for Independence: Domination, Resistance, Nationalism, 1941–1993*. Cambridge: Cambridge University Press.

Kaure, A.T. 1999. *Angola: From Socialism to Liberal Reforms*. Harare: Sapes Books.

Kebbede, G. 1992. *The State and Development in Ethiopia*. Atlantic Highlands, NJ: The Humanities Press.

Kebbede, M. 2001. 'The rehabilitation of violence and the violence of rehabilitation: Fanon and colonialism', *Journal of Black Studies*, 31 (5): 539–562.

Keller, E.J. 1987. 'Afro-Marxist regimes'. In *Afro-Marxist Regimes*, edited by E.J. Keller and D. Rothchild. Boulder, CO: Lynne Rienner Publishers.

Keller, E.J. 1988. *Revolutionary Ethiopia: From Empire to People's Republic*. Bloomington, IA: Indiana University Press.

Lackner, H. 1985. *P.D.R. Yemen: Outpost of Socialist Development in Arabia*. London: Ithaca Press.

Lazarus, M. 1993. 'Disavowing decolonization: Fanon, nationalism, and the problematic of representation in current theories of colonial discourse', *Research in African Literature*, 24 (4): 69–98.

Lefort, R. 1983. *Ethiopia: A Heretical Revolution?* London: Zed Books.

Lewis, G. 1987. *Between the Wire and the Wall: A History of South African 'Coloured' Politics*. Cape Town: David Philip.

Library of Congress Country Studies. c.2005. *Somalia*. Accessed 19 June 2013, http://www.country-studies.com/somalia/siad-barre-and-scientific-socialism.html.

Liebman, M. 1975. *Leninism under Lenin*. London: Merlin Press.

Machel, S. 1980. 'His struggle was the people's struggle'. In *Revolutionary Thought in the Twentieth Century*, edited by B. Turok. London: Zed Books.

Marcum, J. 1969. *The Angolan Revolution Volume 1: The Anatomy of an Explosion (1950-1962)*. Cambridge, MA: MIT Press.

Marcum, J. 1987. 'The People's Republic of Angola: A radical vision frustrated'. In *Afro-Marxist Regimes*, edited by E.J. Keller and D. Rothchild. Boulder, CO: Lynne Rienner Publishers.

Marx, K. 1881. *First Draft of Letter to Vera Zasulich*. Accessed 19 June 2013, http://www.marxists.org/archive/marx/works/1881/03/zasulich1.htm.

Munslow, B. 1986. 'Introduction'. In *Africa: Problems in the Transition to Socialism*, edited by B. Munslow. London: Zed Books.

Nkrumah, K. 1963. *Africa Must Unite*. London: Panaf.

Nkrumah, K. 1964a. *Consciencism: Philosophy and Ideology for Decolonisation*. London: Panaf.

Nkrumah, K. 1964b. 'Some aspects of socialism in Africa'. In *African Socialism*, edited by W.H. Friedland and C.G. Rosberg. Stanford, CA: Stanford University Press.

Nkrumah, K.1973. *The Struggle Continues*. London: Panaf.

Nyerere, J.K. 1964. 'Ujamaa: The basis of African socialism'. In *African Socialism*, edited by W.H. Friedland and C.G. Rosberg. Stanford, CA: Stanford University Press.

Ottoway, M. 1978. 'Soviet Marxism and African socialism', *Journal of Southern African Studies*, 16 (3): 477–485.

Ottoway, M. 1990. 'Introduction: The crisis of the Ethiopian state and economy'. In *The Political Economy of Ethiopia*, edited by M. Ottoway. New York: Praeger.

Ottoway, M. and Ottoway, D. 1986. *Afrocommunism* (second edition). New York: Africana Publishing Company.

Padmore, G. 1964. 'A guide to Pan-African Socialism'. In *African Socialism*, edited by W.H. Friedland and C.G. Rosberg. Stanford, CA: Stanford University Press.

Pool, D. 1979. *Eritrea – Africa's Longest War*. Human Rights Series, Anti-Slavery Society, revised edition, Report No. 3. London: Anti-Slavery Society.

Radu, M.S. and Somerville, K. 1989. 'The Congo'. In *Benin, The Congo, Burkina Faso: Economics, Politics and Society*, edited by C. Allen, M.S. Radu, K. Somerville and J. Baxter. London: Pinter Publishers.

Rivière, C. 1977. *Guinea: The Mobilization of a People*. Ithaca, NY: Cornell University Press.

Samatar, A.I. 1988. *Socialist Somalia: Rhetoric and Reality*. London: Zed Books.

Saul, J. 1985. 'Introduction' and 'The content: A transition to socialism?' In *A Difficult Road: The Transition to Socialism in Mozambique*, edited by J. Saul. New York: Monthly Review Press.

Saul, J. 1990. *Socialist Ideology and the Struggle for Southern Africa*. Trenton, NJ: Africa World Press.

Saul, J. 1993a. 'Introduction'. In *Recolonization and Resistance in Southern Africa in the 1990s*, edited by J. Saul. Trenton, NJ: Africa World Press.

Saul, J. 1993b. 'The Frelimo state: From revolution to recolonization'. In *Recolonization and Resistance in Southern Africa in the 1990s*, edited by J. Saul. Trenton, NJ: Africa World Press.

Senghor, L. 1965. 'African-style socialism'. In *African Socialism*, edited by W.H. Friedland and C.G. Rosberg. Stanford, CA: Stanford University Press.

Somerville, K. 1986. *Angola: Politics, Economics and Society*. Boulder, CO: Lynne Rienner Publishers.

Tronto, J. 2004. 'Frantz Fanon', *Contemporary Political Theory*, 3 (2): 45–52.

Turok, B. 1986. 'The Left in Africa today'. In *Africa: Problems in the Transition to Socialism*, edited by B. Munslow. London: Zed Books.

Waterhouse, R. 1996. *Mozambique: Rising from the Ashes*. Oxford: Oxfam (UK and Ireland).

Woodward, P. 1992. *Nasser*. London: Longman.

Young, J. 1997. *Peasant Revolution in Ethiopia: The Tigray People's Liberation Front*. Cambridge: Cambridge University Press.

8

SOCIALISM AND SOUTHERN AFRICA

John S. Saul

The African continent has been marked by various and remarkably diverse flare-ups of apparent socialist and quasi-socialist intention – from Algeria in the north to Ghana in the west to Ethiopia in the east, with several stops in between. But it is as one approaches the southern cone and moves ever closer to South Africa itself that the intention becomes most marked, not only in rhetoric but also in practice – albeit a practice not as yet concretely realised in any very sustained way. So the question remains: what are we to learn from this southern African regional experience that can provide serviceable lessons for an ongoing struggle to realise equity, social justice and meaningful development in South Africa?

TROPES OF SOCIALIST DEFEAT

After all, one of the stocks-in-trade of African National Congress (ANC)-thinking since South Africa's formal democratisation in 1994 has been to present a negative version of African socialist endeavour elsewhere on the continent and, particularly, within the region. For this version is designed, with varying degrees of caricature, precisely to warn against any feckless dream of a socialist outcome in South Africa itself – however often such an outcome may actually have been invoked by the ANC/South African Communist Party (SACP) itself during the very years of liberation struggle against white dictatorship that it shared with other liberation movements across the region.

Here, one of the favoured tropes – albeit one more often offered in private conversation than in public statement – has been to underscore the lack of realism of the aspiration in general and, in particular, under African conditions and circumstances. This is, of course, a theme sometimes seen in more scholarly offerings. Many decades ago, for example, Roger Murray (1967: 39) queried whether, in Kwame Nkrumah's Ghana, the 'historically necessary' (some form of socialism) was in fact the 'historically possible'. More recently, Giovanni Arrighi would suggest that even in the heyday of 'liberation movement' enthusiasm (the 1960s and 1970s) and despite his own direct involvement in one of them (in Zimbabwe) he had himself been appropriately sceptical as to the likelihood or even possibility of socialist outcomes in a liberated southern Africa (Arrighi 2009; Saul 2011: chapter 6).[1] But the ANC variant of a similar argument, as offered in the private conversations and musings of its leaders (it is difficult to find a paper trail of such utterances), is even more dismissive than this. And this reading of recent history serves, in turn, to underpin an assumption as to the impossibility of the ANC's following any other course than the option of a neoliberal accommodation with global capitalism that it has in fact chosen.

One can see clearly enough the apparently commonsensical nature of this latter choice – evoking, in essence, the explanatory mantra 'globalisation made me do it'. And yet acceptance, overwhelmingly, of the dictates of the so-called 'free market', both locally and globally, has been much more a choice than a necessity: a 'choice' made very consciously in favour of capitalism and against socialism. Perhaps it is enough to recall Thabo Mbeki's own clear statement from the 1980s when he wrote that 'the ANC is not a socialist party. It has never pretended to be one, it has never said it was, and it is not trying to be. It will not become one by decree or for the purpose of pleasing its "left" critics' (Mbeki 1984: 609). And this is the same Mbeki who would note, during the South African transition, that the National Party positions were 'not very different really from the position the movement has been advancing' – and who, after the liberation itself, could even cavalierly assert, as regards his (and the ANC's) chosen economic policies: 'Just call me a Thatcherite' (Green 2006; Mbeki 1991: 2; Saul 2008).[2]

It thus can come as no great surprise that during South Africa's transition from apartheid, Mbeki was quite comfortable (as comfortable in taking such a course as was Nelson Mandela himself, be it noted)[3] in encouraging the ANC to turn its back on any lingering scepticism it might have had as to the virtues of the global capitalist system. Of course, Mbeki also had qualified the argument in his 1984 text suggestively: 'The ANC is convinced that within the alliance of democratic forces … the working class must play the leading role, not as an appendage of the petite bourgeoisie but as a conscious vanguard class, capable of advancing and defending its own democratic interests' (612). Here, indeed, was the apparent promise of some continuing commitment to radical class politics. Yet, in retrospect, the latter sentence seems only to have existed as a pretty perfunctory footnote to his, and the ANC's, continuing rightward turn. Once in power, in fact, he would prove entirely unwilling to work in any way whatsoever to help pull the ANC back onto a leftward track. Quite the contrary.

At the same time, his formulation is suggestive. For precisely the kind of broader class understanding Mbeki purports to acknowledge here may help explain the logic of a formulation of his own which dates from only several years later (although such a statement may now come as a bit of a surprise to those who have lost track of Mbeki's startling ideological peregrinations over the years). Thus, as early as the late 1980s, he could be found (according to William Gumede) 'privately telling friends that he believed the ANC alliance with the Communist Party would have to be broken at some point, especially if the ANC gained power in a post-apartheid South Africa' (Gumede 2005: 38). In Mbeki's scenario, continues Gumede, 'the ANC would govern as a centre-left party, keeping some remnants of trade union and SACP support, while the bulk of the alliance would form a left-wing workers' party'.

'A left-wing workers' party' in opposition to the ANC? This might seem to many of us a possible outcome devoutly to be wished for in the next round of South African history. But what of the choices that actually were made in a post-apartheid South Africa? So careful an analyst as Mbeki's much-cited biographer Mark Gevisser, for example, affirms that by as early as 1985 Mbeki had concluded that 'a negotiated settlement [required] a far more liberal approach to economic policy' than had been the ANC position up to that time. Furthermore, by 1994 '[Mbeki] and his government [felt] forced to acquiesce to the Washington Consensus on macro-economic policy when they implemented their controversial Growth, Employment and Redistribution (Gear) programme in 1996' (Gevisser 2007 quoted in Turok 2008: 57–58; Gevisser 2009).[4] Felt 'forced'? This is a curious choice of words for explaining the ANC's trajectory that bears further discussion, needless to say. Yet the truth is we can also find veteran ANC/SACP activist Ben Turok suggesting something similar in explicitly agreeing with Gevisser as to the 'necessary' nature of the deviation to the right that the ANC had taken.

Yet Turok also knows something more: the particularly grim outcomes likely to follow from a 'choice' so made. In fact, more recently, we can find Turok substantially qualifying his earlier view, now querying just why the ANC government had not 'given equal attention to empowering the masses as to the elite? And why has the insistence of parliament on broad-based empower-ment brought so little success?' (2008: 174). Of course, Turok (263) already knows the answer to this question – and, in consequence, he himself is even willing (in later chapters of the book from which the passages in the preceding paragraphs are quoted) to back away uneasily from the 'new' ANC's hardline capitalist position, and to come, in his words, to 'the irresistible conclusion ... that the ANC government has lost a great deal of its earlier focus on the funda-mental transformation of the inherited social system'.[5] Inevitable? Lost focus? Obviously, a core question remains unanswered here: why was there this ever firmer and untroubled opting for a conservative economic programme on the part of the ANC elite in the first place?

Franz Fanon had one explanation of course. What we have in South Africa, he might have argued, is merely the familiar trajectory of virtually all post-liberation movements in power in Africa: a new middle class that now chooses, in its own class interests, to opt for a junior partnership with capital, quasi-colonial and global. Though now updated to embrace the realities of the ever more 'globalised' workings of capital, the same sad tale could easily be offered as one convincing explanation of the South African case as well. For here, in essence, we see the self-interested embrace by the ANC and its business-oriented cronies of, precisely, the globalising 'logic' of capital; here, in short, is a meek and self-interested submission to the recolonisation of South Africa by diverse capitalists, one facilitated by a new South African elite eager to embrace just such an outcome (Saul 2008 and 2013).[6] True, this would make for a dour reading of what has happened in South Africa – but it is a reading that is quite difficult to refute.

Not, to be sure, that this is the way the ANC itself tells the story. Let us look, then, at the tropes the ANC does draw on in explaining its choices. One explanation favoured by the ANC itself in rationalising these choices is the global collapse of any genuine 'socialist alternative' – the reference here being primarily to the fading away of the Soviet Union and its Eastern European wards from the lists of history. This, it is inferred, left ANC socialists and their aspirations beached, stranded in a sea of capitalist globalisation. And the latter system's stringent global imperatives had therefore, and of necessity, to be taken not merely seriously but as being absolutely prescriptive of policy outcomes in ways they had not quite been in the past. Mark, needless to say, the skewed definition of socialism with which this argument begins, one associated narrowly with the (erstwhile) Soviet style of 'socialism'. Yet that had been a terribly limited, mechanistic and absolutely undemocratic – in short, 'non-socialist'– model if ever there was one and certainly not one that needed to be followed (or relied upon) if a more open and imaginative socialist path were to have been chosen. Instead, even as ruling elites in such countries as China and the new South Africa casually abandoned socialist aspirations, they nonetheless managed to hold to many of the Soviet model's most questionable attributes, notably its formidably arrogant and elite-serving vanguardist mode of politics.

In this chapter, however, it is another trope, crucial to the ANC's retreat from 'socialism', that will be emphasised. This refers, so it is argued, to the 'failure' in practice of any operative socialism elsewhere in Africa. The reference is in particular to those countries in the southern Africa region where ANC personnel, in exile, are said to have witnessed at first hand just such 'failures' of socialism, notably in Tanzania and Mozambique. For these were the states in the region where socialist endeavour had been taken least rhetorically and, for a period, most seriously. It is well known that these two countries (although not so very differently from many other African countries of far less militant initial ideological persuasion) have now been reduced to the status of impoverished supplicants, cap in hand, to global capital. Yet, as we will see below, they do remain eminently discussable cases – both in terms of their strengths and of their weaknesses. Through such a discussion we can discover, clearly revealed, many keys to the meaning of socialist practice in Africa and to the lessons that can be learned from it – lessons not at all illuminated by mere caricature. For in these cases we see both the nobility of the aspiration for a socialist Africa but also, crucially and in the cases of both Tanzania and Mozambique, the weaknesses of the 'socialism' actually practised – weaknesses that tell us more, however, about what might need to be done to make socialism real than they do about the irrelevance of the intention itself.

Not that we will here search further to document the ANC's own implied allusions to the 'failures' of regional socialism – difficult (as noted) as these are to find on the printed page in any case. Instead, we seek here to query these regional projects for ourselves, surveying their practice in order to discover what light their 'failure' might, in fact and not in fantasy, actually cast on the realities of the choice of socio-economic system being made in South Africa itself.

THE FRONTLINE STATES: THE TANZANIA CASE

To have experienced, some fifty years ago and at first hand (as did the present author), the power of the 'Arusha Declaration' years in Tanzania was to see the promise, if not yet the fully realised practice, of socialism in Africa etched in a particularly vivid light (Cliffe and Saul 1972 and 1973; Saul 2013: chapter 2).[7] For there, by the late 1960s, Julius Nyerere – the country's president and the man most closely identified with the dramatic moment of the Declaration itself and the announcement of the country's *ujamaa* project – had announced on behalf of his people the launching of just such a socialist project. Then, briefly but dramatically (and far more so than any other country along the already liberated frontline of the dawning southern African struggle), he and the Tanganyika African National Union (Tanu) held out the prospect of founding a distinctive socialism in Africa, one that could be a touchstone for something quite beyond the kind of 'neocolonialism' and 'false decolonisation' that thinkers such as Fanon had begun to identify as the sobering stigmata of the overall African decolonisation process.

The moment was indeed one of promise, and even promise in the most strictly Fanonist terms. After all, Fanon had seen the post-colonial African political leadership as, in effect, a cadre of usurpers now seen to be working, in their own interests and in those of global capital, and against their earlier assurances of a sustained betterment in their impoverished people's political and economic conditions – a prospect at first presented as being the obvious accompaniment to an attainment of freedom from direct colonial overlordship. And yet here, in Tanzania, there were, in addition to the Arusha Declaration itself, two easily overlooked but particularly striking portents that a more positive outcome would indeed occur there.

One of these moments of promise occurred at a large 1967 rally in Dar es Salaam just after the pronouncement of the Arusha Declaration itself and in the very first days of *ujamaa*-inspired euphoria. Then, in a speech reported in the *Nationalist* newspaper,

Nyerere called on the people of Tanzania to have great confidence in themselves and to safeguard the nation's hard-won freedom. Mwalimu [Nyerere] warned that the people should not allow their freedom to be pawned as most of their leaders were purchasable. He warned further that in running the affairs of the nation the people should not look on their leaders as saints and prophets.

The President stated that the attainment of freedom in many cases resulted merely in the change of colours, white faces to black faces without ending exploitation and injustices, and above all without the betterment of the life of the masses. He said that while struggling for freedom the objective was clear but it was another thing to remove your own people from the position of exploiters (*The Nationalist* [Dar es Salaam], 5 September 1967).

Practical Fanonism in full voice, one might say. Yet there was more. For what of the danger of the successor black elite, now elevated to power, being merely 'in league with global capital'? Here there is a second illuminating statement by Nyerere to consider, one in which he quite self-consciously expanded the import of the anti-colonial nationalist project beyond the merely political realm and onto the terrain of what he termed 'economic nationalism' – and of socialism:

The real ideological choice is between controlling the economy through domestic private enterprise, or doing so through the state or some other collective institution.

But although this is an ideological choice, it is extremely doubtful whether this is a practical choice for an African nationalist. The pragmatist in Africa ... will find that the real choice is a different one. He will find that the real choice is between foreign private ownership on the one hand and local collective ownership on the other, for I do not think there is any free state in Africa where there is sufficient capital, or a sufficient number of local entrepreneurs, for local capital to dominate the economy. Private investment in Africa means overwhelmingly foreign private investment. A capitalist economy means a foreign dominated economy. These are the facts of Africa's situation. The only way in which

national control of the economy can be achieved is through the economic institutions of socialism.

To Tanzania this inevitable choice is not unwelcome. We are socialists as
well as nationalists. We are committed to the creation of a classless society in which every able-bodied person is contributing to the economy
through work and we believe this can only be obtained when the major
means of production are publicly owned and controlled. But the fact
remains that our recent socialist measures were not taken out of a blind
adherence to dogma. They are intended to serve our society (Nyerere
1968: 264–265).

Not, in other words, some 'black economic empowerment' along entrepreneurial lines, but collective action by the overall populace itself (helped to find
focus through a measure of 'leadership', needless to say, but not of any overbearing, all-knowing, unchecked kind). Meanwhile, linked to such general
propositions (genuine popular power, both political and economic) there was
a host of more specific initiatives that then attracted wide attention.

- a leadership code that sought to discipline leaders against their following
  the path of private self-interest into compromising entanglements with
  the private sector;
- a one-party electoral scheme that sought (albeit within quite severe
  limits) to open up the dominant party to public scrutiny;
- a progamme of rural transformation (*ujamaa vijijini*) designed to draw
  peasants together in more organised, cooperative and productive new
  villages;
- an expanded and transformed education system ('education for self-
  reliance') to meet national needs but also to seek to steer students toward
  more selfless and responsible citizenship;
- the *Mwongozo* (Tanu Guidelines) of 1971 that stated its intention to facilitate the attack from below on bureaucratic and politically high-handed
  actions in the country, stating, in its Clause 15, that 'there must be a delib-
  erate effort to build equality between leaders and those they lead' (Tanu
  1971). It was this *Mwongozo* that Walter Rodney once referred to as being
  an 'even harder hitting document than the Arusha Declaration' (Rodney
  1975), momentarily seeming to herald, as it did, a genuine popular
  empowerment from below.

But this latter is one of the most difficult challenges facing those who would create a politics that is at once progressive in import and democratic in substance. There is, of course, a case to be made for the necessity of enlightened leadership – sheer romantic and populist 'spontaneism' is no answer. But, at the same time, no 'leadership' can long go unchecked from 'below' – not if it is to avoid a fall into high-handedness and self-indulgent elitism. Moreover, the resultant contradiction is not one that can merely be 'resolved' easily and once and for all – either in principle or in practice. Instead, it is a tension that must be lived and struggled with in a process of ongoing and challenging democratic politics – leadership winning its case through convincing and responsive argument and practice, on the one hand, and an increasingly enlightened and self-conscious mass base exerting its democratic voice ever more efficaciously and knowledgeably, on the other. As happened in Tanzania, however, the failure to realise the promise of *Mwongozo* – a late addition to the Arusha Declaration package and one that seemed to take the tensions alluded to here with the seriousness they demanded – proved to be one of the key failings of the Tanzanian experiment.

Of course, the dramatic thrust of the *ujamaa* project was stymied in a number of ways, these reflecting additional failures that can be briefly elucidated here. One of these was the failure – for all the talk about 'socialism and self-reliance' – to move with any imagination towards an industrial strategy that could have serviced such a goal and permitted, in Samir Amin's (1985) term, a genuine 'delinking' of Tanzania from the overbearing 'il/logic' of the world of (global) capital. Not that the notion of 'delinking' could ever be interpreted, in Amin's work, as signalling any unrealistic push towards autarky. But – as sympathetic but heterodox economists who had worked in Tanzania such as Clive Thomas (1974) and William Luttrell (1986) argued at the time – what was needed was the forceful assertion of an alternative central focus for the economy, a powerfully internal focus that any external economic links would be expected, primarily, to service.

As Thomas (1974) spelled out the case, this would embody 'the progressive convergence of the demand structure of the community and the needs of the population' – the very reverse, in short, of the market fundamentalist's global orthodoxy. One could then have grounded a 'socialism of expanded reproduction' (in the name of genuine accumulation) and refused the dilemma that has heretofore undermined the promise of the many 'socialisms' which have proven prone to fall into the Stalinist trap of 'violently repressing mass consumption'. For, far from accumulation and mass consumption being warring opposites, the premise would then be that accumulation could be driven forward precisely by finding outlets for production in meeting the growing requirements, the needs, of the mass of the population.

An effective industrialisation strategy would thus base its 'expanded reproduction' on ever increasing exchanges between city and country, between industry and agriculture, with food and raw materials moving to the cities and with consumer goods and producer goods (with the latter defined to include centrally such modest items as scythes, iron ploughs, hoes, axes, fertilisers and the like) moving to the countryside. Collective saving geared to investment could then be seen as being drawn essentially, if not exclusively, from an expanding economic pool. Note that such a socialism of expanded reproduction makes the betterment of the people's lot a short-term rather than a long-term project and thus promises a much sounder basis for an effective (rather than merely rhetorical) alliance of workers, peasants and others – on a democratic road to revolutionary socialism.

But – and here is the rub – this is precisely an emphasis that Nyerere and company chose to turn their backs on. Thus Luttrell (1986), writing quite explicitly within the analytical framework established by Thomas, demonstrates the almost complete failure of Tanzania's 'bureaucratic class' to act in any such way, their continued subservience to the logic of global capitalism and to their own class interest dictating a long-term failure to actually develop the country. He then spells out an alternative track that might have been taken had the elite really wanted to pursue transformation. Moreover, while Luttrell says little about Nyerere himself, another crucial missing link – industrial strategy (to be added to silences about democracy and failures of imagination in the rural sector) – in Nyerere's presumed socialist strategy here stands starkly exposed.

But what of that rural sector, alluded to above? Unfortunately, an active scepticism towards peasants – as towards any genuinely democratic empowerment of the mass of the population from below, be it expressed by workers, peasants, women or students – ran deep amongst the Tanzanian leadership (as would also subsequently prove true of the Frelimo (Front for the Liberation of Mozambique) leadership in Mozambique).[8] Thus, in spite of their many statements about the crucial 'class belonging' (as workers and peasants) of 'the people', such class descriptors were all too readily collapsed into merely populist categories in Tanzania – instead of their facilitating a view of such 'classes' as being potentially empowerable in genuinely radical terms. Any real commitment to an active democracy seems to have been, for the Tanzanian leadership, the catch here. As Leander Schneider (2003, 2004 and 2006) – one of the most careful and incisive of all scholars of the *ujamaa vijijini* initiative – suggests, in this central rural policy,

> several of the most inspiring strands of Nyerere's politics flow together
> – in particular, an exemplary commitment to improving the condition
> of the poor, as well as his theorizing about the nexus of development,
> freedom, empowerment, and participation. However, it is also in the
> field of rural development that problematic dimensions of Nyerere's
> leadership become, perhaps, most starkly apparent. Not only did the
> policy of enforced *ujamaa*/villagisation fail to improve the material
> conditions of Tanzania's rural population, but the adoption of coercive
> means to further it also points to the authoritarian side of Nyerere's rule
> (Schneider 2004: 345).

Nor does Schneider choose the word 'authoritarian' lightly, as witness his use of it with reference to the draconian effacing of the Ruvuma Development Association's experiment in revolutionary rural democracy from below and the conversion of 'rural socialism' into an order, from on high, to villagise. For Schneider's quite self-conscious deployment of the descriptor 'authoritarian' lies at the very heart of his argument. Small wonder that he then concludes his analysis of what he calls the 'statist bent (and the related overtly coercive character observed in 1970s' Tanzania)' with the observation that 'Tanzanian history shows, above all, that turning a blind eye to the tensions of participatory development will neither make them go away nor allow one to avoid the serious costs implied by swiftly reducing participation to near meaningless-ness' (Schneider 2004). Here then is yet another lesson (and there are similar lessons available from the treatment of workers and of students in Tanzania as well) to be learned by anyone of progressive bent who would care to hear such tidings – one that is at once depressing and also, potentially, most instructive.

What of women – and the entire sphere of struggle for gender emancipation and gender equality – whose liberation is perhaps as urgently needed as is those of any other 'social category' in Tanzania (and in the rest of southern Africa)? This was a front of freedom little discussed at the time in Tanzania and, indeed, the record was not an encouraging one. For example, Bibi Titi Mohammed, admittedly no great socialist but a prominent Tanu leader in the early days, underscored some years ago the starkness of the male sense of entitlement that scarred Tanu in those years, the vital role of women militants in the liberation struggle itself soon being more or less passed over:

> When power was transferred to the nationalist government … the story changed. Women's experience was no longer relevant to the postcolonial struggles against neo-colonialism, imperialism and the management of the state apparatus. In [our] discussion Bibi Titi ironically said, 'I started smelling fish' when the first cabinet was named (Meena 2003: 152).[9]

Indeed, Bibi Titi was so incensed by such facts that, by her account, she actually refused Nyerere's offer to co-author with him a joint history of Tanzania's nationalist liberation struggle. Meanwhile, the prevailing silences of that time have continued to scar present-day reality in Tanzania, despite the best efforts of many women activists, then and now, to keep the struggle for gender emancipation alive. But, as we have also seen, the struggle for overall emancipation continues to confront all Tanzanians, male and female, with many of them the poorest of the continent's (and of the world's) poor, as well. This latter struggle is, of course, a struggle – for genuine democracy, for nationally focused and people-centric development and much else – that also confronts the vast majority of similarly deprived South Africans.

THE NEWLY LIBERATED STATES AND THE MOZAMBICAN CASE

Elsewhere in the region and beyond the frontline states, as territories became freshly liberated, the newly empowered former liberation movements (now the ruling parties of their respective countries) made many and various pronouncements of their radical intentions.[10] The currency of their pronouncements was in part a reflex of such movements' long-time hotline to military assistance (via such ostensibly progressive regimes as the Soviet Union and China), in part a manifestation of the trendy (and relatively unreflective) 'leftism' that marked the period (the era of Vietnam, Cuba and the like). Most regimes in the region (Angola, Namibia, Zimbabwe) quickly lost this patina of radicalism and lapsed comfortably into a Fanon-style neocolonial pattern of governance, both political and economic.

Mozambique was, momentarily, the signal exception to this depressing pattern of anti-climax to liberation struggle however – so exceptional, in fact, that Norrie MacQueen, a careful chronicler of 'the decolonization of Portuguese Africa', could firmly state of former Portuguese Africa, that 'the initial plans of Portugal's "guerrilla enemies"' offered 'a clear alternative to the cynical manipulation of ethnicity and the neocolonial complaisance of the kleptocratic elites who increasingly defined African governance in the 1970s and 1980s' (MacQueen 1997: 236–237). In sum, he concluded,

> Whatever their fate, the projects of the post-independence regimes of lusophone Africa were probably the most principled and decent ever proposed for the continent. They have not been superseded in this regard and seem unlikely to be.

And MacQueen argued so with good reason (although he did err, in my view, in quite so uncritically lumping Angola's blighted purpose with the much more genuine promise exemplified, however briefly, by Mozambique).

More immediately, the Tanzanian moment was closely linked to the Mozambican moment as well, not merely by immediate geographical propinquity but by the strong and practical frontline state backup offered by Nyerere. For Tanzania was the main launching pad of Frelimo's cross-border military entry into its own country; Dar es Salaam was the chief nerve centre of the Mozambican struggle throughout the 1960s and early 1970s; and southern Tanzania – Nachingwea camp in particular – was the staging ground for the liberation movement's dramatic initial incursions into the northern Mozambican provinces of Cabo Delgado and Niassa. Not that such support came entirely easily: Nyerere, in the wake of Eduardo Mondlane's assassination in 1969, was forced to press the case for it with impressive zeal in order to win Tanu backing for Samora Machel's progressive Frelimo leadership group, something that had to be asserted against the claims both of a much more opportunist group of alternative pretenders to Frelimo leadership (gathered behind the figure of Uriah Simango) and also of certain senior 'black-nationalist' Tanzanian cabinet ministers (Munyanka, Maswanya, Sijaona) who thought to support Simango.

The result: Frelimo, now firmly under Machel's sway, succeeded in further consolidating liberated zones in the provinces of northern Mozambique adjacent to Tanzania, in also openly contesting fresh areas adjacent to Zambia (in Tete province) and in beginning to press even further south. Moreover, in relatively freed zones the movement would start to build a fledgling social infrastructure of agricultural co-ops, schools and health services. Equally important, it was able to forge an impressive corps of politically conscious and disciplined leadership cadres (Cabaço 2001 and 2009). And then, with Mozambique's independence, Frelimo also launched its own bold experiment in socialist development. The intention: to implement a society-wide programme that would liberate the country's economic potential while also meeting the needs of the vast majority of Mozambique's population.

The movement had clearly matured towards this kind of undertaking – as indicated by the movement's first president, Mondlane (1969 and1983), shortly before his assassination by the Portuguese in 1969. As he argued, in sketching the direction that the movement was increasingly taking,

> I am now convinced that Frelimo has a clearer political line than ever before … The common basis that we had when we formed Frelimo was hatred of colonialism and the belief in the necessity to destroy the colonial structure and to establish a new social structure. But what type of social structure, what type of organisation we would have, no-one knew. No, some did know, some did have ideas, but they had rather theoretical notions that were themselves transformed in the struggle.
>
> Now, however, there is a qualitative transformation in thinking that has emerged during the past six years which permits me to conclude that at present Frelimo is much more socialist, revolutionary and progressive than ever … Why? Because the conditions of life in Mozambique, the type of enemy which we have, does not give us any other alternative … [In fact] the conditions in which we struggle and work demand it (in Saul 2008: 185).

As Mondlane concluded, it would now be 'impossible to create a capitalist Mozambique'. Indeed, 'it would be ridiculous to struggle, for the people to struggle, to destroy the economic structure of the enemy and then reconstitute it in such a way as to serve the enemy'. To 'reconstitute [the economy] in such a way as to serve the enemy': is this not, we might ask, precisely what has happened in South Africa?

In any case, Frelimo then did launch a number of exceptional programmes, not only in spheres such as education, health and women's affairs (see essays by Marshall, Barker and Urdang in Saul 1985), but also in the importance it attached – despite its clearly stated preference for a one-party structure – to practices designed to ensure a genuine voice and presence pressing from below. In this latter respect, it looked to such things as the creation of *grupos dinamizadores* in urban areas and of village committees in the rural areas, these being designed, at the local level, to generalise participation and to concretise an important measure of democracy. It also looked, in workplaces, to Production Councils and such initiatives as its 'Political and Organizational Offensive' in an attempt to counter hierarchy, bureaucratisation and, quite specifically, tendencies towards class formation.[11] In fact, the leadership – despite its above-mentioned commitment to a one-party state, undoubtedly a most debilitating commitment in the longer term – debated strenuously the inevitable tension (recall our discussion of Tanu's *Mwongozo* in the preceding section) it admitted to exist between the vanguard role of the party on the one hand, and 'popular power' intended to find expression from below, on the other.[12]

However, any sense of a creative contradiction that existed and had to continue to be resolved between the respective claims of leadership on the one hand and mass action on the other, did not last long. True, Frelimo distinguished its own practices sharply from the perceived shortfalls of Tanzania's project, privately criticising Nyerere for what it considered to be his all too wispy and romantic evocation of a specifically 'African socialism' – a cultural determinant said to spring relatively unproblematically from the sheer 'Africanness' of a social setting and claimed to serve as guarantor of a benignly univocal and widely shared collective sensibility. Frelimo, in contrast, saw itself as having, thanks to its Marxist–Leninist predilections, a much tougher sense of class contradictions than that. Yet the differences between these two contrasting experiments in post-liberation socialism tended to fade as, in the Frelimo case, the vanguard mode of the armed struggle became the framing carapace of politics during the 'building socialism' period. It thus found itself merely repeating many of the errors – a virtually non-existent domestic industrial strategy, a high-handedness towards the peasantry and workers and a self-righteous leadership style – of Tanzania's socialists.

Take, for example, the area of overall economic strategy, where the choice of an unsuitable Soviet brand of technology-heavy projected industrialisation very soon manifested itself.[13] In Mozambique, as in Tanzania, little was heard of anything like the kind of internally focused and internally driven industrial strategy advocated by Thomas, one that would have been designed to twin more effectively the interplay of rural and urban sectors and to prioritise the meeting of popular needs. And little was heard, either, of genuine peasant empowerment in the rural areas. Instead, the focus was too exclusively on nationalising and rendering productive the abandoned settler estates – throughout the southern part of the country in particular – with, it is true, some allusion to possibilities of a more active kind of workers' control there that were, however, never substantially realised in practice. Meanwhile, a variant of forced villagisation – not unlike that in Tanzania – was the dominant format in the peasant sector per se, one driven forward, as ultimately had also been the case in Tanzania, in a top-down spirit that did anything but inspire confidence.

What then was the reason that Frelimo – and with it, socialist Mozambique – came to stumble? Of course, the likelihood of such a negative result was cruelly overdetermined. The country's inheritance from colonial domination was certainly a poor one, reflected in such weaknesses as the paucity of trained indigenous personnel and an economic dependence that pulled the country strongly towards subordination to global dictate, despite efforts to resist it. There was also the ongoing regional war that made Mozambique the target of destructive incursions by white-dominated Rhodesia and South Africa and of a long drawn-out campaign of terror waged so callously and destructively by these countries' sponsored ward, the Mozambican National Resistance (Renamo) counter-revolutionary movement. But lastly there were, despite Frelimo's own apparently benign original intentions, the movement's own sins once in power, sins of vanguardist high-handedness and impatience and of an arrogant oversimplification of societal complexities and challenges (religious, ethnic, regional). These self-inflicted weaknesses created obstacles of their own to further progress.

Thus – not having the expression of their own voices effectively institution-alised within the space allowed by the vanguardist political model Frelimo had chosen for itself – a popular, self-conscious force from below could, quite simply, *not* be expected to arise to help effectively stem any eventual drive to elitist oppor-tunism and greed on the part of Mozambique's Frelimo-linked elite. Never really invited to take actual, concrete, democratic ownership of its own revolution, the mass of people remained all too passive in its defence of Mozambique's osten-sible revolution, as first – after Machel's death at the hands of the South Africans – Joaquim Chissano and then Armando Guebuza (like Chissano, concerned to enrich both himself and his family in a burgeoning private sector) became presi-dent. In fact, such dramatic examples epitomised the overall leadership's turn to the very brand of self-aggrandisement that Fanon had feared – a trajectory that would also have been unfathomable to either Mondlane or Machel.[14]

Indeed, what we now had, in Alice Dinerman's perfectly accurate description, was nothing less than a:

> rapid unravelling of the Mozambican revolution, with the result that Mozambique, once considered a virtually peerless pioneer in forging a socialist pathway in Africa, … now enjoys an equally exceptional, if dialectically opposed, status: today the country is, in the eyes of the International Monetary Fund (IMF) and the World Bank, a flagship of neoliberal principles.

Moreover, as Dinerman concludes:

> predictably, many of the leading government and party officials rank among the primary beneficiaries of the new political and economic dispensation. Those who enthusiastically promised that Mozambique would turn into a graveyard of capitalism are now the leading advocates of, and avid accumulators in, capitalism's recent, full-blown resurrection (Dinerman 2006: 19–20; Pitcher 2002 and 2006).

Not unlike many amongst the ANC's top brass and their circle, we might again be tempted to add.

What had occurred in Mozambique, Gretchen Bauer and Scott D. Taylor (2005) suggest, was the extremely rapid growth and dramatic spread of corruption (more or less unknown in the initial days of independence) in Mozambique, as well as a fevered 'pursuit of individual profit [that has undermined] much of the legitimacy of Frelimo party leaders, who [have taken] advantage of market-based opportunities, like privatisation, to enrich themselves' (Bauer and Taylor 2005: 135). In short, as these authors then observe,

> the election of Guebuza [as the new president in 2002, and since], holder of an expansive business network and one of the richest men in Mozambique, hardly signals that Frelimo will attempt to run on anything but a globalist, neoliberal agenda – regardless of the abject poverty suffered by most of its electorate.

Is this then a failure of socialism or rather, a sad surrender of Frelimo's once much-trumpeted version of such a project – and a victory for elite-assisted recolonisation? The second of these conclusions seems, to many observers, to be an all too accurate one, unfortunately; it is this kind of sombre conclusion – and sobering outcome – that I have had occasion, albeit with heavy heart, to write about elsewhere (Saul 2009 and 2013, chapter 3).

SOCIALISM IN SOUTHERN AFRICA AND THE SOUTH AFRICAN CASE

The logic of genuine 'economic nationalism', of the refusal of any abject, unqualified surrender to the forces of global capital and of the necessity to link socialism to any such successful refusal was quickly lost on the ANC, that movement/party being able (wilfully or otherwise) to see only the negative dimensions of Tanzania's and Mozambique's failed attempts at a more humane and progressively transformative political economy. But the imperatives of genuine and empowered democracy, of a progressive (non-vanguardist) resolution of the tension between leadership and popular control and of a non-dogmatic economic self-reliance were even more quickly lost on the ANC than they had been, in the long run, on Tanu and Frelimo (Saul 2013: chapter 4; Saul and Bond forthcoming [2014]). As was soon clear, the ANC's momentary toying with the modest measure of transformation that the RDP (Reconstruction and Development Programme) represented soon slipped into Gear and the movement's extremely brief flirtation with the promise of some sustained popular purpose and some sustained popular takeover of the process of transformation was lost.

Indeed, as Michelle Williams (2008) helps make clear, the latter outcome was never really on offer – even from the SACP, much less from the ANC. Thus, in carefully contrasting the South African instance with that of Kerala, she suggests that in the latter case the Indian state's Communist Party premised its activities on what she calls a 'counter-hegemonic generative politics' and 'a reliance on participatory organizing' – a politics that has sought, precisely, to genuinely empower people. In South Africa, on the other hand, the preference of the ANC/SACP grouping has been for 'a hegemonic generative politics' and a reliance on mere 'mass mobilizing' (Williams 2008: 91) – to, in effect, draw a crowd to popularly hail its ascendancy. Small wonder that a saddened, older ANC/SACP cadre like Rusty Bernstein could, shortly before his death, bemoan the fact that when, in the 1980s, mass popular resistance revived again inside the country led by the UDF, it led the ANC to see the UDF as an undesirable factor in the struggle for power and to undermine it as a rival focus for mass mobilization. It has undermined the ANC's adherence to the path [of] mass resistance as the way to liberation, and substituted instead a reliance on manipulation of administrative power … It has impoverished the soil in which ideas leaning towards socialist solutions once flourished and allowed the weed of 'free market' ideology to take hold (Bernstein 2007:144).

A grim balance sheet, in short, albeit one not so very different from that of the recolonised (by the worldwide reach of capital) residues of colonial empires that its neighbours have also become. Indeed, despite its rather higher starting point (thanks to its mineral riches) on the world economic table, the South African populace is firmly lodged well down the world poverty table. For South Africa, in the absence of the imaginative planning that might have sought both an effectively self-centred (but, to repeat, not autarkic) economic model and a possibly transformative developmental future, remains primarily a 'taker' of economic signals from the global corporate world. Its record in terms of providing opportunities for urban employment and rural renewal, in terms of housing, electricity and water supplies, in terms of education and health services, in terms of a progressive package of environmentally sensitive measures and its record in terms of facilitating the growth of social equality more generally, is not markedly better than the records of its neighbours in southern Africa.

In fact, the principal lesson to be learned from recent southern African history, including that of South Africa, is not so much 'what not to do' as it is the high cost to be paid for choosing 'not to dare' – not to dare to be self-reliant and economically imaginative and not to dare to be genuinely democratic and actively committed to the social and political empowerment of the people themselves. For not to so dare is, in our contemporary world, merely to wallow in a stagnant pond of self-serving vanguardism and in a post-Fanonist pattern of elite aggrandisement – even if such attitudes are, in South Africa, sustained within what is now a formally democratic process. And it is to accept passively something else, that 'something else' being most readily epitomised in one harsh, hard and unyielding word: recolonisation. All that struggle, carried out so nobly, against apartheid – and, throughout the region, against a full panoply of arrogant colonialisms – to have come to this: a callous recolonisation, by global capital and, as aided, domestically, by southern Africa's own ostensible once-liberators. Sad, sad, sad.

Not that South Africa has escaped the grim politics of polarisation that the ANC's choice of direction has willed for it. Although the ANC continues to win power (with a roughly similar high percentage of what is nonetheless an increasingly smaller turnout of eligible voters), it has to deal with an increasingly discontented population. As Peter Alexander has noted,

> Since 2004 South Africa has experienced a movement of local protests amounting to a rebellion of the poor. This has been widespread and intense, reaching insurrectionary proportions in some cases. On the surface, the protests have been about service delivery and against uncaring, self-serving and corrupt leaders of the municipalities. A key feature has been mass participation by a new generation of fighters, especially unemployed youth but also school students. Many issues that underpinned the [initial] ascendency of Jacob Zuma also fuel the present action, including a sense of injustice arising from the realities of persistent inequality ... [Moreover,] while the inter-connections between the local protest, and between the local protests and militant action involving other elements of civil society, are limited, it is suggested that this is likely to change (Alexander 2010: 25).

Indeed, Moeletsi Mbeki (2011), Thabo's brother, recently speculated on the possibility of an ever more forceful eruption from below of a genuine, Tunisia-like spring of discontent being likely, eventually, to mark South Africa (he sets the likely date as 2020). Small wonder that even Zwelinzima Vavi, despite the fact that his own trade union central (Congress of South African Trade Unions [Cosatu]) continues to be mired in a demobilising political alliance with the ANC and SACP, can observe: 'We have a constitution which grants people certain rights. Yet in practice millions are denied those rights, especially socio-economic rights, in what has become the most unequal nation in the world' (Vavi 2011).

*   *   *

In short, overall, many of the ingredients for the emergence in South Africa of an effectively counter-hegemonic politics – and, one might hope, for a politics of active, participatory mass empowerment – seem to be in place. In this way South Africa may actually offer a much more promising picture than its fellow, now distinctly anti-socialist, 'false decolonisers' elsewhere in the region: Tanzania and Mozambique. For in South Africa, movements such as the Democratic Left Front give signs of eventually making good the hopes of Fanon himself (and, as quoted above, of Williams). As Fanon (1967: 253) put the relevant point:

> The Third World [including the countries of Southern Africa] today faces Europe like a colossal mass whose project should be to try to resolve the problems to which Europe has not been able to find the answers.

Fanon is still waiting, of course. Indeed, at the moment, the 'answers' (capitalism, growing inequality and extremely straitened structures of democratic aspiration and active participation) of Europe and North America are the structures southern Africa has taken as its own. Nonetheless, as Fanon (1967: 255) tells us, 'For Europe, for ourselves, and for humanity, comrades, we must turn over a new leaf, we must work out new concepts, and try to set afoot a new man [sic]'.

Clearly, the struggle to realise such an outcome continues.

NOTES

1   For a more sceptical view of my good friend Arrighi's account of his own views in the 1960s (reflecting my own rather different memories of the time and of our discussions), see chapter 3, 'Arrighi and Africa: farewell thoughts', in Saul 2011: 53–54.

2   In Saul (2008) see chapter 5, 'The strange death of liberated southern Africa', where I have also cited some of the quotations presented in these pages and a more extended version of a related argument.

3   Recall Mandela's apparent hailing, in 1994, of the free market as a 'magic elixir' in his speech to the joint session of the Houses of Congress in Washington. And his strident statement, in arguing in favour of the Growth, Employment and Redistribution (Gear) strategy to replace the mildly more radical Reconstruction and Development Programme (RDP), that Gear was, as per its august invocation from on-high, 'non-negotiable'!

4   Gevisser (in Turok 2008: 58) also reports that Mbeki's first instructions to Trevor Manuel, upon the latter's taking over as finance minister in 1996, was for a policy that 'called precisely for the kind of fiscal discipline and investment-friendly tax incentives that the international financial institutions loved and that Manuel already believed in'!

5   As Turok (2008: 264–265) continues this thought 'much depends on whether enough momentum can be built to overcome the caution that has marked the ANC government since 1994. This depends on whether the determination to achieve an equitable society can be revived.'

6   On 'recolonisation' see Saul (2008), especially chapter 2, 'Recolonisation and the new empire of capital' (47–80).

7   For my more detailed retrospective reflections on the Tanzanian case see, *inter alia*, Saul (2012) and Saul (2005), specifically chapter 7, 'Julius Nyerere's Tanzania: Learning from Tanzania'. I have drawn directly on some of these materials in preparing this section of the present chapter.

8   On the workers see, *inter alia*, Mihyo (1974) and, in edited form, in *Review of African Political Economy*, 4: 62–84 and Mapolu (1976); on peasants see Schneider (2003 and 2004); on women see Meena (2003: 15–2l), and on the students at the university see Saul (2009), chapter 1, 'The 1960s – Tanzania', and Borbonniere (2007).

9   The interview with Bibi Titi, on which this article focuses, was carried out by Ms Meena in 1988.

10 Once again, I have drawn on some of my own previous writings in preparing this section of the present chapter: notably Arrighi and Saul (1973); my chapter 8, 'Frelimo and the Mozambique revolution' in Saul (1985); the various Mozambique-related sections in Saul (2009); and Saul (2011).

11 See the chapter by Sketchley on Production Councils in Saul 1985 and also, those on urban and rural/agricultural realities, by Pinsky and Dolny respectively, in the same volume.

12 Buyer beware – and see the volume which I edited, *A Difficult Road* (1985). In that volume I myself struggled in its overview chapters (chapters 1 and 2) to evaluate this issue accurately, torn as I was between the claims of Frelimo's apparently benign, even progressive vanguardism on the one hand and the claims of struggle from below on the other. I now feel much more strongly than I did 30 years ago that any stark assertion of the presumed virtues of 'vanguardism' are very questionable indeed – although mere spontaneism is also a weak reed upon which to build a revolution. The fact is that there is definitely a role for leadership – sagacious, clear and forthright – but it must be held, absolutely and openly, democratically accountable. The health and safety of any revolution that seeks to better the lot of the vast majority of the populace is dependent upon that.

13 While teaching, in the early 1980s, in both the Frelimo Party School in Maputo and the Faculty of Marxism–Leninism at the University of Eduardo Mondlane I was shocked at the rigidity of the kind of Marxism that was being urged on Frelimo there by cooperants dispatched from the Eastern bloc countries. This was a 'Marxism' very different in texture from the progressive perspectives I had known within Frelimo in earlier years – although, truth to tell, it fitted all too comfortably with the leadership's own vanguardist and technocratic propensities.

14 Unlike that of Mondlane, Machel's style was indeed far too overbearing for the revolution's own health but there was no sign of corruption; instead, indeed, every sign of his benign dedication to long-term popular well-being; the assassinations of both Mondlane and Machel were costly blows to the country's prospects.

REFERENCES

Alexander, P. 2010. 'Rebellion of the poor: South Africa's service delivery protests – a preliminary analysis', *Review of African Political Economy*, 123: 25–40.

Amin, S. 1985. *Delinking: Towards a Polycentric World*. London: Zed Books.

Arrighi, G. 2009. 'The winding paths of capital' (interview by David Harvey), *New Left Review*, 56: 61–94.

Arrighi, G. and Saul, J.S. 1973. *Essays on the Political Economy of Africa*. New York: Monthly Review Press.

Bauer, G. and Taylor, S.D. 2005. *Politics in Southern Africa: State and Society in Transition*. Boulder, CO: Lynne Reiner Publishers.

Bernstein, R. 2007. 'A letter', *Transformation*, 64: 140–144.

Borbonniere, M. 2007. 'Debating socialism on the hill: The University of Dar es Salaam, 1961–71', MA dissertation, Dalhousie University.

Cabaço, J.L. 2001. 'The new man (brief itinerary of a project)'. In *Samora: Man of the People*, edited by A. Sopa. Maputo: Maguezo Editores.

Cabaço, J.L. 2009. *Moçambique: Identidade, Colonialismo e Libertação*. São Paolo: Editora UNESP.

Cliffe, L. and Saul, J.S. (eds). 1972. *Socialism in Tanzania, Volume I, Politics*. Nairobi: East African Publishing House.

Cliffe, L. and Saul, J.S. (eds). 1973. *Socialism in Tanzania, Volume II, Policies*. Nairobi: East African Publishing House.

Dinerman, A. 2006. *Revolution, Counter-Revolution and Revisionism in Post-Colonial Africa: The Case of Mozambique*. Milton Park and New York: Routledge.

Fanon, F. 1967. *The Wretched of the Earth*. Harmondsworth: Penguin.

Gevisser, M. 2007. *Thabo Mbeki: The Dream Deferred*. Johannesburg: Jonathan Ball.

Gevisser, M. 2009. *A Legacy of Liberation: Thabo Mbeki and the Future of the South African Dream*. New York: Palgrave-Macmillan.

Green, P. 2006. 'The outsider who has measured vision against reality', *Business Report*, 16 February.

Gumede, W. 2005. *Thabo Mbeki and the Battle for the Soul of the ANC*. Cape Town: Zebra Press.

Luttrell, W.L. 1986. *Post-Capitalist Industrialization: Planning Economic Independence in Tanzania*. New York: Praeger.

MacQueen, N. 1997. *The Decolonization of Portuguese Africa: Metropolitan Revolution and the Dissolution of Empire*. London: Longman.

Mapolu, H. (ed.). 1976. *Workers and Management*. Dar es Salaam: Tanzania Publishing House.

Mbeki, M. 2011. 'Wealth creation: Only a matter of time before the hand grenade explodes,' *Business Day*, 10 February.

Mbeki, T. 1984. 'The Fatton thesis: A rejoinder', *Canadian Journal of African Studies*, 18 (3): 609–612.

Mbeki, T. 1991. 'Interview'. *Mayibuye*, March.

Meena, R. 2003. 'A conversation with Bibi Titi: A political veteran'. In *Activist Voices: Feminist Struggles for an Alternative World*, edited by M. Mbilinyi, M. Rusimbi, S.L. Chachage and D. Kiyunga. Dar es Salaam: Tanzania Gender Networking Programme.

Mihyo, P. 1974. 'The struggle for workers control in Tanzania', *MajiMaji* 17, special issue on 'Labour unrest and the quest for workers' control', Dar es Salaam.

Mondlane, E. 1969. *The Struggle for Mozambique*. Harmondsworth: Penguin African Library.

Mondlane, E. 1983. *The Struggle for Mozambique*. London: Zed Books.

Murray, R. 1967. 'Second thoughts on Ghana', *New Left Review*, 42: 25–39.

Nyerere, J.K. 1968. *Freedom and Socialism*. Nairobi and London: Oxford University Press.

Pitcher, A. 2002. *Transforming Mozambique: The Politics of Privatisation, 1975–2000*. Cambridge and New York: Cambridge University Press.

Pitcher, A. 2006. 'Forgetting from above and memory from below: Strategies of legitimation and struggle in postsocialist Mozambique', *Africa*, 76 (1): 88–112.

Rodney, W. 1975. 'Class contradictions in Tanzania'. Accessed 17 July 2013, http://www.marxists.org/subject/africa/rodney-walter/works/classcontradictions.htm.

Saul, J.S. (ed.). 1985. *A Difficult Road: The Transition to Socialism in Mozambique*. New York: Monthly Review Press.

Saul, J.S. 2005. *The Next Liberation Struggle: Capitalism, Socialism and Democracy in Southern Africa*. Pietermaritzburg: University of KwaZulu-Natal Press.

Saul, J.S. 2008. *Decolonization and Empire: Contesting the Rhetoric and Reality of Resubordination in South Africa and Beyond*. Johannesburg: Wits University Press.

Saul, J.S. 2009. *Revolutionary Traveller: Freeze-frames from a Life*. Winnipeg: Arbeiter Ring.

Saul, J.S. 2011. *Liberation Lite: The Roots of Recolonization in Southern Africa*. Dehli and Trenton, NJ. Three Essays Collective and Africa World Press.

Saul, J.S. 2012. 'Tanzania fifty years on (1961–2011): Rethinking *ujamaa*, Nyerere and socialism in Africa', *Review of African Political Economy*, 39 (131): 117–125.

Saul, J.S. 2013. *A False Freedom: Rethinking Southern African Liberation*. Delhi and London: Three Essays Collective and Pluto Press.

Saul, J.S. and Bond, P. Forthcoming (2014). *South Africa's Present as History: From Mrs. Ples to Marikana*. Oxford and Johannesburg: James Currey and Jacana.

Schneider, L. 2003. 'Developmentalism and its failings: Why rural development went wrong in 1960s and 1970s Tanzania'. Unpublished PhD dissertation, Columbia University.

Schneider, L. 2004. 'Freedom and unfreedom in rural development: The theory and practice of Julius Nyerere's rural socialism', *Canadian Journal of African Studies*, 38 (2): 344–392.

Schneider, L. 2006. 'Colonial legacies and postcolonial authoritarianism in Tanzania: Connects and disconnects', *African Studies Review*, 49 (1): 93–118.

Tanu (Tanganyika African National Union). 1971. *Mwongozo wa Tanu*. Dar es Salaam: Tanu.

Thomas, C.P. 1974. *Dependence and Transformation: The Economics of the Transition to Socialism*. New York: Monthly Review Press.

Turok, B. 2008. *From the Freedom Charter to Polokwane: The Evolution of the ANC's Economic Policy*. Cape Town: New Agenda.

Vavi, Z. 2011. 'Keynote address to the SACBC Justice and Peace AGM'. Cosatu press release, 26 February.

Williams, M. 2008. *The Roots of Participatory Democracy: Democratic Communists in South Africa and Kerala, India*. New York and London: Palgrave-Macmillan.

9

UNEVEN AND COMBINED MARXISM WITHIN SOUTH AFRICA'S URBAN SOCIAL MOVEMENTS

Patrick Bond, Ashwin Desai and Trevor Ngwane

The political dynamics of contemporary South Africa are rife with contradiction. On the one hand, it is among the most consistently contentious places on earth, with insurgent communities capable of mounting disruptive protest on a nearly constant basis, rooted in the poor areas of the half-dozen major cities as well as neglected and multiply oppressed black residential areas of declining towns. On the other hand, even the best-known contemporary South African social movements, for all their sound, lack a certain measure of fury.

In the face of the government's embrace of neoliberal social policies since shortly after the fall of apartheid, what are often called 'service delivery protests' occurring many thousands of times a year according to police statistics (Duncan and Vally 2008; Mottiar and Bond 2011) are at once the site of poor people's demands for greater responsiveness to human needs in general, but are also intensely localised and self-limited in their politics. The upsurge of protest since the late 1990s invariably invokes images of the anti-apartheid struggle and thus focuses analysis on continuities and breaks between the old anti-apartheid mass action and the new mass action in post-apartheid society.[1] And yet the majority of community protesters operate in close interconnection with parts of the Tripartite Alliance, composed of the African National Congress (ANC), the trade union movement represented by the Congress of South African Trade

Unions (Cosatu) and the South African Communist Party (SACP) and so the line between insurgencies and governing organisations is not always clear. Yet their geographic and political isolation from one another have contributed to their having little leverage over the Alliance, which notwithstanding some resistance by unions and communists, embraced neoliberal policies in the transition from anti-apartheid resistance to class-apartheid government in 1994.

But beyond the community protests, in many respects, the problems that have faced more traditional radical social movements in South Africa are familiar to students of social movements elsewhere: the problems of moving from movement to governing; of co-optation and shifting roles vis-à-vis the state; of the limits of localism and the problem of how to join community- and workplace-based organising to forge a strong working-class politics. These are all the subject of considerable scholarship, both within and outside of the Marxist tradition and within and outside of South Africa (see for example, DeFilippis, Fisher and Schragge 2010; Katznelson 1981; Piven and Cloward 1979). We argue here, however, that in the South African context, these can be more clearly seen as symptomatic questions of a larger problematic: what we term, following Leon Trotsky, the problem of 'uneven and combined Marxism'.

For Trotsky (1962), 'uneven and combined development' was a fundamentally dialectical framework through which he sought first to theorise the relations among Russia's nascent industrial base (and hence, too, Russia's urban proletariat) and its backward, semi-feudal rural relations and second, following this, the revolutionary potentials for Russia at the time of the Revolution. For Trotsky, this implied understanding the relationship among forms of capital both within Russia and across its borders. Uneven development means that extremely different relations of production coexist within and across territories, while combined development suggests that the 'less developed' are archaic and simply bound, at some point, to 'catch up' with the more advanced, perhaps going through the same 'stages' of development. The South African modernisation narrative since the early 2000s, shared by former president Thabo Mbeki and current president Jacob Zuma, is that the 'two economies' are 'structurally disconnected' – notwithstanding abundant evidence that poverty created in one place directly correlates to wealth accumulated in another (Bond and Desai 2006; Maharaj, Desai and Bond 2011).

Hence, in order to understand the revolutionary possibilities of a given moment, it is important to understand how more and less advanced relations of production are interconnected, how they often reinforce each other and how their contradictions may lead to revolutionary advances in developmentally 'less-advanced' contexts. 'Uneven and combined *Marxism*' implies a way of considering the difficulties of constructing independent left politics in the conjuncture of a long-term capitalist stagnation in a twenty-first-century South Africa in which some sectors of the economy – construction, finance and commerce – have been booming while many other, former labour-intensive sectors of manufacturing were de-industrialised (or shifted from general production for a local mass market to niche production for a global upper-class market, such as luxury autos and garments) and in which large sections of society are still peripheral to the interests of capital, domestic and global – aside from serving as a reserve army of unneeded surplus labour. The unevenness is also geographical, with small areas of South Africa operating within a circuit of luxury consumption and new technologies, but others such as ex-bantustan rural areas continuing their decline. The unevenness of sector and space is no surprise, of course, since capital has always flowed to sites of higher profitability, not to establish equilibrating trends, but on the contrary to exacerbate differentials and enhance inequalities. The word 'combined' is important in South Africa because of the ways capital interacts with the non-capitalist sectors and spaces, including women's reproductive sites and mutual-aid systems, spaces of community commons, state services and nature.

Unevenness is obvious across the cities and townships (and towns and *dorpies* or villages) where battles rage among the sectors of capital and across scales of struggle. The 'combined' part of anti-capitalism is an area we are yet to see fully invoked (in the spirit of, for example, the Latin American mobilisation which foregrounded indigenous movements' struggles), because of the complexities of organising the unorganised – especially women – in shack settlements and rural areas where the act of daily survival in the interstices of capitalist/non-capitalist articulations generates many more collisions of political self-interest than standard Marxist urban theory so far elucidates.

To speak of uneven and combined Marxism, therefore, is to invoke a political project on the South African Left that *cannot but* begin with the contradictory totality of the country's social relations, both internal and external, at multiple geographic scales and at vastly different levels of development. And yet, the beginning cannot also be the end; the challenge for South African left politics is to create from this unevenness a hegemonic formation that is capable of moving toward fulfilling the global Left's hopes in the anti-apartheid struggle, which was, in many respects, an anti-capitalist struggle as well. But to articulate a left politics on this uneven ground is also to enrich the typic-ally imported Marxist analysis, in the sense that the South African experience heightens and encapsulates several otherwise familiar tensions – urban/rural, worker/poor, local/national/global, society/nature, gender and so on – and can therefore show, perhaps more clearly than can other contexts, the essential rela-tions among them.

In what follows, we begin by describing the contemporary contours of protest in South Africa and then return to the problem of the hegemony of the Tripartite Alliance and its embrace of neoliberal policies, even if this has itself been some-what uneven and the source of some tension among Alliance members. We then discuss the development of a strategic impasse among South African social movements and present and critique several theoretically informed alternative routes out of or around the apparent cul-de-sac. We conclude by rearticulating more precisely the stakes in proposing an uneven and combined Marxism and, rather than proposing solutions, we draw upon it to pose the strategic questions for an agency-centred South African Left more sharply.

CONTEMPORARY SOUTH AFRICAN PROTEST

Writing five years after the end of apartheid, Andrew Nash (1999: 61) observed:

> The struggle against Apartheid became at times a focus of the hopes of the revolutionary left around the world. It represents a missed oppor-tunity for the left not only in the more obvious sense that it did not result in a real challenge to the power of global capitalism. It was also an opportunity to transform the historical relationship of Marxist theory and working class politics, and overcome the division which allows a dialectical Marxism to flourish in the universities and journals, while working class politics are dominated by the managerialism of Soviet Marxism or social-democracy.

This sense of a lost opportunity persists in South African politics today. It is found in the widespread discontent in townships and shack-dweller commun-ities on the urban periphery over the rising cost of living and of previously state-provided services such as water and electricity; it is found among the poor in the militant protests for redistricting so that poor areas and rich areas are not administratively separated, thereby hampering the poor's ability to gain access to resources and public services (as in the towns of Khutsong and Balfour); it is seen in the divisions within the ANC, the SACP and Cosatu; and it is seen in the Treatment Action Campaign's successful and well-known battle against Mbeki's AIDS denialism and against Big Pharma's price-gouging of antiretroviral medicines. And yet, in many of the successful instances of protest – for example, the reconnection of water and electricity (Bond 2011c); the rolling-back of privatisation schemes (Bond 2005) and the reduction in the price of antiretrovirals from $15 000 per person to zero (Geffen 2010) – revolutionary Marxists played important leadership roles, suggesting, perhaps, that Nash bends the stick a bit too far.

Nevertheless, the question of how far to bend the stick remains. There is no question that anti-racial apartheid also had within it the seeds of anti-class apartheid. This can be seen in the Treatment Action Campaign's successful attack, not just on price-gouging by Big Pharma, but also on intellectual property rights, which were curtailed by the 2001 Doha exemption for medical emergencies. It can be seen in the Soweto Electricity Crisis Committee's work since 2000, not only to fight against the electricity company's privatisation, rate changes and electricity cut-offs, but also to teach people how to illegally reconnect themselves to the grid. These are only part of what Peter Alexander (2010) calls a 'rebellion of the poor'. In the wake of the introduction of the Growth, Employment and Redistribution (Gear) strategy that marked the Alliance's definitive turn toward neoliberal macro-economic policy, the most militant communities that took to the streets in protest and that formed the new urban social movements were relatively privileged. They already had houses, but were now fighting a defensive battle just to stay on in the urban ghettos. Those who clung on to spaces in the city in shacks appeared to be more patient. The Alliance's promises to the poor included access to the formal ghetto, while at the same time, its municipal officials were evicting those who already had access for non-payment, as employment became precarious when unemployment increased to more than forty per cent of the workforce. For a while, the enormous legitimacy of the ANC explained this patience.

But from the late 1990s, ongoing waves of protests broke across the country's formal townships and shack settlements and the 'new urban social movements' formed in Durban, Johannesburg and Cape Town from 1999. Though the first waves ebbed after a national protest at the World Summit on Sustainable Development in 2002, more surges were noticed from mid-2004 in Zevenfontein, north of Johannesburg, and in Harrismith in the Free State (where repression was marked by shooting and death) and in Durban's Kennedy Road where, beginning in early 2005, shack-dweller protest coalesced into the Abahlali baseMjondolo (shack-dweller's movement).

Yet, in many cases what started out as insurgencies outside the control of the Alliance were siphoned off into calls for participation, legal challenges and 'voice'. Furthermore, one of the striking elements of South African protest is its failure to 'scale up', or join together either geographically or politically. With a few exceptions, the recent upsurge of service-delivery protests have taken the form of 'popcorn protests', that is, movements that fly high, move according to where the wind blows – even in xenophobic directions at times – and then fall to rest quite quickly (Petras and Morley 1990: 53). There have been several attempts at coordination in the mid-2000s: Johannesburg's Anti-Privatisation Forum brought together service-delivery protest groups, students, left polit-ical activists (including, at first, some in the municipal workers' union and the SACP) and independent-left trade unions; the Social Movements Indaba, which from 2002 to 2008 combined community struggles; and since 2011, the Democratic Left Front (DLF) has taken a similar initiative. Despite these efforts, and in part because of continual splintering of independent left forces and a failure to make common cause with the Left of the labour movement, neither common programmes, nor bridging organisational strategies that can challenge neoliberalism on a national level, have developed. Three elements of this failure – reflecting the uneven and combined nature of anti-capitalism in South Africa today – are worth noting here: the importance of access, localism and leadership.

Access

Social movements often organise around sets of demands on the state that are, at least in principle, winnable. Service-delivery protests targeting the privatisa-tion of water supply or high charges for water use by the local water authority, or targeting the regressive kilowatt-per-hour charge on electricity, or the evic-tion of shack-dwellers from squatted land, all imply the possibility of success. In Durban's rebellious Chatsworth community (Desai 2002), for example, in order to achieve de facto recognition and therefore the delivery of services that would keep the movement constituency close to its leadership, move-ment activists increasingly joined with the city council in various committees to administer and monitor the movement's success. A decade after the initial

1999 uprising, political work mainly involved technical issues and oversight over upgrading, liaison with welfare departments and a range of other interventions which pressed, not for radical policy change, but focused instead on merely getting existing policy implemented (Hinely 2009). This also inevitably brought the movement into close working relationships with ANC local councillors and limited the autonomy of the movement, ultimately leading to enormous disappointments in Chatsworth when official promises were broken and municipal contractors engaged in fraud.

Likewise, in Durban's shacklands, in order to get recognition from the local council, shack-dweller activists had to ensure that no more shacks were built. Activists also had to ward off competitors. This was especially so if an organisation defined its role as ensuring delivery. It was paradoxical but increasingly common that movements took political positions sharply critical of neoliberal policies on the one hand, while negotiating for better delivery within those policy frameworks on the other.

Of course, this is a common feature of social movements and of poor people's movements beyond the South African context. There is a recurring question of how to consolidate a movement's 'victories' without demobilising it and how to move beyond the initial 'winnable' demands to more radical ones that cannot be so easily administered. In the South African context, however, this problem is deepened by the sheer weight of the ANC's presence. Though there are a significant variety of political positions taken by local ANC branches and officials, larger matters of policy and financing are settled at the centre, while implementation – and enforcement – depends greatly on authorities at the local level. Reaching the centre, therefore, is fundamentally difficult given the fact that the service-delivery protests tend to limit their demands to locally constituted authorities, with the possible exception of Eskom, the utility that provides ninety-five per cent of South Africa's electricity (Eskom sells energy both to municipalities as well as to four million individual households – mainly in black townships and rural areas – who were retail customers dating back to the apartheid era). Access problems therefore imply a need for protesters to 'jump scale' from local to national and sometimes also to global, for the World Bank has been known to give 'instrumental' advice on matters such as water pricing (Bond 2000 and 2002).

Localism and the geographic scales of protest organisation

Marxist urban theorists, following the geographer Henri Lefebvre, speak of social relations unfolding on multiple geographic scales. Scales combine aspects of people's own construction of the extent of their social relations and bound-aries of the arenas in which they exist. They thus depend, too, on historically accreted understandings of the spatial limitations exerted on these relations and on the physical properties that may inscribe them. As Sallie Marston writes, they 'are the outcome of both everyday life and macro-level social structures' (2000: 221). Finally, the framings of scale – framings that can have both rhetor-ical and material consequences – are often contradictory and contested and are not necessarily enduring. To say, therefore, that contemporary South African protest – with several exceptions such as the Treatment Action Campaign and for a time, the Jubilee South Africa network, as well as some of the more innovative community groups in the major cities – is characteristically *local* in orientation is to make an observation about the scale of the protests.

There is nothing inherently wrong with the localist orientation of protest. To the extent that participants stop evictions that affect them; to the extent that they force local authorities to increase the free allowance of electricity and water and lower fees for anything above the survival allowance; to the extent that a 'residue' of protest emerges as a measure of local institutional safeguard against further abuse; to this extent, they are better off for having protested. From a Marxist perspective, however, limiting protest to the local scale both narrows the immediate transformative potential of social movements and in the longer term, disadvantages both the movements and the people who comprise them. The same can be said about the sectoral narrowness, in which struggles around issues such as the 'water sector', economic reform advocacy, gender, energy justice, climate activism, access to education, healthcare advo-cacy and myriad of more specific struggles fail to connect the dots between one another, both in South Africa and across the world (notwithstanding a World Social Forum movement meant – but apparently unable – to solve this problem) (Bond 2005).

What does going beyond localism mean? To ask the question begs, first of all, a more precise definition of what constitutes the 'local' in the present case. Here, we propose that 'local' in South African protest denotes a focus on administrative and jurisdictional boundaries, on the one hand and on the site of social reproduction, on the other. The extremely vigorous protest move-ments in the country focus most of their attention on the failings of local coun-cils and governments which are themselves both the local enforcers of ANC policies formulated on the national scale – often influenced by the demands of global brokers of capital (the South African Treasury sets great store by its international credit ratings) – and often, political machines in which allegiance to the ANC line at the time is paramount for gaining access to decision-making processes. They are also focused on the circumstances of life in communities in which many people share abysmal living conditions.

As people active in these struggles, we can confirm that these were not originally meant to be narrow and localised. We initially shared the hope that struggles at the community level – at what provisionally could be called the point of reproduction – would have a quality and depth to them that would enable radical social antagonisms to flourish in ways that were unthinkable in the world of regular wage-work, at the 'point of production'. As an idea, it makes sense. People live in communities 24 hours a day. With a huge mass of unemployed people stuck in these ghettos, many with experience in previous struggles, including that against apartheid, it would be easy for demands made from these sites to be backed up with the force of mass organisations. All that was needed was a focus on bread-and-butter township or shack issues and then an ideological extrapolation to broader political questions. Or so our thinking went, along with that of various segments of the independent (non-ANC, non-SACP) Left.

Focusing on the site of reproduction made sense in another way. In fact, the townships, shack-dweller communities, flat-dweller communities and *dorpies* of South Africa are collectively the site of a vast amount of economic activity and the unemployed are, as often as not, also the marginally employed, the unofficially employed and the precariously employed, which also means that they play no role in the pre-eminent labour organisation in the country, Cosatu, which has its base in the country's heavy and extractive industries and public sector. Only the narrowest view of the working class would ignore the precariat.

And yet, the local community as a site of post-apartheid resistance to neoliberalism has been much more difficult to sustain. Partly this is because of an assumption, seldom made by those actually living in townships, that there exists substantial ground for unity flowing from merely living under the same conditions. One version of this assumption, as articulated in Latin American cities by James Petras and Morris Morley (1990: 53), is that:

> The power of these new social movements comes from the fact that they draw on the vast heterogeneous labour force that populates the main thoroughfares and the alleyways; the marketplaces and street corners; the interstices of the economy and the nerve centres of production; the exchange and finance centres; the university plazas, railway stations and

the wharves – all are brought together in complex localized structures which feed into tumultuous homogenizing national movements.

In the South African context, however, while localism produced militancy, it did not necessarily produce solidarity on any regular basis. Indeed, shack-dwellers often face the ire of those with a tighter, but still precarious, hold on stable tenure in the townships. Township residents can be mobilised for violence against shack-dwellers and immigrants as much as they can be mobilised for solidarity.

Another source of optimism for the fusing of proletarian and precariat identities is alluded to by John Saul (1975: 175), recalling arguments made nearly four decades ago:

> In a capitalism in crisis the 'classic strengths of the urban working class' could become 'more evident,' with the 'the upper stratum of the workers [then] most likely to identify downward [to become] a leading force within a revolutionary alliance of exploited elements in the society'.

In the South African context, therefore, the mobilisation of communities could, in theory, join up with the existing organisation of workers through Cosatu, provided the latter could peel itself away from allegiance to the ANC and the Alliance's embrace of neoliberalism, especially in the light of clearly deteriorating conditions.

But beyond the disappointments generated by a Cosatu much changed by its entry into the Alliance and the decline of the shop-steward leadership that had provided much of its strength during the anti-apartheid struggle, local communities were themselves difficult to coalesce around consistent analyses of the problems that led to their oppression. Abstraction from the local to *multiple* scales proved difficult once the problems of evictions, electricity, sewerage and potable water were addressed.

Finally, it must be said that from a strategic point of view, there is some value in being able to organise at a scale commensurate with that of one's adversary's organisation. The ANC is organised at the national level and it staffs its organisation by the positioning of cadres in local areas. This means that it centralises power and is able to exert significant – though far from total – control over local cadres. Thus although some local councillors, for example, are more 'trigger happy' when it comes to repressing service-delivery and shack-dweller protests (and there have been more than a dozen deaths of protesters at the hands of police and non-official enforcers), the ANC's centralised organisation, which is extremely averse to criticism, has set a policy of repression while also trying to channel protest into the least threatening, least direct forms, such as marches, as opposed to land occupations. The ANC's factional violence against its own cadres is notorious, such as in Durban where in mid-2011 the party's leader was assassinated. But by December 2011 the ANC city manager and political elites were sufficiently united to unleash violent young party members on DLF activists who staged a march of more than 5 000 against the United Nations climate summit and who put up signs a few days later in the City Hall, during a visit by President Zuma.

Leadership

Another set of problems that arises from contemporary South African protest is also familiar to students of social movements and revolutionary politics, namely, the problem of leadership and particularly, the role of intellectuals in the movement. Antonio Gramsci's analysis of intellectuals is apposite here. Gramsci (1971) argues, in essence, that intellectuals are those who give shape, through mental labour, to specific sets and sites of social relations. Those he calls 'traditional' intellectuals are those whose roles as intellectuals were formed in earlier periods and thus appear as separate from and above contemporary class relations and antagonisms, such as clergy and the professional scholars and teachers. 'Organic' intellectuals, by contrast, are those whose intellectual labour shapes the projects of entire groups of people, such as industrialists and union militants. By virtue of their social position, traditional intellectuals can make claims about universals, whereas organic intellectuals allegedly articulate particularities. But as Gramsci (1971: 4–23) makes clear, traditional intellectuals are just as moored to class as are organic ones and in fact newly dominant groups work not only through their own organic intellectuals, such as managers and consultants, but also through traditional intellectuals. In South Africa, many organic intellectuals arose out of the anti-apartheid struggle. Many were linked to the trade union movement, others to the ANC, still others to the SACP and others to the Trotskyist and other independent left-wing formations. Even since the apartheid period, the boundary between organisations of traditional intellectuals – for example, the universities and NGOs – and the organisations that produced and were produced by organic intellectuals in and of social movements has been porous. Student militants were enormously important to the anti-apartheid struggle and post-apartheid South African universities have been home to some academics who have aligned themselves closely with, and worked within, the social movements. The question this has raised within social movements, however, is that of vanguardism.

In some social movement efforts, significant participation by university-based and foundation-funded scholar-activists and NGOs seemed to other participants to reproduce inequalities. Accusations of 'ventriloquism' and 'substitutionism' by academics within movements have been traded (Bohmke 2009a, 2009b, 2010a and 2010b).[2] Some university-based intellectuals have argued that since 'the poor are the embodiment of the truth', the role of traditional intellectuals is to reflect their positions to the world and simply act in concert with the poor (see critical discussion initiated by Walsh 2008). This kind of analysis sometimes results in the romanticisation of urban social movements and also denies the complex articulations of movements and the education of their leaders. There is no doubt about the dangers of vanguardism. The question is whether a populism that homogenises 'the poor' is capable of building the necessary coalitions to bring protest up to a regularly coordinated non-local scale.

The question of leadership has also led to the involution of protest, especially divisions within social movements and their networks, including the Anti Privatisation Forum, the Soweto Electricity Crisis Committee, the Western Cape Anti-Evictions Campaign, the Landless People's Movement, Jubilee South Africa and the Social Movements Indaba. These divisions are, however, more a symptom than a cause of the strategic impasse faced by South African urban movements today. Scholars of movements have noted that internal tensions often come to the fore when the there is no clear way forward for externally oriented action (Polletta 2005).

Together, the contradictory tendencies of access, localism and leadership have produced a movement sector that is at once extraordinarily militant in its actions and profoundly moderate in its politics. The increasing turn away from electoral politics in poor areas in favour of protest politics signals a strong disenchantment with the apparatus of representative government and with the actual governance of the (mostly) ANC officers. On the other hand, in spite of this disenchantment, South African movements are nowhere close to articulating alternatives and doing so would require movement leaders to engage in the sustained dialogue necessary to abstract from local concerns to national and even international ones. The potential is there: the Treatment Action Campaign's successful demand for decommodified and locally made (generic) AIDS medicines and the Campaign against Water Privatisation's fight against

Johannesburg Water's outsourcing management to Suez, took activism in these sectors out of tired social policy or NGO-delivery debates and set them at the cutting edge of the world's anti-neoliberal backlash.

TRIPARTITE ALLIANCE HEGEMONY

Another inescapable feature of South Africa's contemporary politics is the continued – though increasingly fragile – hegemony of the ANC. The ANC enjoys an enormous amount of legitimacy and ongoing prestige, in spite of the fact that nearly twenty years of ANC rule has resulted in deepening poverty and inequality, and in spite of the visible divisions within the ANC, as for example, in the clashes between President Zuma and his predecessor, Mbeki, and between Zuma and the ANC Youth League leader, Julius Malema. The ANC was the main organisation of the international anti-apartheid struggle and even though it was banned within South Africa from 1963 to 1990, it quickly reasserted itself as the largest, best-organised group capable of taking the reins of power during the early 1990s transition. In establishing its hegemony at the local level, it supplanted already-existing organisations with its own (for example, women's organisations and youth groups) and has dominated electoral politics since the first post-apartheid elections in 1994.

The Tripartite Alliance is dominated by the ANC, which, under Nelson Mandela, began to separate the ideological strands that had undergirded the most militant elements of the anti-apartheid movement, both in South Africa and abroad. Capital flight increased after the democratic elections of 1994 and, in reaction, in early 1995 the ANC government relaxed exchange controls to prove its new loyalty to the Washington Consensus. By the mid-1990s, indeed, ANC leaders had distanced the party from the interventionist currents in the movement. In his first interview after winning the presidency in 1994, Mandela stated: 'In our economic policies ... there is not a single reference to nationalisation, and this is not accidental. There is not a single slogan that will connect us with any Marxist ideology' (interview with Ken Owens, *Sunday Times*, 1 May 1994). Although he inexplicably missed the nationalisation mandate he was given in the 1994 *Reconstruction and Development Programme* (African National Congress 1994: 80), Mandela's specific reference to Marxist ideology in many senses reflects the strong strand of anti-capitalist thinking that linked into resurgent struggles against apartheid from the early 1970s. Through its policy and slogan of Black Economic Empowerment (BEE), moreover, the ANC deracialised capitalism – albeit for a very few billionaires – and separated the profitability dynamic of South African capitalism from racial domination. The latter has remained strong, of course, but more notable is the rise of class apartheid techniques (Bond 2005).

Mandela's avowed anti-Marxism did not, however, so alienate the SACP and Cosatu that they abandoned the coalition. To the contrary, the initial redistributive promises in the ANC platform, eclipsed by Gear in 1996 as well as by numerous White Papers starting in mid-1994, gave the SACP and Cosatu power in administering what might, in other circumstances, have been the development of a managerialist, social-democratic welfare state. The SACP chairman, after all, was Joe Slovo (prior to his death in early 1995) and his 1994 U-turn towards a fully neoliberal housing policy (Bond 2000; Republic of South Africa 1994), as the World Bank explicitly recommended, was the main signal that the Reconstruction and Development Programme was finished before it had even begun. Slovo reversed nearly every major mandate he was provided.

Though centralised, corporatist bargaining was not part even of the initial coalition deal, Cosatu had a prominent place at the table to represent the concerns of the organised working class. It did so with enough friction with the ANC to ensure that it could boast of putting up a fight, even while lauding the not-really-corporatist arrangements of the Alliance *as* corporatist, suggesting that it in fact had codetermination powers (in sites such as the National Economic Development and Labour Council) and that the working class was more institutionally powerful than it patently was. After all, in the post-apartheid era the share of profits to wages shifted in favour of capital by nine per cent. And the SACP gained some power over the state's redistributionist functions, with the Mandela era witnessing central committee members in positions that included the ministers or deputy ministers of trade and industry, public works, housing, transport, public services and even defence. At once, this meant that the SACP had something to lose from challenging the ANC within the coalition too strongly and it was consistent with the party's long-standing line that racial democracy had to precede the larger economic project of socialism. It also meant that the party would be at the frontlines of managing a rapidly changing urban landscape as the lifting of residency laws under apartheid resulted in the vast growth of shack communities both on the urban periphery and in already urbanised township areas. That the party endorsed Gear and the neoliberal Africa strategy (the New Partnership for Africa's Development) and supported a platform that put private investment at the centre of its housing strategy – in a period characterised by capital flight – suggests that it was a comfortable member of the publicly anti-Marxist ANC-led coalition and that its constant support for the coalition's neoliberal macro-economic initiatives at multiple scales in 1996, 2001 and 2010 should not surprise (Bond 2000).

Nevertheless, the Alliance's cohesion and hegemony has not been rock-solid. There have been tensions, from the start, both between Cosatu and the ANC and within Cosatu *about* the ANC and the union federation's role in the Alliance and what it gets out of it. These tensions extend backwards in time to before Cosatu's founding in 1985 and speak both to the shop-floor militancy of 1970s unionism in South Africa and to the tensions around the integration of the union movement into the nationalist project. But these tensions were raised with the introduction of Gear by the ruling party's neoliberal bloc and ultimately resulted in Cosatu's support for Jacob Zuma's successful bid for ANC leadership against Thabo Mbeki in the 2007 ANC National Conference and the ANC's humiliating firing of Mbeki as president in September 2008.

And yet Zuma's government has done little better than Mbeki's and has not changed the country's neoliberal macro-economic course (Maharaj, Desai and Bond 2011). A three-week strike of public-sector workers in 2010, most of whom were members of Cosatu, which both imposed real hardship and threatened to spread to other sectors of the economy, signalled the ripening of the contradictions of Cosatu's continued alliance with the ANC. Cosatu's membership has become older and more skilled as neoliberalism has resulted in segmented labour markets and the proliferation of informal work and a growing proportion of its members are employees of the state. For this – and for the access to a different lifestyle for leaders who move into government positions – Cosatu depends on the ANC-dominated state. On the other hand, continued austerity and attempts to squeeze public-sector workers – visible from Johannesburg to Wisconsin, from Durban to Athens – in the face of already desperately inadequate services and a massive and visible gap between rich and poor (even among Africans), has led at least one Cosatu leader to criticise Zuma's government as becoming a 'predator state' (Vavi 2011).

The fraying hegemony of the ANC with respect to its Alliance partners and the simple refusal of many township and shack-dweller communities to engage in the formal political process any longer, signify South Africa's deep crisis. Nevertheless, the protests raise the question of whether dissent is solely about the delivery of services, or whether it signifies a bigger dissatisfaction with the social order as such. Do protesters see continuity between the anti-apartheid struggle and the struggle today? Even in extreme cases of struggle (such as the disputes over district boundaries in Khutsong), the lead activists retained connections to the Alliance that, through its legitimacy from the anti-apartheid struggle and its patronage networks, were more durable than the centrifugal pressure to disconnect. And if a crisis consists in the fact that 'the old is dying, but the new cannot yet be born' (Gramsci 1971: 276), it begs the question of what 'the new' is and what its birthing process could look like.

THEORISING THE STRATEGIC IMPASSE

The question of how to move out of the crisis to a renewed revolutionary politics that separates the nationalist project from the politics of neoliberal development has garnered several answers. Each is partial and each, as we will argue, is inadequate to the task. In this section of the chapter, we will examine three that have particular currency: the expansion of rights through litigation; the claim for 'the right to the city', which is distinct from juridical rights-talk; and the creation of spaces for 'participation'. In the following section, we will revisit the question of the impasse with reference to a reformulated Marxist account of uneven and combined development.

Rights

Community-based social movements have repeatedly gone to court to enforce their rights. And actual 'victory' in court is beyond our quibbling and indeed some offensive victories (nevirapine to halt HIV transmission during birth) and defensive successes (halting evictions) are occasionally recorded. Never-theless, we consider insidious the constitutionalist discourse that envelops individual cases in an overall strategy: the idea that 'the turn to law' is a good or beneficial thing to do with the energies, affinities, possibilities and power of a movement.

The 'turn to law' discourse bears the unmistakeable scent of reform without a strategic sense of how to make more fundamental demands that bring into question barriers as large as property relations. The result is the kind of 'reformist-reform' (as Gorz [1967] put it) that entrenches the status quo. (In contrast, non-reformist reforms work *against* the internal logic of the dominant system and strengthen rather than co-opt the counter-hegemonic challengers.)

In this sense, the illegal occupation of land is far more powerful than a court's ultimate granting of tenure to the occupiers. The turn to constitutionalism also has consequences for movement leadership; it is based on the conception that a certain professional legal caste among us can secure in the Constitutional Court meaningful precedents (and consequent compliance by the executive) that advance the struggle of the poor in a fundamental way.

To clarify: we are not opposed to going to court. This may be useful from time to time. But as a strategy – rather than as a tactic – it is limited and unable to compensate for weaknesses in protest organisation and militancy. For example, the Treatment Action Campaign's victory against Mbeki in late 2003 was spurred, to some extent, by a mid-2001 Constitutional Court ruling that compelled his government to provide nevirapine to HIV-positive pregnant women in order to prevent mother-to-child transmission. In general, it is fair to say that the rights narrative was important to reducing stigmatisation and providing 'dignity' to those claiming their health rights. Also successful in the Constitutional Court was Durban's Abahlali baseMjondolo shack-dwellers' movement, which in 2009 won a major victory against a provincial housing ordinance justifying forced removals. Such removals continue unhindered, unfortunately, and at nearly the same moment that Abahlali baseMjondolo won the court victory, they were violently uprooted from their base in Kennedy Road.

Thus, as Gerald Rosenberg (1993) indicates, writing in the critical legal studies tradition, rights depend on their enforcement and courts cannot compel this. Further, court judgments can be reversed: a crucial rights narrative test came in the struggle to expand water provision to low-income Sowetans. A victory had been claimed by the Anti-Privatisation Forum in 2006 because after community struggles, water in Johannesburg is now produced and distrib-uted by public agencies (the multinational firm with Soweto's water contract, Suez, was sent back to Paris after its controversial 2001 to 2006 protest-ridden management of municipal water). In April 2008, a major constitutional lawsuit in the High Court resulted in a doubling of free water to 50 litres per person per day and the prohibition of pre-payment water meters. But the Constitutional Court reversed this decision in October 2009 on grounds that judges should not make such detailed policy and that the prevailing amounts of water and the self-disconnection delivery system were perfectly reasonable within the ambit of the South African Bill of Rights. Once again, this meant that activists were thrown back to understanding the limits of constitutionalism: they recom-mitted to illegal reconnections if required (Bond 2011c).

We therefore object simply to the subordination of a political discourse to a legal discourse – even if superficially an empowering one, in terms of 'rights' narratives – and therefore to the subordination of a radical discourse to a liberal one. As Alan Hunt and Gary Wickham argue, discourse 'structures the possibility of what gets included and excluded and what gets done and what remains undone. Discourses authorise some to speak, some views to be taken seriously, while others are marginalised, derided, excluded and even prohibited' (1994: 8–9). By flirting with legalism and the rights discourse, movements have seen their demands watered down into court pleadings. Heartfelt pleas are offered but for the observance of the purely procedural: consult us before you evict us. Demands for housing that could be generalised and spread, become demands for 'in-situ upgrading' and 'reasonable government action' and hence feed the politics of local solutions to the exclusion of demands that can be 'scaled up'.

Right to the city

An alternative formulation of 'rights' is given by Lefebvre and David Harvey's 'right to the city' argument. Harvey (2008: 23) is clear that the 'right to the city' is a *collective* right, rather than a liberal-individualist one and is based on the idea that 'the freedom to make and remake our cities and ourselves is … the most precious yet most neglected of our human rights'. Because Harvey links urbanisation and therefore the way of life of an increasing majority of humanity to the absorption of capitalist surplus, the 'right to the city' implies empowering the mass of people to take the power from capitalists to produce their way of life and learn to wield it themselves. The current crisis of global capital has led to some of the uneven developments to which we have already referred in South Africa. The explosive price of real estate (nearly four hundred per cent from 1997 through to a 2007 peak) was facilitated by not only local over-accumulation but by the inflows of surplus global capital, thus contributing to the boom-bust dynamic in the construction trades even as the rest of the economy stagnated or worsened. 'The results,' Harvey (2008: 32) writes, 'are indelibly etched on the spatial forms of our cities, which increasingly consist of fortified fragments, gated communities, and privatised public spaces kept under constant surveillance'. He continues, quoting Marcello Balbo:

> [The city] is splitting into different separated parts, with the apparent formation of many 'microstates'. Wealthy neighbourhoods provided with all kinds of services, such as exclusive schools, golf courses, tennis

courts and private police patrolling the area around the clock intertwine with illegal settlements where water is available only at public fountains, no sanitation system exists, electricity is pirated by a privileged few, the roads become mud streams whenever it rains, and where house-sharing is the norm (Harvey 2008: 32).

Harvey sees the 'right to the city' as a 'both a working slogan and political ideal' to democratise the 'necessary connection between urbanization and surplus production and use' (Harvey 2008: 40). However, in the South African context, the slogan has been taken up both by proponents of legalistic means of struggle and by the more autonomist-oriented shack-dweller campaigns and so the 'right to the city' can be seen as a kind of ambiguous hinge that joins quite different political orientations. For example, Marie Huchzermeyer argues that the South African Constitution mandates 'an equal right to the city' and that this requires movements to pursue marginal gains through the courts: 'Urban reform in this sense is a pragmatic commitment to gradual but radical change towards grassroots autonomy as a basis for equal rights'. After all, she argues,

> three components of the right to the city – equal participation in deci-sion-making, equal access to and use of the city and equal access to basic services – have all been brought before the Constitutional Court through a coalition between grassroots social movements and a sympathetic middle-class network.

Nevertheless, she also argues that human-rights 'language is fast being usurped by the mainstream within the UN, UN-Habitat, NGOs, think tanks, consultants etc., in something of an empty buzz word, where the concept of grassroots autonomy and meaningful convergence is completely forgotten' (Huchzermeyer 2009: 3–4).

Unfortunately, given the power imbalances, Huchzermeyer and others who make the 'right to the city' claim run the risk of merely extending a slogan, rather than a strategic vision, to the question of the current impasse in South African social movements. The danger here is particularly felt in the ways in which 'the city' can be taken to mean 'particular cities' (which, on one level, they must) and therefore to privilege local politics and local solutions, without a larger-scale analysis that could provide a kind of standard by which locally generated choices and strategies could be subjected to criticism. One result is that like-minded groups often accept one another's political stances while discounting the possibilities of coalition across types of community: hence, for example, 'Abahlalism' – 'shack-dwellerism' – arises as a kind of autonomistic-populist practice in which the deep suspicion of *non*-shack-dwellers, even if sometimes merited, finds its mirror image in the idea that political ideas are invalidated or validated simply by virtue of their issuing from 'the poor' (Desai 2006).

'Participation'

A clause in the Constitution as well as various laws compel municipalities to involve residents in 'community participation' processes to enable people to directly influence decisions that affect them. John Williams (2006: 197), reporting on research in the Western Cape, finds that '[m]ost community participation exercises in post-apartheid South Africa are largely spectator politics, where ordinary people have mostly become endorsees of pre-designed planning programmes, [and] are often the objects of administrative manipulation'. As a result, formal municipal governance processes are 'a limited form of democracy [that] give[s] rise to an administered society rather than a democratic society' since there is no real debate of policy or of social programmes by the working-class electorate and government officials (198). In Durban, a study of community participation in local economic development processes by Richard Ballard and his colleagues reveals that such processes allow ordinary people 'to demand accountability' from 'elected representatives and sometimes quite senior officials'. However, they are 'consultative rather than participatory' and 'invariably become conspicuous for the issues they leave out, and for the voices they did not hear' (Ballard, Habib and Valodia 2006: 4).

This was particularly apparent in the way that the Durban 'Citizen's Voice' process was handled by the city and the main water NGO (Mvula Trust), invoking participation by what might be termed 'civilised society' as a way of encouraging poor communities *to consume less water* just after the municipal prices had doubled in real terms over a period of six years (Bond 2011a).

In a different vein, Williams (2006: 197) concludes that 'community participation in South Africa is informed by the memory of community struggle – a radical form of participation – against the racist apartheid State' and that this must be harnessed. 'It is precisely this repertoire of radical strategies that can and should be revisited and adapted, to advance the interests of the materially marginalized communities at the local level'. Luke Sinwell applies a theoretical approach first developed in the South African context by Faranak Miraftab (Sinwell 2009: 31), based on a distinction between 'invited' versus 'invented' spaces of popular participation. The ward committees, *imbizos* (government-initiated public forums) and integrated development plans of invited participation contrast with spaces invented through 'self-activity' such as community self-organisation, direct action and other non-official mechanisms of exerting pressure. Based on extensive research conducted in Alexandra, one of the country's oldest and poorest black working-class townships, he concludes that progressive change is more likely to emanate from the use of invented than from invited spaces. However, Sinwell laments that community activism in the invented spaces also fails to question power relations and social structures in a fundamental way. Community organisations tend to work within budgetary constraints set by the state and as a result community groups end up competing among themselves for limited resources rather than questioning the neoliberal framework and its ideological underpinnings (Miraftab 2004).

COMBINED AND UNEVEN DEVELOPMENT, COMBINED AND UNEVEN MARXISM

The importance of Marxist criticism is to uncover, in particular situations, what is 'systematic' and what is 'conjunctural', as Gramsci (1971: 177) put it. This, in turn, helps to distinguish – and, therefore, to both facilitate and structure discussion about – short- and longer-term demands. The 'pure militancy' of an immediate politics of the poor does not do this easily. It is rather through dialogue, not just among the poor but among the several sectors of society caught at various points in the contradictions of neoliberalism, that a larger political formation capable of a sustained revolt against capital and the creation of a new order can be built.

Here, Trotsky's understanding of 'combined and uneven development' is useful. Though it can be read somewhat more broadly, most interpretations of Trotsky understand him to have meant 'combined' development to refer to the relations among different levels of development *within* a given nation (Barker 2006; Trotsky 1962). In South Africa, the logical corollary is to 'articulations of modes of production', a concept promoted by Harold Wolpe to explain race–class politics linking sites of surplus value extraction to bantustans (where impoverished women provided for the reproduction of cheap labour power at a vast distance), but which is even more relevant in post-apartheid South Africa given enhanced migrancy, xenophobia and adverse gender power relations (Wolpe 1980). Geographers such as Harvey and Neil Smith have emphasised that even within nations, the combined unevenness of development is given spatial expression. Apartheid was, in its nature, both a racial order and a spatial one and it enforced uneven *and* combined development in almost caricatured forms. The systematic separation of racial groups, the profound underdevelopment of black areas and the racial segmentation of labour markets suggested to many on the Left (including us), as we noted earlier, that the fight against apartheid was coterminous with the fight against capitalism. Though we were correct that capitalism and racism were mutually reinforcing during the twentieth century, the conventional mistake by radicals was in thinking that the defeat of one durable but ultimately conjunctural manifestation of racism, apartheid, would bring the capitalist system to its knees.

Accordingly, we found that apartheid was conjunctural, but uneven and combined development is systematic (Bond 2005; Maharaj, Desai and Bond 2011). The particular spatial manifestations of uneven and combined development are also conjunctural, though, again, they can be extremely durable. Hence, fights against eviction or for clean and affordable water, even while encountering the severe power of state coercion, and sometimes taking years to resolve, do little to change the systemic dynamics of uneven and combined development that are deepened in new ways in neoliberal South Africa.

Trotsky also marshalled the theory of uneven and combined development to argue against 'stageism' or the idea that revolutionary politics depended on a given country's going through the specific, drawn-out processes of capitalist development found in other countries. What this meant, however, was that coalitions among workers across space *and* across situations in the process of capital accumulation (for example, industrial workers, peasants) were central to revolutionary potentials, but that these potentials were *realisable*, even if with difficulty. The contemporary conjuncture in South Africa, beset by entrenched neoliberalism imposed by a weakening-but-still-present ruling Alliance dominated by the ANC, has seen the accumulation of protests by township residents over services, by shack-dwellers over evictions and services and by the relatively 'privileged' public-sector workers over pay and the quality of services they provide. Though the public-sector workers' strike was suspended without winning the union's key demands, it came close to bringing out private-sector workers – all in the formal sector – as well.

The question for an 'uneven, combined Marxism' is how to *take advantage* of the unevenness and particular conjunctural combinations of social relations in South Africa and beyond. The present period in South Africa exemplifies the dynamics of uneven and combined development and its spatial and social consequences. Within South Africa, it is important to think about how, for example, shack-dwellers' struggles and public-sector workers' struggles could be linked up, even as the latter's relative privilege and operation in the formal labour market may make them wary of such an alliance and as the former's distrust of co-optation creates an equal hesitancy. The Durban climate summit – the Conference of the Parties 17 – illustrated how very difficult it is to conjoin labour, community and environmental considerations, especially in the context of a set-piece 'Global Day of Action' march (3 December 2012) when distances between constituencies, political traditions and issue areas remain debilitating (Bond 2011b).

How could a joined-up movement respond to the conjunctural pressures upon it, such as the apparent advantages to the unemployed of labour-market flexibilisation schemes or to the quality of life of township residents of evicting shack-dweller settlements? What kind of ways can – or should – Marxists talk about to take on the systemic problems of uneven and combined development with people who are located in different, and even sometimes opposed, areas of this combination? What organisational forms might be applied to start this conversation and yet keep it focused on the systematic elements of the present? How do we move beyond the concern for access, the localism, the constitution-alism and the anti-political populism of contemporary protest – even as these sometimes yield concrete results – while also moving beyond the ambiguity of a simple slogan? To us, the protests represent a profound critique of neoliber-alism by working-class communities. But are protesters aware of the greater significance of their protests? And to what extent do protesters' demands require solutions that challenge neoliberal policy and even entail a challenge to the capitalist mode of production? Or is it the case that the overarching neolib-eral economic framework constrains the realisation of not only the people's aspirations, but their ability to think beyond capitalism?

We agree with Nash that the answers to these questions will not come through the elaboration of a new, 'proper' Marxist line by mainly university-based, white intellectuals and that the great task of a renewal of South African Marxism will depend on the elaboration of a new stratum of organic intellec-tuals from the movements (though not necessarily bypassing the universities) who can, perhaps, move among them in ways that enable them to abstract from the local without abandoning the reality of it. Being able to do this partly depends on the ability of South African movements to look beyond themselves, to a world increasingly resistant to neoliberalism and to contribute to, and take from, a growing global movement. The successes of the Treatment Action Campaign were one such contribution, although this movement also teaches the dangers of self-liquidation into state-conjoined service delivery and narrow sectoral politics, as well as a seeming over-reliance on foreign funding.

In encountering similar-but-different movements and contexts, movement intellectuals gain new perspectives on the possibilities of coalitions and on the similar-but-different permutations of combined and uneven development elsewhere; these can enhance their capacity to reinterpret local conditions by denaturalising existing political categories and divisions. Indeed, in calling for a 'combined and uneven Marxism', we intend to suggest that the way forward cannot lie in the search for the pure revolutionary subject, whether the worker, the township 'poors', the shack-dweller, the organic feminist, the red-green social environmentalist, or anyone else and it cannot lie in the search for the perfect location, whether the household, community, farm, benefits office, oil refinery or factory. Combined and uneven development makes clear that if the Marxist view that people are a 'nexus of social relations' holds, a combined and uneven Marxism must draw on the interdependence of locations in these relations in order to reinforce our interdependence, rather than accept the capitalist combination of unevenness and mutual social antagonisms among those from whom capital is extracted. Of course this is to state a problem rather than to proclaim a new strategy. The development of organic intellectuals from within the movements, and their discussions and alliances with one another as well as with 'traditional' Marxist intellectuals, are the only way to move forward on this front.

AFTERWORD: MARIKANA'S MEANINGS (by Patrick Bond)

The prior words, drawn from consecutive (not synthetic) presentations to a Wolpe Lecture at the University of KwaZulu-Natal in 2010, were drawn together as an essay in 2012, prior to the Marikana massacre. There has not been occasion since for the authors to generate a coherent, joint approach to the massacre, but a few ideas follow the logic of the argument above. First, most obviously, when a ruling party in any African country sinks to the depths of allowing its police force to serve white-dominated multinational capital by killing dozens of black workers so as to end a brief strike, it represents an inflection point. Beyond just the obvious human-rights and labour-relations travesties, the incident offered the potential for a deep political rethink, unveiling extreme depths of ruling-class desperation represented by the fusion of Cyril Ramaphosa's black capitalism, Lonmin's collaboration (through Ramaphosa) with the mining and police ministers, the brutality of state prosecutors who charged the victims with the crime, the alleged 'sweetheart unionism' of the increasingly unpopular National Union of Mineworkers (NUM) and the fragility of a Cosatu split between Zuma/Ramaphosa loyalists and those with worker interests at heart.

The site of the immediate conflict was the platinum belt. South Africa's share of world platinum reserves is more than eighty per cent. The belt stretches in a distinct arc around the west side of the Johannesburg–Pretoria megalopolis of ten million people and up toward the Zimbabwe border. The area also has vast gold and coal deposits and the nine main mining firms operating mostly in this region recorded $4.5 billion in 2011 profits from their South African operations. In this context, there are six basic factual considerations about what happened at Marikana, 100 kilometres north-west of Johannesburg, beginning around 4 pm on 16 August 2012.

First, the provincial police department, backed by national special commando reinforcements, ordered several thousand striking platinum mineworkers – rock drill operators – off a hill where they had gathered as usual over the prior four days, surrounding the workers with barbed wire and firing teargas. Second, the hill was more than a kilometre away from Lonmin property; the mineworkers were not blocking mining operations or any other facility, and although they were on an 'unprotected' wildcat strike, they had a constitutional right to gather. As they left the hill, 34 workers were killed and 78 others suffered bullet-wound injuries, all at the hands of police weapons, leaving some crippled for life, with some shot dead while moving through a small gap in the fencing, and the others murdered in a field and on a smaller hill nearby, as they fled. Third, no police were hurt in the operation – although it appears that a sole miner with a pistol fired as he entered the gap – and some of the police attempted a clumsy cover-up by placing crude weapons next to the dead bodies of several men after their deaths.

That day, 270 mineworkers were arrested, followed by a weekend during which state prosecutors charged the men with the 'murder' of their colleagues (under an obscure apartheid-era 'common purpose' doctrine of collective responsibility), followed by an embarrassed climb-down by the national prosecutor after major social constituencies registered utter disgust. There was no apparent effort by police to discipline errant troops in subsequent months, even when massacre-scene photographs showed that weapons were planted on dead mineworker bodies and indeed the police moved into Marikana shack settlements again and again to intimidate activists in the wake of the massacre, including fatally shooting – with rubber bullets one Saturday morning – a popular local councilwoman (from the ruling party) who sided with the protesting mineworkers and communities.

The details about how the massacre unfolded were not initially obvious, for mainstream media were embedded behind police lines (unaware at the time of the 'killing kopje') and it was only a few days later that observers – the September Imbizo Commission, University of Johannesburg researcher Peter Alexander and his research team (Alexander et al. 2012) and *Daily Maverick* reporters (especially Greg Marinovich and Sipho Hlongwane) – uncovered the other shootings. Most journalists relied on official sources, especially the police and the National Prosecuting Authority, even when they were discredited by the revelation of persistent fibbery. Such media bias allowed the impression to emerge in conventional wisdom that police were 'under violent attack' by irrational, drugged and potentially murderous men from rural areas in the Eastern Cape's Pondoland, as well as from Lesotho and Mozambique, who used *muti* (traditional medicine) to ward off bullets. Plenty of press reports and even the SACP's official statement refer to the workers' pre-capitalist spiritual sensibilities to try to explain why they might have charged toward the police, through the five-metre gap in the barbed wire, with their primitive spears and wooden sticks. In April 2013, the Farlam Commission that Zuma mandated to investigate the massacre was anticipating testimony from the mineworkers' main *sangoma* about his influence, but just before the scheduled appearance, he was murdered in his Eastern Cape homestead by someone shooting with an R5 rifle, the same make as the police use.

Another layer of complexity is related to the prior murder of six workers, two security guards and two policemen close by, when a march on 11 August 2012 by striking workers against the NUM – accused of selling out the workers – was met with gunfire, apparently from NUM officials. Tension in the area mounted quickly and when the security guards and police were killed by some of the Marikana mineworkers, this generated a sensibility of vindication; gruesome footage of the murdered policemen had circulated amongst the police who were on duty on 16 August. Later, the assassination of NUM shop stewards increased in pace, as well. But it must be recalled that this was not brand new conflict, for strike-related violence over the prior year at Lonmin and the other major platinum mining operations had left scores of other workers dead, with 50 murders just six months earlier when 17 000 mineworkers were temporarily fired nearby at the world's second-largest platinum firm, Implats, before gaining wage concessions.

South Africa learned a great deal about labour's desperation in subsequent days, because explaining the intensity of the Lonmin workers' militancy required understanding their conditions of production and reproduction. The typical rock drill operator's take-home pay was said to be in the range of $500 (ZAR4 000 in 2012) per month, with an additional $225 (ZAR1 800) per month as a 'living out allowance' to spare Lonmin and other employers the cost of maintaining migrant-labour hostels. Most workers were from Lesotho, Mozambique and the Eastern Cape's Pondoland; many therefore maintained two households, having families to support in both urban and rural settings. At the same time, structural changes in the mines were blurring the distinction between shop steward and foreman, hence drawing NUM local leaders into a cosy corporatist arrangement with the mining houses. But controlling the workers would be another matter, and NUM found itself challenged by a new union that had come from its own dissident ranks the Association of Mining and Construction Union (Amcu).

Indeed, tens of thousands of workers who subsequently went on wildcat strikes in the North West, Limpopo, Free State, Mpumalanga, Northern Cape and Gauteng provinces did not do so out of the blue. They began leaving NUM in droves from late 2011 because of its worsening reputation as a sweetheart union, mostly moving to Amcu. The workers had participated in various forms of labour- and community-based protests over the prior few years, as the three hundred and fifty per cent price increase for the metal during the 2002 to 2008 boom left the main companies – AngloPlats, Implats and Lonmin – extremely prosperous, without evidence of trickle-down to the semi-proletarianised workforce. So it was that 3 000 Lonmin rock drill operators demanded a raise to $1 420 per month as a basic gross 'package' amount; they struck for over a month (three weeks beyond the massacre) and ultimately received what was reported as a twenty-two per cent wage package increase, which in turn catalysed prairie-fire wildcat strikes across the immediate mining region and then across other parts of the country in the period September to November. Similar militancy was soon evident in trucking, the auto sector, municipal labour and other sectors.

But as with a vast proportion of ordinary South Africans, this was a time of extreme household indebtedness. It soon became clear that the Marikana workers were victims not only of exploitation at the point of production, but also of super-exploitative debt relations. Financial desperation was compounded by legal abuse, carried out by the same race/gender/class power bloc – white male Afrikaners – who had, in their earlier years and in the same geographical settings, been apartheid beneficiaries. Microfinance short-term loans that carry exceptionally high interest rates were offered to mineworkers by institutions ranging from established banks – one (Ubank) even co-owned by NUM and another (Capitec) replete with powerful ANC patrons – down to fly-by-night 'mashonisa' loan sharks. The extremely high interest rates charged, especially once arrears mounted, were one of the central pressures requiring workers to demand higher wages.

Still, none of this labour–capital conflict – implicating mining houses and financiers – would have flared into such an explosive situation at Marikana, many believe, were it not for the relationships between state, ruling party and trade union elites that had developed over the prior two decades with the major mining houses. These cosy relations, even relegitimising companies with very low morals which regularly engaged in labour-broking, apparently incensed the ordinary workers, raising their staying power to such high levels. For example, Lonmin's successful public relations onslaught and tight connections to the ruling party probably gave its executives confidence that long-standing abuse of low-paid migrant labour could continue – with NUM itself having become so co-opted that shop stewards were reportedly paid three times more than ordinary workers. NUM general secretary, Frans Baleni, earned $160 000 per year at that stage, and gained notoriety when he advised Lonmin to fire 9 000 of the same Marikana mineworkers at its Karee mine in late 2011 because they went on a wildcat strike. Of the 9 000, 7 000 were rehired but they quit NUM and joined the rival Amcu. One result was that of the 28 000 workers at nearby Implats, seventy per cent had been NUM members in late 2011, but by September 2012 the ratio was down to thirteen per cent.

On the ecological front, the entire platinum belt contributes to the toxicity and overall pollution that means South Africa's 'Environmental Performance Index' slipped to fifth worst of 133 countries surveyed by Columbia and Yale

University researchers in early 2012.[3] The Mineral Energy Complex's prolific contribution to pollution is mainly to blame, including its coal mining that generates coal-fired power used in electricity-intensive mining and smelting operations. In this context, Lonmin might have considered its ongoing destruction of the platinum belt's water, air, agricultural and other ecosystems to be of little importance – within a setting in which pollution is ubiquitous.

Moreover, the North West provincial and Rustenburg municipal governments were apparently rife with corruption. Emblematic was the 2009 assassination of a well-known ANC whistle-blower, Moss Phakoe, which a judge found was arranged by Rustenburg mayor Matthew Wolmarans. Again, in this context, Lonmin and the other big mining houses in the platinum belt might have considered South Africa just one more Third World site worthy of the designation 'resource cursed' – a phrase usually applied to sites where dictatorial and familial patronage relations allow multinational capital in the extractive industries to, literally, get away with murder. Around two dozen anti-corruption whistle-blowers like Phakoe were killed in the first few years of Zuma's rule.[4]

Family enterprise suited the Zumas, who had a reported 220 businesses. It was not surprising to learn, for example, that along with the Gupta family – generous sponsors of Zuma's patronage system – son Duduzane was co-owner of JIC, the platinum belt region's largest firm specialising in short-term labour outsourcing (sometimes called 'labour-broking', though JIC denies this, and NUM has a recognition agreement with the firm). Nor was it a secret that the president's nephew, Khulubuse Zuma, played a destructive role in nearby gold-mining territory as Aurora co-owner, along with Mandela's grandson and Zuma's lawyer. Indeed, that particular mining house had perhaps the single most extreme record of ecological destructiveness and labour conflict in the post-apartheid era, reflecting how white-owned mining houses gave used-up mines with vast acid mine drainage liabilities to new black owners who were ill-equipped to deal with the inevitable crises.

South African observers thus learned a great deal as a result of the massacre and a growing realisation about the socio-economic, political and ecological context. The stage was set, immediately after Marikana, for renewed debates over whether the Tripartite Alliance was a progressive or now regressive political arrangement, especially between the centre-left unionists and communists who are close to official power and thus defensive of the political status quo, on the one hand, and on the other, critical, independent progressives convinced that South African politics could become more acutely polarised. Overlaying the crisis and these debates was the internal ANC split between pro- and anti-Zuma forces, which spilled over into Cosatu prior to its September 2012 congress before, at the Mangaung electoral conference of the ruling party, Zuma squashed his opponent and then deputy president, Kgalema Motlanthe, with three quarters of the vote. It was this political battle that initially paralysed labour leadership, given the danger that Cosatu would unleash centrifugal forces that its popular leader Zwelinzima Vavi could not control. There was even talk of NUM opening up a leadership challenge to Vavi, on grounds that the 300 000-member union (Cosatu's largest single member) was strongly pro-Zuma and insisted on the official Cosatu support that Vavi had initially resisted.

Such political manoeuvring left Cosatu mostly silenced about Marikana, as NUM's weight and the parallel subversion of other union leaders made it too difficult for the federation to visibly back the upstart platinum, gold and other mineworkers. In any case, what these wildcat strikers were doing might, more conservative unionists believed, even throw the institutions of central-ised bargaining into chaos. The demand for higher wages was both extreme, and thus opposed by NUM, and ultimately successful in the case of Marikana's courageous workers. The twenty-two per cent raise – at the time inflation was around six per cent – that the workers won after a month of striking was remarkable. It inspired the country's labour force to look at their own pay packets askance. But by failing to issue immediate statements about Marikana, much less mobilise workers for solidarity against the joint onslaught of multi-national capital and the state, Cosatu was simply unable, in late 2012, to inter-vene when so many cried out for a shift from the proverbial 'war of position' to a 'war of movement'. Cosatu's longing gaze to Zuma for a genuine relationship reminded many of its support for him during the darkest 2005–2007 days of corruption and rape charges. Yet it was now, in the Marikana moment, even more apparent that Cosatu's conservatism was the principal barrier to social progress. Its weakness was tangible at two levels.

First, and in sharp contrast to Cosatu's posture, there was the partial filling of the void by Malema, the ANC's former youth leader. Malema himself had been partially discredited by his alleged implication in corrupt 'tenderpre-neurship' (insider deals for state contracts) in the neighbouring province of Limpopo. Yet he managed to gather 15 000 angry people at Marikana two days after the massacre and voiced powerful critiques of Zuma, Lonmin and their associated black capitalist allies, such as Lonmin part-owner Ramaphosa. Meanwhile, the second way in which Cosatu's weakness was manifested was in the subsequent rise of Ramaphosa to renewed power within the ANC. Any such rebirth of Ramaphosa had seemed virtually inconceivable immediately after the Farlam Commission began. There, a startling series of revelations emerged about Ramaphosa's 'smoking-gun' emails sent to other Lonmin executives and government ministers exactly 24 hours before the massacre. To further contextualise this, recall that Ramaphosa's company, Shanduka, was the majority shareholder of the Lonmin black empowerment subsidiary, which gave him nine per cent ownership in Lonmin and a seat on the board. In 2012, Shanduka was being paid $360 000 per annum by Lonmin for providing 'empowerment' consulting, not to mention Ramaphosa's board salary and dividend returns on Lonmin share ownership.

This was not a bad arrangement for the mining house, for one of Ramaphosa's emails on 15 August 2012 reflected the power relations that Lonmin gained in its association with the former mineworker leader: 'The terrible events that have unfolded cannot be described as a labour dispute. They are plainly dastardly criminal and must be characterised as such. There needs to be concomitant action to address this situation'. Ramaphosa wrote to Lonmin's Albert Jamieson:

> You are absolutely correct in insisting that the Minister, and indeed all government officials, need to understand that we are essentially dealing with a criminal act. I have said as much to the Minister of Safety and Security. I will stress that Minister [Susan] Shabangu should have a discussion with Roger [Phillimore, Lonmin chairman].

Revealing these emails, the lawyer for the 270 arrested mineworkers, Dali Mpofu, explained:

> It's a long line of emails under, in the same vein, effectively encouraging so-called concomitant action to deal with these criminals, whose only crime was that they were seeking a wage increase ... At the heart of this was the toxic collusion between the SA Police Services and Lonmin at a direct level. At a much broader level it can be called a collusion between the State and capital and that this phenomenon is at the centre of what has occurred here ...
>
> This collusion between State and capital has happened in many instances in this country. In 1920 African miners went on strike and the government of Jan Smuts dealt with them with violence, and harshly,

and one of the results of that was that they reduced the gap between what white mineworkers were getting and what black mineworkers were getting … and the pact that had been signed in 1918 of introducing the colour bar in the mines was abandoned. That abandonment precipitated a massive strike by the white mineworkers in 1922 and that strike was dealt with by the Smuts government by bringing in the air force – and about 200 people were killed. This is one of the most important happenings in the history of this country, and in 1946 under the leadership of the African Mineworkers Union, the African workers, 70 000 African workers, also went on a massive strike and the government sent 16 000 policemen and arrested, like they did to our, the people we represent, some of the miners under an act called the War Measures Act.

So this has happened, this collusion between capital and the State has happened in systematic patterns in the history of, sordid history of, the mining industry in this country. Part of that history included the collaboration of so-called tribal chiefs who were corrupt and were used by those oppressive governments to turn the self-sufficient black African farmers into slave labour workers. Today we have a situation where those chiefs have been replaced by so-called BEE partners of these mines and carrying on that torch of collusion (cited in Farlam Commission 2012: 218–220).

The BEE billionaire Ramaphosa's collaboration with white elites was also reflected in his attempt a few months earlier to purchase a prize buffalo at a game auction for $2.3 million, an event underscored by Malema as indicative of the gulf between the new South Africa's one per cent and the workers. Not surprisingly, Malema was quickly rewarded with overwhelming support from Marikana miners on two occasions – including a memorial ceremony he arranged, at which he kicked out several of Zuma's cabinet ministers who had come to pay respects. But on his third visit, police denied him his constitutional right to address another huge crowd. Even while contesting fraud charges in his home base (where facilitating provincial tenders had made him rich) Malema thus became, briefly, an unstoppable force across the mining belt in the North West and Limpopo provinces, and even in Zimbabwe, calling for radical redistribution. At one point three weeks after the massacre, the South African National Defence Force was declared to be on 'high alert' simply because Malema addressed a group of disgruntled soldiers.

Yet money still talks in South Africa. By December 2012, Malema's own apparent power had ebbed. And Ramaphosa had won the ruling party's deputy presidency against Malema's two main allies – with more than three quarters of the vote. Cosatu was also very clearly in retreat, with Vavi nervously appealing to Ramaphosa not to act like a capitalist. And Malema was completely out of the national political equation, humiliating himself with a co-authored letter to the ANC leadership just before the Mangaung conference began, begging that he be allowed back into the organisation. This request was simply rebuffed by Zuma's team.

In addition to expressing relief at Malema's fate, business openly celebrated Ramaphosa's defeat of anti-Zuma candidates Tokyo Sexwale and Matthews Phosa. The vociferous endorsements of Ramaphosa by big business at the end of 2012 meant the ANC's economic talk-left-so-as-to-walk-right strategy was well understood. The potential for Ramaphosa to act in the interests of South Africa's untransformed business-in-general coincided perfectly with his own personal portfolio's tentacles, from his firm Shanduka, spreading right across the South African economy: Macsteel, Scaw Metals SA, Lonmin (through Incwala Resources), Kangra Coal, McDonald's SA, Mondi Plc, Lace Diamonds, Pan African Resources Plc, Coca-Cola, Seacom, MTN, Bidvest, Standard Bank, Alexander Forbes, Investment Solutions and Liberty Group. Ramaphosa also held the chairs of the Mondi paper group and MTN cellphones, and was on the board of SABMiller, which he formerly chaired.

With Zuma re-elected ANC president at Mangaung and with Ramaphosa as his deputy and presumed replacement in 2019 after Zuma's second term ends, the ruling party's political turmoil appeared to stabilise, and the stage shifted again to the issue of civil society versus state and capital. An early 2013 call for a national strike from the most militant of mineworkers reflected ongoing frustrations. But the forces for genuine change had not, by the end of 2012, been properly gathered from below. Prospects for labour and community activists unifying at the base needed more attention, for to exist in Marikana and similar mining towns was to face incessant police repression bordering on unqualified brutality.

Nonetheless, the brief emergence of a women's mutual-aid movement amongst mineworker wives and girlfriends, as well as other women from the impoverished Marikana community was one reflection of a new bottom-up politics. At least one martyr emerged from their ranks: Paulina Masuhlo, an unusually *sympatico* ANC municipal councillor in Marikana, who sided with the workers, was shot in the abdomen and leg with rubber bullets during a police and army invasion of Nkaneng on 15 September. She died of the wounds on 19 September. Yet for the subsequent week and a half, police and malevolently bureaucratic municipal officials refused the women's attempts to memorialise Masuhlo with a long protest march from Nkaneng to the Marikana police station. Persistence and legal support prevailed, so 800 demanded justice in a women's-only trek from Nkaneng to Marikana police station on 29 September, dignified and without casualties.

But the political opportunities that might fuse worker, community and women's interests in improving conditions for the reproduction of labour power – perhaps one day too joined by environmentalists – were fragile and easy to lose. Male migrant workers typically maintained two households and hence channelled resources back to the Eastern Cape, Lesotho, Mozambique and other home bases. This process of mixing short-term residents with long-term Tswana-speaking inhabitants was fraught with potential xenophobia and ethnicism, not to mention gendered power relations. Migrancy has also facilitated syndicates of illicit drugs, transactional sex (even forced sexual labour), traditional patriarchy, dysfunctional spiritual suspicions (for example, the use of traditional medicine *muti* against bullets which allegedly wears off quickly in the presence of women), widespread labour-broking and other super-exploitative relations. An uneven and combined politics would be needed to sort through the complications.

After a month on strike, the Lonmin mineworkers won a twenty-two per cent wage increase based on a determination forged from frustration and anger, but they lacked a sufficiently strong and clear political agenda to follow through against the deeper structural oppressions. Yet some such agenda would be necessary to mobilise the tens of millions of disgruntled South Africans into a force capable of breaking sweetheart relations between state, ruling party, labour aristocrats, parasitical capital and the London/Melbourne mining houses. For some, Marikana was potentially the breakthrough event that independent progressives had long sought, one that could reveal more graphically the intrinsic anti-social tendencies associated with the transition of the ANC Alliance's elite from revolutionaries to willing partners of some of the world's most wicked corporations. Such a narrative was indeed the one promoted by the otherwise extremely fractured South African Left.

For example, some factions associated with the relatively broad-based (though labour-less) DLF and the Marikana Support Campaign, did sponsor regular political meetings in Johannesburg and Cape Town and also solidaristic activities in the platinum belt. These efforts included a rally in Rustenburg a month after the massacre when more than 10 000 workers were mobilised by the Workers Committees and DLF. The extraordinary spread of labour militancy to other mines, to the transport sector and to the Western Cape farms was in part a function of DLF cadres' energy and vision.

Nonetheless, because the first such DLF meeting at the University of Johannesburg a week after the Marikana massacre provisionally included a leading NUM representative on the programme (he was shouted down and chased from the hall), another left faction led by Johannesburg's Khanya College broke away to found the 'We are all Marikana' campaign. Resolutely opposed to any legitimation of Cosatu's Alliance unionism, this network also gathered ordinary workers for educational events (although momentum appeared to slow within a month of the massacre). In contrast, one other small revolutionary party in Marikana engaged in much higher-profile recruiting and consciousness-raising: the Democratic Socialist Movement (associated with the Committee for a Workers' International) and its allies – numbering just twenty at the founding meeting – launched a 'Workers and Socialist Party' in late 2012.

Excellent intentions notwithstanding, none of these efforts were adequate to the task. Even though it may often have seemed that a 'pre-revolutionary' situation existed in a South Africa that had one of the highest protest rates in the world, the lack of connection between those with grievances remained the most crippling problem. And this disconnect continued amongst traditional critics of ANC neoliberalism in late 2012. One critical example was the lack of any real attempt to coordinate international solidarity. Here, in fact, was a huge void in Marikana-related political work, an opportunity lost by South Africans despite the willingness of NGOs to call on the World Bank to divest from Lonmin just one day after the massacre and the fact that at least a dozen spontaneous protests broke out at South African embassies and consulate offices across the world in subsequent days.

There was, though, the hope that, as another example, the women of Marikana, organising across the divides of labour and community, could set the example so desperately needed by the broader Left. Their organising efforts ranged beyond Marikana itself, as they briefly helped connect the dots elsewhere, in nearby terrains ranging from mining *dorpies* to sites of land struggle in North West, Limpopo and Gauteng provinces. However, these women were as diverse and ethnically divided as the broader society: wives, girlfriends, mothers, daughters, sisters, health-workers, educators, sex-workers, cooks, cleaners, salespersons.

Moreover, they had the additional burdens of handling trauma counselling for victims of violence and providing mutual aid to the many community members who were suffering, directly and indirectly, because of the reduction in available immediate cash – one of the side effects of the wave of wildcat strikes. In short, as in other sectors of the society, much political work was needed in order to create a truly coherent oppositional voice amongst women.

The same could be said of 'progressives' more generally. Such people had long been associated with the ANC because of the century-old party's liberatory, social-democratic and deep-liberal orientation, but after 1994 many of them continued their determined work of liberation mainly from within civil society. In this political space, one found organisations that jumped into the Marikana political breech with much-needed support activities. These included, for example, the Socio-Economic Rights Institute, Sonke Gender Justice, Studies in Poverty and Inequality, Students for Law and Social Justice, the Treatment Action Campaign and Section 27 (which is named with reference to the country's Bill of Rights). Yet, here again, where was the coherence, organisational and ideological, that could render this a cumulative and defining force?

As for the official 'Left': there was, to be brutally frank, absolutely nothing worth salvaging. As *Business Day*'s Peter Bruce (2012) wrote four days after the massacre:

> What's scary about Marikana is that, for the first time, for me, the fact that the ANC and its government do not have the handle they once did on the African majority has come home. The party is already losing the middle classes. If they are now also losing the marginal and the dispossessed, what is left? Ah yes, Cosatu and the communists – Zuma's creditors.

It was almost surreal to find Cosatu and communist leaders anxiety-ridden at the prospect of widening worker revolt.

The worker revolt continued rising through to 2013, despite narratives about social 'leadership'. Truck drivers received an above-inflation settlement in October 2012 after resorting to sometimes intensely violent methods to disrupt scab drivers, in the process creating shortages of petrol and retail goods in various parts of the country. With Durban's Toyota workers, municipal offices and then the farm workers of the Western Cape all also engaged in wildcat strikes, no one was taking the signals from Pretoria seriously. This was not new, of course, for in September 2012, the World Economic Forum's *Global Competitiveness Report* (Schwab 2012) placed South Africa in the number one position for adverse employee–employer relations (in a survey done prior to the Marikana strikes), whereas using the same measure of class struggle in 2011, South African workers were only in seventh place out of the one hundred and forty-four countries surveyed (Schwab 2012). By February 2013, the farm workers had won a fifty-two per cent wage increase after ongoing strikes had threatened the vineyards' viability and reputation.

Partly as a result of labour militancy, major ratings agencies began downgrading the country's bond rating – for example, to BBB level by Standard & Poor's. The resulting higher interest rates to be paid on the country's prolific foreign borrowings – about five times higher in 2012 in absolute terms than what was inherited from apartheid in 1994 – created yet more fiscal pressures as well as household and corporate repayment stress. Given Europe's crisis and South Africa's vulnerability, much lower GDP growth rates in 2013 and beyond were anticipated. And instead of countering that prospect with an interest rate cut by the South African Reserve Bank in late 2012, as was projected, the country's shaky financial standing put countervailing upward pressure on rates.

Thus in the period after Marikana, the situation remained fluid and it was impossible to assess which forces would emerge from the chaos. It was here that contemporary South African narratives from within – 'nationalism', 'populism', 'Stalinism', 'Trotskyism', 'autonomism', 'black consciousness', 'feminism', 'corporatism', 'liberalism' and 'neoliberalism' – all appeared inadequate to the tasks at hand, be it on the platinum belt or in so many other workplaces and communities. No ideologues posed a vision that could rescue South Africa from the intense pressures that seem to be growing stronger each week.

What was definitive, though, was the waning of any remaining illusions that the forces of 'liberation' led by the ANC would take South Africa to genuine freedom and a new society. Marikana had that effect, permanently, and Ramaphosa's December 2012 elevation could do nothing to restore faith in the ruling party – just the opposite. In coming years, protesters are likely to keep dodging police bullets as they move the socio-economic and political-ecological questions to centre stage, from where ANC neoliberal nationalism will either arrange a properly fascist backlash or, more likely under Zuma's ongoing misrule, continue shrinking in confusion with regular doses of necessary humility.

ACKNOWLEDGEMENT

The authors thank John Krinsky for fusing the authors' three disparate arguments, made originally at a Harold Wolpe Lecture in Durban in mid-2010. His care and sophistication in identifying solutions to our own conceptual problems remind us of the merits of internationalist collaboration and comparative Marxist praxis.

NOTES

1   For a sample of the debates on the independent left see Alexander 2010; Ballard, Habib and Valodia 2006; Bond 2005; Desai 2002; Duncan and Vally 2008; Maharaj, Desai and Bond 2011; Runciman 2011; Sinwell 2011 and Williams 2006.
2   See reactions to Bohmke's debates on *PoliticsWeb* and *Pambazuka*.
3   See Yale University and Columbia University. 2012. *Environmental Performance Index*, http://epi.yale.edu/.
4   For updates on this facet of the crisis, see http://www.corruptionwatch.org.za/.

REFERENCES

African National Congress. 1994. *Reconstruction and Development Programme.* Johannesburg: Umanyano Publications.

Alexander, P. 2010. 'Rebellion of the poor', *Review of African Political Economy*, 37 (123): 25–40.

Alexander, P., Lekgowa, T., Mmope, B., Sinwell, L. and Xezwi, B. 2012. *Marikana: A View from the Mountain and a Case to Answer.* Johannesburg: Jacana.

Ballard, R., Habib, A. and Valodia, I. (eds). 2006. *Voices of Protest: Social Movements in Post-apartheid South Africa.* Pietermaritzburg: University of KwaZulu-Natal Press.

Barker, C. 2006. 'Extending combined and uneven development'. In *One Hundred Years of Permanent Revolution*, edited by B. Dunn and H. Radice. London: Pluto Press.

Bohmke, H. 2009a. 'The branding of social movements in South Africa'. Accessed 14 June 2013, http://www.librarything.com/work/11812265.

Bohmke, H. 2009b. 'The white revolutionary as a missionary?', *New Frank Talk* 5. Accessed 10 July 2012, http://www.scribd.com/doc/31891005/The-White-Revolutionary-as-a-Missionary-Contemporary-travels-and-researches-in-Caffraria.

Bohmke, H. 2010a. 'Between the halo and the panga', *Dispositions* 2. Accessed 14 June 2013, http://dispositionsjournal.blogspot.com/.

Bohmke, H. 2010b. 'Don't talk about us talking about the poor', *PoliticsWeb.* Accessed 10 July 2012, http://www.politicsweb.co.za/politicsweb/view/politicsweb/en/page7 1619?oid=206254&sn=Detail&pid=71616.

Bond, P. 2000. *Cities of Gold, Townships of Coal.* Trenton, NJ: Africa World Press.

Bond, P. 2002. *Unsustainable South Africa.* Pietermaritzburg: University of KwaZulu-Natal Press.

Bond, P. 2005. *Elite Transition*. Pietermaritzburg: University of KwaZulu-Natal Press.

Bond, P. 2011a. 'Durban's water wars, sewage spills, fish kills and blue flag beaches'. In *Durban's Climate Gamble,* edited by P. Bond. Pretoria: Unisa Press.

Bond, P. 2011b. *Politics of Climate Justice: Paralysis Above, Movement Below.* Pietermaritzburg: University of KwaZulu-Natal Press.

Bond, P. 2011c. 'The right to the city and the eco-social commoning of water'. In *The Right to Water,* edited by S. Farhana and A. Loftus. London: Earthscan.

Bond, P. and Desai, A. 2006. 'Explaining uneven and combined development in South Africa'. In *Permanent Revolution*, edited by B. Dunn. London: Pluto Press.

Bruce, P. 'The thick end of the wedge', *Business Day,* 20 August 2012. Accessed 14 June 2013, http://www.bdlive.co.za/opinion/columnists/2012/08/20the-thick -end-of-the- wedge-the-editors-notebook.

DeFilippis, J., Fisher, R. and Schragge, E. 2010. *Contesting Community*. New Brunswick, NJ: Rutgers University Press.

Desai, A. 2002. *We Are the Poors.* New York: Monthly Review Press.

Desai, A. 2006. 'Vans, autos, and Kombis and the drivers of social movements'. Paper presented at Harold Wolpe Memorial Lecture, University of KwaZulu-Natal Centre for Civil Society, Durban, 28 July. Accessed 14 June 2013, www.ccs.ukzn.ac.za/ default.asp?11,22,5,2258.

Duncan, J. and Vally, N. 2008. 'National trends around protest action'. PowerPoint presentation, Centre for Sociological Research, University of Johannesburg, Johannesburg.

Farlam Commission. 2012. 'Transcription of the commission of inquiry: Marikana – days 1 to 7, 1 to 31 October 2012'. Accessed 14 June 2013, http://www.seri-sa.org/ images/stories/marikana_consolidatedtranscript_days1-7.pdf.

Geffen, N. 2010. *Debunking Delusions*. Johannesburg: Jacana.

Gorz, A. 1967. *A Strategy for Labor*. Boston: Beacon Press.

Gramsci, A. 1971. *Selections From the Prison Notebooks*. Translated and edited by Q. Hoare and G. Nowell Smith. New York: International Publishers.

Harvey, D. 2008. 'The right to the city', *New Left Review,* 53: 23–40. Accessed 14 June 2013, http://newleftreview.org/?view=2740.

Hemson, D. 2005. 'Can participation make a difference?' Durban: Human Sciences Research Council.

Hinely, R. 2009. 'Poors of Chatsworth take charge', *The Mercury,* 16 September.

Huchzermeyer, M. 2009. 'Does recent litigation bring us any closer to a right to the city?' Paper presented at the Workshop on Intellectuals, Ideology, Protests and Civil Society, University of Johannesburg, 3 October.

Hunt, A. and Wickham, G. 1994. *Foucault and Law*. London: Pluto Press.

Katznelson, I. 1981. *City Trenches*. Chicago: University of Chicago Press.

Maharaj, B., Desai, A. and Bond, P. 2011. *Zuma's Own Goal*. Trenton NJ: Africa World Press.

Marston, S. 2000. 'The social construction of scale', *Progress in Human Geography*, 24 (2): 219–242.

Miraftab, F. 2004. 'Invited and invented spaces of participation', *Wagadu,* 1 (1): 1–7.

Mottiar, S. and Bond, P. 2011. 'Social protest in South Africa'. Paper presented to the International Society for Third Sector Research, Stellenbosch University, 24 August.

Nash, A. 1999. 'The moment of Western Marxism in South Africa', *Comparative Studies of South Asia, Africa and the Middle East,* 19 (1): 61–72.

Petras, J. and Morley, M. 1990. *US Hegemony under Siege*. London: Verso.

Piven, F.F. and Cloward, R. 1979. *Poor People's Movements*. New York: Vintage Books.

Polletta, F. 2005. 'How participatory democracy became white', *Mobilization*, 10 (1): 271–288.

Republic of South Africa. 1994. *A New Housing Policy and Strategy for South Africa*. South African Government Information Service. Accessed 14 June 2013, http://www.info.gov.za/whitepapers/1994/housing.htm.

Rosenberg, G. 1993. *The Hollow Hope*. Chicago: University of Chicago Press.

Runciman, C. 2011. 'Questioning resistance in post-apartheid South Africa', *Review of African Political Economy*, 38 (130): 607–614.

Saul, J. 1975. 'The "labor aristocracy" thesis reconsidered'. In *The Development of an African Working Class*, edited by R. Sandbrook and R. Cohen. Toronto and London: University of Toronto Press.

Schwab, K. (ed.). 2012. *Global Competitiveness Report 2012–2013*. Geneva: World Economic Forum. Accessed 20 June 2013, http://www.weforum.org/reports/global-competitiveness-report-2012-2013.

Sinwell, L. 2009. 'Participation as popular agency', unpublished PhD thesis, University of the Witwatersrand, Johannesburg.

Sinwell, L. 2011. 'Is "another world" really possible?', *Review of African Political Economy*, 38 (127): 61–76.

Trotsky, L. 1962. *The Permanent Revolution and Results and Prospects*. London: New Park Publications.

Vavi, Z. 2011. 'Address by Cosatu general secretary at the Anti-Corruption Summit', Johannesburg, 8 December.

Walsh, S. 2008. 'Uncomfortable collaborations', *Review of African Political Economy*, 35 (116): 255–279.

Williams, J.J. 2006. 'Community participation: Lessons from post-apartheid South Africa', *Policy Studies*, 27 (3): 197–217.

Wolpe, H. (ed.). 1980. *The Articulations of Modes of Production*. London: Routledge.

CHAPTER

10

CRITICAL REFLECTIONS ON THE CRISIS AND LIMITS OF ANC 'MARXISM'

Mazibuko K. Jara

At the heart of South Africa's national liberation struggle was the constitution of a future South African nation in which white domination would be defeated. From the 1960s the Oliver Tambo-led African National Congress (ANC) increasingly used Marxist tools to develop its analysis of the South African social formation that had been shaped by three centuries of colonial dispossession and close to a century of capitalist development. The ANC defined and characterised this social formation as a 'colonialism of a special type' (CST) in which all classes and strata of black people were oppressed on the basis of their race. According to the ANC, what was needed to free black people from this national oppression was a multi-class revolutionary front uniting all the oppressed in prosecuting a national democratic revolution (NDR). This ANC theorisation of the social formation and the required political strategy also asserted the crucial and leading role of the working class in the revolutionary process and that the struggle for national liberation would be incomplete without fundamentally and systematically shaking the roots of racialised capitalism in South Africa, even though the ANC did not necessarily mean, or accept the necessity of, a transition to socialism. In essence, the ANC's use of Marxism was vanguardist and shaped by Stalinised/sovietised influences that were transmitted to it through leading members of the South African Communist Party (SACP) who, from the 1960s, dominated ANC theoretical perspectives.

What has become of the ANC's use of Marxism? What do the nineteen years of post-apartheid ANC rule and nation-building say about the scope and limits of the ANC's 'Marxism'? This chapter critically engages with the CST thesis and shows that the ANC's continued use of Marxism has been transformed into attempts to hegemonise and marry the working class to a project to transnationalise and deracialise South African capitalism. This has been through what the chapter describes as an Afro-neoliberal project that defines the ANC in government today. In addition to this critique of the limits of Afro-neoliberalism in resolving the national question, the chapter takes the argument further by reviewing how the ANC's nation-building project has failed to grapple with racialised post-apartheid social struggles over housing in the Western Cape. The chapter provides a second case study, which reviews sustained ANC government legislative efforts to retribalise the former bantustan countryside against the logic of a progressive nation-building project. Both these case studies show that the ANC has not been able to realise even its own limited notions of nation-building from the pre-1994 era and that these go against the progressive resolution of the national question. How the ANC has acted on race and nation in the post-apartheid period has opened the door to the reproduction of apartheid racial categories and regressive forms of nationalism including the return of ethnic identity, white supremacist arrogance, regressive racial polarisation, narrow black elite solidarity and Africanist chauvinism, particularly in relation to the so-called Indian and coloured racial 'minorities'.

This chapter concludes that the ANC's NDR theory is an exhausted Marxism that is denuded of both its radical impulses and emancipatory logics, particularly when it comes to resolving the national question. The ANC's nation-building project, whether in its 'rainbow nation' or 'home for all' or 'liberation of Africans in particular' versions, has not been based on a conscious political strategy which understands and addresses the structural socio-economic base of national oppression. Where critical structural interventions could have been made, we saw equivocation and even a retreat to racialised strategies. On this basis, the chapter argues for a post-ANC, post-national liberation Marxism relevant to the constitution of a new historical bloc of forces that can resolve the national question on the basis of transforming South Africa away from racism, white supremacy, racial privileges, narrow Africanism and capitalism.

THE 'COLONIALISM OF A SPECIAL TYPE' THESIS

At least since the early 1960s, the SACP-inspired CST thesis has been the pre-eminent theoretical framework used in the analysis of the South African national question. Applied to the apartheid period, the CST thesis held that South African society was a form of colonialism where the colonial community occupied the same territory as the colonised people. The CST thesis argued that white nationalism in South Africa was a unique form of colonialism in which the colonial seat of government was not in a parent country in Europe but inside the country (Holiday 1988). The CST thesis assumed that a white oppressive nation came into being with the 1910 Constitution, which excluded blacks, and this laid the basis for regarding South Africa and its population in general as an emerging single national entity (Pomeroy 1988). In this way, the CST thesis defined black South Africa as a nation which was shaped by the trajectory of a specific path of racialised capitalist development based on national oppression. In general, Marxist discussion of the national question acknowledges that capitalism tends to group a population with all its various classes into a single nation in a single territory (Mzala 1988). South Africa manifested this tendency throughout the entire period of CST.

This emerging black nation included coloured (the majority of whom reside in the Western Cape) and Indian South Africans who 'despite deceptive and often meaningless concessions … share a common fate with their African brothers (and whose) … own liberation is inextricably bound up with the liberation of the African people' (ANC 1969, unpaginated). In other words, the strategy aimed at liberation of the black majority (of which coloured and Indian people were considered a part) from national oppression and exploita-tion challenged and largely undermined a 'negative minority' approach (that is thinking of one's group as a separate entity). To have adopted such an approach would have led down a cul-de-sac (Pahad 1988). However, in my analysis the CST thesis did not sufficiently explain the development of, nor develop strategies to address, racial identities in colonial and apartheid South Africa together with the concomitant fears and perceptions of working-class coloured people about the reduction of their privileges due to deracialisation. The short-lived non-racial moment achieved amongst wide layers of thousands of political activists under the umbrella of the United Democratic Front (UDF) in the 1980s was also overstated because it had its own weaknesses, such as allowing people to orga-nise in groups based on apartheid-imposed racial identities, as if the non-racial

moment had already overcome entrenched racial identities, fears and perceptions. In addition, the CST thesis imposed the concept of African leadership on
the Western Cape in the 1980s without a rigorous understanding of the nature
and character of coloured identity, including its African roots. This led to fundamental mistakes in the subsequent ANC Western Cape strategy and tactics.

The above notwithstanding, the internal CST conditions allowed for the
principle of non-racialism to play a revolutionary organisational and ideological role. Thus, the CST social formation was resisted and challenged with
ideologies that gave priority to democratic majority interests and non-racialism,
thus going beyond a narrow racialised majority–minority dichotomy (Van
Diepen 1988). Consequently, the CST thesis posited the concept of the NDR,
which would destroy apartheid-era social and economic relationships and lay
the basis for a new and deeper internationalist approach (Pomeroy 1988). In
terms of the CST thesis, the central aspect of the national question in South
Africa was about the defeat of this special type of colonialism through the self-
determination of oppressed people in South Africa, the essence of which would
be the emergence of a new, sovereign and non-racial South African nation
in which race, ethnicity and nationality were no longer indices of difference.
According to the CST thesis, this concept of 'nation' was 'not defined by skin
colour or racial designation' (Jordan 1988: 118). In the CST thesis the sovereignty of a nation originates and is legitimated by the 'people' as a whole. In
this regard, Pallo Jordan cited a 1983 speech by former ANC president, Oliver
Tambo, wherein Tambo argued that 'sovereignty will come from the people as
a whole, and not from a collection of bantustans and racial and tribal groupings organised to perpetuate minority power' (Jordan 1988: 117). For the post-
apartheid period, this conceptualisation of sovereignty should challenge how
we understand the different neo-apartheid power and spatial groupings in the
Western Cape and how far the post-apartheid period has failed the non-racial
project which the ANC regarded as not only an idealised goal, but an essential
part of the concept of a new, united, South African nation (Jordan 1988).

According to Harold Wolpe (1988), the South African national question
reflected the interrelation between class and race. This was to argue for a class-
based approach to the resolution of the national question, which was different
from both an accommodation of national liberation within the exploitative structures of capitalist South Africa (Van Diepen 1988), and a narrow nationalism
in which an elite group amongst the oppressed gains ascendancy (ANC 1969).
This required the introduction of a revolutionary subject to bring about 'national

sovereignty ... and [the turning around of] the social order' (Van Diepen 1988: 10). However, despite the manifestation of such a revolutionary subject through sustained and widespread black working-class political action from the mid-1970s on, the reality of the 1993 political settlement did not manage to make a fundamental break with capitalism (DLF 2011; Marais 2001; SACP 2006).

LEFT CRITIQUES OF THE CST THESIS

The CST thesis was challenged by other left schools of thought. Bill Freund (cited by Mare 2003) argued that to see the struggle against apartheid as anti-colonial was to miss the mark because South Africa had been effectively independent for decades despite its colonial roots. This then suggested that the South African social formation had to be seen in class terms primarily, in which race, racism and apartheid were functional to capitalism. Variants of this view character-ised the social formation as racial capitalism. These left critiques suggested that CST promoted nationalism, which is an ideology that can corrupt the working class, divide it and prevent its unity at a time of crucial class struggles. This critique was linked to strategic perspectives for an explicitly socialist revolution, and not an NDR, which would ultimately resolve the national question. These views argued that a national liberation struggle stage would mean that the struggle for socialism is permanently postponed. Another critique by Neville Alexander (1986) argued that the CST thesis obstructed the drive towards single nationhood by adopting apartheid racial categories instead of rejecting them, mobilising the oppressed and exploited on the basis of their class positions and fostering a new national identity on the basis of unifying characteristics and the class struggle for socialism.

There was something overly deterministic in the CST thesis about how nation-building would take place post-apartheid. Mzala (1988) categorically stated that, after liberating themselves from apartheid, the people of South Africa would gravitate irresistibly towards integration. Yunus Carrim (1996, unpaginated) put it this way: 'As the process advances, the culture, values and interests of the African working class and its allies will increasingly come to constitute the core of the new South African'. As argued in this chapter, this linear path predetermined by Carrim has not been realised.

There is still no rigorous theoretical conceptualisation on the dynamics of race and class in the post-apartheid reality from a Marxist perspective.

Perhaps this is not surprising, given that Marxism has been criticised for its weak conceptualisation of the national question. These critiques have pointed to the problematic relationship socialist governments had with nationalism; the tendency for Marxism to emphasise the economics of capitalism at the cost of attention to the racial, psychological, philosophical, identity, cultural, linguistic, territorial and physical aspects of nationalism. Further, the absence of a coherent Marxist theory of nationalism has often led to half-baked attempts by left forces to merely paint nationalism red by overemphasising the revolutionary potential of national liberation struggles (Dexter 1996). These weaknesses of Marxism have given space to the rise and consolidation of a problematic ANC approach on the national question, which may still capture nationalist loyalty amongst the formerly oppressed without an appreciation of the interconnectedness between race and class.

AFRO-NEOLIBERALISM, POST-APARTHEID CAPITALISM AND A FLOUNDERING NATION-BUILDING PROJECT

In order to secure long-term conducive conditions for profitability, the ruling capitalist class has actively determined and shaped the substance of the new South African nation. In essence, South Africa is now a post-apartheid nation based on a liberal democratic constitutional dispensation in which the free market and the right to private property are fundamental. This is what the 1994 political settlement ultimately achieved. To play its part in the bargain, the new government also acted swiftly to adopt neoliberal economic policies that facilitated the financialisation, transnationalisation and globalisation of the South African economy. This included a significant restructuring of work that worsened working conditions, retrenched more than a million workers, evicted more than a million farm workers, increased labour productivity and increased capital's share of national income at the expense of the working class. The working class affected by these processes remains overwhelmingly black and the capitalist class driving them remains overwhelmingly white (the racial capital–labour regime from the apartheid era remains intact) albeit somewhat deracialised at the upper echelons with the absorption of a handful of black capitalists and a larger layer of black managers in the middle to upper echelons of the state and the economy. This process of economic change has significant implications for the resolution of the national question. In essence, addressing the legacy of national oppression is increasingly constrained by the capitalist character of the South African economy post-apartheid. The perpetuation of national oppression is not now in the form of formal apartheid laws that discriminate against black people. White privilege and racism are now maintained and reinforced by the accommodation of formal liberation and democracy within the exploitative structures of South African capitalism.

For the post-apartheid political dispensation to protect the interests, social positions and property rights of capital is to leave intact colonial and apartheid dispossession, destruction of socio-economic systems, national oppression, gender oppression and economic exploitation. The protection of the above stands as a barrier against a progressive resolution of the national question and other much-needed socio-economic transformation. In Joe Slovo's (1988: 148) words, 'The basic objectives of liberation cannot be achieved without undermining the accumulated political, social, cultural and economic white privileges. The moulding of our nation will be advanced in direct proportion to the elimination of these accumulated privileges.' The emerging post-apartheid state and the nation-building project have not come close to what Slovo had envisaged.

Post-apartheid capitalist restructuring (coinciding with the resolution of the profitability crisis of late apartheid through the significant restoration of capitalist profitability in South Africa) has effectively reduced the social weight of the working class in ways that marginalise it from defining the essence of the nation-building project. Ironically, under CST it was the process of proletarianisation that helped to break down tribal divisions and to lay the basis for an emerging black nation, whereas in the era of capitalist globalisation the working class is subject to division and atomisation. This has huge implications for working-class consciousness, self-agency and class struggles for the resolution of the national question.

In Wolpe's view (1988), the basis of the national question lies in the economic structure. Informed by this view, Edward Webster, Jacklyn Cock and Michael Burawoy (2005) raise the questions: what are the contours of the new post-apartheid racial order and how do they reflect the changing labour supplies, the informalisation of work and the emergence of an African bourgeoisie? In what ways does liberal democracy conserve/restore or challenge/dissolve the racial division of labour and racialised property relations? The national question remains incomplete in many African states because bourgeois strata amongst the oppressed held the reins of state power after the defeat of colonial rule

(Pomeroy 1988). Likewise, the post-apartheid state has inspired the growth and development of such a black bourgeois strata whilst also restoring profitability to the main section of capital (white capitalists). This shows the limitations of South Africa's liberal democracy in challenging the racial division of labour and racialised property relations, which would be essential for resolving the national question.

Like other ruling classes, the South African capitalist class has a deep interest in exploiting class and racial divisions from the unresolved national question as a means of retaining its control. This essentially white ruling class, whilst not directly and expressly appealing to loyalties for national unity on the basis of race or colour, has effectively exploited racial and colour loyalties to foster a comprador black section and has overtly and covertly induced racial tensions between the different racial categories of South African workers. Within this overall framework, white workers continue to occupy a special role in this racial division of the working class. Despite their desertion by the ruling class goal of securing the restoration of capitalist profitability post-1994, the white working class has essentially defended its colonial and apartheid privileges by opposing affirmative action, employment equity and refusing to join political forces with its numerically larger and politically organised black working-class sisters and brothers. Under CST, the white working class had occupied an important 'seat at the ruling table of the capitalist class helping in the domi-nation of the black working class' (Mzala 1988: 38). Under such conditions, the white working class had an objective interest in maintaining the inferior political, social and economic status of black workers. It is only logical that the liberal democratic framework has not yet shaken the white working class out of this ideological corruption despite its increasing exposure to the restruc-turing of work under capitalist globalisation and the associated neoliberal labour market policy. In fact, the crumbs it received from the capitalist table helped it to consolidate skills, expertise, good lifestyles, financial assets and amenities, which the majority of black workers still do not have. This places the white working class in an advantageous position where it can meet its socio-economic needs and allow itself to be used on a racial basis to block the work-place and socio-economic empowerment of black workers. A 2006 Western Cape National Union of Metalworkers of South Africa (Numsa) conference on non-racialism provided many examples of how the white working class conducts itself in relation to black workers on a daily basis throughout the Western Cape (Numsa 2006). These examples confirm the emergence of a new form of white chauvinism amongst white workers. This chauvinism is worsened by the fact that there is no progressive conscientisation and organisation of white workers on a progressive anti-capitalist and anti-racist basis. Further work is required to analyse the socio-economic profile of white workers in order to identify similarities and differences between them and black workers. Such empirical information would be the basis for non-racial trade union and political work amongst white workers in order for them to recognise their common class interests with black workers.

Given the foregoing analysis of white workers and how post-apartheid capitalism has continued to benefit white people, it is useful to consider where white consciousness is in terms of nation-building. Anthony Holiday (1988: 85) described white South Africans as being caught in a profound 'spatio-temporal disorientation', which prevented them from understanding where and when they are living and who they could be within a broader conception of the South African nation. This disorientation is still a barrier to nation-building and means that they have not become Africans in Africa, à la Tambo (1979). Instead, they have held on to and defended their apartheid privileges. The organised political forces amongst them have also sought to actively block and delegitmise any change. This reproduction of white arrogance and supremacy can survive and even get emboldened primarily because of the shortcomings and limits of Afro-neoliberalism.

The above does not represent the totality of race and class dynamics within post-apartheid South African society. Jeremy Seekings and Nicoli Nattrass (2002) show that inequality has increased within races in the post-apartheid period. This challenges the understanding of privilege in terms of old approaches to race and class. It is not far-fetched to suggest that for the 1.5 million or so black middle-class beneficiaries of the post-apartheid dividend, whatever remains of a national grievance is not about its structural foundations but essentially about further deracialisation of the capitalist market. For these sections, their concrete material reality as black people has changed significantly in relation to the wealth of the country, the political institutions of administration, education, opportunities and public prestige. This has significant implications for how the ANC and sections of the black elite understand and pose issues of inequality and blackness, particularly as it is not in their strategic interests for the black working class to assert its own interests, which may potentially challenge capitalism. In other words, the entrenchment of a deracialised capitalism in the era of neoliberal globalisation fails to resolve the national question in so far as the national question is about the complete social, economic and political liberation of the black working-class majority. To reaffirm, post-apartheid capitalist relations continue to deepen racial contradictions and class inequalities even within the previously oppressed black majority in ways that leave the national question unresolved.

Further, instead of creating an independent black capitalist class, the post-apartheid period has created a black section of the capitalist class that has, internally, a compradorial-type relationship to the white capitalist class, thus deepening the hold of white local and international monopoly capital over the South African economy. This is likely to become a new form of internal colonialism, reflecting itself less through the political, but increasingly through economic forms of subjugation and domination. The emergent black capitalist stratum is not galvanising a transformative national developmental effort. Whilst it has gained hegemony over the ANC and the state, it is incapable of uniting a historic bloc behind a progressive nation-building project. Instead, at moments when its progress is blocked, it is likely to retreat to subjectivist and overly psychologised explanations for persisting injustices and white racism. It is incapable of connecting white racism with the deeply entrenched, structured character of capitalism and its systemic reproduction of the peripheralisation, underdevelopment, or the persisting poverty and marginalisation of the majority of black people. Its Afro-neoliberalism is narrow and limited.

Instead of achieving predetermined outcomes, we have seen, amongst other things, the reproduction of racial identities to the detriment of the nation-building project. These include the narrow essentialist racialisation of transformation, inequality, capitalism, the HIV/AIDS epidemic and criticism in a manner that shows degeneration of the national debate to the level of race populism (Mare 2003), a far cry from the limited and non-transformative 'rainbowism' and even further from a radical project. To understand this new form of regressive racialisation, it is useful to refer to what Carrim (1996) has identified: on the one hand, the impetus for the evolution of a broad, non-racial identity and, on the other hand, the emergence of ethnic and racial identities in new forms. Philip Dexter (1996) explains these developments in terms of the limited transition occasioned by the 1993 political settlement. According to Dexter (1996, unpaginated), 'The pressure to revert to old, comfortable identities that are primarily based on perceived racial ethnic identities' becomes great in light of the limited transition, 'even if these identities were artificially created'.

AFRICAN–COLOURED SOCIAL RELATIONS IN THE WESTERN CAPE

The Western Cape Province presents the most complex manifestations of an unresolved national question. This province, which post-1994 has seen sharpened racial conflict, is populated by a majority of 'coloured' people with 'Africans' and 'white' people as significant minorities while 'Indians' and migrants from other African countries are generally considered an even smaller minority. According to Statistics South Africa's Census 2011 results, 49.6 per cent of people described themselves as coloured, 33.4 per cent as black African, 16 per cent as white, and 1.1 per cent as Indian or Asian (Stats SA 2012). As the 2006 Numsa conference on non-racialism noted, in the Western Cape, the capitalist class continues to divide and weaken the unity of African and coloured workers. In this regard, appeals are made to the previous intermediate position occupied by coloured workers in apartheid racial hierarchies (Numsa 2006). This is done at two levels. The majority of African workers are made to resent and begrudge their fellow coloured colleagues who normally occupy more senior positions across the board (Numsa 2006). The second level is where white social and political forces such as the Democratic Alliance (DA) have paternalistically become political champions of the line that coloured people are considered by the democratic dispensation as 'not black enough' and therefore classifying them as losers in democracy (Numsa 2006).

In the African townships in the Western Cape, the housing crisis is visible everywhere: dense and ever-expanding urban sprawls of shacks. In contrast, in the coloured townships this housing crisis is deceptively invisible as it is hidden in backyards of formal good-quality housing. National, provincial and local housing policy has not provided sufficient housing units to meet the ever-growing backlog and has prioritised the reversal and rolling back of apartheid spatial planning. As a result, the Delft Township, far away from the Cape Town economic centre, is the only post-1994 settlement which can be claimed as significantly racially mixed. The perpetuation of apartheid spatial patterns limits interracial social integration and the emergence of deracialised identities. This is against the earlier experience in South Africa's capitalist development which, from the beginning of the twentieth century, formed a single national market binding various black groups by economic location (Mzala 1988). These processes undermine the potential for nation-building based on creating conducive material, infrastructural conditions for a united and emancipated nation – overcoming apartheid geography and addressing the massive inequalities of decades of combined and uneven development. Existing political organising efforts have not yet resulted in systematic, sustained and effective social mobilisation of shack- and backyard dwellers in a common movement of the homeless staking their claim for a social wage. The contestation of charity mobilised for the victims of regular fires (which destroy informal housing) at the Joe Slovo camp and the intense disputes over who has the rights to benefit from the N2 Gateway Housing Project have exposed this glaring absence of non-racial homeless people's solidarity and social mobilisation. This has also resurfaced old tensions between *amagoduka* (migrant workers) and established residents of Cape Town's African townships. Under these conditions, black working-class unity, as the bedrock of a progressive nation-building project, is far from a reality. Instead, the entrenchment of racial identities, mutual fears and mistrust are the order of the day. In addition, profound processes of thorough-going transformation, such as nation-building, are likely to be deformed and stunted without being buttressed by organic processes of popular self-empowerment, without self-agency. In the 1980s, the anti-apartheid struggle was characterised by extensive and grounded political education of activists and the mass base on a wide variety of societal concerns including non-racialism and nation-building. In contrast, the post-1994 period has been marked by a virtual absence of such political education. Such consciousness-building would also have needed to address the structural socio-economic base of national oppression and liberation. By their very nature, 'rainbowism' and the 'home for all' variants of the nation-building project are incapable of driving a systematic consciousness-building programme of the kind required, and which would not simply soothe racial animosity but actually address it systematically.

In response to the housing and other socio-economic crises in the Western Cape, Afro-neoliberalism opted to effectively aggravate tensions and conflicts between coloured and African people in a province where white capital is extremely manipulative and fairly well politically organised. The rise of a narrow Africanism within the ANC in the Western Cape, on the back of the older ANC concept of African leadership (see below), can be seen as the beginnings of the tendency towards national exclusiveness which must be understood as, à la Mzala (1988: 51), 'a drive by the bourgeois elite among the oppressed to take over the role of the new exploiter' instead of addressing colonial working conditions on the wine farms and other such racially subjugating systems that continue to persist in the Western Cape.

The concept of African leadership or hegemony referred to in the above paragraph has been described by the ANC (1997) to refer to the hegemony

271

of indigenous Africans over national life and the character of the new nation. There are three problems with this formulation. Firstly, 'African' consciously and deliberately implies the exclusion of Khoi and San heritage, which includes a history of slavery, genocide and ignored but heroic anti-colonial resistance. This is to miss an important opportunity to embrace and reaffirm the African origins of large sections of coloured people in the Western Cape (Ozinsky and Rasool 1993). Secondly, 'African' is used loosely to paper over class differentiation amongst the diverse African communities in South Africa. African leadership can end up as a narrow nationalistic concept if it is not related to its class content (Carrim 1996). To be controversial, there is no doubt that a white but communist Joe Slovo was a far better representative of black working-class interests than a black but capitalist Patrice Motsepe. The third problem has to do with the imagery of a timeless pre-colonial African society, which can be transmitted as a whole to a twenty-first-century capitalist South Africa. This has opened the doors for moribund feudal forces and practices to rear the ugly head of reactionary nationalism based on ethnic and tribal identity (see below).

Narrow and racialised Africanism is strategically incapable of structurally rolling back apartheid geography, socially mobilising a non-racial homeless people's movement and decommodifying basic services as the basis for building integrated communities. The emergence of this kind of Africanism is founded in how ANC strategy and tactics are defined in class terms. For example, Joel Netshitenzhe (1996, unpaginated) narrowed the scope for national liberation to the removal of 'barriers that have been set by apartheid in terms of black people and Africans' (in particular) access to the economy and services', leaving intact the economic structure of society. In the same piece, he also sought to equate the role of the working class in national liberation together with that of the 'middle strata'. Such Africanism could rise in the Western Cape given the relative political marginality of organised working-class formations in the body politic of the province. In general, narrow and racialised Africanism stands against the logic of a progressive and working-class-based nation-building project.

PROVINCIALISM AND RETRIBALISATION

Another outcome of the 1994 political settlement was the break-up of South Africa into nine provinces largely coinciding with ethnic and language boundaries. In my analysis, the creation of these provinces has diluted the goal of building a united non-racial South Africa. As a result, tendencies to provincialism, regionalism and ethnicity have been entrenched and in the future they may become centripetal forces against national unity. The creation of provinces may have removed bantustans, but more significantly failed to move away from the social content of these spaces (Mare 2003). These were spaces of extreme discrimination and inequality. It is in these spaces that social reproduction is tenuous for the black working class. It is in these same spaces that there has been extremely limited racial and social integration because apartheid geographies have been reinforced by post-apartheid spatial development patterns. No wonder it then becomes easy for creeping racialisation to become a national expression of provincialism, regionalism and ethnicity.

The compromises the ANC government made with traditional leaders are another factor which can potentially reinforce the narrow and chauvinistic rise of ethnic identities, cultural practices and undemocratic rule by an unelected and parasitic elite. This perpetuates the 'subject' status of rural people, thus denying them their 'citizenship'. How can rural 'subjects' be part of a progressive twenty-first-century African nation? Surely it is only free 'citizens' who can be such? Indeed the Freedom Charter recognised the cultural diversity of South Africans but this did not imply that cultural identities are eternally frozen categories and that the expression of different identities must ultimately serve to foster national unity (Carrim 1996). The African Renaissance project and the invoking of African identity has had the effect of freezing these categories as if they were in some timeless pre-colonial Africa which has not even reached the stage of evolving into an oppressed black nation. Even worse is the establishment of forums of traditional leaders in the cosmopolitan and largely urbanised African constituency of the Western Cape. This can have the effect of further ethnicisation of communities, thus threatening broader integration.

When it comes to how rural areas of the former bantustans are governed in the post-apartheid period, the ideology of segregation continues. Tradition, custom and welfare are now instruments to govern rural areas and are used to perpetuate the logic of segregation and second-class citizenship for the people who live in these rural areas. They remain citizens of the bantustans and not of a democratic South Africa. No matter what their personal preferences, they must still pay their dues and loyalty to unelected and ethnic-based tribal rulers. Full citizenship, rights, democracy and development are not what drive state policy in rural areas.

It is useful to remember that the 1996 Constitution established wall-to-wall elected municipalities across every inch of South African territory. This new local government mandate was a break with the colonial and apartheid periods where local government in the former homelands combined and concentrated administrative, judicial and executive power in a single state functionary, the tribal authority. It is completely forgotten today that the overwhelming majority of traditional leaders were perverted and co-opted as instruments of colonial and apartheid rule. This was through a process of conferring statutory powers upon them: traditional leaders were conferred with statutory powers over Africans in 'black areas'. These powers and the statutory structures within which they were exercised formed the building blocks of the homeland system. The new constitutional framework dismantled the homeland system and removed governmental powers given to tribal chiefs. However, what the 1996 Constitution provided for was reversed in subsequent, post-1996 laws – the Communal Land Rights Act, Act 11 of 2004 (CLARA) and the Traditional Leadership and Governance Framework Act, Act 41 of 2003 (Framework Act).

The Framework Act allows all former tribal authorities to continue in the post-apartheid period under their new identity as traditional councils. In other words, the Framework Act does not discontinue the previously hated tribal authorities that were established by the apartheid-era Bantu Authorities Act, Act 68 of 1951. This entrenches apartheid-era tribal boundaries and authorities in virtually all rural areas in the former apartheid homelands, even in areas where there were no longer chiefs. The Framework Act essentially refashions the old tribal authorities as 'traditional councils' without much transformation of their content, purpose, functions and powers. It gives traditional councils the very kinds of unaccountable governance powers tribal authorities had under the 1951 Bantu Authorities Act. These powers contributed to various abuses and ultimately led to the loss of legitimacy of tribal authorities in many areas. The Framework Act seeks to locate traditional leaders as the primary institutions of power in rural areas. The Framework Act also enables government to devolve governance powers and responsibilities to traditional councils in fourteen areas of responsibility, including land administration; natural resource management; registration of births, deaths and customary marriages; justice; safety and security; and economic development. In practice, the powers are exercised on such a large scale that it renders the traditional councils an impermissible fourth sphere of government.

The preservation of tribal boundaries and authorities makes post-apartheid South African citizenship and the depth of rural democracy dependent on geography. People living in former homelands are made tribal subjects under a separate legal regime and form of governance from other South Africans. They become insulated from the reach of the laws applying to other South Africans and are subject to customary law as defined and interpreted by tribal chiefs. The consensual nature of customary law is now also undermined when it is applied within fixed jurisdictional boundaries derived from the Bantu Authorities Act, as is done in the Framework Act. With the Framework Act, traditional leaders have begun to circumscribe the power and agency of the majority of rural dwellers, features which are an essential part for the development of consensual customary law. This is inconsistent with undoing the legacy of apartheid laws.

The anti-bantustan revolts that exploded during the 1980s were struggles to be part of a united South Africa and a rejection of the ethnic identities that were perverted, frozen and imposed by apartheid. The post-apartheid legal framework on traditional leaders betrays those struggles and attempts to impose a map of neatly delineated separate 'tribes' on the 17 to 22 million South Africans living in former homeland areas. Current attacks on 'outsiders', whether labelled foreigners, *AmaMfengu*, 'Pedis' or 'Shangaans', illustrate the direction things could take. To justify this slide, the state has used a discourse laden with phrases such as the '*recognition* and *promotion* of the *institution* of traditional leadership', 'status, role and place' and 'institutionalising traditional leadership'. Absent from state discourse are 'rural democratisation', 'democratic transformation of rural social relations', 'empowering communities', 'self-agency and self-empowerment of rural communities', 'sustained social mobil-isation of rural communities', 'people-driven rural development', 'detribalising the former bantustan countryside' and so on.

To conclude this section, it is useful to refer to ANC president Jacob Zuma's role in emboldening tribalised identities. In his political fight to become ANC president, Zuma combined the use of victimhood with the strategic deploy-ment of ethnic appeals. In KwaZulu-Natal, Zuma was central in rolling back the Inkatha Freedom Party (a Zulu nationalist movement implicated in apartheid rule and violence). He did not do this on the basis of organising a working class movement into a solid democratic popular support base, using the slow and painstaking methods of persuasion (Horn 2008). He led a group in the ANC that courted the Zulu king (King Zwelithini) and other important cultural symbols (such as the popular Shembe church) as quick-fix personalities to bring with them all their subjects/believers as voters (Horn 2008). Such an appearance has a powerful effect on locals who are searching for identity and popular welfare in light of growing immiseration. After his June 2005 dismissal as the deputy president of South Africa, Zuma continued to publicly court the Zulu king and other Zulu cultural symbols. He went beyond Zulu ethnicity to actually cultivate and entrench ethnic identity and symbols of other cultural groups. He did this to communicate a powerful but reactionary message: the modernising Thabo Mbeki is a threat to the traditions that the majority of the people hold dear. When such an accessible Zuma is now seen as victimised by a modernising Mbeki, the choice is clear for a Shembe church follower: 'Zuma is my man'.

CONCLUSION: TOWARDS A POST-ANC, POST-LIBERATION MARXISM

This chapter has argued that post-1994, the ANC used 'Marxism' to justify and codify a neoliberal revolution and the containment of contradictions. Containing contradictions has been a key feature of the politics of the ANC. The ANC-in-government has been able to square a number of circles, pursuing the promise of a massive social-delivery programme whilst sustaining neoliberal economic policies that reproduce the worst of the colonial and apartheid economic order.

One of the most disquieting aspects in South Africa today is the absence of coherent Marxist and other liberatory responses to the crisis of the ANC's 'Marxism', particularly when it comes to the national question. Where they exist, radical analyses have been largely limited to academic debates and have also been marginalised in the wider public discourse and policy process (Du Toit 2005). Yet it is possible to change this and go so much further than what is allowed by dominant ideological frameworks. This is extremely important if a Marxist analysis is to 'illuminate, not simply the extent and nature of existing problems, but also the scope and possibility for agency, change and transformation' (Du Toit 2005: 20). This will depend on the extent to which Marxist analysis can go beyond charting broad outlines and features of the structure of South African society and start contributing to enabling ordinary people to make sense of their situations in order to act upon them (Du Toit 2005).

This situation also creates opportunities for theoretical innovation. Specifically, attention needs to be paid to the nascent seeds of a progressive national project, as was seen in the broad ethnic and racial unity during the working class strikes at Marikana and De Doorns at the end of 2012 and in the solidarity with African migrants who bore the brunt of the May to August 2008 outbreak of Afrophobia. An important arena for innovation in theory and political action concerns the sphere of production and reproduction, particularly when it comes to social reproduction and the need to build and fight for alternative political economy spaces in order to build working-class power across narrow divides. What is required are fine-grained narratives, praxis and alternatives that engage with, challenge and enlarge the space for poor people's agency (Du Toit 2004). As Webster, Cock and Burawoy (2005) argue, much-needed Marxist intellectual and political work would aim to examine and challenge the capitalist nature of post-apartheid South Africa and pose the question of socialism. I add that the unresolved national question is an essential part of such intellectual and political work. In other words, the door is open for 'building Marxism' in a way that is indigenous and creative as it pays attention to the unresolved national question.

According to Webster (2006), the approach of 'building Marxism' means that Marxism is seen as a social theory designed to understand dilemmas and possibilities of social transformation. This approach tries to understand a capitalist society and identify possibilities for transforming it. Inherent in this approach is the need for Marxism to be subject to continuous challenge, including the need for it to acknowledge its historic failure to grapple with the national question. 'Building Marxism' means reconstructing Marxism. For the unresolved national question, a reconstruction of Marxism means the need to understand post-apartheid nationalism, race, racism and tribalism as a first step towards the reconstitution of a historic bloc capable of advancing its post-capitalist class interests in ways that go beyond narrow economic determinism; in ways that also go to the heart of race and racism and white supremacy as a separate category even if it still originates from economic relations.

South Africa is in desperate need of a radical and transformative political and economic project. Such a project should be about new values that underpin national identity, wealth-creation and ownership and redistribution and it should also be about transforming the power dynamics of social relations. It is such a project that provides the most conducive conditions to resolve the national question, transform society as a whole and build an alternative to capitalism. These are tasks that the ANC's 'Marxism' is incapable of discharging.

ACKNOWLEDGEMENT

I wish to acknowledge critical input and encouragement from Vishwas Satgar. The ideas in this chapter were also tested in a 2006 unpublished paper that was presented at the Harold Wolpe Memorial Trust's Tenth Anniversary Colloquium ('Engaging silences and unresolved issues in the political economy of South Africa', 21–23 September 2006, Cape Town, South Africa) as well as several public speaking events hosted by the Goedgedacht Forum for Social Reflection and Democracy Development Programme between 2008 and 2010.

REFERENCES

Alexander, N. 1986. 'Approaches to the national question in South Africa', *Transformation*, 1: 63–95.

ANC (African National Congress). 1969. 'Strategy and tactics of the South African revolution'. *Forward to Freedom*. Sechaba: London. Accessed 2 July 2013, http://www.marxists.org/subject/africa/anc/1969/strategy-tactics.htm.

ANC. 1997. 'Nation-formation and nation-building: The national question in South Africa'. In *Umrabulo: Discussion Documents for ANC National Conference*. Johannesburg: ANC.

Carrim, Y. 1996. 'The national question in post-apartheid South Africa: Reconciling multiple identities', *African Communist*, 145. Accessed 2 July 2013, http://www.sacp.org.za/main.php?ID=2375.

Dexter, P. 1996. 'Marxism and the national question in a democratic South Africa', *African Communist*, 145. Accessed 2 July 2013, http://www.sacp.org.za/main.php?ID=2375.

DLF (Democratic Left Front). 2011. *Declaration of the Democratic Left Front: Adopted by the First National Conference*. Accessed 11 June 2012, http//:www.democraticleft.za.net.

Du Toit, A. 2004. *Forgotten by the Highway: Globalisation, Adverse Incorporation and Chronic Poverty in a Commercial Farming District*. Chronic poverty and development policy series, no. 4. Bellville: Programme for Land and Agrarian Studies, University of the Western Cape.

Du Toit, A. 2005. *Chronic and Structural Poverty in South Africa: Challenges for Action and Research*. Chronic poverty and development policy series, no. 6. Bellville: Programme for Land and Agrarian Studies, University of the Western Cape.

Holiday, A. 1988. 'White nationalism in South Africa as movement and system'. In *The National Question in South Africa*, edited by M. van Diepen. London: Zed Books.

Horn, P. 2008. *Populism: What Happens When the Terrain Shifts?* Unpublished discussion notes. Amandla Publishers (Durban Editorial Collective).

Jordan, P. 1988. 'The South African liberation movement and the making of a new nation'. In *The National Question in South Africa*, edited by M. van Diepen. London: Zed Books.

Marais, H. 2001. *South Africa: Limits to Change: The Political Economy of Transition.* New York: Palgrave-Macmillan.

Mare, G. 2003. 'The state of the state: Contestation and race re-assertion in a neo-liberal terrain'. In *State of the Nation: South Africa 2003-2004*, edited by J. Daniel, A. Habib and R. Southall. Cape Town: HSRC Press.

Mzala. 1988. 'Revolutionary theory on the national question in South Africa'. In *The National Question in South Africa*, edited by M. van Diepen. London: Zed Books.

Netshitenzhe, J. 1996. 'The national democratic revolution: Is it still on track?', *Umrabulo*, 1 (1). Accessed 2 July 2013, http://anc.org.za/show.php?id=2968.

Numsa (National Union of Metalworkers of South Africa). 2006. *Report of the NUMSA Western Cape Non-Racial Conference.* Cape Town, 21–23 July. Cape Town: NUMSA.

Ozinsky, M. and Rasool, E. 1993. 'Developing a strategic perspective for the coloured areas in the Western Cape', *African Communist*, 133: 39–47.

Pahad, E. 1988. 'South African Indians as a national minority in the national question'. In *The National Question in South Africa*, edited by M. van Diepen. London: Zed Books.

Pomeroy, W. 1988. 'What is the national question in international perspective?' In *The National Question in South Africa*, edited by M. van Diepen. London: Zed Books.

SACP (South African Communist Party). 2006. *Bua Komanisi! Information Bulletin of the Central Committee of the SACP*, May (Special Edition).

Seekings, J. and Nattrass, N. 2002. 'Class, distribution and redistribution in post-apartheid South Africa', *Transformation,* 50: 1–30.

Slovo, J. 1988. 'The working class and nation-building'. In *The National Question in South Africa*, edited by M. van Diepen. London: Zed Books.

Stats SA. 2012. *Census 2011.* Pretoria: Stats SA.

Tambo, O.R. 1979. 'Message on January 8'. *Sechaba.* London.

Van Diepen, M. 1988. 'Introduction'. In *The National Question in South Africa*, edited by M. van Diepen. London: Zed Books.

Webster, E. 2006. Unpublished input to a workshop on developing the research agenda of the Chris Hani Institute. Input recorded by the author.

Webster, E., Cock, J. and Burawoy, M. 2005. *A Research Agenda for the Chris Hani Institute.* Johannesburg: Chris Hani Institute.

Wolpe, H. 1988. 'Race and class in the national struggle in South Africa'. In *The National Question in South Africa*, edited by M. van Diepen. London: Zed Books.

CONCLUSION

Vishwas Satgar

For the past four decades historical Marxism as a body of social thought and radical practice has been systematically attacked. The cold war, the triumphalism of the liberal world after the collapse of the Soviet Union, the spread of a hegemonic common sense naturalising financialised capitalism (in everyday life as credit-driven consumption and as unadulterated greed), the prejudice of the liberal media and the weaknesses of authoritarian vanguardist Marxism have all contributed to discrediting Marxism and even erasing its presence in public discourse, in many countries. However, the deep anti-Marxism of our time is unhinging in the midst of the deepest and most multifaceted systemic crises of modern capitalism. Not only are the limits and contradictions of globalised capitalism apparent for all to see, but the making of deep inequalities, hunger, mass unemployment, ecological crisis and growing violence are reaffirming a class politics and understanding of our social world.

The spectre of Marxism is back but this time freed from the cage of orthodoxy or dogma. Although those who believe Marxism is always right, does not have weaknesses and has all the answers ('zombie Marxists'), will continue to exist and will also make an appearance in this conjuncture. The world, however, is no longer starry-eyed in the presence of such a radicalism. In the ferment of transnational activism, within the World Social Forum and with the rise of a new Global Left, a heterodox anti-capitalism has come to the fore, open to various resources of critique, imagining different ways of exiting capitalism and consciously seeking a democratic way forward rather than the 'correct line'. A non-dogmatic and democratic Marxism is finding its way in this context. This volume has provided a glimpse of such a Marxism: its new axes of renewal, themes and challenges.

BEYOND VANGUARD MARXISM

Marxism being in crisis is not new. Even its death has been proclaimed many times in the last century. At the beginning of the twentieth century, the first crisis of Marxism emerged in the context of mass working-class politics and movements. The looming onset of World War I and positions on imperialist war – reform versus revolution, vanguard versus mass party – were all sources of deep contention and contributed to the crisis of Marxism at that time. After 1917, the Russian Revolution spawned a society that became an object of critical enquiry on the Left. For such a thinking and critical Left the collapse of the Soviet Union did not come as a surprise. The makings of the crisis of vanguard Marxism were long observed. However, the crisis of vanguard Marxism was more than Soviet orthodoxy and the failings of communist rule. In fact, the lineage of vanguard Marxism and its crisis extends to China, anti-colonial movements and national liberation movements, mainly in Africa.

In the late twentieth century various currents of academic Marxism have also entered into crisis. This includes structuralist and anti-humanist Althusserian Marxism, rational choice Marxism with its attempt to marry methodological individualism and analytical philosophy to Marxism and regulation theory with its grounding in post-Fordism and new social structures of accumulation. While South Africa has generally received its Marxisms from the outside (for example, Marxism–Leninism, Trotskyism, English Marxism, Poulantzian, Althusserian), many in the tradition of academic Marxism have long retreated and taken flight on the wings of postmodernism, the latest intellectual import into South Africa. Such post-Marxists have immersed themselves in postmodernism's fetish for deconstruction, philosophic discourse and its obsession with individualism; the latter something postmodernism has in common with neoliberalism.

However, outside the academy and in the mainstream of South African politics a national liberation vanguardist Marxism looms large; it struts around the weak foundations of a post-apartheid society, claiming to be making history. South Africa is one of the last bastions of such a jaded Marxist imagination. Its future is in question as it displays morbid signs of exhaustion within national liberation politics, as it degenerates into authoritarian populism and as it champions carbon-based and globalised industrial state capitalism. More fundamentally, vanguardist Marxism, as represented through the ruling African National congress (ANC) Alliance in South Africa, has engendered its own orthodoxy: the ubiquitous and ever-present march of the 'national democratic revolution'. It is within this imagination and through its doctrinal framing that reality is engaged by the ANC-led Alliance. It is the window that mediates the real world.

Despite the exceptionalism sometimes claimed by national liberation doctrine, like all vanguardist orthodoxy it is easy to hold on to its doctrinal certainties while practice displays the opposite; it becomes the crutch for the ignorant or the arrogant, even when the interests, dreams and passions of the working class, the poor and victims of capitalism generally, are not realised. Moreover, the ideologues of such a Marxism are more about legitimating the 'correct line' of 'scientific socialism', handed down from above, than critically making intelligible the actual state of things and allowing a collective interrogation of the contradictions of contemporary South African capitalism. This is not new or exceptional and has generally been how vanguard Marxism brings about its own obsolescence; Marxism becomes ritual and obfuscation in its ossification. This volume reaches for a renewed Marxism that is an alternative to orthodox and vanguard Marxism.

THE AGE OF MANY MARXISMS

Marxism derives its resilience from the continued existence of capitalist social relations and oppressions. It is the dialectical Other of capitalism; the subterranean red mole. For Marxism to cease to exist, capitalist social relations have to be extinguished. Karl Marx, alongside other great modern thinkers such as Charles Darwin and Sigmund Freud, made a profound contribution to social thought by unlocking the inner workings of capitalism, its contradictions and historical specificity. Marx recognised capitalism as a historical social system; it had an origin and would not last forever. Marx's contribution to critical social thought has not been surpassed, but instead has thrown up many Marxisms each with different analytical strengths, theoretical emphases and in some cases practical approaches to challenging capitalism. Such a proliferation of perspectives with different degrees of proximity to Marx's categories and inflections is a sign of strength and vitality. The originality of Marx's social thought, his dialectical and historical materialist critique of modern capitalism lends itself to the making of different forms of anti-capitalist critique. It is a fertile resource to engage capitalism and its contemporary oppressions while thinking with and going beyond Marx. However, it is also important to recognise that many critical social theorists and theories, including feminism and ecology, have developed powerful critiques of contemporary capitalism. This has developed mainly from outside Marxism. In this context the embrace of and cross-fertilisation with critical contemporary social thinkers and currents of radical social thought become important in the remaking of contemporary Marxism. This volume is a collective effort to demonstrate this.

Many Marxist schools of thought and analytical approaches have also come and gone. The cartography of Marxisms is beyond the scope of this short reflection; suffice to say that it is a cartography of keeping critical thought alive and in some instances engendering anti-capitalist practice. In this volume we also affirm that a crucial source for the renewal of Marxism comes from its place in contemporary struggles against globalised capitalism. Such a location of Marxism takes it beyond the academy or the global North and reshapes the cartography of Marxism in relation to myriad struggles and the global South. For Michael Burawoy in this volume (see chapter 2), unorthodox and engaged Marxism has to be the thin edge of the wedge in the struggles against the commodification of nature. But even without such a precise positioning of Marxism, new forms of capitalist oppression and critical learning from past experiences of Marxism, including socialist projects it spawned, such as those in Africa, are also crucial sources for inciting a renewed role for Marxism. In short, and as we demonstrate in this volume, the journey of Marxism in the twenty-first century is beyond the cage of orthodoxy; it is about Marxisms that have escaped and are being remade through new adventures within contemporary struggles unfolding on the planet.

THE ADVENTURES OF DEMOCRATIC MARXISM

Without orthodoxy what is left of Marxism? This is a crucial question. It is similar to asking: would Marx have been a Marxist today? Marx would certainly not have been a Marxist in the dogmatic mould, guarding orthodoxy. Instead, he probably would have been a Marxist in the sense of being alive to the changing structural, agential and historical conditions of capitalism. This means the inherent categories of Marxism (for instance, class, class struggle, exploitation, value, capital, alienation and metabolic rift) would be put to work to make sense of our contemporary globalised capitalist world, grounded in Marx's dialectal and historical materialist method. These categories would be used to engender new meanings and understandings about the global capitalist political economy, its crisis tendencies and trajectories. This is the task of democratic Marxism, one of the Marxisms journeying freely beyond the iron cage of orthodoxy. It is a task also begun in this volume but with a long way to go as part of a new and exciting adventure.

As part of such an adventure this volume also, in a bold way, tries to place the ship of historical Marxism on a new journey to find its association with democracy. While democratic theory itself is struggling to define democracy, a crucial departure for democratic Marxism is recognising that classical Marxist and vanguardist understandings of democracy do not assist us in the present. The reclaiming of democracy, from below, is happening beyond notions of 'dual power' and is inventing pluralities of power. The street politics and power of Tahir Square, of the *indignados* (unemployed youth) in the plazas of Barcelona and Madrid and the Occupy Movement, for instance, are shifting global political consciousness in ways beyond instrumentalist understandings of conquering state power. For instance, the notion of the '99 per cent versus the 1 per cent' articulated by the Occupy Movement has become more than a moral rallying call against the super-rich transnational capitalist class: it is now actually part of global common sense as a discourse of delegitimation and for the needs of the majority. Assertions of symbolic and material capacities, through grassroots expressions of direct and participatory democracy, are inciting us to think against capitalism in a transformative manner. Moreover, the liberal appropriations of democracy ring hollow as transnational corporate power poses challenges to all forms of sovereignty and citizenship. At the same time, the face of contemporary capitalist empire is increasingly fascist in its imposition of neoliberal managerial rationality in every sphere of the global political economy. In this context, reclaiming democracy from below is a necessary political imperative. Democratic Marxism in the twenty-first century has to re-engage with the task of making contemporary democracy the political and economic means for transformation, while redefining it in practice to ensure it is about democracy *by the people*. Hence democracy is about a non-elite form of democracy that strengthens direct and participatory democracy and gives these democratic practices a primacy within the overall logic of democratisation. In fact, a grounding in a conception of democracy as being *by the people* is even more radical than what any of the 'isms' have to offer, whether Left or Right. This is a crucial message of this volume.

Finally, democratic Marxism, through democratic practice, has to constitute a transformative historical subject, as opposed to a subaltern subject of financialised neoliberal capitalism, in order to advance change. Such a transformative historical subject expresses a capacity for self-emancipation through championing alternatives to a broken capitalist world and a crisis-ridden society. It is also a historical subject, conscious of the need to marshal all the material social forces and intellectual resources of anti-capitalism. In its practice it is about constituting a counter-hegemonic democratic left unity, even if the purity of Marx's categories and orthodox Marxist discourse has to be diluted with broad left perspectives of how to understand and resist the oppressions of contemporary capitalism. All of this simply means that the adventures of democratic Marxism, in the twenty-first century, will only have meaning as a critical theory if defined through social struggle, grassroots-led democratisation and transformative change. Only in these ways will it be a crucial resource to make the world a better place.

CONTRIBUTORS

Patrick Bond is professor of Development and the director of the Centre for Civil Society at the University of KwaZulu-Natal. He has published numerous books on South Africa and Zimbabwe.

Michael Burawoy is professor of Sociology at the University of California, Berkeley. From 2010 to 2014 he served as the president of the International Sociological Association (ISA) and he has published widely on Marxism, South Africa and economic sociology. His books include *Manufacturing Consent* and *The Politics of Production*.

Jacklyn Cock is professor Emerita in the department of Sociology and an honorary research associate of the Society, Work and Development Institute (SWOP) at the University of the Witwatersrand (Wits). She has published widely on South Africa, including *Maids and Madams: A Study in the Politics of Exploitation* and *The War against Ourselves: Nature, Power, and Justice*.

Ashwin Desai is professor of Sociology based at the Centre for Sociological Research, University of Johannesburg. He has published widely on South African politics.

Daryl Glaser is associate professor in the department of Political Studies at Wits University. His publications include *Twentieth Century Marxism: A Global Introduction* (edited with David Walker).

Mazibuko Jara is a freelance writer and activist and was senior researcher at the Law, Race and Gender Research Unit in the Law department at the University of Cape Town. He has published widely on South African politics, Marxism and agrarian issues.

Meg Luxton is professor and director of the graduate programme in Gender, Feminist and Women's Studies at York University in Canada. She has published widely on feminist theory, gender, women's work – paid and unpaid and Marxism, including *More Than a Labour of Love: Three Generations of Women's Work in the Home* and (edited with Susan Braedley) *Neoliberalism and Everyday Life*.

Trevor Ngwane is a community activist and leader who has written extensively on South Africa's social movements and local politics.

Devan Pillay is associate professor in Sociology at Wits University. He has written widely on South African politics, including regularly for leading newspapers.

Vishwas Satgar is senior lecturer in the department of International Relations at Wits University and serves as chairperson on the board of the Co-operative and Policy Alternative Center (COPAC). He has published widely on Africa's political economy, South African politics and Marxism.

John S. Saul is professor emeritus of Social and Political Science at Toronto's York University. He is a leading intellectual and activist with reference to Africa-related issues, having written some 20 books on southern Africa and on more general development issues; he has been an author and expert on Marxism and the liberation movements since the 1960s.

Ahmed Veriava has recently completed a PhD in the department of Political Studies at Wits University. He has written on South African municipal service delivery, local politics and social movements.

Michelle Williams is associate professor in Sociology at Wits University and is the chairperson of the Global Labour University Programme, also at Wits. Her books include *The Roots of Participatory Democracy: Democratic Communists in South Africa and Kerala, India* and *South Africa and India: Shaping the Global South* (co-edited with Isabel Hofmeyr) and *Labour in the Global South: Challenges and Alternatives for Workers* (co-edited with Sarah Mosoetsa).

INDEX

Page numbers in italics refer to information in illustrations.
Page numbers with 'n' refer to information in notes.

Printed in the USA
CPSIA information can be obtained
at www.ICGtesting.com
JSHW082122211124
74056JS00003B/15